Timothy Bax was born in Dar-es-Salaam, Tanganyika in 1949. He attended boarding school in Lushoto from the age of six and in 1963 moved to England to continue his schooling. A year later he moved with his mother and two sisters to Toronto, Canada, where he completed his education. At the age of nineteen he returned to Africa, living first in South Africa then in Rhodesia (Zimbabwe). He joined the Rhodesian Army in 1969 and was commissioned two years later as a Lieutenant in the Rhodesian Light Infantry. A year later he was wounded while engaged in the first ever 'Fire-Force' deployment mounted by the Rhodesian Security Forces. In 1974, Tim was asked by the legendary commanding officer of the Selous Scouts, Lt. Col. Ron Reid-Daly, to join his unit. After successfully completing the selection course, Tim was given command of a pseudo-terrorist group tasked with seeking out and destroying real terrorists groups operating both inside and outside Rhodesia. In 1975 Tim commanded the first Rhodesian vehicle-borne raid ever mounted against guerrilla camps situated deep inside neighbouring countries. A year later he was seriously wounded while taking part in a similar raid. Tim was later appointed second-in-command of the Selous Scouts Reconnaissance Group. He was married to his wife Carol in 1977. In 1980 he and his wife left Rhodesia to settle in South Africa where with the rank of major, he was appointed second-in-command of South Africa's 5 Reconnaissance Regiment. Tim resigned from the army in 1982 and later served on the board of a multi-national company in South Africa. Their daughter, Jennifer, was born in June 1982. In 2002 Tim moved to the United States. He currently resides in Lake Placid, Florida.

THREE SIPS OF GIN

Dominating the Battlespace with Rhodesia's Elite Selous Scouts

Timothy Bax

Helion & Company

Co-published in 2013 by:

Helion & Company Limited
26 Willow Road
Solihull
West Midlands B91 1UE
England
Tel. 0121 705 3393
Fax 0121 711 4075
Email: info@helion.co.uk
Website: www.helion.co.uk
Twitter: @helionbooks
Visit our blog http://blog.helion.co.uk

and

GG Books UK
Rugby
Warwickshire
Tel. 07921 709307
Website: www.30degreessouth.co.uk

Designed and typeset by Farr out Publications, Wokingham, Berkshire
Cover designed by Euan Carter, Leicester (www.euancarter.com)
Printed by Henry Ling Ltd, Dorchester, Dorset

Text © Timothy G. Bax 2013
Photographs © as individually credited

ISBN 978-1-909384-29-3

British Library Cataloguing-in-Publication Data.
A catalogue record for this book is available from the British Library.

Front cover: Selous Scouts pig blown up in a landmine. (Dennis Croukamp). Rear
cover: Tim Callow, Selous Scouts Reconnaissance expert. (Tim Callow).

For details of other military history titles published by Helion & Company Limited
contact the above address, or visit our website: http://www.helion.co.uk.

We always welcome receiving book proposals from prospective authors.

To my parents, for encouraging me down the road to my destiny

And to my family and friends, for sharing my journey.

Contents

List of photographs   ix

Acknowledgements   xiv

Glossary   xv

Map   20

Prologue: A Most Worrisome Exposé   21

1   A Case for the Prosecution   24

      East Africa   27

2   The Road   35

      Magamba   39

      Lushoto School   49

3   Dar-es-Salaam   60

      Mr. Deppetawalah's Villa   66

      England   72

4   Canada   74

      Europe   83

      Lumberjack   86

5   London   95

      The Atlantic   99

      South Africa   103

6   Recruit   114

7   Trooper   124

      Border Control   130

8   An Officer I Wanted to Become   141

9   An Officer I Became   151

10   Subaltern Officer   176

      Mukumbura   176

      A Girl in my Soup   183

      A Walk in the Dark   188

      A Lady in the Attic   196

11   Mozambique   203

      A Port Too Many   211

      Brush with Fire   216

	Early Bird Catches the Worm	223
	The Doctor and the Cane Rat	228
12	An Unconventional Wisdom	235
	Selection	235
	The Regiment	240
	Moses	243
	Mechanized Raids	252
13	Passage of Fire	259
14	Matriarchic Matron	274
	The Mess	278
	A Rocky Engagement	285
15	Interlude	291
	Honeymoon	297
	An Angry Brigadier	302
16	Melting Pot	307
	Third Sip of Gin	314
17	Conduct Unbecoming	323
	Betrayal	334
18	Division of Cultures	342
	Wild Coast	349
19	White Mischief	365
20	Farming Frolics	376
21	Caravan of Camels	389
	A Laborious Union	398
22	Monkey Business	406
	Mikhail Kalashnikov	412
	Where Danger Lurks	414
	Post Scripta	418
	Index	421

List of photographs

Colour section

Mr Smith and his staff, Lushoto School. (Tim Bax) 1

Pupils on a hike at Lushoto School. (Tim Bax) 1

Trevor Kirrane. (Jacqui Kirrane) 2

Officer selection. (Terry Griffin) 2

Officer selection tracking course at Kariba. (Terry Griffin) 3

Selous Scouts Tracking Wing, Kariba. (Noel Robey) 3

Rehearsing for Passing Out Parade. (Terry Griffin) 4

The author carrying the colours. (Terry Griffin) 4

The author carrying the colours in the RLI. (Terry Griffin) 5

Part of my Troop. (John van Zyl) 5

RLI soldiers testing weapons before deployment. (Dennis Croukamp) 6

A view of a K Car. (Dennis Croukamp) 6

Early SAS border control operations. (Carol Doughty) 7

A Fire Force deploys. (Dennis Croukamp) 7

Sergeant Major Peter McNeilage, SCR. (Selous Scouts Association c/o Tom Thomas) 8

Members of the Selous Scouts Reconnaisance Team. (Dennis Croukamp) 8

Selous Scouts preparing to deploy into Mozambique. (Dennis Croukamp) 9

Bax and Collett on parade after being wounded. (Tim Bax) 9

Lt. (later Captain) Dale Collett. (Selous Scouts Association c/o Tom Thomas) 10

Neil Kriel, Ron Reid-Daly and Jerry Strong in the Selous Scouts Officers' Mess. (Phee Fletcher) 10

The author home from the bush on R&R. (Tim Bax) 11

Tim Bax, Tom Thomas and Keith Samler. (Selous Scouts Association c/o Tom Thomas) 11

Captain Athol Gillespie. (Selous Scouts Association c/o Tom Thomas) 12

Bob Wishart, in wheelchair. (Selous Scouts Association c/o Tom Thomas) 12

Selous Scouts standard being paraded at 5 Reconnaisance Regiment. (Noel Robey) 13

Peter Donelly, Selous Scouts soldier extraordinaire. (Pete Donelly) 14

Author with Pete Donelly on his farm. (Pete Donelly) 15

COIN formal dinner. (Debbie Patching)   15

COIN Security Group managers. The author is seated at the centre.
(Debbie Patching)   16

Black and white photographs

Our first house: a thatched roof with walls of mosquito netting. (Tim Bax)   25

Constructing one of Father's 'domino houses'. (Tim Bax)   29

Construction of Father's 'rambling Spanish villa. (Tim Bax)   32

Father watching me and Janet swim in a rock pool. (Tim Bax)   33

Father's Peugeot with Mother's Escort behind. (Tim Bax)   36

Waiting for Abdullah to fix the broken car spring. (Tim Bax)   37

Ladywood Cottage: Mother, Janet and Tim. (Tim Bax)   41

Tim and Janet having a break from home classes. (Tim Bax)   42

German Bridge near where the car broke down. (Tim Bax)   47

Lushoto. (Tim Bax)   49

Lushoto school. (Tim Bax)   52

Sports ground Lushoto school. (Tim Bax)   53

The road to Lushoto school. (Tim Bax)   54

Dar-es-Salaam harbour with British warship. (Tim Bax)   64

Mr Deppetawalah's pink villa. (Tim Bax)   69

Mother, Tim, Shelagh and Janet on the beach in Dar. (Tim Bax)   70

Vikki (Tim Bax)   71

George Thorley. (Terry Griffin)   126

Arriving at Deka Base Camp at night, Zambezi Valley. (Terry Griffin)   135

WO2 Trevor Kirrane. (Jacqui Kirrane)   140

School of Infantry. (Terry Griffin)   146

Trevor Desfountain. (Jacqui Kirrane)   150

Major Dick Lockley, Officer Cadet Course, Course Officer. (Dick Lockley)   154

Jerry Strong receiving the Sword of Honour, Sandhurst. (Jerry Strong)   155

Jerry Strong, Officer Cadet Course Instructor (Jerry Strong)   155

3 Commando boxing team. (Jacqui Kirrane)   157

Cadet course, air operations. (Terry Griffin)   159

Officer Cadet Course. Standing from left: Martin Pearse, Tim Bax,
Deon Kriel, Athol Gillespie, Terry Griffin. Seated from left:
Theo Williams, David Rawlins, Andy Chait, Colin Willis. (Terry Griffin) 161

Andy Chait. (Carol Doughty)   169

Andy Chait's final resting place. (Carol Doughty) 169

Colin Willis, SCR, C Squadron, SAS. (Colin Willis) 170

Relaxing whilst on an officers' course. (Terry Griffin) 171

Confrontation with an Elephant at the watering hole. (Dennis Croukamp) 173

Officer Cadet Course Passing-Out Parade. (Terry Griffin) 174

Officer Cadet Course, course photo. (Terry Griffin) 174

Two officers from our course, Colin Willis and Martin Pearse,
    joined the Rhodesian SAS. Martin, seated seventh from left,
    was later killed in action. (Carol Doughty) 177

Winston Hart. (Winston Hart) 179

Winston Hart and the Land Rover destroyed by a landmine. (Winston Hart) 179

Resting beneath a parachute canopy during an external operation.
    (Winston Hart) 185

3 Commando being briefed for operations in the Zambezi Valley.
    (D. Scott-Donelan) 190

Deploying along the Zambezi. (Dennis Croukamp) 190

General Coster, Lt Col MacIntyre and WOI Tarr. (Jacqui Kirrane) 193

A break during early border control operations. (D. Scott-Donelan) 194

Deploying into Mozambique. (Dennis Croukamp) 194

Early border control operation. (Doug Lambert) 196

Frolics in the officers' mess. The author with Colin Willis. (Phee Fletcher) 199

RLI officers (author back row centre). (Terry Griffin) 201

Ian Smith reviews a parade. (Jacqui Kirrane) 204

Major Doug Lambert. (Doug Lambert) 206

Members of JOC Hurricane. (Terry Griffin) 206

Para drop during Fire Force deployment. (Dennis Croukamp) 209

RLI deploying on operations inside Mozambique. (D. Scott-Donelan) 209

RLI patrol resting up. (D. Scott-Donelan) 211

RLI soldiers resting during a vehicle-borne raid into Mozambique.
    (D. Scott-Donelan) 212

RLI soldiers taking a break during external operations. (D. Scott-Donelan) 213

RLI soldiers troop for a fire-force deployment. (Dennis Croukamp) 214

An RLI Fire-Force waiting to be called out. (Dennis Croukamp) 219

A Fire Force helicopter refuelling in the bush (Dennis Croukamp) 219

K Car. (Dennis Croukamp) 220

Helicopter deployment into Mozambique. (Dennis Croukamp) 221

Issuing orders – RLI soldiers in Mozambique. (D. Scott-Donelan) 222

Dr Charlee Griffiths. (Dr Charlee Griffiths)   224

Dr Charlee Griffiths – my first sip of gin! (Dr Charlee Griffiths)   225

Dr Charlee Griffiths and his newly-issued rifle. (Dr Charlee Griffiths)   231

Helicopter deployment of a Selous Scouts reconnaissance team.
    (Dennis Croukamp)   233

The first group of Selous Scouts instructors. (Noel Robey)   238

Captured weapons after a Selous Scouts raid. (Dennis Croukamp)   239

Chris Schulenburg, GCV. (Dennis Croukamp)   243

Lt Col Ron Reid-Daly. (Phee Fletcher)   249

Selous Scouts pseudo-team with their command element. (Dennis
    Croukamp)   250

Selous Scouts pseudo-team. (Noel Robey)   254

Selous Scouts pig blown up in a landmine. (Dennis Croukamp)   254

Selous Scouts column refuelling before launching attack in
    Mozambique. (Dennis Croukamp)   255

Selous Scouts operator. (Dennis Croukamp)   256

Sergeant Major Peter McNeilage, SCR. (Selous Scouts Association,
    c/o Tom Thomas)   257

Pete McNeilage. (Selous Scouts Association, c/o Tom Thomas)   257

Tim Callow, Selous Scouts Reconnaissance expert. (Tim Callow)   262

Tim Callow on a reconnaissance. (Tim Callow)   263

A mechanized raid into Mozambique. (Dennis Croukamp)   266

A mechanized raid into Mozambique. (Dennis Croukamp)   268

Colonel MacIntyre and Ian Smith. (Jacqui Kirrane)   277

Neil Kriel, Ron Dick and Jerry Strong in the Selous Scouts Officers'
    Mess. (Phee Fletcher)   281

Ron Reid-Daly and his wife Jean with Philippa Fletcher. (Phee Fletcher)   282

Pre-deployment briefing at a Selous Scouts' fort. (Dennis Croukamp)   293

Keith Samler. (Keith Samler)   304

Selous Scouts reconnaissance patrols were seldom compromised.
    (Dennis Croukamp)   326

A two-man reconnaissance team, Selous Scouts. (Dennis Croukamp)   344

Port St Johns. (Kathryn Costello)   350

Port St Johns bridge. (Kathryn Costello)   351

Port St Johns lighthouse and river-mouth. (Kathryn Costello)   353

Port St Johns river-mouth. (Kathryn Costello)   354

Radio 604 Capitol Radio in Port St Johns. (Kathryn Costello)   354

Brian Hulley's Umgazana cottage. (Dr Brian Hulley)   356

Fishing with Brian Hulley. (Dr Brian Hulley)   358

Andy Samuels. (Debbie Patching)   360

Ben Dekker at a party. (Kathryn Costello)   363

Ben Dekker. (Kathryn Costello)   363

Pete Donelly blowing his bugle. (Pete Donelly)   386

John and Yvonne Bishop. (Debbie Patching)   391

COIN head office. (Debbie Patching)   392

A COIN formal dinner. (Debbie Patching)   397

John Bishop aghast at seeing monkeys wearing COIN corporate
    t-shirts! (Debbie Patching)   408

Andy Samuels and John Bishop at a COIN conference. (Debbie Patching)   409

Returning from a conference in the COIN corporate jet. (Debbie Patching)   410

Trevor and J.P. Beard. (Debbie Patching)   411

Acknowledgements

My family and many of my friends have been ceaseless in their endeavors at getting me to write this book. More often than not they have done so while unashamedly imbibing my limited stocks of wine. While I was unsuccessful in my endeavors at getting any of them to help with the manuscript, I am grateful for their unfailing support during the time it took me to complete it. Without their support, the book would never have been written. I am particularly grateful to my daughter Jenni, her mother Carol, and to my good friend Charlie Aust for persuading me to begin the book, and encouraging me to finish it.

A few have given freely of long periods of their valuable time in making the book a reality. I would like to thank Andrew Mackay for tirelessly going through each chapter to improve its literary content. Also to Jeremy Strong, Doug Lambert, Charlee Griffiths, Dick Lockley, Vic Walker and Tom Thomas for keeping the project headed in more or less the right direction. I would like to thank the Regimental Associations of the Rhodesian Light Infantry and the Selous Scouts for giving their blessing to the publication of this book. I am deeply saddened that my good friend and colleague, Lieutenant Colonel Ron Reid-Daly, passed way before the book could be published. I would like to thank him posthumously for his untiring assistance in correcting the detail in many of the chapters.

Many thanks, also, to Marco Gollino for all his work in establishing my website. He gave freely of his time and expertise for which I am extremely grateful.

Finally, and in particular, I would like to thank my editor, Gail Adams, for the many hours she devoted to trawling through each chapter for errors while reclining on a beach near her Portuguese villa successfully resisting drinking vast amounts of cheap Spanish plonk.

I am deeply indebted to them all.

Glossary

AK	automat Kalashnikov. Automatic assault-rifle used by terrorists/guerrillas.
Afrikaans	language spoken by Afrikaner
Afrikaners	native of South Africa, of European (especially Dutch) descent
askari	guard
ayah	nanny
BBC	British Broadcasting Corporation
BOSS	Bureau of State Security
BSAP	British South Africa Police; official name for the Rhodesian Police
basha	sleeping structure made of poles and thatched grass
batman	a servant or 'valet' assigned to an officer
bergen	large 'H' frame back-pack
bliksem(ed)	seriously chastised or beaten up
boet	brother, a term of endearment
boma	small thatched lodge
CLM	Commander of the Legion of Merit
COIN	Counter Insurgency
COMOPS	Combined Operations Headquarters
CSM	Commando Sergeant Major
catch a glide	catch a ride
casevac	casualty evacuation
chibuli	beer
clap	to hit; pronounced 'clup'
culled	killed
DSO	Distinguished Service Order (British medal)
dhobi	person who does laundry
dop	alcoholic drink; RLI slang
ek sê	"I say" (Afrikaans); pronounced "ek say"
Engelsman	An Afrikaners way of referring to any white person not of their own.

FN	Fabrique National; 7.62 semi-automatic assault rifle used by Rhodesian Army
FRELIMO	Frente de Libertação de Moçambique; Liberation Front of Mozambique
fade	disappear
Fire-Force	airborne quick-reaction force
flat	angry, cross; RLI slang
flatdog	crocodile
floppie	dead person, normally refers to a dead terrorist
frantan	napalm-like substance
frozen area	area prohibited to all government forces except Selous Scouts
G car	troop-carrying helicopter
gangen	bush veldt
gat	rifle
gomo	hill or mountain
gonk	sleep
gook(s)	guerrilla; an American expression born out of the Vietnam war
goose	woman
graze	eat
grazing irons	eating utensils
grimmie	girl of questionable character
HQ	headquarters
hondo	war or revolution
houtie	indigenous black person
ishe	sir
JOC	Joint Operations Center
jesse bush	thorn bush
johl	to have a good time
jislaaik	good grief
KIA	killed in action
K car	helicopter gunship
kaffir	African; derogatory
kaffir pot	black cast iron cooking pot favored by rural Africans
kak	shit
kanzu	lightweight, white, ankle-length robe worn by household

	servants
kepi	French military cap
kit	personal items of army equipment or clothing
knobkerrie	wooden club with a knob on the end, used as a truncheon.
koppie	hill; Afrikaans
kunjan	hullo
LZ	landing zone for a helicopter
lekker	nice; Afrikaans
lighty	young person; Rhodesian slang
MAG	general purpose machine-gun
MBE	Member of the British Empire
MLM	Member of the Legion of Merit
making tracks	to leave quickly; Rhodesian slang
mampoer	home-distilled brandy brewed by Afrikaners
mealies	corn, maize
memsahib	lady of the house; usually European lady
mombie	cow
mooi	very nice
mooshie	nice
NCO	Non-Commissioned Officers
oke	person
ouen(s)	guy(s)
pamberi	forward with
para-military	Non-military person trained in military procedures
pasi ne	down with
pseudo-team	counter-gang; patrol of Selous Scouts disguised as a terrorist gang
puza	drink
RLI	1st Battalion, Rhodesian Light Infantry. A second battalion was never formed.
RPG	rocket-propelled grenade
RSM	Regimental Sergeant-Major
RV	rendezvous
recce	reconnaissance
SAP	South African Police
SAS	Special Air Service. This book refers mainly to 'C'

	Squadron, the Rhodesian SAS.
SB	Police Special Branch
sadza	finely crushed maize meal
shambok	cowhide whip
shona	tribe of Africans in Zimbabwe
sies	yuk
sing	weapon set on automatic fire
Sitrep	situation report
skeem	think
skafe	cigarette
skuzapu	pick-pocket, name used by terrorists when referring to the Selous Scouts
skiver	somebody who is lazy
slay	kill
slayer	rifle or machine gun
slot	to hit, or to kill
smaak	to like
snyed	cheated
snyed by the rays	sunburned
spoor	animal or human tracks
stable belt	belt manufactured from thick nylon weave in the colors of the regiment, often with the belt buckle being in the form of the regimental badge
start	money; RLI slang
stengah	whisky and soda in a tall glass; popular drink in the tropics
sterk	big
subaltern	a junior officer
sunray	unit or sub-unit commander
TMH	anti-tank mine with anti-handling devices
takkies	terrorist, 'Tame Terr' is a terrorist who has been captured and turned
toto	small child
tribal trust land	TTL: area reserved for settlement by rural black tribesmen
troopie	trooper in the RLI
trop	wall

tune(s)	to tell
UNIMOG	German-made military utility vehicle
valley	Zambezi Valley
vellies (Veldskoen)	desert shoes made from soft suede leather, worn without socks
vlei	low-lying, open grassland; Afrikaans
wafa-wafa	you're dead, you're dead
ZANLA	Zimbabwe African National Liberation Army; Chinese-backed Rhodesian terrorist movement.
ZIPRA	Zimbabwe People's Revolutionary Army; Russian-backed Rhodesian terrorist movement.

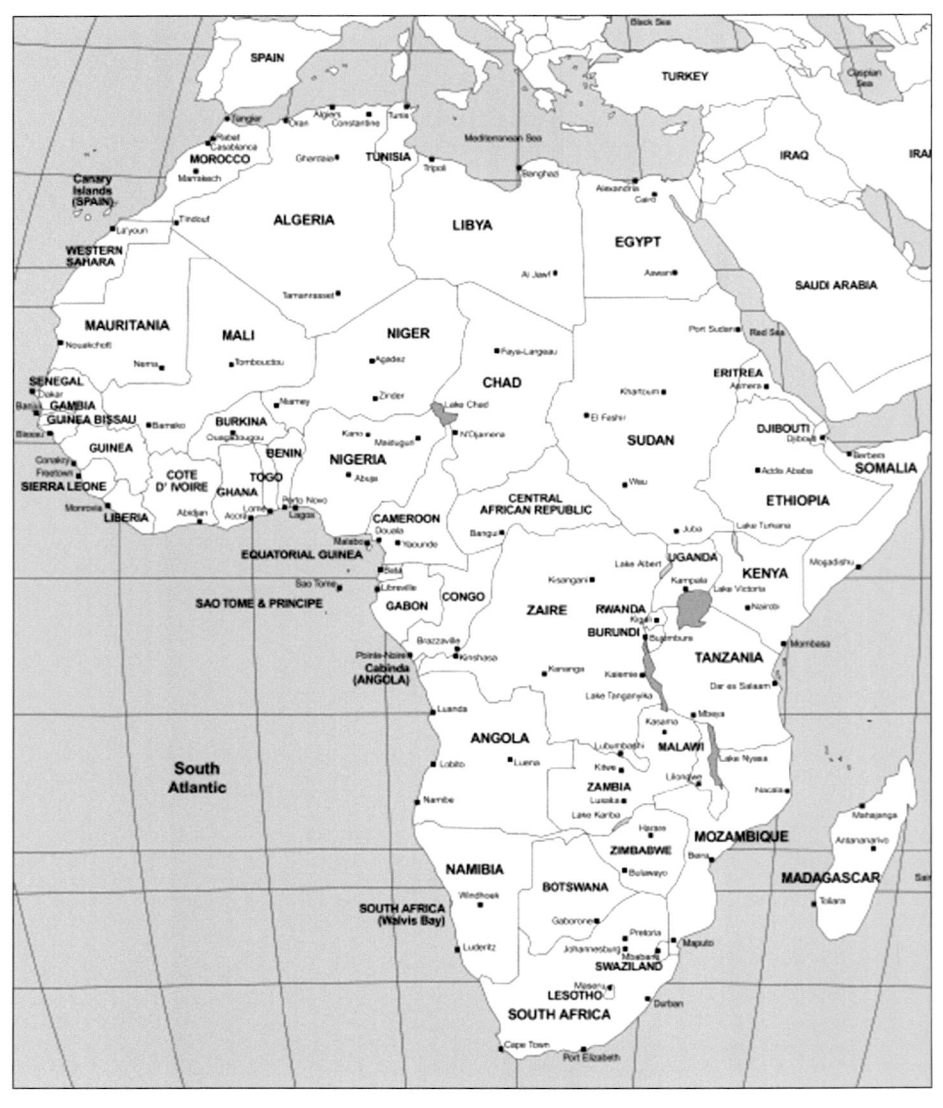

Prologue
A Most Worrisome Exposé

"**M**other, I'm writing a book."

"Oh, how lovely, dear," replied my unsuspecting mother. "About what?"

"About my life in Africa." Almost as an afterthought I added, "And about our impossible family and friends."

"Oh dear, do you really think that's a good idea?" Mother looked concerned. She was reclining in an old wicker chair at the assisted living facility in which she was living in Ottawa, Canada. "People might find us a little. . .uhm, well you know, a little odd."

"Yes, I know. But I really can't help that. I'll try to recount at least a semblance of normality. After all, we seem to have got through our lives relatively unscathed."

I was being kind. The sight of my twin sister Janet drifting down the corridor with hair looking like an exploding fireworks display and wearing a long floral dress that made her look like a Chelsea flower show arrangement bore testimony to our eccentric family. She was talking in animated fashion to some startled patrons as if having known them for her entire life. Behind her on a leash was her large and ungainly looking Labrador, Milo, who was busy devouring food from the trays on the dinner trolley.

"Well, I think you should speak to your sisters first," cautioned Mother.

As if by some magical cue, Janet arrived dragging Milo behind her. She had abandoned the group of patrons who were probably wondering where their next meal was coming from.

"You're looking worried," soothed my twin to Mother, brushing a strand of white hair from her forehead.

"It's Tim, he's writing a book about us, and Africa, and all of his friends."

"No, you jolly well are not," said Janet, giving me a withering look. "I don't want my name being associated with any of those outrageous people you refer to as your friends!"

Janet had recently been appointed to a directorship with the Canadian government and was clearly uncomfortable at the thought of such a potentially intrusive exposé being uncorked from our family's past.

"Perhaps you could write mainly about *your* friends," suggested

Mother, anxious to broker some sort of resolution to this sudden and unexpectedly troublesome dispute within the family.

"I can't write a book about my life in Africa without saying something about my family," I persisted. "Anyway, it's your fault, Mother. You should have known better than to try and raise a family in the middle of the African bush. It's a miracle any of us survived."

"Well, don't go writing anything unkind about your sisters or your friends," warned Mother with finality. "I won't have it."

As if wishing to dismiss any further talk on the matter she added, "Now take me down to the lounge, it's cocktail time and I don't want to keep the staff waiting."

Having grown up and lived most of my life in the decadence of colonial Africa, I could recall "cocktails" being more than just a peripheral activity of the daily African landscape. Life seemed a constant blaze of parties, and no luncheon was complete without the discreet presence of a uniformed native carrying a tray of gin and tonics.

෬

The idea of writing a book was arrived at one morning after a traditional South African New Year's breakfast of kippers, washed down with copious amounts of beer. I had returned to South Africa from my new home in the United States to spend Christmas and New Year's with my daughter Jennifer, and her mother Carol, to whom I had been married for some twenty years.

"Dad," said my daughter, nonchalantly swigging back her third beer of the morning. "I think you should write a book."

"About what?" I asked, somewhat taken aback by the consummate ease with which she was disposing of the family's limited supply of alcohol. The liquor stores would be closed for another two days.

Jennifer was relaxing on a garden chair on the porch of the Johannesburg home she shared with her mother, her feet resting on the limb of a pink and white and very out of control bougainvillea bush that was threatening to devour the entire porch.

"About us, Dad, and Africa, and all of those outrageous people you refer to as our friends," replied my daughter, waving a half-empty bottle of beer vaguely towards the skyline of another glorious African morning.

Ↄↄ

This book is certainly not intended as an autobiography, or even as an historical account of my life. It is merely a loose recollection of stories, anecdotes and incidents, some amusing, others outrageous, but all entirely real, that I shared with my family and friends in the course of my life's journey in Africa and which I have attempted to string together in some sort of sequential order. I am entirely unsure in the writing of this book as to whether or not I have complied with Mother's request to be kind to my sisters! As to whether or not I have been kind to our friends, I am equally unsure. To the best of my recollection all of the facts recounted are real as, dare I admit, are all of the characters. I hope that they will be graceful in any condemnation of my recording for public consumption the extraordinary and comical events as they unfolded.

However, I am enormously grateful to all of them. For they have collectively contributed in making my life rich in laughter.

Timothy G. Bax
Lake Placid, Florida

1

A Case for the Prosecution

"I see you, Old Man." "I see you, too."
"Is everything well in the village?"
"It is well."
"Is the lion still nearby?"
"Yes. But I am not afraid, for I still have my lantern."
—*Conversation with an African villager: 1971*

Darkness had fallen. A cacophony of shrieks and sounds heralded the excitement of yet another of Africa's nocturnal awakenings. There was an urgent knocking on the screen door.

Inside, shrieks of laughter and the tinkling of cocktail glasses dulled even the relentless shrill of the cicada beetles. Mother and Father were enjoying sundowners with friends inside a screened 'boma' which served as our family's living quarters. The knocking went unheard.

"Memsahib … *Memsahib!"* whispered the African askari, opening the screen door just enough to poke his head through. As a night guard, it would have been impolite for him to have intruded any further into the sanctuary of his master's home. He was an old man with white hair and a face deeply etched by years of toil in the African bush; quite how many years, he was incapable of remembering. He looked deeply concerned.

"What is it?" asked Mother, momentarily distracted from her guests. She was standing close to the door and was worried by the grave look on the old man's face.

"Watoto na maliza. Simba iko karibu sana!" rasped the askari, his voice raised in alarm. He was sweating profusely in the sweltering, heavy night air; his luminous eyeballs contrasting starkly with the moist sheen of his black skin. He wore an oversized khaki tunic and a matching pair of oversized shorts which ballooned over his spindly legs like the sails of an Arab dhow. In his sinewy hand he clutched a wooden club, or knobkerrie. It was a far cry from the Lee Enfield he had carried while proudly serving with the King's African Rifles.

Our first house: a thatched roof with walls of mosquito netting. (Tim Bax)

"What's worrying the poor man?" asked Father, suddenly aware of the askari's presence.

"He says the children are crying," replied Mother, hastening to the door. "He says there's a lion nearby."

As if to punctuate her remark, the unmistakable deep-throated grunt of a black-maned lion reverberated menacingly through the still, black night. The surrounding bush fell immediately into a deep and uneasy silence. A startled hush enveloped the boma. Even the cicada beetles ceased their chorus, as if silenced by some mystical stroke of a conductor's baton.

Tonight as with every night, the askari had been guarding the open-sided sleeping boma which I shared with my two sisters. It was nestled under the canopy of a large acacia tree a few hundred feet from the living quarters where Mother and Father were now entertaining. Except for a waist high screen of thatch that surrounded the boma, burgeoning white mosquito nets hanging from a makeshift roof of palm fronds provided the only protection between us and the surrounding bush.

"Well, tell him to chase the damn thing off." Father was helping himself to another whisky. "We can't have it upsetting the children."

Mother quickly reached for one of the smoking kerosene lanterns that were providing the only light and stepped outside. The dutiful askari followed close behind.

"I'll be back as soon as I've settled the kids." Clutching her cocktail, she moved quickly into the stillness of the dark, moonless night.

The party resumed.

So did the persistent call of the cicadas.

It was another routine night in the decadence of Colonial East Africa.

ري

Recounting that and other stories of our early childhood, Mother seemed entirely unrepentant. Our family comprising Mother, my twin sister Janet, older sister Shelagh and me had just finished a lazy Sunday morning breakfast in the regulated security of our second floor apartment in Toronto, Canada. Outside, the swirling, wind-driven snow of another bleak Canadian winter had collected in thick drifts on the window ledges. A thin icy layer of condensation had formed on the inside of the windows. The cold, blustery weather seemed far removed from the tropical warmth of Africa which we had left two years before.

"Mother!" exclaimed Janet indignantly. "It's jolly lucky we weren't all dragged to our death by some ferocious wild animal. It's very irresponsible of you to have left us sleeping miles out in the bloody bush while you and Daddy stayed up partying all night!"

"Now don't exaggerate, dear. You children were only a short way off and Daddy had hired an askari to protect you. Besides, we didn't stay away from you all night."

"Fat use the askari would have been with just a knobkerrie against a whole bloody pride of lions!" Janet persisted. "How we all managed to survive I'll never know."

"Well, your father always had a gun with him. He would have shot anything that came too close," sighed Mother, becoming a little exasperated.

"Oh, that's great! Then we would really have been in mortal danger, Daddy blasting a bloody great elephant gun in our direction with just a mosquito net for us to hide behind."

"Now stop it, dear. Your father was a highly-decorated soldier who knew how to handle guns."

Janet was not to be stopped. "Mother, there's a big difference between shooting at some Germans, and staggering out into the African bush after a few whiskies at night shooting at a pride of hungry lions walking between our beds. I'm appalled!"

"Janet, I do wish you would stop exaggerating." Mother was unsuccessfully trying to escape further persecution by engrossing herself in the Sunday crossword.

"Well, I think that at the very least, you and Daddy could have waited until you had a proper roof over your heads before starting a family."

Janet had sanctimoniously curled herself up on the couch surrounded by great wads of tissues into which she was relentlessly blowing an extremely red, snotty nose.

Outside the snow had turned to wind-driven sleet which beat a rhythmic tattoo against the icy window.

East Africa

"I became terribly bored. I wasn't even allowed to make myself tea.
There was a servant to make it, another to serve it."
"What did you do?"
"I started drinking my husband's gin."
—Tanganyika settler's wife: 1955

Mother and Father arrived in East Africa in 1947. With them was my sister, Shelagh, who was a year old. Father had been sent by the British Colonial Office after the war to take part in a scheme to grow groundnuts near the palm-fringed port of Dar-es-Salaam, the capital city of the British-controlled colony of Tanganyika. The scheme was to bring untold wealth and prosperity to the impoverished region.

Before its official launch the scheme had to be given a name, one that would capture the spirit and boldness of such an imaginative enterprise. After much deliberation a name was finally chosen. It was to be called 'The Groundnut Scheme'. (They were British, after all.)

Finding volunteers to participate in the scheme wasn't a problem. There were thousands of recently demobilized servicemen anxious to leave the gloom of Britain's post war economy for the excitement and glamour of Britain's East African colonies. Among them was my father, a decorated and flamboyant armored corps cavalry officer who had demobilized from the British Army with the rank of Lieutenant Colonel. Commissioned in the field, he was the recipient of the Military Medal (MM) for bravery and had been invested as a Member of the Order of the British Empire (MBE) for his exploits on the battlefield. But he knew nothing about farming, much less of growing groundnuts. Neither apparently did anyone else.

The torrential rains which lash the coastal plains of East Africa through the summer were a phenomenon that had escaped the attention of the Foreign Office. It was only when the squadrons of heavy plant machinery shipped from England began getting bogged down in a seething quagmire of mud that alarm bells began to ring. By then it was too late.

When the rains subsided, the scorching tropical sun baked the ground to the consistency of dried concrete. It could barely be penetrated by a jack-hammer much less the struggling groundnut seedlings trapped below.

The Groundnut Scheme's collapse was almost as dramatic as its grandiose beginning. Its only legacy was a large number of families from Britain who suddenly found themselves in East Africa devoid of a living; Father amongst them. Undaunted, they did what the British have always done when faced with such adversity—they flocked to the club for a pink gin.

Father at least had the wisdom to abandon the sinking ship before the official pronouncement from London to "scuttle the bilges." By that time the ship had already sunk. The Foreign Office had always been slow in admitting its mistakes; it was slower still in making public pronouncements about them.

Into this crucible of doubt and confusion was born my twin sister, Janet. I followed rather belatedly some 20 minutes later. It was 1949.

My African journey had just begun.

അ

Even after the failure of the Groundnut Scheme, large numbers of families continued to pour off the ships at Dar-es-Salaam. They all needed a place to live so Father started building houses. But it wasn't quite like a duck taking to water. He knew little about house construction. In fact, he knew nothing.

But the devil is in the detail, and Father proved nimble at avoiding the many stumbling blocks that lay strewn along his way. Where there wasn't a European way to circumvent a building problem, there was always the uncomplicated African way. Kiln-dried bricks were in short supply and came with a price tag bigger than Father could afford. But the clay earth that had so effectively torpedoed the Groundnut Scheme was like gold dust to a builder.

Constructing one of Father's 'domino houses'. (Tim Bax)

Father recruited a small army of unskilled laborers to form clay bricks in wooden handmade molds that were left to bake under the hot tropical sun. He leased a large tract of land close to the tranquil Indian Ocean, cleared it, and began building.

Father's office consisted of an old canvas chair and makeshift folding table placed under the shade of a large umbrella tree. Upon it each morning he would arrange his rough building plans, a thermos of tea laced with whisky, and a large tin of Erinmore flake pipe tobacco. It was from here that he directed building operations, like a film director overseeing a cast of unrehearsed amateurs. He was never without his old meerschaum pipe. He said it kept the sand flies away.

Slowly, very slowly, the houses reached completion. Soon row upon row of little rectangular brick and stucco houses sprang from the ground looking like neatly placed dominoes.

There was no shortage of families wanting to take occupancy. Business in the colonies was as likely to be concluded over a handshake and a pink gin in the cordial atmosphere of the Dar Club as in a banker's office. To Father, the passing of cheques was a bothersome and irksome formality which seldom got in the way of allowing families to take ownership of a new home. The result was that his cash reserves began receding as quickly as the outgoing tide.

But there was always the hope of a better tomorrow. It was the glorious days of colonial clubs and gymkhanas, of pink gins and stengahs, of bored memsahibs and lavish cocktail parties and of servants … legions of them. For the newly arrived housewife from England there were servants to take care of her every need. One only needed to clap one's hands and shout "Boy!" to have a splendidly-attired native discreetly appear like a genie from a lantern. A strict 'pecking order' ensured that each servant knew his or her place within the hierarchy of the household.

At the top was the 'houseboy' whose function was to all but manage the home; sometimes he did that as well. Below him were cook boys, laundry boys (or dhobis), garden boys, night guards and the ubiquitous 'ayah', or nanny. No household with children was ever without an ayah.

For want of anything else to do, the 'memsahib' would usually spend her day at the gymkhana club playing tennis, or golf, or 'something'. If the tropical sun proved too bothersome, she could order a cocktail in the bar and catch up on the latest scandal. Sometimes there might even be a scandal to indulge in as there was no shortage of attentive young officers from England on attachment to the King's African Rifles. Living with the family of a bored memsahib provided relief from the mundane monotony of the barracks. In England, the question would often be asked, "Are you single, married … or from the colonies?"

The first 'real' house Father built for the family was quite luxurious compared to our previous dwelling. Much to Mother's relief it had real windows, doors and a thatched roof. But the thatch leaked mercilessly when it rained and during the summer it rained continuously. There was no plumbing and the toilet was a 'throne' or 'thunder box' perched precariously over a deep hole outside and to the rear the house. It was situated under a large acacia tree and was surrounded by a shoulder-high grass fence which gave only a modicum of privacy. Even that was never assured.

During the day, the tree teemed with troops of marauding monkeys who would stare inquisitively down at any unfortunate person sitting below. Occasionally they would start squabbling and screaming at each other like precocious children. It wasn't unusual to have a mischievous monkey hanging from a lower limb by one arm while unraveling the toilet paper with the other. Worse, they might abscond with the entire roll.

One evening, Father saw a leopard stretched out on one of the lower limbs. After that we stopped using the throne at night. We used chamber pots instead.

During the day my sisters and I would see nothing of our parents. From the moment we awoke until we were put to bed we were under the constant supervision of our ayah. The only time we saw Mother and Father was after our bath in the evening when we would be paraded before them like tin soldiers on a toy parade. After checking that we had 'cleaned behind our ears' we would be hastened to bed. If Mother and Father were entertaining we were not allowed to utter a word except to offer a polite "Goodnight." Children were to be seen and not heard.

Once in bed we would be tucked under a billowing mosquito net that hung from the ceiling like the sail of a beached galleon, and the ayah would walk around pumping voluminous clouds of choking insecticide, almost gagging us. Then the lights would be turned out. Later a lizard or small gecko might succumb to the noxious fumes and drop from the ceiling to splatter on the floor below.

As the dying embers of the sun flickered below the horizon a hyena might give an hysterical cackle followed immediately by the deep, menacing grunt of a lion warning its arch enemy to stay clear. The comforting sound of boots crunching against gravel outside the window would indicate the presence of the night guard, or askari, patrolling around the house while the encompassing shadows of night fell across the uneasy, ever-watchful African landscape.

❧

Flushed with the success of his 'domino houses', Father decided to build an elaborate new house for us close to the beach. The result was a rambling Spanish-styled villa with a roof of Spanish shingles, wrought iron gates and terracotta walkways built around an open courtyard. With the great influx of families from England had arrived an even greater influx of petty thieves anxious to share in the colony's newfound wealth. They would walk off with anything that wasn't secured … and much of what was.

One night shortly after taking occupancy of our modern new home, a thief brazenly stood outside Shelagh's bedroom window and, using a long pole, removed most of her belongings, including mosquito net and bed sheets. He almost succeeded in removing her pajamas as well.

Father was furious, "Damn fatheads!" I seldom heard him swear.

Our days were carefree and the beach our oyster. Our contentment was interrupted one day by Mother announcing that Shelagh, aged six, would soon be leaving to attend boarding school somewhere up-country at a place we had

Construction of Father's 'rambling Spanish villa. (Tim Bax)

never heard of and cared about even less.

Getting her to the school was no easy feat. The entire family would pack into Father's car and set off for the train station with the Peugeot looking like an overloaded taxi from a crowded Arab bazaar. On the roof rack would teeter a pyramid of metal trunks packed with everything Shelagh would need for her first year as a boarder. Upon our arrival at the station we would bid her a tearful farewell and wave frantically as she boarded the train, followed by her luggage which was hoisted onto the train by a disinterested porter. There would be a shrill whistle and the train would jerk, jerk again, and start shunting hesitatingly down the platform. We would follow it trying to touch Shelagh's outstretched hand as the train gathered speed, its hissing engine lost to view amid plumes of billowing steam. Then she would be gone and we would start crying.

An overnight train would take Shelagh to a dusty inland town called Morogoro situated some 80 miles away. Although it was a relatively short distance the trip took all night. The train stopped at every road crossing, junction and village along the way. Sometimes it stopped for no apparent reason at all, the driver alighting to go somewhere, to do something. From Morogoro her luggage would be transferred onto an old bus for the eight-hour

Father watching me and Janet swim in a rock pool. (Tim Bax)

trip along a badly corrugated dirt road to the school in Lushoto, high in the foothills of the Usambara Mountains. There was seldom adult supervision. At best she would be under the care of some of the older children who had made the trip before.

Janet and I made a sacred pact that if we were ever sent away to the same school we would run away. We made a list of food we planned to steal during our 'great escape' and hid it in a shoebox together with sketches of our escape route. The details of our escape and evasion plan didn't extend farther than running to a secret cave we had discovered close to a disused bridge near our house and 'lying low' for a short period. After that we didn't know what we would do.

Under threat of informing Mother that we had once caught him peeing on her cabbage patch, we blackmailed the garden boy into becoming part of our plan. He was to make daily trips to the bridge bringing us bread, jam and water. We told him that if our parents hadn't found us within two days he was to tell them where we were.

We were brave, but not that brave.

The sadness at losing our big sister to the clutches of boarding school soon dissipated. Each day the ayah would shepherd us down to the beach wearing little more than colorful sunhats and great swaths of suncream smeared on our faces. Coral reefs with tidal pools that nestled along the beach teemed with aquatic life. The rock pools became our playground, and Janet and I would spend hours wading through the shallow turquoise waters in search of starfish, sea urchins and other exotic creatures. They would scuttle away at our intrusive approach and hide in dark nooks in the coral, peering at us through large, translucent eyes.

Our freedom was shortlived. One day Mother informed us that our family was to relocate upcountry to be closer to Shelagh. "You two will shortly be old enough for school and we've decided to send you to the same school as your sister."

Our fate was sealed.

A few weeks later we set off for what was to be our new home in the Usumbara Mountains. We travelled in two cars: Janet with Mother in her car and me and Abdullah, the cook, travelling with Father. Amongst my belongings on Father's roof rack was the shoe box containing the escape plans to our hiding place under the bridge.

It had been a bridge too far.

2

The Road

"Where will you rest tonight?" "Upon my sleeping mat." *"Don't you have a home?"* "The plains are my home."
—Excerpt: The Nomadic Masai

I was horribly carsick for almost the entire journey.

A rusty chain hanging from the rear bumper of Father's car thrashed and jerked against the dusty road like an angry serpent. Father explained that its purpose was to dissipate static electricity from the car. It was the electricity, he said, that was making me sick. I didn't believe him because my sickness seemed to worsen. It wasn't helped by the thick clouds of red dust that billowed behind us like a rolling avalanche. Each time we slowed or stopped we became engulfed in a swirling red miasma of choking red powder.

The 80 miles of road to Morogoro were tarred. The remainder of the 250-mile journey was along a dusty, corrugated road with a surface like a washboard. The only rule of the road was to stay ahead of the vehicle behind so as not to become enveloped in its rolling clouds of red dust. Old buses, their rivets busting under the weight of mountainous loads, would career full throttle down the centre of the road refusing to give way to anything to avoid being overtaken.

We had been trailing behind one such bus for some time when Father decided he had had enough. The inside of the car was already awash with clouds of choking dust and foul-smelling Cavendish smoke which belched from Father's meerschaum pipe like acrid plumes from a smoke stack. Throwing caution to the wind he propelled us headlong into the red morass like a comet into a cloudbank. I wondered if we would ever emerge from the dark, churning cauldron. I was aware only of the reverberating clatter of the bus's overworked diesel engine as we rattled past it, unseeing. There was no way of knowing whether at any moment we might crash headlong into oncoming traffic.

"Bloody fools!" exclaimed Father, as we emerged unscathed from the churning avalanche of dust. "Damned natives haven't a clue about the rules of the road."

Father's Peugeot with Mother's Escort behind. (Tim Bax)

I breathed a sigh of relief. I was feeling nauseous beyond belief. I began to wonder what fate might have befallen Mother and Janet who had been traveling behind us. We had just shaken ourselves free from the dust when there was a loud 'twang', and the rear of the Peugeot settled back onto its rear axle with an ominous thud. A coil spring had snapped on the suspension. The next bump propelled us into the air and the car skewered sideways like a glider in a crosswind. Father just managed to bring it to a bone-jarring landing when the bus we had overtaken exploded past in vengeful fury.

We were eventually joined by Mother and Janet who emerged from their car looking like disheveled clowns. They were covered head to toe in a thick film of red, powdery dust which gave their eyeballs a luminous appearance and made their teeth look bleached. We collapsed on the side of the road like rag dolls, watching ruefully as Abdullah the cook disappeared under Father's car with an alarming assortment of jacks, blocks, pliers and coils of baling wire.

We had broken down in the middle of the dry thorn scrub of the Masai plains. Across the road two Masai tribesmen were standing like motionless sentinels watching us with disdain. They were standing in their traditional posture; balanced precariously like storks on one leg, using the slender shafts of their spears for balance. Each wore an ochre-colored blanket caked with dirt

Waiting for Abdullah to fix the broken car spring. (Tim Bax)

draped over one shoulder. The strands of their long hair were braided into place with a mixture of red clay and cow dung. Although they were standing some way off, the sharp rancid odor of their unwashed bodies was overpowering and made me gag. Everything about them had an ochre hue, even their rich, dark skin. It gave them an odd, alien look as though they might recently have arrived from another planet.

The two Masai had been tending their cattle which provided their daily sustenance of curdled milk mixed with cow blood. The blood was obtained by driving a hollow reed into the cow's jugular vein and allowing it to spurt into an earthenware gourd. The wound would then be plugged with a paste of mud and cow dung and the indignant animal let loose to rejoin the herd.

"Mommy, pleeeease tell them to leave, I have to do a pee!" grimaced Janet, her knees clasped together like a vice.

"I can't, they'll just wait around to watch you."

"But I can't wait!"

"It's rude to pee in front of strangers."

The Masai, oblivious to Janet's distress, had meandered down to the cars and were busy preening themselves in the dusty reflection of the windows. The clanging under Father's car stopped. Abdullah had suddenly become aware of their presence and lay inert under the car not daring to move. One of the Masai lifted his spear aiming its sharp, pointed tip downwards. For a moment I thought that Abdullah might be impaled before our very eyes! I wondered vaguely if we might be next and decided it couldn't possibly feel worse than the nausea I was already feeling. Luckily, it was the car tyre that had caught the tribesman's interest. He was inquisitively prodding at it with the razor tip of his gleaming spear.

"Do something," chided Mother, looking in Father's direction. Sensing that he needed to establish his authority over a rapidly deteriorating situation, Father drew himself up on the steep, sandy bank like an officer about to chastise lagging soldiers from the trenches.

"Abdullah!" he shouted in an authoritative voice. It was almost as if the poor cook himself might be responsible for the imminent demise of the Peugeot's front tyre. "Tell those bloody fools to leave the tyres alone."

Father might just as well have been talking to the man in the moon. Abdullah didn't speak English and nor, curiously, did the Masai. Mother tried vainly to translate, but Abdullah was having none of it. He remained mute and unmoving in his hiding place.

Eventually the Masai got bored and ambled back to their herd. The clanging under Father's car resumed, Janet had a pee, and the broken spring was jury-rigged to last a few more miles.

The remainder of the wearisome excursion through barren scrubland was relatively uneventful. We passed scattered villages with huts made of wattle saplings packed with mud and thatched roofs of dried grass. Young 'totos' dashed into the middle of the road like dusty urchins to make us stop, oblivious to any danger of being run over. When we did pull over they would thrust their dirty, cupped hands through the open car windows, their snotty noses full of crawling flies and beg for something... anything.

Eventually we reached the little village of Mombo and started climbing the long, narrow, winding escarpment road to our new home in the Usumbara Mountains.

Magamba

"Did you hear?" she whispered in shocked indignation.
"What?"
"She ran off with a young Hussar."
"Who?"
"The District Officer's wife."
"Oh!"
—Anonymous memsahib, Tanganyika: 1956

Father had purchased a picturesque hilltop house on a large acreage of ground overlooking the gently rolling hills and luscious valleys of Magamba in the central highlands of Tanganyika. Each morning the cool valleys would become awash in soft, willowy seas of milky-white mist, and the hills would rise starkly behind like the remote islands of an archipelago. In the evening the hills and valleys would become bathed in veils of soft yellows, pinks and blues, as the filtered shafts of sunlight began to set behind the thickly-wooded mountains behind.

The house was called Ladywood Cottage. It seemed an odd name to give a sprawling complex consisting of three separate wings, two sitting rooms, two dining rooms and a guesthouse. Included in the purchase were a large herd of gawking dairy cows, an unruly gaggle of aggressive ducks and geese, a vast sea of squawking chickens, wild dogs, tame dogs, acres of unkempt fruit orchids, a wattle plantation, wild garden, flower gardens and vegetable gardens.

Not part of the purchase but very much in attendance were the monkeys. The countryside teemed with undisciplined troops of squabbling Colobus monkeys which would launch forays into the vegetable and fruit gardens plucking them clean of all that was edible and much of what wasn't.

Mother decided she needed to fast track Janet's and my education in order to gain us entrance into the school Shelagh was attending. It had previously been referred to as the German school but the new British Governor, in a moment of rare inspiration, had decided to drop the word 'German' and it then became known as the 'Lushoto Preparatory School'. Some of the German staff had remained and no amount of British influence had been able to eradicate the culture of strict discipline that had previously prevailed.

"You're both behind in your education," announced Mother one morning over breakfast. "I'm going to keep you at home to do correspondence courses

I've arranged to have sent from England."

I had heard frightening stories from my elder sister of the draconian discipline and canings which took place at her school and was elated at this unexpected but welcome reprieve. Each morning after breakfast, Janet and I would sit at the dining room table with HB pencils freshly sharpened and listen attentively as Mother endeavored to teach us a baffling array of English public school lessons. But correspondence courses taught in the middle of the African bush were fraught with complexities.

One morning we were trying to unravel the mysteries of basic mathematics when there was a deafening barrage of gunfire from the area of the chicken coop. A troop of baboons was making a foray into the pen of Mother's prize egg-laying hens. We rushed down to find Father blasting away at half a dozen fang-baring baboons he had managed to corner inside the coop. The baboons proved more nimble than Father's aim was good, and with each explosive discharge from his heavy caliber shotgun a portion of the coop would come crashing down, together with another chicken in a squawking eruption of shredded feathers.

The final tally after the smoke had cleared was one baboon killed, eight chickens dead, and the chicken coop partially destroyed. Father's face was blackened by cordite making him look as if he had just emerged from a confrontation with Ali Baba and the forty thieves. The garden boy who had rushed to Father's aid sustained a minor flesh wound on his calf. Father had the dead baboon gutted and strung up like a crucifix on a pole near what remained of the coop. It was a grim reminder to the rest of the baboon troop of the folly of further raids.

There was always something to disrupt Mother's attempts at creating a tranquil atmosphere in which to study. The sudden appearance of a posse of natives chasing a wild boar through her favorite hibiscus bushes would end an attempt at teaching us the alphabet. On another occasion, a volley of rifle fire punctuated an intricate lesson in grammar. Father was gamely trying to repel a raid by a pack of jackals on the pen of the luckless geese; they always seemed to attract unwanted attention from foraging predators.

Learning the alphabet seemed terribly mundane by comparison.

☙

The centre of social activity, in fact of every activity, was the 'Club'. In Magamba ironically it was called the 'Magamba Club'. It was the 'headquarters' of the

Ladywood Cottage: Mother, Janet and Tim. (Tim Bax)

district; the rallying point for the colors, the place of news, of gossip, of intrigue and of scandal. If the Club was the hub of activity, its *sine qua non* was the bar. Each noon the European community would flock to it like parched ducks to an inviting pond. Janet and I would be deposited unceremoniously on the floor of the foyer with strict instructions to be seen but not heard. From there we would crawl unnoticed on to a wide windowsill overlooking the front entry from where we would secretly observe the parade of odd and eccentric characters that would invariably arrive like actors to a pantomime.

One such person was a very old and very retired Air Vice-Marshal by the name of Harrison. He was a tall, slim man who would arrive at the Club each day precisely at noon driving a bright red MG sports car which he never drove faster than twenty miles an hour. He was always immaculately dressed in twill trousers, tweed jacket with leather elbow patches, plaid hat and an overstated bow tie. Having parked his car, he would slowly emerge from its cramped interior looking like an Indian charm snake rising to its owner's flute. Once unlimbered from his car he would take time brushing down his jacket and trousers before combing a finger through an immaculately trimmed moustache. Then he would bend down and dust a large red cravat over a pair of shoes already polished to a mirror finish. Having completed his grooming

Tim and Janet having a break from home classes. (Tim Bax)

he would snap himself to attention, insert a swagger stick under his arm and totter upstairs to the bar—and his waiting stengah. His departure some hours and many stengahs later tended to be a more comical and less dignified affair.

Another frequent patron to the Club was the community's ranking nobility, an eloquent lady who had married into British aristocracy and settled in Magamba after the war. After the death of her husband, Lady Mary Lead had chosen to remain in her lavish, nine-bedroomed mansion situated on acres of rolling, landscaped gardens. It was staffed by a complement of household servants rumored to be greater in number than were employed by the local hotel. She regularly threw lavish cocktail parties at which dozens of attentive servants would circulate carrying silver trays laden with dainty hors d'oeuvres. It was customary for the servants always to be bare-footed as it was considered disrespectful for them to wear shoes in their master's house, even if the master happened to be a *memsahib*.

One day there was a scandalous rumor that the Air Vice-Marshal had prodded his swagger stick into Lady Lead's bosom to emphasize a point while both were enjoying noon drinks at the Club. The resulting slap to the Air Vice-Marshal's cheek had hushed the bar into silence and almost put paid to the poor man's reputation as an officer and a gentleman.

Couples would arrive at the Club together—and sometimes leave alone. Worse—they might leave with someone else. Unmarried District Officers sent from England lived an isolated and lonely life, as did some of the wives. The Club provided a welcome interlude.

Mother was never to be drawn by us into any discussion on the matter.

ல

We had been at Magamba for almost a year when my pajama-clad Mother rushed into my bedroom one night shaking me from a deep sleep and pulling me from my bed.

"Hurry up," she urged. "Follow me and don't worry about your slippers."

She took my hand and half dragged me through the open courtyard into our living room at the far side. Janet was already there, huddled under a blanket at one end of the couch. Also in the room were a number of armed European policemen.

"Now don't be frightened children, but we've just been told that there are two gangsters roaming around the neighborhood. They have already shot and killed two of our neighbors."

Mother spoke in a business-like tone, as if making a report on the state of the cabbage plantation. "We're going to spend the rest of the night here in the living room. The police will stay and protect us."

Two of the policemen duly remained behind while the remainder slipped out into the still, dark night.

The next morning we heard that two gangsters called Assailo and Appailo had burst into a number of households a few miles from us ransacking the homes and murdering three Europeans in an indiscriminate fusillade of fire. For the rest of that day we remained constantly in sight of Mother who had armed herself with one of Father's hunting rifles. As luck would have it, Father had gone to Dar a few weeks earlier to start a new business importing Helena Rubenstein products from England, leaving the rest of the family behind. Shelagh had just returned to boarding school which had now been locked down by a large militia of European police reservists while the hunt for the killers was mounted.

There were not enough reservists to guard each home, so families were urged to evacuate each night to the safety of the local hotel which was guarded by a contingent of police. Mother however, was made of sterner stuff. She decided she did not want to abandon the house to be ransacked by two renegade killers, and that if they wanted a fight she was game to give it. That night she ushered Janet and me into her bedroom, secured the house, and bundled us into her bed together with Father's fully loaded hunting rifle. We had just slipped into a fitful sleep when we were awakened by the sharp, staccato sounds of rifle fire coming from the driveway.

Mother calmly removed the hunting rifle from under the sheets, cocked it, and positioned herself at the bedroom window.

"Now don't worry," she whispered. "If I start shooting I want you both to crawl under the bed, is that understood?"

It was. We were both under the bed before she had finished speaking.

A commotion in the front garden followed by another volley of rifle fire was all Mother needed to let lose a fusillade of her own. The bedroom filled with smoke and the acrid smell of cordite. To add to the commotion, the percussion of the shots dislodged a large picture from the wall that fell heavily on to the bed we were lying under. I thought it was Mother and worried in case she had been hit. My fears were allayed when I heard her fire off more shots into the night followed by a rapid volley of profanity that must have had the two killers wondering who they were up against.

Just then we heard the welcome sound of a high-revving police Land Rover speeding up our driveway spewing flying stone and gravel. This caused the gang to have second thoughts about pressing home their attack, and after firing a few more desultory shots in the direction of our house they skulked off into the night. The next morning we heard that after leaving us they had ransacked a farm three miles away which belonged to a very eccentric retired old doctor who lived alone. The two killers had walked through the house firing into each room in an endeavor to kill the old man. Miraculously he had survived. Not so lucky was a bottle of his favorite tipple. By the time the police arrived they found the irate doctor angrily bemoaning the fate of a bottle of Dimple Hague Scotch whisky which lay shattered on his bedroom floor.

Not even the wily old Air Vice-Marshal was immune from the attention of the gang. We went to see him the day after they had broken into his modest home, a small cottage situated on a wooded hill overlooking the golf course. We sat in his living room which was cluttered with mementos of a bygone era. One wall was awash with plaques and badges of proud squadrons which had long since flown their last mission westward into the sunset. A Spitfire's propeller hung on a wall above a large fireplace that dominated the far end of the room. The propeller's hub had been bored out and replaced with an ornate brass clock which had stopped a few seconds short of midnight on a day long forgotten. To its left under a small window with tiny wood-framed panes was a glass-topped drinks trolley on which were clustered crystal liquor decanters and fine crystal cocktail glasses. Next to them was a silver soda siphon and ice bucket.

"Pink gin?" he asked Mother, reaching for the decanter. "Keeps the wits honed and the aim good."

"Yes, please. What happened when the gang broke in?"

"I was having my evening ablution when I heard a scuffle in the dining room. I came out to see what the devil was going on and was confronted by these two rascals looking like they had just emerged from a month in the forest."

"Were they armed?" asked Mother, reaching for her gin.

"I should say so. Looked like German Mausers to me. They had one apiece."

"What did you do?" asked Mother, shocked.

"Would have rugby-tackled the blighter closest to me but wasn't dressed for the occasion." The Air Vice-Marshal's moustache bristled as he spoke.

"Dressed for the occasion … ?"

"I was still in my altogether!" "Altogether?"

"Afraid so. You know, naked—flying the Jolly Roger." His eyes twinkled and he gave Mother a sly wink. "Think it must have given them a bit of a fright but it gave me a bit of leeway to make my next move."

"Goodness me, what did you do next?"

"Turned on my wing and flew back to my quarters as quickly as I could." He gestured his square jaw in the direction of his bedroom. "I locked the door behind me and quickly got dressed. By the time I retrieved my shotgun from the closet the bastards had slipped out through the back door. Must have known I was ready for a fight."

"Did you call the police?"

"Police? Heavens no, a stiff shot of whisky was what I needed. By Jove, it seemed to do the trick, so I sat down and had another. If they come again I'll have my guns cocked and ready. They won't catch me unawares next time. I've taken to sleeping with my britches on."

Assailo and Appailo were hunted down two weeks later by a small patrol of European Police Reservists who had relentlessly tracked them through the dense forest at the foothills of the Usumbara Mountains. The patrol had eventually come across the two killers sitting around a fire under a thick canopy of trees. It was early evening and they were busy devouring part of a lamb slaughtered from their last homestead attack and which was now roasting on the fire before them.

It was to be the last meal they ever tasted. Their final tally of murders was thirteen.

℔

With the demise of the gang, social activities in Magamba were able to resume. There was little to do for entertainment, so isolated families tended to create their own. Cocktail parties, for which one was always expected to dress in evening wear, were *de rigueur* in Colonial Africa. Magamba was no exception. Because of the remoteness of the houses and the vast distances involved, a great deal of logistical planning was required before setting off for a function at a neighbor's home. Roads were bad and often became impassable after a sudden tropical downpour. Bridges and culverts could wash away and the rocky surface of the roads made punctures an occupational hazard on even the shortest of trips.

"We've been invited to a cocktail party at the new District Officer's residence. He and his young wife have just arrived from England," announced Mother, after a particularly tedious lesson in English grammar. "I want you kids to help the houseboy load the car after lunch, so don't run off too far."

That afternoon my two sisters and I duly helped the houseboy load Mother's car. It was a small station-wagon into which we packed an array of shovels, ropes, winches, foot pumps, and puncture kits—all standard paraphernalia when traveling to a cocktail party in Colonial Africa. The back seat was let down and a mattress laid on top where the three of us could sleep. With Assailo and Appailo gone we were at least able to dispense with loading Mother's rifle and ammunition.

That evening with Mother in a long evening dress and high heels and Shelagh, Janet and me in pajamas, we set off for the six-mile journey to the District Officer's house. It wasn't long before the motion of the car lulled me to sleep. Some time later I was wakened by Mother shaking me. The car had stopped in the middle of nowhere and it was pitch black outside.

"Out you get, the back wheel has a puncture. Let's get it changed quickly, we're already running late."

We had stopped in the middle of a dense forest and the incessant chirping of cicada beetles made my ears ring. It had been raining and the ruts in the dirt

German Bridge near where the car broke down. (Tim Bax)

road had turned into rivulets of mud. Mother quickly changed out of her high heels and slipped into a pair of Wellington boots which she kept in the car for just such an emergency. Then shucking her long evening dress up around her waist, she waded out into the mud and opened the rear hatch door.

"Come on you three, out you get. Roll the bottoms of your pajamas up and jump out in your bare feet."

We jumped out, the slimy mud oozing between our toes. The mattress was rolled back and the spare wheel, jacks and wheel spanners removed from their storage bin beneath the floor boards. Shelagh held a flashlight while Mother jacked up the car, unscrewed the wheel nuts and tried to wrestle the wheel off. It suddenly came free and she lost her balance, falling against Shelagh who was sent tobogganing down the slippery embankment into the ravine below. Only the faint glow of her torch gave any indication of where she had landed.

"Mummy, don't just stand there, do something!" Janet was always guaranteed to inject a dose of panic into an already chaotic situation.

"Do stop your shouting," whispered Mother, still struggling with the spare wheel. "We won't be able to hear your sister."

We stood silently, straining our ears for any sound which might indicate where Shelagh was. Even the insects seemed to hold their breath in sympathy. Suddenly from the ravine below came the faint sounds of Shelagh sobbing. It spurred Mother into action.

"Hop into the car you two while I go looking for your sister. I don't want you wandering off into the night while I'm gone."

We had no intention of wandering anywhere and scampered quickly into the back of the car while Mother, her cocktail dress still up around her waist, disappeared into the ravine. The insects resumed their shrill call and from deep within the forest came the raucous lonely cry of a bush-baby. It sounded like someone being strangled. Janet and I hardly dared to breathe! About half an hour later with Janet and me peering nervously through the back window like two distraught chimpanzees, Mother and Shelagh re-emerged from the ravine looking disheveled but otherwise unharmed. They finished changing the tyre and after wiping the mud off themselves with Shelagh's pajamas, pronounced the job complete. Mother quickly changed back into her high heels and we sped off down the road arriving at the District Officer's residence late but without further incident.

"You kids remain in the car and try to get some sleep. I've parked close enough to the front entrance to hear you if you need me."

"But what happens if we need to do a pee?" Shelagh seemed to have an innate capacity to think ahead and plan for any critical, life-threatening emergency.

"It's quite alright for you to pee outside the car." As an afterthought she added, "Just don't go outside if the dogs are barking."

"Are they vicious?" asked Janet nervously.

"No, but if they start barking it means there are leopards nearby. I don't want you wandering off to have a pee in front of a prowling leopard."

That night we took turns peeing in one of Mother's Wellington boots.

∽

A year after arriving in Magamba, Mother informed us that we were ready to begin our formal education. At six years of age, Janet and I were to be incarcerated as boarders at the Lushoto Preparatory School. We started to cry.

"Don't worry, you'll be allowed home at half term," said Mother. "Before you know it the first school term will be over."

Each school term was of four months' duration. Even with a half-term break in between, four months seemed an awfully long time to be away from home.

Lushoto. (Tim Bax)

Lushoto School

Come to Lushoto, come to Lushoto, it's the school of misery.
When you get there, there's a notice saying " Welcome unto Thee." But don't
believe it, don't believe it, for they're always telling lies. If it wasn't for the prefects
it would be a paradise.
Build a bonfire, build a bonfire, put the teachers on the top; Put the prefects in
the middle and burn the whole damn lot!
—Lushoto School Song: 1956

The next three years of my life revolved around the constant clanging of a school bell, a severe and humorless German matron called Miss von Kauffman, and an austere French mistress called Zoë Goodwin. Zoë was not a 'mistress' in the classical sense of being an indulgent inamorata … but perhaps she could have been.

She would display flashes of the indulgent and debonair one day, and the next be the antithesis; a juxtaposition of a stern, severe pedagogue of discipline.

The Lushoto Preparatory School was a co-educational boarding school situated in a remote area of woodlands some five miles from the small town after which it was named. The steep majestic peaks of the Usambara Mountains provided a scenic backdrop to the school buildings which at first glance might have been mistaken for a military barracks. Fraternization between girls and boys was discouraged in the classroom; at all other times it was strictly frowned upon.

Mother deposited me with my metal trunk inside the entrance to a wide, gloomy corridor that ran the length of what she said was the boys' dormitory and instructed me to wait for the matron. Then she bent down, kissed me goodbye, and was gone. Mother never believed in prolonging the inevitable. I didn't have to wait long.

"Follow me und zer must be silence, you hear? Zer must be silence at all times."

I might have been forgiven for thinking that Mother had inadvertently deposited me at a German order of a Franciscan retreat. Miss von Kauffman was a thin slip of a woman with pinched features and a permanent scowl etched into her scrawny face. A relic of the school's German past, she had found the transition from German to English a bitter pill to swallow. What better way to extract retribution than on English schoolboys.

"Zis vill be your bed vor ze next term."

I found myself in a spartanly-furnished room that had eight beds, four down either side. Next to each was a small wooden locker into which had been carved the names of countless previous inmates. In the centre of the room was a bare wooden table and against one wall was an old wooden cupboard shared for the storage of school uniforms. No casual clothes were allowed. Hanging on the wall above each bed was a cotton valise for the storage of socks, hankies, underwear and the few personal effects that each pupil was allowed to keep. Tucked into the top of the valise was the bottom of a mosquito net, yellow with age, that hung from a wire strung the length of the room. There were ten similar rooms situated down either side of the long hallway.

"You vill vait until ze rest of ze boys com and zey vill tell you vot to do."

Having inducted me into the school routine, the matron turned on her heels and I was left to my own devices. I was petrified. The rest of the day was a haze of incomprehensible sounds, instructions and routines which numbed my senses and convinced me of one thing: I was determined to run away. At last the day ended and I was able to crawl into bed and escape into the oblivion of a deep sleep.

I was awakened early the next morning by the loud, incessant clanging of a bell. Everyone scrambled out of bed and began groggily to form a line inside the dormitory. Another rancorous clang and lines of boys from each room began merging into one to start shuffling towards the bathrooms. Afterwards we had to form another line to return to our rooms. There we dressed, made our beds and prepared ourselves for breakfast. The whole time we would be under the constant supervision of the unhappy matron.

I soon realized that the school bell was the only arbiter of time. No watches were allowed and no wall clocks or other time pieces displayed. Just as time was measured by the school bell, movement was managed by walking in line like mindless sheep. When we weren't in class we were waiting in line, or walking in line, or doing something in line. Nothing could be done unless it was in a line.

No sooner had I scrambled to get dressed and make my bed, when the incessant bell had us forming a new line to walk to the dining room. This was a large and uninviting hall filled with roughly-hewn wooden tables with benches on either side on to which we were squeezed like rag dolls. At one end of each table sat a glowering schoolmaster who watched over our every move ready to cuff any boy who dared misbehave, just as a lioness might cuff a recalcitrant cub.

The master's function, apart from enforcing strict silence during meals, was to ensure that the contents of our plates were ingested through our mouths and not secretly deposited into our blazer pockets to be discarded later in the day. Any boy unlucky enough to be caught with a pocket full of congealed scrambled eggs while stumbling over a recital of *mensa, mensa, mensam* in Latin class was likely to feel the sudden heavy 'thwack' of the master's flat-bladed wooden ruler across his knuckles. Then would come the dreaded, "Boy, report to the headmaster's office for the cane!"

Upon our return from the dining room we were shepherded into another line to walk to the assembly hall, boys through one door, girls through another. Sitting at a piano on the elevated stage was quite the most bizarre-looking woman I had ever seen. She had the appearance of a ghoulish mannequin that a makeup artist with a warped sense of humor had worked on with the specific intention of frightening children. Cold blue eyes glared piercingly out of a proud but haggard face caked in layers of white powder. Her pale, ghostly appearance was dramatized by large pools of shocking red rouge smothered on her cheeks and her lips were smeared with lipstick of a matching color. A lathering of thick black eyebrow paste completed her bizarre appearance. She

Lushoto school. (Tim Bax)

could have been mistaken for a clown except, as I was later to learn, there was nothing clownish or comical about Zoë Goodwin.

Standing in the assembly hall I was beginning to wonder what fate might befall us when Zoë began pounding the piano keyboard in the opening bars of *Lord Behold Us With Thy Blessing*. Moments later she thrust her arm into the air and began whirling it around like a propeller. This was apparently a signal to galvanize the assembly into song. It was also the cue for the headmaster to stride purposefully on to centre stage followed by a posse of sinister-looking masters who glowered at us as if we might be lambs awaiting slaughter.

Morning classes were interrupted at 10 a.m. by the clamor of the persistent bell. It would have everybody spilling out of their classrooms into a courtyard adjacent to the assembly hall for morning tea. This consisted of sweet black tea and thick slices of bread smeared with globs of butter. Then it was back to class until noon when the same bell would hasten us back to our dormitory to wash our hands in preparation for lunch. We would be joined at lunch by the headmaster, Mr. Smith. He would sit alone at a small round table at the front of the dining room surveying the boys for any infringement of manners such as talking, eating with mouths open, or trying to cram their dumplings into their pockets, or worse, into somebody else's pocket. We would have to pretend to listen attentively to a crackling noise on an old short-wave wireless through which snatches of the BBC news could be heard through the static … and

Sports ground Lushoto school. (Tim Bax)

as we listened we would ponder how best to dispose of our bread and butter pudding without being noticed. Everybody hated bread and butter pudding.

After lunch we would return to the dorms in another orderly line and have to lie on our beds feigning sleep for an hour before the start of afternoon classes. These would end at 4:30 p.m. to be followed by tea in the dining room and an hour of segregated sports on a large playing field at the bottom of a steep slope in front of the school: girls at one end, boys the other. Afterwards we would drift back to our dormitories to prepare for our baths.

The baths weren't really baths at all but heavy concrete tubs in which two boys would bathe at a time. When the first two had finished, two more would take their place and so on until everyone had finished. If you happened to be among the third or fourth lot in, the water would be tepid and dirty. The entire time we would be presided over by the matron who stood on a raised platform made from two wooden pallets stacked one above the other. From this vantage point she could peer into each bath, making sure we got on with what we were suppose to be doing and not deriving any enjoyment from the experience like normal children. She seemed unconcerned at being surrounded by such a large group of naked boys, something that struck me as odd some years later when I started becoming self-conscious of my own body. In fact, she seemed to revel in the occasion.

Dinner followed after which we would return to the classroom for an hour of prep. Then it was back to the silence of the dormitories and the solitude of sleep.

The road to Lushoto school. (Tim Bax)

❡

The days seemed to roll together in an endless routine of clanging bells, snaking lines and scratchy blackboards. Eventually I began to feel like a robot waiting to react instinctively to the next bell that rang, or the next thwack of a ruler on my knuckles, or the feel of the next rawhide cane against my bottom. The terms came and went punctuated only by welcome trips home and the brief respite from the regimented routine of the school.

It was during my fourth term that things took a decided turn for the worse—I came face to face with the person who was to become my nemesis at the school, Zoë Goodwin. I had hitherto managed to avoid any personal contact with the grim-looking woman who smirked at us from behind her piano each morning, and I was startled to see her enter our class one day.

She strode in like an indomitable legionnaire on parade and told us that, henceforth, she was to become the chief architect of our ability to make anything out of our lives by teaching us conversational French. It didn't take her long to realize the enormity of my incompetence for learning foreign languages. Thereafter she became for me a 'femme fatale' of almost tyrannical proportion.

Prep every Monday evening involved reading pages of French literature followed by a written test to see how much we had assimilated. The following day Zoë would stride grandly into our class and announce the results of our written endeavors. Each time, my name would be read out last with a score of zero out of ten. On the third successive week of my failing to score even a solitary mark, she must have arrived at the conclusion that I was beyond redemption.

"Repeat after me," she said, striding towards my desk like a harbinger of doom. "Je suis un espèce d'imbecile."

She spoke slowly, enunciating each word clearly, so that perhaps even I might understand the meaning. I didn't, but the resulting laughter within the class convinced me that if I was to retain any vestige of credibility with my peers, revenge would have to come ... and it would have to come quickly. Luckily it came quicker than I could have hoped.

Zoë lived in a small two-roomed flat beneath my dormitory, accessed by a door situated directly beneath a dormitory window. She owned a horse named Sox that was stabled on the school grounds, and she rode most afternoons. Sometimes after her ride she would alight from her horse directly outside her flat and have a groom return the horse to the stable. I happened to be standing at the dormitory window one day as she dismounted to walk inside her flat. Without thinking, I leaned out the window and spat on her head.

In my haste, I didn't notice the close proximity of the native groom standing nearby; a groom who a few days previously I had used as target practice while showing some of the more junior boys my prowess with a catapult. After a quick consultation with the groom, Zoë came flying up the stairs like a witch on a broomstick. No amount of protestations as to my innocence or of the 'wrongful accusations' by the groom could sway her from her verdict of 'guilty'. The summons to the headmaster's office was as swift as the punishment was severe. Six lashes from a rawhide cane left painful welts on my bottom but enhanced my reputation as one of the 'old and bold' at school.

I had just turned seven years old.

My next caning was also the result of negligent observation, a technique I was to learn the hard way but which, having eventually honed, would stand me in good stead later in my adult life. Miss von Kauffman's low regard for the discipline of English schoolboys was vindicated one afternoon when she walked into the dormitory and found four of us proudly displaying our lower appendages on a table top to see who had the longest. We were engaged in the very important competition of deciding who could claim bragging rights to the enviable title of 'King Willie'. It was an extremely prestigious honor surpassed in importance only by the boy who owned the most marbles. Marbles to a schoolboy were like cattle to the Masai; without them you had little influence and even less leverage.

We had made the unfortunate mistake of not posting a guard while engaged in such an important endeavor. The first that we were aware of the matron's presence was when the sole of her shoe came crashing down on our four willies in a blaze of agony. Before we could react, her shoe came crashing down again in what was a blatant application of double jeopardy. Not satisfied with the severity of her punishment and sensing an opportunity of seeking further retribution for English boys having invaded the sanctity of a former German school, she formed us outside the headmaster's office to await further punishment.

Welts on one's bottom were displayed like badges of honor at bath time. They subjected the wearer to considerable status amongst subordinates and seniors alike. Little regard was attached to an ability to recite the French alphabet, or recite the Latin version of Caesar's address to the Gauls in Pompeii in 58 BC. This was the realm of the remote boarding school where status among schoolboys was determined not from within the classroom, but by deeds more worthy of schoolboy lore.

෴

I had just returned home on the completion of another term when Mother informed the family that we would be leaving Magamba at the end of the following term to return to Dar. Shelagh, who had already left the school having completed its academic curriculum, was attending a Catholic boarding school in England.

Three months later we packed up our household belongings and left Magamba, returning to Dar along the same dusty road we had travelled four years before. Father had bought a house in an exclusive suburb of the city called Oyster Bay and it was there that Janet and I were to enjoy our first holiday at the coast. We spent our days basking in an endless summer of deserted sandy beaches fringed with coconut palms, or surfing on the graceful 'curlers' that rose up slowly from the Indian Ocean to roll gently up the sparkling white sand in shimmering carpets of foam.

The holiday ended too quickly and before we knew it we found ourselves making the long, torturous journey back to Lushoto by rail and road. Although it was only a distance of some 250 miles the trip took over eight hours during which time I was both homesick and carsick the whole way. Living in Dar meant that I would be unable to return home during the half-term breaks, and it would be many months before I would see my parents again.

℘

Back at school I continued to struggle through the seemingly impossible intricacies of French and Latin.

"Boy, give the verb-pronoun infinitive of mensam!" would gloat the Latin master while hovering over me like a vulture. I was clueless. He was a lanky man with an impossibly long beak nose and tiny, close-set eyes partially hidden beneath a dense foliage of unkempt eyebrows. Perched on the end of his long nose was a small pair of wire-framed spectacles with thick lenses through which he would glare menacingly at anything and anyone that caught his eye. His shoulders were constantly hunched and he lived in constant fear of conspiracies being hatched behind his back as though Brutus himself might have been lurking in some dark recess of the class.

Finding the language almost impossible to fathom, I would occupy my mind with something more worthy such as making 'bombers' to flick at some studious-looking girl sitting a few rows up. Bombers were wads of tightly folded paper that could be catapulted with great accuracy over a considerable distance using a rubber band stretched between two fingers. They were a weapon of choice in the classroom and were also a favorite way of conveying secret messages over considerable distances. On one occasion during a particularly tedious lesson in Latin vocabulary, a bomber streaked like a missile directly in front of the Latin master. Thinking that I was responsible for its launch, he came striding toward me, ruler in hand to extract vengeance. Just then another bomber struck him on the back of his balding head. He whirled around fixing his beady eyes on a small fat boy who was unsuccessfully trying to stifle a snigger.

"Boy, how dare you play the fool behind my back!" He strode to the fat boy's desk, glaring down at him like a buzzard from a lofty perch. "Extend your fingers," he leered, and with his wooden ruler landed a crushing blow on the poor boy's knuckles twice in quick succession. Having dispatched the unfortunate fellow to the headmaster's office for the cane, the master fixed his darting eyes back to me, convinced that I must somehow have contributed to the painful welt on his bald patch. I was saved from another certain caning by the timely intervention of the school bell.

☙

Weekends were relatively free and unsupervised. Pupils were allowed free reign in the large common area that sloped up from the back of the school. However, entering the forest beyond was discouraged; it was in the forest that most of the boys chose to spend their weekends. This thickly-wooded area became the scene of epic battles between groups of boys formed into different 'regiments,' each headed by one of the seniors. We would send out patrols into an opposing regiment's area, probing through the thick bush for vulnerable lines of defence so that attack plans could be made and battle plans hatched to capture ground. Here the catapult was the weapon of choice and it was wielded with great effect. Sometimes necessity required that our regiments band together to 'fight' against bands of African children who attended a school in a tribal area across a small river that formed our school's boundary. One weekend we received information that a group of African schoolchildren was planning a foray across the river to try and occupy an area of our forest and, if possible, capture one of us as prisoner.

We had an excellent intelligence network in the form of a native who tended the sports ground and who lived in the same location as many of the black schoolchildren. He would give us information in exchange for food which we would sneak out of the dining room in our blazer pockets. He informed us the Africans intended 'attacking' the following Sunday. Their plan was to walk down the road that ran parallel to the boundary river and then up a steep hill to attack one of the forts we had built to safeguard the school's rear flank.

At the appointed time, two of our combined regiments comprising some thirty schoolboys lay in ambush halfway down the hill, taking cover in thick bush. The plan was for us to lie low and upon a signal from our lead scout, rise and fire our catapults to scatter the attackers. We had been waiting for about an hour when we heard the sound of voices coming down the road. We crouched expectantly waiting for the signal to attack. There was a sudden shrill blast from the scout's whistle that had been stolen the night before from the sports master. We rose as one to unleash a volley of pebbles into the mass of bodies below. There was a moment's silence followed by shrieks of anguish from a group of schoolgirls running helter-skelter down the road with their large and buxom matron, Miss Buckle, panting in hot pursuit behind them.

It was like a carnival gone badly wrong. There had been a terrible mistake. We had fired at a group of our own schoolgirls on their way to the river for a Sunday picnic. Our scout, not wanting to compromise the entire operation by being seen, hadn't properly identified the target before giving the signal to attack. It was yet another lesson that, even as I felt the first whack from the headmaster's cane, I resolved never to forget.

Towards the end of that term we received a letter from Mother saying that we would not be returning to the school. Janet was to join Shelagh at the Catholic boarding school in England and I was to remain with my parents in Dar-es-Salaam.

My academic future remained uncertain.

3
Dar-es-Salaam

The objective of the Club is to promote social intercourse between gentlemen.
Jackets and ties for gentlemen are mandatory after 6 PM.
Women are required to dress appropriately except in the bar.
—Club Rules, Dar-es-Salaam Club: 1965

I was elated at having been taken out of boarding school and wasn't at all worried by the fact that my parents seemed unable to find a school in Dar-es-Salaam that would accept me.

Father had recently been appointed Secretary of the Dar-es-Salaam Club, a prestigious 'Members Only' establishment steeped in colonial tradition overlooking the city's tranquil, palm-fringed harbor. Most of the Club's public rooms were the exclusive domain of gentlemen members; women were allowed by invitation only. At noon the men would gravitate to the bar and drink gin and tonic as they deliberated beneath swirling ceiling fans on the growing emergency in Kenya, or some other bothersome native insurrection within the colonies. The women would cluster beneath the shade of thick canopies of lush, pink and white bougainvillea on the Club's expansive verandah and sip chilled glasses of fruit-laden Pimms as they gossiped about the latest scandal. There was always something to gossip about … even if it was as mundane as some new colonial officer's wife from England who might have breached some unforgivable protocol at last night's ball. Splendidly-attired native servants dressed in white, ankle-length kanzus, red cummerbunds and fezzes would loiter discreetly nearby waiting for a signal from the women to have their drinks replenished. Drinking provided a pleasant escape from the boredom of the cloistered society of the colonies.

The Club's opulent dining room was the personification of elegant sophistication and superlative service and was reputed to serve the finest cuisine in the colony. Each evening after dinner, members and their guests would congregate on the upper balcony overlooking the blinking lights of the harbor where invariably a British warship would be at anchor. There they would sip liqueurs and smoke cigars taking solace in the presence of such a powerful symbol of Britain's naval might … and pontificate over the invincibility of the Empire.

❧

One of the perks that came with Father's job was a family dwelling within the Club grounds into which our family had moved. It was staffed by the usual bevy of cooks, houseboys, dhobis and garden boys, all of whom would fall over each other ensuring that no one, especially the memsahib, had to lift a finger doing menial household chores. Janet and I only had to snap our fingers to have the servants scurrying to the Club to obtain anything we desired, from soufflés to sodas. We became terribly bored while Mother and Father were at work and would keep the servants occupied by compiling creative 'chits' for them to deliver to the Club demanding such exotic childish delights as 'Coca-Cola mixed with peanuts.'

Even though we had our own cook, our family would often have meals delivered from the Club's dining room. A lovebird called Kiki who lived in a cage in the dining room foyer would screech in indignation each time a Club waiter arrived to serve our meals. One day at lunchtime Kiki remained silent, so Father got up to see what was wrong. The bird was lying on the floor of its cage in a state of paralytic intoxication. Earlier that morning I had filled its water dish with Bombay Gin. Father's reservoir of patience was not unlimited and I was confined to my bedroom for the rest of the day on a diet of bread and water.

❧

I had been living in Dar for some months enjoying a carefree lifestyle when things took a decided turn for the worse. Mother mentioned a word I had been dreading ever since leaving Lushoto—*school*!

Mother and I were walking along the beach one afternoon when she asked what I thought I might like to do when I grew up. She was particularly worried by the fact that my teachers had all appeared vexed as to what I might be *capable* of doing. "Not capable of applying himself to anything involving maths or science" had written my algebra teacher in a glib reference to my having failed to grasp even the basic rudiments of fractions.

I had no idea what I wanted to do, so Mother adroitly turned the conversation to what she thought *she* might like me to do.

"I think it would be a good idea if you followed in your father's footsteps and joined the army," she said, stepping gingerly over a large starfish that had been left stranded on the beach by the outgoing tide.

"What do people do in the army?" I asked, bending down to examine the speckled pink creature.

"They live in special barracks and train to shoot guns and things." Then in an apparent effort at not wanting to create an impression that it was *all* she thought me capable of doing added, "I think it's something that all young men are required to do at some time in their lives."

"What if I don't want to join the army?" I asked, guardedly. I certainly didn't want to be cornered into something which sounded worse than boarding school.

"Then you might have to go to jail," responded Mother gravely.

"Well, going to jail sounds better than shooting guns at people." I was rather pleased at the ease with which the problem of my future seemed to have been disposed. Mother seemed less enthusiastic.

"Then we'll just have to hope you do a little better at the local convent where your Father and I have decided to send you. They deal with children who have special needs."

I was almost tempted to ask if I could change my mind and join the army, anything to keep out of school. But I was only nine years old and the thought of shooting guns scared me. Mother went on to explain that Shelagh would soon be returning on holiday from the convent she was attending in England. Then upon her return to England, Janet would go with her to attend the same convent. I was to remain behind to begin the next phase of my hitherto unsuccessful academic journey.

I was elated that I still had at least a few more months of freedom.

❦

The big event on the Dar social calendar was a visit to the harbor by a British warship for the purpose of what the British ostentatiously referred to as 'Showing the Flag'. This involved anchoring the ship at a prominent anchorage, bedecking it in a colorful extravaganza of flags and colored lights, and holding a series of non-stop cocktail parties for everyone who was anyone. Sometimes a whole squadron of warships would arrive throwing the entire city into a carnival of decadent partying. It sent a strong warning to the natives not to try and usurp the power of their colonial masters.

The prize amongst the social elite in the city was to be invited to a midday cocktail party hosted by the Captain. Invitations would be sent out on gold embossed cards: "Captain Fothergill-Adams, Royal Navy, O.B.E., D.S.M., on behalf of her Britannic Majesty, cordially invites you to … ." Attendance would include the Governor, District Commissioners, District Officers, Privy Judges, Judge Advocates, and, on one occasion, our entire family. I had never been on a warship before and Father secretly hoped that if I wasn't to join the army, the visit might encourage me to become a swashbuckling sea rover.

After a brief tour of the vessel, guests assembled on the foredeck where a band of the Royal Marines sat sweltering beneath a red, white and blue canvas awning playing *Rule Britannia* while sailors circulated carrying trays of gin and tonics and hors d'oeuvres. Precisely at noon the Captain rose to propose a toast to the Queen, and guests rose unsteadily to their feet … only to duck in fright a moment later when a celebratory gun was fired from the ship's aft gunnery deck. Nobody had thought to warn the startled guests about the fusillade and some though it might be the start of a native insurrection. It quickly became apparent that it was: just moments later soldiers of the 2nd Battalion, King's African Rifles, based in their barracks a few miles away decided to mutiny against their British officers and non-commissioned officers. With typical British composure, the cocktail party on the frigate was allowed to finish before its decks were cleared of the clutter of revelry and replaced with the accoutrements of war. I secretly hoped the ship might shed its anchor and steam off with guests still clinging to the quarterdeck as eager spectators for what might follow. Alas, we were shepherded into a longboat tied alongside and taken to the Queen's Wharf where we eagerly gathered to wave the frigate off as she sailed through the harbor mouth at full speed to meet this new menace to the Empire.

The mutineers had taken control of the barracks, locking the handful of European officers and NCOs in a small ante-room adjacent to the Officers' Mess. They were in the process of setting up roadblocks leading into the city when the first salvo from the frigate exploded outside the barracks in a profusion of smoke and shrapnel. It was as if somebody had thrown a cobra into a chicken coop. By the time the frigate's only helicopter clattered noisily overhead with a small contingent of Royal Marines still dressed in their band uniforms, the mutineers had scattered. The only mopping up to be done was removing a few of the diehard mutineers from the soldiers' canteen. Their main priority had been to lay siege to the canteen's liquor supply, a task they had performed with admirable efficiency.

Dar-es-Salaam harbour with British warship. (Tim Bax)

By a remarkable stroke of good fortune, the Officers' Mess steward had decided against joining the mutiny and had remained stoically behind the bar during the entire fracas. He was still there when the officers were freed from their brief imprisonment and was able to serve them stiff tots of gin.

So ended the first ever mutiny by the King's African Rifles.

❧

Sensing that the incident with the naval frigate might have perked my interest, Father decided to take my exposure to seamanship to a new level. I was already spending much of my time at the Yacht Club, which was within easy walking distance of our house, gazing at the sleek yachts as they sliced effortlessly through the turquoise sea, their beautifully-colored mainsails pulled taut against an offshore breeze and their full spinnakers reefed tight against the mast.

"I've decided to build a sailing boat," Father grandly announced one morning. I was elated. The prospect of my being able to put to sea in the company of such graceful sloops as *Sea Breeze* and *Ocean Queen* was more than I could ever have dreamed.

"But Daddy, there are some lovely yachts for sale at the Yacht Club, why can't we buy one of those?"

"Because I'd like us to try building one of our own," replied Father firmly. "That way we can design it to our own specifications."

I would have preferred to buy a ready-made sloop but the prospect of building a yacht to our own design sounded exciting enough. "When can we start Daddy?"

"The hull is due to arrive tomorrow morning so there's no reason why we can't start the following day."

That night I couldn't get to sleep thinking about my sudden stroke of good fortune. There were so many questions to be answered: What would I call her? Who would I invite on my maiden voyage? Could she be rigged for a genoa? Eventually, I fell into a fitful sleep and dreamed of roaming the seven seas.

The next morning I could barely contain myself. Father had left for work at the Club and I spent my time hounding the house servants as to where they thought the best place might be to build the boat. They appeared as excited by the great undertaking as I was, and Ali even suggested it would be a good idea if he came along as chief cook and bottle washer on my first voyage. I informed them that the hull would be arriving later in the morning and that it would probably necessitate a crane driving on to the premises. Ali, who now considered he had a stake in the enterprise, suggested that we should cut down a large betel nut tree that grew outside the back door. We eventually decided that such a capital project would probably require the consensus of my parents, so we compromised and utilized our time clearing the shrubbery from under the tree so that at least we would have shade to work under.

Just before lunch Father phoned to tell me that the hull was arriving that afternoon. Barely able to disguise my excitement I told him about having cleared a place to put it under the betel nut tree. This seemed to please him and it seemed that everything was falling into place. Soon after lunch, I saw two Club employees staggering down the interleading walkway between the Club and our house carrying a large oak barrel which they placed under the tree. I couldn't imagine building a yacht large enough to carry such a large barrel but it seemed a trivial matter. Eventually Father arrived and I couldn't disguise my excitement any further.

"Daddy, when's the hull arriving?"

"That's it under the betel nut tree," he replied, pointing to the barrel. He seemed perplexed that I should even have asked.

"But what's the barrel got to do with the hull of our yacht?" I was beginning to feel the first qualms of apprehension that something might be amiss.

"The barrel *is* the hull, fat-head. We're simply going to cut it in half and use one side as the hull. The other half we can cut up to make seats, a rudder, and whatever else we decide to put on her."

My dream of being able to sail away in a seafaring sloop evaporated as quickly as the morning mist off the Masai plains. I started to cry. Ali started to laugh, as Africans tend to do when confronted by the absurd.

Eventually the barrel was sawed in half and after a few days of Father doing his best to craft something that resembled a floating vessel, he pronounced it ready to launch. It looked exactly like what it was; a blunt nosed, wooden wine barrel cut in half! Father had fashioned a mast from an old deck railing and Mother had donated an old mop handle to be used as a boom, and another as a tiller. The final touch was to cut up a white linen tablecloth that Father had commandeered from the Club's dining room and which Mother had sewn into something resembling a sail.

On the day of the launch some African servants were corralled from the Club to carry the newly-commissioned 'yacht' to the beach. Not thinking that it was deserving of a name too grand, I decided to call her *Betel-Nut*. She was floated in the water and held steady by the intrigued servants as I gingerly climbed aboard. Then to much applause from Father and amused laughter from the Africans, I was pushed to sea on my maiden voyage. Apparently Father's limited knowledge of naval architecture hadn't extended to a realization that barrels have a propensity to roll over when placed in water; half a barrel has a propensity to roll over and sink. Luckily, *Betel-Nut's* blunt nose prevented her from travelling more than a few feet out before she turned turtle and disappeared beneath the waves.

My venture into the mysterious realms of the sea had ended in abject failure.

Mr. Deppetawalah's Villa

Later that year, Shelagh returned from England to spend Christmas with the family. Mother decided it would be as good a time as any for us all to get away on holiday. Father was unable to join us as Christmas was a busy time at the Club and there was much to be planned in the way of seasonal festivities.

Mother was working for the Federation of Tanganyika Employers and had struck up a business acquaintance with an Indian trader who enjoyed a colorful reputation among the business fraternity in Dar. Mr. Deppetawalah made his money and his reputation selling illegal bounty under the guise of being a respectable importer/exporter. He preferred to be known as an Indian 'merchant', though his business cards, of which he carried a variety, described him alternatively as being a 'Gentleman Trader' and a 'Purveyor of fine imported goods'. He reminded me of an accomplished conjurer trying to bewilder an unsuspecting audience into believing the unbelievable on the pretext of an impeccable reputation for honesty … Mr. Deppetawalah was anything but honest.

He owned a large pink villa on the beach of an historical Arab slave-trading town north of Dar-es-Salaam called Bagomoyo. It was from there that natives had been herded into dhows to be dispatched as slaves to the Arabian Peninsula. Rumor had it that Mr. Deppetawalah might have had family connections to the slave trade, lending some authenticity to his ambiguous designation of 'Gentleman Trader'.

The villa was a two-storey brick and stucco building painted in a shade of pink which locals within the town called 'Deppetawalah Pink'. Years of exposure to the tropical sun had faded it to a sad and melancholy complexion that couldn't really be described as anything. A chaotic tangle of white bougainvillea had clawed its way up the outside walls in a desperate attempt at camouflaging its fading luster. Upstairs, sea-facing bedrooms opened on to a spacious balcony that ran the entire length of the villa with a panoramic view of the sea. It was an idyllic place to spend a holiday.

"I hope no slaves had to work here," said Janet, looking suspiciously around the living room. It was congested with heavy furniture carved from teak beams which had been removed from Arab dhows. Magnificently-carved teak bookcases containing an entire library of books covered the length of one wall.

"Don't be silly, dear. Of course slaves didn't work here. They were kept in jails in the town until being loaded on to the dhows bound for Arabia." Mother seemed anxious to deflect any association the villa might have had with the slave trade.

"Well, I certainly wouldn't want to sleep under the same roof that any poor slave had to toil under," responded Janet piously.

"You don't have to worry about that, dear. Now, if you're all ready let's go down to the beach before it gets too hot."

"Mummy, it mentions the slave trade in this book I'm reading," injected Shelagh, paging through a voluminous, dust-covered book she had extracted from a bookcase. It was entitled, *The Bagomoyo Slave Trade: 1874 -1905*.

"Read it out loud so we can all hear," said Mother, relieved at having proof to quell Janet's concerns. "I don't want anyone thinking we've come to a slave house on holiday."

Shelagh began reading … "Bagomoyo: the name of a large pink villa owned by a legendary Indian slave trader whose cruelty to slaves chained within its walls led them to refer to it as *Bagomoyo*, meaning *the place we gave away our souls*. The name was later given to the nearby harbor town from where slaves embarked on their voyage to the Arabian Peninsula."

Further thought of the beach quickly evaporated as Mother disappeared into the kitchen to pour herself a stiff gin!

જ

Christmas and New Year came and went; so did Janet and Shelagh. It was another tearful farewell as they boarded an ageing Dakota aircraft for their exhausting three-day flight to London via Benghazi and Rome. Shelagh, age 16 and Janet, age 12, would have no one to take care of them during the long flight, and once they landed in England would have to find their own way to the Catholic convent at which they were enrolled in Deal, Kent.

I remained behind to attend the local Catholic convent a few blocks away from where we lived. My academic progress remained depressingly slow while Mother and Father wracked their brains as to what could be done to improve it. They eventually managed to find a lady tutor who agreed to take on the herculean challenge of improving my grades. Unfortunately, she happened to be rather an attractive and voluptuous lady who had a cleavage which ignited my imagination more than the mathematical equations she spent endless hours trying to get me to unravel. After four months of agonizing effort, she eventually had to admit defeat and I was left to labor in the wake of my more accomplished classmates at the convent.

જ

Each afternoon after school Mother would drive me and our German shepherd, Vikki, to the beach in Father's old Peugeot whereupon we would waste little time plunging into the surf. Vikki loved the sea as much as I did and would seldom leave my side for as long as I remained in the water. She would paddle around me in tight circles keeping me as close to the shore as she could. It was as if she had taken it upon herself to become my personal lifeguard. Afterwards

Mr Deppetawalah's pink villa. (Tim Bax)

we would race each other back to the car, where, no sooner had I opened the passenger door, then she would jump in and vigorously shake herself dry. Everything in the car, including Mother, would be covered in a deluge of seawater and beach sand. Then Vikki would curl her wet body on the front passenger floor and we would wait patiently until Mother had calmed down enough to drive us home.

It wasn't long before the floor of the car began to rust badly and one day it fell out completely. I was sitting in the passenger seat with Vikki between my feet when all of a sudden she disappeared from view and I was left staring through a gaping void in the car floor. Thinking that my seat might follow, I shouted to Mother in alarm. This caused her to swerve into the path of an oncoming bicycle being ridden by an old and very dignified-looking African. He managed to avoid being struck by veering off the road into a ditch, where he was set upon by Vikki, who thought him responsible for her sudden and unexpected exit from the car.

Motoring behind us was an elderly family friend called Major Reg Field, who stopped to see if he could be of any assistance. He was never without a

Mother, Tim, Shelagh and Janet on the beach in Dar. (Tim Bax)

hip flask of gin tucked into the inside pocket of his worn tweed jacket and it was the gin that saved the day. The fiery liquid had an immediate calming effect on the old African who was quite happy to have both his pride and his ego restored by a few hefty swigs. Having milked the occasion and the flask of everything he could, he tried to remount his bicycle, but succeeded only in falling back into the ditch. Mother seemed unsure about what to do.

"We can't just leave the poor man lying there, he might be unconscious," she worried.

"I think now would be as good a time as any to take a page from the French as they were fighting the Hun on the Maginot line … *always take advantage of a lull in battle to beat a hasty retreat*," suggested the Major. "Might I suggest we rendezvous at the bar for a drink?"

"We can't just leave the old man lying by the side of the road," gasped Mother.

"He seems quite peaceful right now," persisted the Major. "He might feel less magnanimous when he wakes up a little later with a hangover and with the anaesthetizing effects of the gin no longer numbing his dog bites. I don't think

Vikki (Tim Bax)

we should be around when that happens."

Deciding to heed his advice, Mother herded Vikki and me into the back of the Peugeot and we set off for the Club, leaving the old man slumbering peacefully by the side of the road.

❧

Two years after our return to Dar-es-Salaam the unthinkable happened and Tanganyika decided to cut the bonds of the yoke which had kept her tied to England's bosom for the past twenty-two years. Not even the lavish cocktail parties aboard Britain's mighty battle cruisers had been able to prevent the sun from setting on her once-proud empire. The Union Jack was lowered from the Club's flag pole for the last time, and crowds of joyous, chanting natives spilled into the streets of Dar-es-Salaam in a chaotic celebration of *uhuru*. It was 12 October 1962 and I was twelve years old.

Unfortunately with the unraveling of the empire also came the unraveling of my parents' marriage. Father and I left for England shortly after independence and eventually settled in a small town in Kent called Tunbridge Wells. Later, we were to be joined by Shelagh and Janet on holiday from the convent.

Mother remained in Africa for a short period to tidy up her affairs. Her intention was then to return to her native Canada via England, collecting Shelagh, Janet and me on the way. The four of us would then catch a voyage across the Atlantic leaving Father behind in England.

I wondered whether I would ever see Africa again.

England

Father and I arrived in England during the middle of a cold, wet and soggy winter.

I found myself inducted into an English school system I knew little about and liked even less. My only noticeable achievement was after Father insisted I join the school's Cadet Corps, the Royal West Kents. I was on the rugby field taking part in a Bren gun firing practice using blank ammunition when I inadvertently sent a volley of *live* tracer bullets arcing past the teachers' staff room. Quite how a magazine of live rounds ended up in my particular gun was never fully established, even after an exhaustive inquiry. I was reasonably certain, even with the dislike I had for some of my teachers, that I hadn't personally been responsible.

The cadet training officer was an old major named Mackenzie Halethorpe-Jones whose only claim to fame during the war was spending a week at an El Alamein bar acquiring a taste for gin after being rescued from a desert oasis called Sidi-el-Bish. He had become stranded there while reconnoitering German airfields as a member of the Long Range Desert Group. His taste for gin had never deserted him.

"Damn oasis was as dry as a skeleton in a teetotaler's closet," the Major would recount for the umpteenth time as we lay behind our Bren guns. "Not enough water to wet a robin's whistle."

With that he would unhitch a dented aluminum canteen which he wore on his belt and take a long swig before smacking his lips and wiping his mouth with the back of his leathery hand.

"By Jove, you've never tasted water until you've really needed it," he would gasp, taking another long swig. Only later did we realize that the canteen was full of *gin*. It was after he had taken a number of nips from his canteen while instructing us in the firing techniques of a Bren gun that my accidental discharge occurred. The Major had acquired some live Bren gun tracer rounds to compare to the blank rounds we had previously been using. I can only imagine that in his befuddled, gin-fueled mind he must have inadvertently put a belt of live rounds into my gun instead of blank rounds. When I eventually pulled the trigger and the Bren rattled into life spewing an arc of tracer bullets toward the school, the old Major seemed quite excited.

"By Jove, lad, that'll keep their ears pinned back for a bit. They'll think the Hun has arrived at their door," he said, taking another swig from his canteen. "Another burst like that and I'll wager they'll be digging their foxholes deeper."

Miraculously the only injury which resulted from the mishap was to the village vicar, who also happened to be the school's religious studies master. It was rumored he had fainted on being confronted by the sight of a schoolmistress's knickers as she dived for cover beneath the coffee table.

I really liked the old Major. He inspired me with tales of redoubtable exploits against the Germans with impossible odds and in the harshest of conditions. I asked him one day what it felt like to be old.

"I don't feel old. I don't feel anything until noon; then I have a nip of gin!"

The comment on my first *and* last report card from the school was, "Timothy's academic standard upon being accepted into the school was below average. Unfortunately, it has continued to deteriorate." I left the school still unable to recite my multiplication tables with any degree of accuracy, but knowing precisely where Sidi-el-Bish was located in the North African desert.

の

Five months after arriving in England, I embarked on the SS *Sacramento* with Mother, Shelagh and Janet destined for a new life in Canada.

4

Canada

"Success is assured through achievement. Fame through spectacular failure."
—Graffiti, boys' washroom, Northern Secondary School,
Toronto: 1966

"Tim, you'll have to start concentrating a little harder on your studies. Your exam results are appalling." At the age of sixteen I had just completed my third term at Toronto's Northern Secondary School and my report card was less than flattering. Mother was not impressed. She would have been less so had she seen it before I had forged it into something a little more respectable!

I had arrived in Toronto from England the year before with Mother and my two sisters. Father had remained in England. Our voyage across the North Atlantic had been well timed to coincide with the onset of a bitterly cold and ferociously stormy winter. Gales whipped the tumultuous seas into a frenzy and the small freighter on which we had secured our passage was tossed about so badly we had to strap ourselves into our bunks to prevent being flung against the opposite bulkhead. It was strapped into our bunks that we remained for most of the voyage. The first meal we enjoyed shortly after leaving harbor also happened to be our last. A heaving stomach and rolling seas are not conducive to fine dining, even if one did feel inclined to take a stab at one of the bowls of mulligatawny soup that skidded across the dining room table as the ship ploughed down the side of another huge wave. We were rather pleased to see the cold, barren shores of Nova Scotia appearing through a blizzard of snow some fourteen days after leaving England.

Sick and disheveled, we caught a train to Toronto where we were met by my startled grandparents. They had been unsure of what to expect of a family who had lived for so long 'amongst the savage natives in Africa' and were aghast at our motley appearance.

"You'd better stay with us for a while so we can put some meat on your bones," scolded Grandma, taking in our skeletal appearance.

Fourteen days of retching on the high seas had left us looking like hungry refugees. Three months later, bloated and fat, we were glad to hear Mother announce that she had acquired a small two-bedroomed apartment for us. My initial excitement at being able to move into a place of our own was quickly tempered when I realized it was situated obscenely close to a drab-looking secondary school which loomed menacingly outside our lounge window like a harbinger of doom. Mother took pride in telling us that it was Northern Secondary School, her old Alma Mater.

"It's a new school with extremely high educational standards. I was one of the first pupils to enroll at the school and I think it would be nice if you children could follow in my footsteps."

Alarm bells instantly started ringing in my mind. We had only been in Canada a few months; surely it was unduly hasty to be thinking of a return to school! As if reading my mind Janet came to my rescue.

"Mother, it could hardly be considered a new school if you attended it forty years ago. It looks rather bleak and forbidding now. Isn't there somewhere a little more modern we could attend?"

"Don't be silly, dear. Your grandmother says it still enjoys a good academic reputation and besides, I can remember it had wonderful outdoor sporting facilities." Mother seemed resolute.

I couldn't imagine my elderly and somewhat absent-minded grandmother knowing much about anything, let alone the academic standards of the city's schools. The only sporting facility visible outside our window was a barren parcel of land buried beneath four feet of snow.

A week later I found myself being ushered into the Deputy Principal's office for an assessment on which school curriculum might best suit me. He was an unhappy-looking individual who sat hunched behind a large mahogany desk peering uncertainly at an open file containing a record of my academic history. His brow was furrowed and he looked gravely concerned.

"Yes Timothy, I see that you've had … uhm, shall we say, a challenging time as far as your … uhm, academic achievements are concerned."

He leaned back in his reclining chair with his hands clasped tightly under his chin, looking at me as if I might have been some unwelcome alien who had suddenly appeared to make his life miserable. He waited for me to offer a response to his astute observation.

I was at a loss to explain my dismal academic performance, so focused instead on a group of longhaired youths I could see through a window situated behind the Deputy Principal's chair. They were lounging on the grass and appeared to be taking turns inhaling from a cigarette that was being cautiously passed between them as if it were some illegal contraband. Perhaps the school wouldn't turn out to be so bad after all. The Deputy Principal, who thought I was staring vacantly at him, sat patiently waiting for me to respond. He must eventually have begun to wonder whether I even possessed an ability to communicate, so he coughed nervously into his hand and continued.

"What we ... uhm, normally do," he coughed again, leaning forward in his chair to peer closer at the unwelcome file. "What we normally do is to try and fit our new pupils into a ... uhm, an academic stream that would best complement the subjects they had previously excelled in." He paused, his eyebrows knitted in concentration. "But I see in your case we have ... uhm, shall we say, very little to go by."

Clearly, excelling in catapult fights and raking machine-gun tracer bullets past teachers' staff rooms were not aptitudes the Deputy Principal had been confronted with before.

"I think ... uhm, we should look at starting you off in the ... uhm, four year science and technology course. It's tended to be ... uhm, a successful area into which to place students who we have been ... uhm, shall we say, unsure of in the past." He looked at me gravely, almost with pity.

Scribbling a few notes in the file he hurriedly closed it and pushed it with some relief to the far corner of his desk. It was as if he were pushing away a distasteful and particularly obnoxious plate of food. He was obviously relieved at having protected the integrity of the school's more noteworthy academic streams by placing me into the school's melting pot of 'challenged students'.

"Welcome to Northern Secondary School," he offered with trepidation.

I was rather pleased at having navigated myself through the interview with at least a modicum of success. I had been accepted, albeit reluctantly, into the school—even if it wasn't into one of its more acclaimed courses.

However, my spirits were dampened later that evening when Mother informed me that my twin sister had been accepted into the school's five-year university entrance Arts and Business Science course at a grade higher than mine.

഑

During my first school assembly I was relieved not to see anybody resembling Zoë Goodwin scowling down at me from the stage. When I asked a boy seated next to me if pupils were allowed to be caned, he looked at me as though I was quite mad. Discipline in the school appeared quite lax, with few rules pertaining to anything. The only attendance rule was that a note signed by a parent had to be produced explaining any absence from school. What I didn't realize was that the notes ended up in the Deputy Principal's office to be kept on file.

One of my classmates was a mischievous, blonde-haired urchin who had an uncanny ability of being able to extract from his mother an unending reservoir of scribbled letters explaining his habitual absence. He would constantly try to entice me into skipping classes to join him on a foray into town to do something—anything rather than sit in a classroom listening to a subject we both found loathsomely boring and mostly incomprehensible. The problem was that my mother was nowhere near as naïve as his must have been so I would end up having to fabricate my own notes. I eventually became quite adept at forging Mother's signature, and my attendance at school began dropping in proportion to the number of bogus notes that began accumulating in my file.

One day we both skipped school to avoid writing a math exam that neither of us had any expectations of passing. We decided that a more worthy way of spending the day would be to explore one of the more 'risqué' neighborhoods in the city. Catching first the subway and then the bus, we eventually found ourselves standing in front of a seedy-looking striptease club advertising a nonstop procession of 'free to look, pay to touch' scantily-clad women. Never having seen a bare bosom before, I suggested to my friend that now might be as good a time as any to expand our knowledge of the female anatomy. A lesson in biology seemed a reasonable substitute for the mathematics class we were missing. Our only obstacle was a sign on the front door '18 Years and Older'.

Not wishing to miss out on such a golden opportunity, I led my friend down the street to a disreputable-looking bookstore advertising avant-garde adult literature. The storekeeper was hesitant about allowing us in, but I convinced him that all we wanted to purchase was a dark-colored pen. He hastily sold us one in order to hasten our exit from the store. We slipped into a nearby alley and spent the next few minutes inking on to each other's faces what we hoped looked like beard stubble, but which probably just accentuated the adolescent acne we both suffered. Armed with our new disguise, we walked back to the strip club, purchased our entrance tickets from the sleepy-looking attendant, and slipped excitedly into its cavernous interior.

We found ourselves inside a dark, stale-smelling hall full of filthy vinyl-covered seats with a stage projecting into the center. A soiled red velvet curtain was pulled across the back of the stage from where presumably the ladies would make their *entré de grande*. There weren't many people inside, so we sat as close to the stage as we dared without becoming too conspicuous. Then we waited in breathless anticipation of what might follow. A few minutes later a hollow-sounding speaker started blasting a scratchy rendition of *Love Potion Number Nine* and the stage curtains slowly began to part. My excitement was just beginning to mount when I felt myself being unceremoniously jerked from my seat by two vice-like grips locked on to each side of my shirt collar. I was half carried and half dragged back up the aisle I had just walked down with my feet dragging along the threadbare carpet. Outside the front door I found myself unceremoniously deposited on the pavement, to be joined a few seconds later by my disheveled-looking friend. We lay sprawled on the cracked concrete like two rag dolls at the feet of two of the ugliest creatures I had ever seen.

"If we catch you two tadpoles in here again we will keep you until your parents come and collect you," said the man closest to me. He didn't appear to have any eyes, just two small slits where his eyes should have been, and his teeth, or what was left of them, were stained a dirty brownish-yellow. His arms, chest, and bulging neck were a smudge of dark tattoos. I desperately wished I was back in the security of my school. My math teacher seemed almost angelic by comparison. The two hulks continued chastising us as we scampered away, feeling like two delinquents who had been caught peeking through a bedroom keyhole.

The following morning I arrived at class early and placed my carefully-crafted 'sick note' on the teacher's desk. There was still some time before class started and I was determined to reap at least some profit from the previous day's fiasco. With an aura of great conspiracy, I fished my ticket from my shirt pocket and proudly displayed it to the boy sitting next to me. On it in large bold letters was printed, 'Welcome to the Victory Burlesque Theatre – Toronto's Premier Sex Club'.

"What's a burlesque theatre?" he asked.

"I don't know, but there are lots of naked girls inside," I whispered, deciding to remain mute about the fact I hadn't actually seen any. Nor did I feel inclined to allude to details of my premature eviction.

"You mean whores?" gasped the boy in awe. Before I could correct his somewhat erroneous description word buzzed around the class like wildfire.

"Wow, you went inside a whore-house? What's it like? What did you do? The entire class swarmed around me like bees to a honey pot. I was just beginning to bask in my newfound notoriety when I suddenly felt the ticket being plucked from my fingers. Standing above me was Mr. Baginski, the class teacher.

"Your sick note says you were suffering from sore eyes and a sore throat," he said with the smugness of somebody about to expose a major fraud. "Did your eyes get sore before or after you attended the strip show?" Obviously he had been eavesdropping on our conversation. I began to get a distinct sense of foreboding that I had not heard the end of the previous day's debacle.

That afternoon, my feelings of misgiving deepened when into the history class walked the Deputy Principal's secretary. "Timothy Bax would you follow me to the Deputy's office, please." She paused for effect ... *"Immediately!"* My heart began to sink.

Downstairs I was quickly hustled into the Deputy Principal's office and I was horrified to see Mother already in attendance. She looked anything but happy. My immediate reaction was to flee, but a clicking sound indicated the door being closed behind me; my options were looking perilously limited. On the Deputy Principal's desk was an untidy pile of scribbled notes which I immediately recognized as being my forged sick notes. I was shocked at how many there seemed to be. My sense of foreboding deepened when I saw clasped between the Deputy's fingers the infamous ticket I had been relieved of earlier that morning. He held it at arm's length as if it might be the most unsavory thing he had ever touched in his life.

"Could you ... uhm, explain how you came into possession of this ... uhm, ticket? It ... uhm, seems to have been purchased on the same day you were ... uhm, shall we say, incapacitated by sickness." He frowned in distaste. Not wishing to subject either himself or Mother to any sordid explanation I might offer, he quickly continued, "Your ... uhm, mother seems to be ... uhm, unaware of the existence of ... uhm, some of these sick notes."

"All of them!" corrected Mother.

My fate was sealed; my compromise complete.

The following morning two things happened. Mother decided that I should spend my spare time as a member of the local militia, and she also decided that I should travel to England at the end of the school year to visit Father.

"Janet will have completed her schooling so she can travel to England with you. When you return to finish your schooling, Janet will remain in England to attend university."

Janet had already been accepted into the London School of Economics after which she planned to travel to Belgium to study at the University of Europe. She would complete her embrace of the elite European tertiary institutions by attending three semesters at the Sorbonne in Paris. Her academic achievements made mine look like something from the 'Parthenon of the Failed'. I was still struggling to get through high school, an accomplishment which was by no means assured.

It was decided that while we were in England visiting Father, and before Janet entered university and I returned to Canada, we would do a bicycle tour of Europe so Janet could get the 'lie of the land'. It all sounded terribly exciting.

I thought I had got off rather lightly from my misdemeanors.

༚

Mother made the necessary arrangements for me to join the militia at the Toronto Armory and the following week I found myself walking into its drab interior to commence training with the Royal Regiment of Canada. I spent most of my weekends for the next few months being taught the rudiments of basic drill. This involved the complex procedure of getting my feet to work in conjunction with my arms while being hounded around a Parade Square by a maniacal drill sergeant. What made the experience particularly disconcerting was the fact that his shrill commands, shouted into my ear at close range, were accompanied by enormous amounts of spittle.

The Drill Sergeant suffered from an extraordinary inability to remember anyone's name, a problem he overcame by referring to everybody as 'shithead'. One evening while marching in a squad, I made the grave mistake of turning left when I should have turned right. The reaction from the Sergeant was as if I had caused an insurrection within the Regiment. He suffered an apoplectic fit of anger. His face and neck became so swollen and red I feared he might have a stroke.

"Halt!" he eventually bellowed, sounding like a mortally wounded buffalo.

Halt was the magical word to stop everything in its tracks. We froze where we were like granite statues barely daring to breathe. I was weighing up my chances of making a dash for freedom through the Armory gates when my senses were numbed by the noise of the Sergeant barking into my ear. The accompanying spittle made it seem like he had sneezed at the same time.

"What's your name, shithead?" "Bax, Sergeant."

"I'm trying to turn this bus right and you have it skewered across the road pointing in the wrong direction, you shithead. What did you say your name was?"

"Bax, Sergeant."

"You get back on to that bus, shithead, and next time it turns right you make sure you turn right with it! Understood?"

"Yes, Sergeant."

"What did you say your name was?"

ↄ

One weekend I was sent as part of a squad on an overnight bivouac to a Canadian Forces training base at Camp Petawawa. Any misguided thoughts I might have entertained of an exciting weekend were dashed when I heard we were to be accompanied by the screeching Sergeant. Upon our arrival at the camp we were taken to a remote pine forest to be taught how to make temporary shelters and set up patrol bases. That night we had to take turns doing guard duty. I was awakened just before 2:00 a.m. by somebody tugging at my feet.

"Wake up," came a whispered voice from the dark. "You're on guard." I slipped groggily from out of my sleeping bag feeling slightly disoriented. The forest seemed alive with sound. A chorus of shrills and chirps enveloped my senses and an owl hooted from somewhere above me. Eventually, I got to my feet and felt my way to a large tree on the perimeter of the camp where I sat with my back against its trunk staring vacantly into the night. I almost died of fright a few minutes later when I heard a voice from somewhere in the inky blackness behind me. It was the Drill Sergeant.

"Guard, identify yourself! Where are you?" I heard him tripping and stumbling toward me sounding like a disorientated rhinoceros. I thought he must be checking to see if I was awake.

"Here, Sergeant," I hissed as loudly as I dared, trying to sound alert.

ↄ

"Where?" he grunted, bumbling closer toward me through the thick underbrush. I was glad it was only an exercise. Had we been at war every enemy within a mile would have known of our presence.

"Here, Sergeant," I repeated, getting to my feet and stepping from behind my tree. He stumbled his way to where I stood, steadying himself breathlessly against the trunk.

"Name?" His voice rasped loudly in the night. "Bax, Sergeant."

"Who?" It was as if he had never heard the name.

"Bax, Sergeant."

"Shithead?"

"Yes, Sergeant."

"I'm going into the trees for a shit parade," he announced in a voice louder than modesty might have necessitated.

It seemed that everything in the army had to be done as a 'parade', even a natural body function performed at 2:15 in the morning. The owl which had been hooting in indignation at the clamor became suddenly quiet, as if stunned into silence by the Sergeant's dramatic announcement. Even the insects and frogs gave momentary pause from their incessant chirping.

"I'll be back in a minute. Keep your eyes open for when I return." He stumbled past me carrying a shovel and a toilet roll and then disappeared into the night. The last thing I heard was a loud fart as he crashed and stumbled deeper into the forest.

After a few minutes I thought I heard a noise coming from deep within the forest and wondered what might have become of the Sergeant. I was tempted to shout out. Once I thought I might even have heard him calling out, but thought it might be the owl. Then there was silence. As time went on I began to get worried. I wasn't sure what to do and wondered if I should go in search of the poor man, but doubted my ability to find my way back. After some thirty minutes I decided that I had better do something. So I crawled to the shelter of the Lieutenant in charge of our squad.

"Sir, Sir," I whispered urgently through the flap of his shelter.

"What is it?" he muttered from inside his sleeping bag.

"It's the Sergeant, Sir. I think he's lost!"

"Pull yourself together, boy. What do you mean the Sergeant's lost? Where did he go?" The Lieutenant sounded agitated.

"Shit parade, Sir. About forty minutes ago and he hasn't returned yet!"

"Shit parade? What are you talking about? You're not making any sense, boy!"

Never having spoken to an officer before I wondered if "shit parade" might be an expression they were unfamiliar with.

"The toilet, Sir. I think he went to the toilet and got lost." "You've been awake for too long, boy. There are no toilets in the

forest. Go and wake the next guard and get some sleep. The Sergeant is probably in his shelter sleeping." With that the Lieutenant rolled over and went back to sleep.

I wondered how the Sergeant could possibly have returned to his shelter without my having heard him. Feeling rather foolish, I did as I was told and woke the next guard. Then I went to sleep. The following morning it was discovered that the Sergeant was indeed missing.

"What was the last thing you heard from the man?" asked the lieutenant, preparing to send out a search party.

"A fart, Sir!" 'A fart?'

"Yes Sir, a fart."

Operation "Lost Fart" was launched. The Sergeant was found around noon that same day looking cold, dehydrated and distinctly embarrassed. Obviously his bushcraft and night navigation skills were not up to the standard of his drill. The incident affected him badly and he lost a lot of his verve and passion. Not long after, he was transferred from being a drill sergeant to manning the armory's logistics stores. I hoped he would have greater luck remembering what was in his stores than who was on his parade.

Europe

Erma's Bordello
Discount for hotel residents. Bookings available at reception.
Closed for religious services on Sunday.

—Notice above Reception desk,
Hilltop Pension, Arenas de Mar

The following summer at the ages of 17, Janet and I arrived in England to visit Father who was managing a small country hotel in Kent. Shortly after our arrival he drove us into the little village close to the hotel to purchase two new bicycles with which we could start preparing for our tour of Europe. The following morning Janet and I set off down a country road to test our new bikes and see how far we could cycle in a day. We hadn't traveled far when we came to a steep hill. Ignoring Janet's cautionary remarks about the judicious use of brakes when freewheeling downhill, I took off like a champion cyclist intent on winning Olympic gold. Half way down the hill my front wheel started wobbling so badly I lost control and fell off, sliding the rest of the way down headfirst. I came to a stop—minus shoes, trousers and a good portion of my skin—at the feet of a grizzled old Kentish farmer who peered down at me in disbelief as though doubting his own eyes. Just then I was joined by what remained of my bike which tumbled through the air like an elongated flying saucer. Janet arrived shortly after, thinking I might be dead.

"Is he still alive?" she asked, looking down it my prostrate body. Not waiting for a reply, she added, "Don't you think we should try and find his trousers?"

"Never mind his trousers," growled the farmer. "You'll have to find a doctor who can graft some skin back on to his hands and knees." With that he picked me up, pitched me across his shoulder and started striding toward his farmhouse. "But first we'll get the wife to throw him into a tub of hot water to disinfect his wounds."

I spent the next two weeks as a guest of Britain's health services being attended to by a Pakistani doctor barely able to speak English. He informed me through an interpreter that it would take another month for my skin to heal. It took considerably longer for Father to weld my bike back together.

Eventually, Janet and I with our bikes in tow were able to catch the ferry across the Channel to Oostende in Belgium. We spent the next three weeks pedaling through Belgium, Holland and Germany staying in youth hostels, or where these were not available, sleeping on roadsides or beneath bridges. One day after a particularly grueling climb up a steep mountain pass in Germany Janet suggested we get rid of our bikes and hitchhike the rest of the way. I readily agreed, but changed my mind two days later when the truck driver with whom we were traveling stole our backpacks. By then it was too late; we had already sold our bikes.

With few possessions other than the clothes on our backs and feeling distinctly disenchanted, we were picked up on the side of the road by a swab young Englishman driving a new Jaguar. He agreed to drive us a considerable way down the Spanish coast to the little resort town of Arenas de Mar on the Costa Brava. Having lost most of our money and much of our gear, we decided that this would be as far south as we would venture. After spending a few days soaking up the sun we would return to England.

The only affordable accommodation we could find was a rambling, open-style Spanish villa with its spacious bedrooms converted into dormitories. It was full of young travelers who lay sprawled about in varying stages of undress seeking respite from the heat. The Spanish lady who ran the establishment seemed as laid back as she was uninhibited.

"Se, se … sleep anywhere. Girls and boys together in the same room, in the same bed, I don't care. Give me 5 pesos a day and sleep anywhere."

Her attractive olive face was framed by a mane of jet black hair which cascaded around her shoulders in waves of soft curls and she wore a striking red dress with plunging neckline that left her breasts almost completely exposed. I wondered if she might also be the Madame of the bordello which was audaciously advertised on the wall behind her. I decided against asking when I remembered the precarious state of our finances. Purchasing some sunscreen seemed a wiser investment if we intended spending time on the beach. I followed Janet upstairs to find two beds which we could call home for the next week.

Walking to the beach the next morning, we stopped at a tiny store selling beachwear to replace the towels we had lost during our journey. Standing amongst the locals we must have looked like English tourists just emerged from hibernation after a long, bleak winter. I suggested to Janet we buy some tanning cream.

"Don't be silly," she replied, scooping up a big bottle of olive oil. "That's far too expensive. We're in Spain now. How do you think all these people keep such lovely tans?"

"These people were born on the beach and haven't moved off it since. We haven't had our bodies exposed to the sun since before the onset of the last Canadian winter." I was not convinced that olive oil was the answer for a painless transition from a lily-white complexion to a deep Spanish tan.

"Tim, you're talking as if we're going to be in the sun all day. Olive oil is less than half the price of sunscreen and if we put enough on, it will give us all the protection we need. The secret behind not burning is to drink lots of liquid. The wine here is cheaper than bottled water. A gallon or two should be enough to keep us well hydrated throughout the day."

Janet's knowledge seemed all embracing and I felt ill inclined to argue.

We spent the rest of the day drenching ourselves in olive oil as we soaked up the bright Mediterranean sun, quenching our thirst with copious amounts of cheap Spanish plonk. We spent the next week confined to our beds looking like lobsters freshly plucked from a pot of boiling water then seared over an open fire.

A week later we were back at London's Heathrow Airport with me bidding a fond farewell to Janet and Father. I was sorry to be leaving my sister and it was a sad parting. She hadn't even turned eighteen and would have to remain behind to fend for herself with little financial support in getting herself through university.

The following day Mother collected me from the Toronto Airport to complete my last year at school.

Lumberjack

Women are prohibited from the bunkhouses.
Women living in the bunkhouses will be charged for accommodation.
—Notice: Bunkhouse #1
Island Lake Lumber Company
Chapleau: 1966

"Mother, I think I'd like to return to Africa after my schooling." "To do what?" she asked, looking startled. "You kids have done nothing but complain about how primitive Africa was; now you're telling me you want to return!" We were sitting in the living room of our Toronto apartment and I was glancing through a newspaper advertisement exhorting new immigrants to settle in South Africa.

"The South Africans are advertising for qualified artisans and professionals. They'll even pay the passage for those who meet their criteria," I said optimistically.

"Well, don't let them have sight of your academic qualifications. They'll probably pay to keep you out," responded Mother skeptically. "What do you intend doing once you get there?"

"Architecture. My teacher says I have a flair for designing buildings, and it's one of the fields listed as qualifying for a free passage."

"Well, you're hardly a Frank Lloyd Wright in the making and I would think they're looking for someone with a bit more than just a high school diploma. It's by no means certain you will achieve even that." Mother clearly wasn't sharing in my enthusiasm. "Even if they do pay for your passage, you'll need money once you arrive. You need to find yourself a job this summer to put aside a nest egg."

A month later I was surprised to receive notification from the South African Embassy in Ottawa that my application for free passage to South Africa had been accepted. My date of departure was set for four months after the end of my final school year. A week later Mother announced that she had managed to secure a summer job for me working at a lumber camp in Northern Ontario.

"They've agreed you can continue working at the camp after you graduate from school while you wait for your passage to South Africa. It should enable you to save enough money to sustain yourself over there until you can find a job."

Toiling in a lumber camp in the middle of the Canadian wilderness wasn't quite how I had envisaged earning money during my summer holiday. I was thinking more in terms of being a waiter, or washing dishes—anything but a lumberjack. Unfortunately, I failed to make an impression on the many restaurants I visited and sixteen weeks later found myself boarding a Canadian National Railways train for an overnight journey to a northern Canadian lumber camp. I certainly wasn't feeling very lumberjackish!

&

The 'Island Lake Lumber Company' was situated on the edge of a pristine lake about eight miles west of the small railhead town of Chapleau. I alighted from the train at dawn the following morning not having a clue how I was supposed to get myself to the camp. Hitching my backpack over my shoulder I started walking along a dusty road which I hoped would lead me into town where I could ask for directions.

I had walked about three miles and the sun was just beginning to cast its pale glow over the eastern horizon when I reached Chapleau. I continued walking towards the centre of the town, along sleeping sidewalks littered with empty beer cans. It looked as if the numerous bars and saloons I passed had done a brisk business the night before. Nothing moved. It was as if the town itself might still be sleeping off a terrible hangover. A thin, middle-aged man looking badly in need of a shave and a clean set of clothes lurched toward me from a side street. He reeked of stale whisky and cigarettes.

"Excuse me, could you tell me the direction to the Island Lake Lumber Company?" I asked hopefully. He stopped to lean against a street light which was still emitting a feeble glow in the morning light, then retched into a storm drain already clogged with trash.

"What?" he replied, gazing indignantly at me through pale, watery eyes. His skin was a dull, ghostly grey.

"The Island Lake Lumber Company, do you know how I can get there?" He vomited again, shook his head and stared at me for a long moment as if trying to focus his tired eyes.

"Yeah, down the road two miles, left at the stop street and eight miles further down the dirt road," he spluttered, coughing fitfully. He was still swaying unsteadily against the street lamp as though not trusting his balance.

"I work there myself. Tell them I'll be a bit late … be at the mill as soon as I can clear the cobwebs." I wondered if he meant today or tomorrow, or even next week.

He extended a clammy, limp hand towards me. "Sean Connor O'Connor, friends call me Connie." I shook it reluctantly noticing it was shy two fingers, then turned and set off in the direction he had indicated.

He stopped me. "Careful of them bears, there's plenty in the woods. But they don't like the smell of whisky; here … take a slug, it should get you there safe enough."

He reached into his back pocket and extracted an almost empty bottle of Scotch. I wasn't sure whether or not to take it. I had never slugged neat whisky before. I took a swig which burned down my throat like liquid fire. If I was going to be a lumberjack, now was the time to start learning. I took another slug and tossed the empty bottle back to the unsteady man. I was barely old enough to shave.

I started walking. By the time I arrived at the lumber camp it was well past midday and I was soaked in sweat. I made my way to a small log cabin with a sign 'Administration Centre' painted on its door. Inside was a large, French Canadian woman with a smile as large as her ample bosom.

"Bonjour, M'sieur," she beamed. "Comment ça va mon vieux?" "Excuse me?" I replied. I must have looked perplexed because she continued in broken English.

"We expectant de boy on de passengaire train, you mast be de l'enfant Bax?" Not waiting for a reply she embraced me warmly as if my identity had never been in doubt. "Welcom to Lac de l'embâcle."

I thought I might have arrived at the wrong camp. "Lac de l'embâcle?" I queried.

"Tis de nam of de camp dey call Island Lac," she said reassuringly, writing my name into the staff register. "You will join de gang at de sawmeel tomorrow wit olde man Pierre Laframboise. Today you be settle in de bunk, dat be bunkhouse number un."

She pointed in the direction of a row of neat looking bunk houses on a small rise overlooking the camp. I contemplated telling her about my meeting with Sean Connor O'Connor and passing on his message but wasn't sure who he had wanted me to give it to, so decided against it. I was on my way out when she added, "Tomorrow you meet with M'sieur de Rosie, de millwright for Lac de l'embâcle."

Bunkhouse number one was empty when I arrived. A loud buzzing from the direction of the sawmill indicated that everyone was still at work. Four steel beds, each with a thin mattress, were arranged down one side of the wooden cabin with a small basin set in one corner. I placed my backpack on the only empty bed which was against the far wall, and extracted the limited bed linen that Mother had allowed me to bring. The only storage space was a narrow wooden shelf above the bed upon which I placed a few toiletries, including a bottle each of expensive aftershave and cologne; everything else I placed under the bed. The bunk house was to be my home for the next three months. I hadn't been there very long when in walked Sean Connor O'Connor.

"Knew there was a young-un moving into the bunk house," his breath still reeked of alcohol. "Didn't realize it would be you. Sean Connor O'Connor's the name, friends call me Connie."

I shook his clammy, limp hand for the second time that day. Then he collapsed on the bed next to mine and fell asleep.

ও৲

When I awoke the following morning, my entire body was swollen in itchy, red welts. Lying on the floor next to Connie were my bottles of aftershave and cologne. Both were empty. Connie was sitting on his bed looking at me through hazy, blood-shot eyes.

"Sorry, woke up in the night with a terrible thirst, that's some fancy stuff you had in those bottles. I see the bedbugs gotcha. Need to put some birch branches under that mattress of yours. Keeps the bedbugs away." Not only did Sean Connor O'Connor have an insatiable fondness for drinking men's toiletries, but he was proving to be a walking encyclopedia on how to survive in a lumber camp.

Breakfast in the cookhouse consisted of huge plates piled high with eggs, bacon, sausages, steaks, chops, pancakes dripping with maple syrup and toast. Jugs of steaming hot coffee were circulated around the tables like gourds of beer at an African wedding. The cookhouse appeared to be the centre of social activity within the camp and it seemed that just as one meal was ending, another would be beginning. Lumberjacking in the Canadian wilderness was hungry work.

Not long after breakfast I heard a huge diesel engine below the mill cough into life. It spluttered belching clouds of blue smoke and then settled into a steady, clanking rhythm. The engine was the power source for the mill, driving its many saws, conveyer belts and chipping machines. I was waiting near the mill wondering how I would get to meet the millwright, M'sieur de Rosie, when I felt a heavy weight on my right shoulder. I turned to be confronted by the biggest man I had ever seen. Removing his enormous hand from my shoulder he gripped mine in a bone-crunching grip.

"Bonjour de yong man an' welcom to you, my nam is Jean Bateese de Rosie." He continued grasping my hand, almost crushing it. "Com wit me for to show you de plas dat we call, Lac de l'embâcle. I show you around all over de plas, an show you de work dat we do. Den when we is don, I tak you down to de lac to work with M'sieur Pierre Laframboise."

With his lilting French Canadian accent he sounded almost poetic. I was soon to learn that there was nothing poetic about M'sieur Jean Bateese de Rosie. Before joining the Island Lake Lumber Company he had been a soldier with the Royal Canadian 22nd Regiment, the famous 'Van Doos'. This French Canadian mechanized infantry regiment, whose battle honors scattered the globe, had an airborne company attached to its 3rd Battalion. Bateese de Rosie, as he liked to be called, had been the company's bull-nosed Sergeant-Major. He had been present during many of the Regiment's more recent skirmishes and was known for 'taking no prisoners'.

He explained to me the importance of knowing all the job functions in the mill.

"De man she wok in de mill each day, be dronk most all of de tam. From de town dey com most all of de day, drinking w'isky blanc and rum." I wondered at the abundance of signs that were displayed around the mill prohibiting the intake of alcohol. "Dey lose de finger in de saw, not good for dem at all. So you l'enfant de job you tak, when fingers dey 'ave no more."

It seemed that my new responsibility was to replace anybody whose fingers had been lopped off by one of the numerous saws that whirred inside the mill. I decided that it would be a good idea to avoid alcohol while working at the camp and wondered whether Sean Connor O'Connor might be one of the first workers I might have to replace.

I followed Jean Bateese de Rosie attentively around the mill as he explained the workings of every saw, sorter and chipper. As we walked through the mill it became evident that the one thing he hated more than anything was cats. This was unfortunate as the mill seemed infested with cats of all shapes and sizes.

"Dam cats dey be all over de plas. Dey be no use at a'll. If you catch dem it be grande affaire, for into de debarquer dey go."

Luckily, the cats appeared more nimble-footed than the hulking millwright was agile. If they suffered the misfortune of being caught they would end up being thrown into the chipper machine to be incorporated into sheets of prime Canadian plywood.

We ended up walking down to a large wooden jetty jutting out into the deep waters of the lake, next to which floated an unimaginable tangle of huge logs. Across the lake constant streams of logging trucks disgorged yet more logs into the water. They were prevented from floating away by long booms of old logs tied end-to-end with metal chains. As each boom became full, the logs would be towed across the lake by a powerful diesel-powered boat to be added to those already at the mill.

There was an old man working on the jetty with a battered briar pipe clamped firmly in his mouth from which billowed plumes of strong-smelling Cavendish. He was wielding a long fourteen-foot aluminum pole called a pike, on one end of which was a sharp metal spike and a claw-like hook used for untangling logjams. The pike was used to push the floating logs on to a moving conveyer chain which carried them into the mill. Jean Bateese de Rosie greeted the man before introducing him to me.

"Dis be M'sieur Pierre Laframboise wit whom you will work most all of de tam." The man paused from his work just long enough to grip my hand in his vice-like fingers. For the second time that morning I thought my fingers might snap. The millwright explained that helping M'sieur Pierre Laframboise push logs on to the conveyer chain would be my job when I wasn't temporarily replacing someone who had had their fingers sliced off in the mill. He impressed upon me the importance of the job.

"If no log dey com up to de debarquer, de mill she shot right down. Den all of de tam the work she is stopped, there be no recompense."

It seemed a terribly responsible job to be giving a young schoolboy and more alarmingly, seemed like frightfully hard work. My sense of unease wasn't helped the following morning when I learned that the man who I was replacing had had his foot amputated falling through a log jam. Pierre Laframboise soon taught me that it was not brute strength that was required to dislodge the tangled logs, but a knowledge of which particular log was causing the jam. Except for brief periods in the mill I spent the entire summer on the jetty working with Pierre Laframboise. He taught me how to 'read' a log jam, how to nimbly step on to the jams in order to dislodge a troublesome log and most important, how to keep the pointed end of my pike sharp. He taught me how to read the weather from the direction the loons were facing as they called plaintively from the lake, and how to judge the next day's temperature from where the whippoorwills roosted for the night.

We would be on the jetty before daybreak, untangling the logjams that had formed in the night so we could feed them into the mill as soon as it started. The work was backbreaking and constant and we stopped only when the saws stopped for 'early breakfast'. This was followed by 'late breakfast' around mid-morning then lunch. Food at the lumber camp was hearty and plentiful and never in short supply.

Each evening after work a huge dinner was served in the cookhouse. Later the men would drift back to the bunk house or sit in a common room to watch television. Few of the workers had cars and the town was too far away to walk every evening. I would sit on the side of my bed listening avidly as Connie talked of endless days spent in lumber camps too numerous to recall. His was a sad tale of a misspent youth and opportunities lost.

"It's the devil in the whisky that makes a fool of me," he would lament sadly, his hands shaking, "and a fool and his money are easily parted."

Sitting on a bunk on the far side of the room, a lonely man with no family or future would play a sad and melancholy lament on a battered six-string guitar he kept beneath his bed. The sun would decline slowly below the horizon and a loon would give a plaintive call from far out on the water. One by one the men would lie back on their beds and stare vacantly up at the ceiling until sleep brought them respite from another day's toil.

No baths or showers existed at the camp. The only means of bathing was a large communal sauna constructed on a wooden platform extending into the lake. Each Saturday morning with the mill shut down for the weekend the sauna would be fired up and we would drift into its hot, steamy interior with crates of beer. There we would sit naked, consuming vast quantities of beer as we sweltered in the intense heat. When it became unbearable, the door would be flung open and we would jump into the icy waters of the lake looking like a gaggle of freshly-plucked ducks.

After the sauna we would dress in our cleanest pair of dirty jeans, a checkered shirt, and hitch a ride into town. The bars and taverns did a thriving business each Saturday night relieving the mill workers of their weekly wages. Whatever was left over was eagerly scavenged by the multitude of prostitutes who guarded every street corner like garish sentinels of the night.

❧

I worked at the camp for three months before returning home to finish my final school term.

When I returned the following year with the great ordeal of my education finally behind me, I was surprised and saddened to hear that Pierre Laframboise had been killed. He had been doing what he loved best: balanced atop a log jam with his long pike thrust down into the cold, deep waters of the lake trying to find the elusive log that would unravel the rest. He had found it as he always did, but the logs had unbundled quicker than he had expected. He lost his footing and quickly slipped between the logs into the icy waters below. His body was not recovered until the following day.

"He still be der, like a phantome on de jam, be Pierre Laframboise. I still see him der mos' every tam, shak'in de head and smokin de pipe, be the spirit of M'sieur Laframboise." I had never seen Bateese de Rosie show any emotion, but when he told me of the drowning a tear trickled down the gritty paratrooper's cheek. He walked up to me placing his huge hand on my shoulder.

"Take up de pike of Pierre Laframboise and leesten closly to wot 'is spirit say. You no more a l'enfant, but homme de Jeune, so good luck to feed de debaquer."

With that he thrust Pierre Laframboise's pike into my hands, turned his back and was gone. From that day I worked on the jetty alone, with only the spirit of Pierre Laframboise's to guide me.

I worked for another four months at the mill keeping its hungry saws fed with logs. Eventually the day of my departure to South Africa neared and I had to return to Toronto. I said my final farewells to M'sieur Jean Bateese de Rosie, to Sean Connor O'Connor and to the many others in the camp who had become my friends. I decided to walk to the train station, just as I had walked the day I arrived. I wished I had remembered to ask Connie for a swig of Scotch before I left.

It was a sad day as I climbed aboard the train for my final departure. In my backpack was the end of the pike that had belonged to Pierre Laframboise and which I had used for the past four months, its metal tip still razor sharp. It was given to me by Jean Bateese de Rosie as a lasting memento of my stay at the camp.

"You mus never forget de lumberjack day ... de day you spend on Lac de l'embâcle. An never forget de spirit of de man, de man dey call M'sieur Pierre Laframboise."

☙

Two weeks later I said goodbye to Mother at the Toronto International Airport. I was nineteen years old as I boarded the plane for my return to Africa.

5
London

Prophylactics are not to be thrown out of windows. It is unhygienic for people passing below.
Use litter bins provided.

—Sign behind the door,
Hotel Venus, London

Landing at London's Heathrow Airport in the late afternoon I quickly cleared the formalities of Passport Control and Customs. I felt elated with my newfound freedom. After eighteen years I was finally released from the yoke of parental control … and of my alma mater. I was young and adventurous, soon to be nineteen and about to embark on my own voyage of discovery. I flagged down a taxi.

"Where to, skipper?" asked the cab driver.

"Cheap hotel, close to the night life," I replied in an authoritative voice. I was determined to have a memorable start to my voyage.

"That puts you in Soho. Take my advice and keep with a crowd. I've seen too many young boys like you walk away minus their trousers and wallets."

I had no intention of losing either. My tone of voice and sallow complexion obviously hadn't left much of an impression. The salty old cab driver had seen it all before. I wasn't too sure where Soho was but if it was good enough for him, it was good enough for me. Let my voyage begin!

Darkness was already beginning to spread its shadowy veil as we circled around Piccadilly Circus and turned turned up towards Oxford Street. The thoroughfare was ablaze with an extravaganza of flashing neon lights and beckoning signs.

"Is this Soho?" I was becoming somewhat concerned. It all looked terribly expensive and somewhat out of the league of my meager wallet.

"Up the road and to the left, skipper. You'll know when we get there." I could see him shaking his head at me through his rear view mirror.

Four blocks later we left Oxford Street and several streets later turned left on to Archer Street. The comparison was as instant as it was stark. We had just turned off a broad thoroughfare awash with bright lights and glittering shop windows and were now immersed in the gloom of a narrow street lit only by the pale glow of sleazy red signs offering questionable services by the shadowy figures loitering beneath. The signs blinked their tired, repetitive messages as if badly in need of sleep.

My taxi pulled up next to a drab double-storey building boldly advertising itself as the *Hotel Venus*. A handwritten notice inside the front window announced the hotel's hourly rates as being the cheapest in town. The notice was illuminated by a bare red light bulb hanging from ceiling.

"This is it, skipper. Cheapest 'otel on the strip."

The two-way radio inside the taxi crackled into life as the driver announced our arrival. I felt distinctly uncomfortable. The *Hotel Venus* was not the type of hotel I had envisioned in spending my first two nights of freedom.

"I'm not too sure that I really like this area very much. Do you suppose we could try looking for something a little nicer?"

"Listen laddie, I have another fare waiting for me. I warned you about the area. Now gimme thirteen quid and 'op out so I can get moving." My sudden demotion from 'skipper' to 'laddie' didn't bode well for my being able to negotiate a more respectable hotel.

"Perhaps you could take me back to Oxford Street," I suggested hopefully.

"Laddie, each minute you keep me waiting is costing you another nicker. Now gimme *fourteen* quid an 'op out." My earlier feeling of déjà vu was rapidly receding.

"You can just drop me somewhere on your way to your next fare … ."

The taxi driver didn't even let me finish my sentence. "That'll be *fifteen* quid, laddie. Gimme a twenty and I'll be happy with a fiver tip. Now go on, 'op out so I can get moving." I realized I was on the losing end of a futile and very expensive argument.

Inside the hotel I paid for a single night's accommodation. "Where's the lady you're with?"

"I'm by myself." The landlady looked at me suspiciously but agreed to show me upstairs to a room. I was feeling decidedly in need of a drink. The evening wasn't going as I had planned.

"Do you have a bar downstairs?" I asked, as she followed me up the stairs. She eyed me suspiciously, as if intent on making sure I didn't steal any of the hotel's fittings on the way to my room. There didn't seem to be many fittings left to steal.

"What d'ya think we are then, the Ritz?" The old lady was wheezing from the climb and seemed on the verge of an imminent attack of asthma. "There are plenty of bars outside along the strip. You pay to watch a show and the drinks are free."

We had reached the top of the stairs and she was leaning against the balustrade, gurgling noisily in quick, shallow breaths. Having satisfied herself that I wasn't going to steal anything she turned around and wheezed slowly back down, sounding like a tired steam engine. She turned at the bottom of the stairs.

"If you bring a lady back tonight it will be another 20 quid."

My room was small and musty. The bed sheets looked as if they had successfully escaped the attention of the laundry lady for some time. The *pièce de résistance* was a pink prophylactic dispensing machine screwed to the wall above a tiny sink in the far corner of the room. On it was a sign warning against discarding its contents under the beds or out the window. A similar sign was situated behind the door where one would normally expect to see emergency evacuation procedures.

The thought of some drinks while being entertained to an adult show in London seemed like sweet revenge for my ejection from the Toronto strip club some years before. Perhaps my stay in London would not turn out to be so bad after all. I quickly showered, changed into some clean clothes, and walked downstairs into the dimly-lit street. Not wanting to venture too far from the doubtful security of my hotel room, I opted for the first club I came to. It didn't look very welcoming but boasted the services of a bar. The entry was barred by a steel grill gate. Behind it stood an unfriendly-looking individual who looked like he would be more at home inside a wrestling ring.

"May I come in?" I inquired politely.

"You a member?" he snarled, unsmiling. His bare tattooed arms were crossed over his large, barrel chest.

"No, I don't want to become a member. I'd just like a drink, please."

"Two pounds membership." He wasn't the type to engage in frivolous conversation.

"But all I want is a drink at the bar," I persisted. "Two pounds membership."

He unclasped his muscular arms in a clear sign that he wasn't inclined to prolong the conversation much longer. I hurriedly extracted the money from my wallet and placed it into his open hand. The grill gate opened and he nodded in the direction of a narrow, dimly-lit passage.

Walking along the passage I came to yet another grill gate behind which stood what appeared to be the first man's twin brother. It was only after I had been relieved of a further two pounds 'entrance fee' and another eight pounds to watch a floor show, which would include free drinks, that I was allowed to proceed into the gloom of the club's inner sanctuary. I groped along, barely able to see anything. Feeling my way to an empty seat, I sat down and waited for my eyes to become accustomed to the dark.

I soon realized that I was the only person in the room and was beginning to wonder whether a show would be put on solely in my honor, when I felt the presence of somebody sliding into the seat next to me. I turned my head to see an extremely attractive and well-proportioned blonde girl smiling at me through a smudge of red lipstick. She placed a long slender arm around my shoulders.

"Why are you sitting by yourself?" she purred.

"I'm here to watch the show," I responded, sounding rather foolish. I forgot to mention anything about wanting a drink.

"Well, I'm the dancer ... " she whispered, leaning closer so that her lips touched my ear. "And I don't do shows just for one person." Her tongue began to flicker inside my ear. "But ... I have a room upstairs and I give a very, very good private show ... ."

"But, I've really just come for a drink."

"Then ... why don't you give me twelve pounds, come up to my room for a drink and I'll give you a show that you'll never want to tell your mother about."

By now she was almost sitting astride my lap. I was already pretty sure I didn't want my mother knowing anything about my first night in London. But to get my 'free' drink I gave her twelve pounds.

"All you need do is wait for a few minutes while I go upstairs and prepare myself. Then walk to the man at the second steel gate and ask for the key to Susan's room."

My evening's investment was beginning to look perilously shaky. It seemed I was now entwined in more than just her slender arms. It was double or quits! When I arrived at the steel grill gate to ask for the key, Mr. Helpful was his usual polite self. There was no Susan working in the establishment, no keys and no private rooms. I was shown to the front door.

No one even bothered to wish me a 'good night'.

The Atlantic

"Are you on leave from your Regiment?" "No, not exactly!"
"What do you mean?" "I'm on furlough." *"Furlough?"*
"Yes. Got into a spot of trouble with the commanding officer's daughter."
—Conversation aboard SS *Windsor Castle*: 1969

By six o'clock the following morning I had booked out of the *Hotel Venus*. By eight o'clock the same morning, I had put as much distance between the hotel, Archer Street and Soho as I could manage. Dragging my two large suitcases behind me like reluctant dogs on a leash I headed towards Victoria Station. Here I managed to find a more salubrious lodging at an establishment called the *Vicars Landing* close to the train station from which I was to depart the following morning. I didn't set foot outside the hotel until it was time for me to leave.

Early the next day I walked to the station and boarded the train. In my pocket was a one-way ticket issued by the South African government for the fourteen-day voyage to Durban aboard the *SS Windsor Castle*. Four hours later I arrived at the Southampton docks and was relieved to see the majestic pink-hulled liner lying peacefully rigged at her mooring. Perhaps my luck since leaving Canada might be about to change for the better.

I quickly dispensed with boarding formalities and was shown to my cabin by an obliging steward. He indicated that it would be worth my while to tip him for the voyage in advance. "To assure you of my very best services at all times, sir!"

Inside the cabin the person with whom I was to share my accommodation had already arrived and was busy unpacking his bags. He was a young artillery lieutenant from the British Army and was about six years my senior.

"Worthington-Thomas, Lieutenant, 3rd Queen's Horse. Roger's the name. Not a bad billet considering. A bit cramped for four but I'm sure we'll manage."

I had no idea what he was talking about. A double bunk was situated on one side of the cabin which, although not luxurious, seemed adequately comfortable for two.

"Four? I hope not, there are only two bunks."

"Ah, yes, but you know, a bit of female company what, what. Been on these voyages before, you know. It takes a day or two to get the sleeping arrangements all tidied away but … " he gave me a sly wink, "it doesn't take long for the sea air to take effect."

I was beginning to wonder whether I might be allowed any say in my cabin mate's plans to play musical beds when he continued. "Now, what we need to do is arrange some sort of a code between us if either wants to be alone with, you know … a lady companion. It will have to be something that won't give the game away to others."

He gave me another lecherous wink. Without even waiting for a response he continued, "Why don't we stick to my old tried and tested?"

"What's that?"

"Off to 'unlimber the canon', old boy."

"What?"

"Army expression. Nobody else will understand. I'll tell you I'm off to unlimber the canon and you lie low until I give you the all clear."

I later learned that Worthington-Thomas, Lieutenant, 3rd Queen's Horse, was on forced furlough from his Regiment for scandalous behavior unbecoming an officer and a gentleman of the Queen's Horse Artillery. He never alluded to the exact nature of the scandal; only that it had involved his commanding officer's daughter.

It didn't take long for Roger to start his cabin frolics. I was enjoying a pre-dinner aperitif at the bar on the first evening we were at sea when the barman slipped me a folded piece of paper. He nodded across to the far side of the bar where Lieutenant Worthington-Thomas was sitting engrossed in the company of an attractive older lady. She was gazing at him in awe, obviously enchanted by the story he was spinning her. I unfolded the note. On it was scrawled, "Target within range. Off to unlimber the canon … drinks on me until I see you later, old boy. Best regards, Roger."

The barman gave me a knowing look and slid another drink in my direction. It was going to be a tedious fourteen days.

The recent rebuke from his Regiment seemed to have had little effect on the Lieutenant. By the third day of our voyage he had befriended the wife of a couple who sat each evening at the same dinner table to which we had both been assigned. Gail was young, petite, and vivacious. He husband was older, very portly and had an unfortunate propensity for sweating profusely. He was also an avid imbiber of alcohol and a chronic gambler. When he wasn't eating, he was in the ship's casino in a doubtful state of sobriety, presiding over a mountain of gambling chips and a clutter of empty gin glasses.

Early on the morning of our fifth day the ship docked at the island resort of Las Palmas. Her starboard stabilizer was vibrating and would have to be repaired. Passengers who wanted to disembark were allowed to do so but were warned against drinking at the dockside hotel. The locally-made wine was a potent brew known as *Vino Collapso*. It had proven the undoing of many a passenger during the ship's previous stops at the Island. Passengers were cautioned that the ship was scheduled to leave port by six o'clock that evening. Anyone who hadn't made it on board by that time would be left behind. I asked Roger if he intended to disembark.

"Absolutely, dear chap. Might never get another chance to taste that native brew they're talking about. You coming along?"

"Afraid not, you're on your own." I was still reeling from my misadventure in London the week before. I certainly didn't want to be stuck at a hotel in Las Palmas clutching a bottle of *Vino Collapso* as I watched my ship sail into the night.

"Ah, I say, that's rather fortunate. In that case, I wonder if I could prevail upon you to do me a small favor?"

I became a bit worried. I had got to know Roger well enough to realize that nothing he involved himself in was small or uncomplicated. He explained that he was to go ashore in the company of his married lady friend, Gail, and would I mind covering if her husband started looking for her. I replied I was sure that neither of them had anything to worry about. The husband would probably be ensconced all day at his normal spot in the ship's casino.

"None the less, dear chap, wouldn't want to bump into the old man as I walk back up the gangway with his wife on my arm. Perhaps you could linger around the gangway an hour or so before our scheduled departure. You can give me the thumbs up if the coast is clear for us to come aboard."

I wasn't too sure what I was supposed to do, or what the Lieutenant and his lady friend intended doing if the coast wasn't clear.

Two hours before we were due to sail, I positioned myself at the top of the ship's gangway having had a quick look into the casino. I was relieved to see the familiar figure of the portly, sweating husband placing piles of chips all over his roulette table, completely oblivious to his wife's absence. At his elbow was a freshly poured gin and tonic. An hour before we were due to sail there was a loud blast from the ship's horn. A second blast followed thirty minutes later. I began to worry. There was no sign of the wayward Lieutenant—or his mistress. Fifteen minutes later a ship's officer standing close by gave the order to raise the gangway.

"Excuse me, but my friend isn't back from shore yet." I didn't want to mention his mistress. That would lend an air of tackiness to what seemed an extremely serious matter.

"Can't help you, Sir. Maritime rules. Ships can't wait for late passengers."

There was a loud clank as the gangway was secured against the ship's side and the lines were cast off. The vibrations through the decking intensified as her huge diesel engines inched her away from the dock. We were underway. There was still no sign of the two recalcitrants.

Feeling extremely anxious I wondered what to do. I thought I had better tell somebody about the missing passengers, but I wasn't sure I wanted to be the author of a scandal when the lurid details began to unfold. Eventually I decided that I would confide in the ship's purser, perhaps he would know what to do. I was busy walking toward his office when over the ship's intercom there was an announcement:

"The ship will be slowing down. The Port Captain's launch will be coming alongside to drop two passengers who missed the ship's departure."

I ran upstairs to the top deck. Sure enough, plunging its way toward us in the choppy sea was a spiffy-looking white launch. Waving at the ship with a bottle of *Vino Collapso* grasped firmly in his hand was a very inebriated and unsteady Lieutenant Roger Worthington-Thomas. He was singing at the top of his voice, "I'm the Jolly Roger." Standing next to him with her arm around his shoulder was the equally disheveled figure of Gail.

As the launch came alongside, two bosun's chairs were lowered from the davits on the upper deck on which passengers had gathered to watch the spectacle of the two errant passengers being winched aboard. Amongst them wondering what all the commotion was about, was the portly figure of Gail's husband! As it turned out, the first person that the luckless Lieutenant bumped into as he was winched aboard was the very person he had sought to avoid. And it was into her startled husband's arms that Gail lurched as she was being helped from the bosun's chair.

I saw very little of Gail after that … as did Roger. After recuperating for a day or so in our cabin he emerged as if nothing had happened. Not being able to find his lady companion he set his sights on new hunting grounds. It wasn't long before the barman started passing more notes about the artilleryman having found new targets that required his presence on the firing line. My old routine of sitting at the bar sipping free drinks while I waited for the firing to end resumed.

Fourteen days after we had put to sea in Southampton we arrived off the coast of South Africa. After brief stopovers in Capetown, Port Elizabeth and East London we arrived in Durban. I disembarked from the *Windsor Castle* with some trepidation. I didn't know a solitary soul on the continent. Neither did I have any family to fall back on.

But I was back in Africa, and to a new beginning.

South Africa

"Are you visiting South Africa, or do you intend to settle?"
"I intend to settle."
"Do you have family here?"
"No." *"Friends?"* "No."
"What will you do?"
"I don't know."

—Conversation with immigration official,
Durban Harbor: 1969

The South African government had unwittingly agreed to put me up in a hotel in Durban for a month while I looked for a job. For the first two weeks after my arrival finding a job was not a priority: I was having too much fun. The Springbok was a sumptuous holiday hotel situated a block from the beach front. It was full of young immigrants from England wanting to shed the cloak of their predictable past for the excitement of an unpredictable future. Like me, they were staying in the hotel for free.

There were simply not enough hours to enjoy the abundant nightlife that spilled from the numerous clubs scattered along the beachfront. Each dawn we could be found on the beach with copious amounts of champagne spilling from our glasses, toasting the first rays of the sun. As the city began to stretch itself awake from a fitful night, we would be singing our way back to our hotel … and to the welcoming embrace of another day's slumber.

It took me about two weeks to appreciate that the decadence of my lifestyle was fast outstripping the resources of my bank account. I realized that I had better do what I had intended doing the first day I stepped off the boat—get a job. With my high school drafting diploma tucked firmly into my top pocket and carrying some architectural drawings that I had kept from school, I confidently started plodding the streets of Durban looking for job opportunities. The tepid responses I received after my first week of job hunting convinced me that it would probably be a good idea to move into cheaper accommodation until I established myself, especially as the kind hospitality of the South African government was due to expire within a few days.

During my fourth week I bade farewell to my friends at the Springbok and moved into some cheap lodgings at the Bay View pension, a dilapidated building on the outskirts of the city that had originally been built as a nunnery. The nuns' financial predicament must have been as precarious as mine was becoming. There had been no repairs to the building in the thirty years the nuns had occupied it; a tradition the new owners had decided to maintain. By the time I arrived it was in the process of being devoured by hungry tropical vegetation that clung to the walls and roof like the tentacles of a giant green octopus. Green creepers had even found their way inside the windows and were laying siege to the interior of the building.

Once established in my new digs I resumed my search for work. Getting into town each morning and returning in the late afternoon was no easy feat. Bus routes in the area were limited, necessitating having to walk a lot of the way. I had almost given up hope of securing employment in the architectural field when my luck unexpectedly changed for the better. Stanley & Stanley was one of Durban's most prestigious architectural firms with offices situated on the top floor of the city's highest building. I had previously avoided seeing them, thinking they might be out of my league. One afternoon I was walking past the building and decided, on a whim, to pay them a visit.

I took the elevator to the top floor and stepped into the foyer. There I found myself standing in an opulent and lavishly-furnished rotunda that looked like it might be the foyer of a grand hotel. Facing me at the far end was one of the loveliest ladies I had ever seen. She stood up and asked if she could be of assistance.

"Well, actually I've come to see if there are any employment opportunities available?"

She extended her hand toward me. "Brenda's my name, Brenda Watson. Welcome to Stanley & Stanley. Do you have an appointment?"

"No." I felt like bolting back into the elevator, but heard its doors closing behind me with a solid 'thump'.

"Would you like to see one of our partners, sir? I'm sure it can be arranged."

I must have stammered something in reply.

"Why don't you take a seat? May I have your name, please?"

I gave it to her, finding it difficult to take my eyes off her well-proportioned bottom as she walked toward a far curve in the rotunda. A minute or two must have passed before she reappeared. Her smile was dazzling.

"Mr. Stanley, our senior partner, will see you in a moment, Mr. Bax." She returned to her desk and sat down.

I was just beginning to contemplate my options of remaining and making a spectacle of myself with my limited architectural experience, or leaving— when Mr. Stanley appeared. He was a slim wisp of a man, wearing brown corduroy trousers, a bright pink shirt and a large bow tie decorated with prints of red and white balloons. A bushy black moustache and goatee completed his rather absurd appearance.

"Earnest Stanley's the name. I understand you might be interested in joining our company." His greeting was warm and effusive. "Why don't you come into my office and we can see whether we might be of mutual benefit to one another."

I followed him into a room which looked like something out of Star Wars. One might easily have mistaken his office for a large capsule suspended in space; round portholes with electronically-operated reflectors directed moving shafts of bright light around the room giving a sense of perpetual motion.

After taking some time to study my meager portfolio he looked up and smiled.

"You have a limited grounding in architecture, but perhaps we can help you develop and grow. One of our draftsmen is leaving us in two months. Perhaps you would like to fill his shoes?" I explained that I was presently unemployed and that while his offer sounded very attractive I was hoping to start work sooner.

"See if you can find something temporary for the next two months and we'll keep the position open for you."

The interview was over.

On the way back to my hotel that afternoon I bought a copy of the Durban Chronicle. That night I scanned it for something I might be able to do while waiting to begin work with Stanley & Stanley. An advertisement caught my eye: "Earn unlimited money selling Durban's hallmark of quality clothing."

The next morning I was knocking on the door of Richard Eberhardt's Quality Clothing situated in a suite of offices on the second floor of a squat-looking building off Smith Street.

"We sell quality clothing by catalogue," explained a brash young man introducing himself as the sales manager. "The only requirement of the job is that you have to reach a sales target of eighty items of clothing per month."

The man went on to explain that all I had to do was walk the streets to which I was assigned each day and sell items of men's and women's apparel from a large catalogue. With the catalogue came an accompanying briefcase … anda metal tape measure.

"What's the tape measure for?" I inquired.

"Made-to-measure suits."

"But I've never measured for one before."

"Nothing to it. Concentrate on the vitals: arms, shoulder, waist, chest, inner and outer legs. You'll get the hang of it. Just use your common sense. The main thing is, look like you've done it a thousand times before."

"With a metal tape measure?" "Do you want the job or not?"

With my induction into Richard Eberhardt's Quality Clothing complete, I was sent on my way. An hour later I had caught the bus to my assigned area and was making my first hesitant steps into an Indian jeweler's store to attempt a sale. I wasn't very well received. The shop was quite busy and the jeweler looked annoyed by my presence. I hung around awkwardly for a few minutes clutching my briefcase and wondering what to do. Eventually, a shop assistant hustled me into a back room to get me out of the way. He must have felt sorry for me because he had the courtesy to ask to look at my catalogue. The made-to-measure suits caught his eye. One in particular he thought he might like.

"Are they really made-to-measure?" he asked.

"Yes."

"Who does the measurements?"

"Me."

"How long before delivery?"

"Two weeks," I lied. They had omitted to provide me with this vital piece of information during my induction training. To my horror he decided to order one. I had hoped to begin my sales career by selling something more mundane—a shirt perhaps, or a pair of shorts. The shop assistant looked distinctly unhappy as I unsheathed my metal tape measure almost decapitating him in the process. Having taken all the measurements I could think of, I gave him a smile and an order to sign.

"Is that it?" He looked skeptical.

"That's it. All you need do is give me your color preference and sign the order."

Color selection was another minor detail overlooked before I was sent out on to the road. I learned later when the order was returned by the manufacturer tagged 'incomplete information' that I should also have specified 'material'.

He hesitated before signing. My performance must have appeared somewhat cavalier. Reluctantly he put his signature on the order form. I hoped that I wouldn't be around when his made-to-measure suit eventually arrived. I beat a hasty retreat before he could change his mind or ask any further questions.

Unfortunately, the sale of my first suit didn't prove to be a harbinger of a successful sales career to come. For the rest of the month my sales were woefully poor. It was a day before the month's end and I was still thirty items of clothing short of making my sales target. My continued employment with Richard Eberhardt's was not looking promising.

That evening I was back in my hotel feeling rather dejected when I received an unexpected phone call. It was Brenda, the receptionist from Stanley & Stanley. She told me that she had left the company in anticipation of relocating further north to be close to her family.

"I'm going to be leaving town in a day or so. Why don't we have lunch tomorrow? You could catch up on a bit of the company's corporate culture."

"I'd love to but tomorrow is my last opportunity to make my sales target and it isn't looking terribly hopeful." I explained my predicament.

"Come on. Let's do lunch anyway. Perhaps I can help you make some sales."

"Well, so long as it's quick. I can't afford to be another month without work."

I didn't really feel that I could afford the time for lunch but neither did I want to miss out on the prospect of having lunch with such a beautiful lady. It was agreed that we would meet at noon the next day at the Edward Hotel.

I arrived at the hotel on tenterhooks. I was nervous at not having made a single sale that morning and was even more nervous at the prospect of meeting Brenda. I settled myself by thinking that she probably wasn't as attractive as I had initially thought. I was ushered through the door and into the lobby by a tall, regal-looking sheik wearing a white turban. He asked my name then beckoned me through to a small private alcove. Brenda was already seated sipping a gin sling. My heart almost stopped. She was wearing a tiny red dress that made little pretense of covering anything but a modicum of her tiny frame. I couldn't imagine a more beautiful lady.

"Now," she teased after we had both settled on a couch with our second gin.

"Let's have a look at some of this clothing you're selling."

I produced my catalogue and showed it to her. Leafing through the women's section she suddenly leaned back on the couch with a squeal of delight.

"Just what I've been looking for, you should have told me you sell women's lingerie."

I was a bit embarrassed. I hadn't paid much attention to that particular section. She closed the catalogue with a loud clap. "That's it. You and I are off to my apartment. I want to spend some time looking at my wardrobe and deciding what more I need to buy for my move up north."

"But it will take two weeks for the clothes to arrive," I stammered. Events seemed to be moving quickly out of my control.

"That's fine. They can be mailed to my new address. Come on, let's skip lunch and I'll fix us something at my apartment. I want to take my time looking through the catalogue."

Thirty minutes later we were ensconced on the couch of her North Beach penthouse apartment discussing the vagaries of women's underwear. Two gin slings later I was being led through to the cool, darkened interior of her sumptuous boudoir … .

That evening I returned to my hotel with thirty pieces of women's undergarments written into my order book. The sale of fifteen pairs each of women's knickers and brassieres wasn't as noble an endeavor as selling a handful of gentlemen's suits. Nor would it bring me the 'Achiever of the Month' award. But at the very least, my job with Richard Eberhardt's was secure for another month.

❧

Toward the end of the following week a young, rough and ready Australian called Rod Moore moved into the room next to mine at the pension. He hailed from a sheep farm somewhere close to Alice Springs and was about as rough and unfinished a product of humanity as could be imagined. His parents must have completely neglected to arm him with any social graces before he left the sheep farm and he hadn't acquired any since.

I was becoming distinctly disillusioned with seeing my name at the bottom of the 'Weekly Sales' chart at Richard Eberhardt's. The only time someone's name appeared below mine was when an Indian salesman decided to take a fortnight's leave. One evening while we were sitting on the verandah of the pension enjoying a cold beer Rod told me that he was taking time off work to drive to Rhodesia.

"I hear it's fair dinkem up there, mate. Being screwed up by a few armed gollies running around the outback, but the Rhodesians seem an OK bunch. Why don't you come with me, we can share the driving."

Travelling a thousand miles north with the likelihood of being chased through the bush by armed thugs didn't sound a particularly appealing prospect, especially with someone as rough and ready as Rod.

"Don't worry, mate … just anchor my ass to a well-stocked bar and I'll try not to behave like a skunk at a wedding. It'll all be fair dinkem, you'll see."

"Fair dinkem" seemed an all-embracing Australian term for anything upwards of "OK."

"How long are you going for?" I had three weeks remaining before I started work with Stanley & Stanley. It was a boat I couldn't afford to miss.

"Just a coupla weeks, mate. We'll have you back here by the end of the month."

With the aid of my fingers I did some quick sums on the precarious state of my financial situation. I had overcome my inability of being able to do basic mathematics in my head by using my fingers the way a Chinaman would an abacus. Barring any major unforeseen expenses, I could just string out my cash reserves to last until my first pay cheque from Stanley & Stanley.

"I'm in." I replied. "When do we leave?" "Tomorrow morning, mate. At sparrow fart."

By mid-morning the next day we had vacated our rooms at the pension and were on our way north with our worldly possessions packed neatly into the back of Rod's old Ford Escort. Two days later we crossed the border bridge spanning the wide expanse of the Limpopo River and drove into the sleepy Rhodesian border town of Beit Bridge.

The white colonial-style building which housed Passport Control was pristine. Inside, large ceiling fans slowly circulated the hot, dry air making the stifling heat just manageable. Occasional gusts of air would swirl through the open windows carrying pieces of tumbleweed or blades of dry grass. The two Rhodesian officials who attended to us from behind a polished teak countertop were the epitome of politeness and decorum. They were obviously of British heritage and in spite of the heat were smartly dressed in crisply starched white shorts, long socks and tunics.

"Where are you gentlemen headed?" the Passport Control officer asked politely, extending a hand to take our passports.

"Salisbury, if we can beat the heat and the buzzards. This place is hotter than an overcooked dingo on a barbie." A bead of sweat running down Rod's face dropped on to an open page of his passport as he handed it across the counter.

"Visiting or staying permanently, sir?"

"Loitering for two weeks, mate. First thing I need to do is pour some amber liquid down my parched throat. It's feeling as dry as the shriveled arse of a thirsty camel stranded in a dry oasis." My Australian travel companion seldom felt moved to express himself in simple, polite terms.

"Beg your pardon, sir?"

"I think he wants to know where we can stop for a cold beer," I interjected.

"Moore's Hotel, just around the corner, sir. Or if you can wait another hour or so, the Zambezi Bar in Bulawayo. It's quite popular with the younger set. It's on your route about two hours' drive away."

"A beer in the Zambezi Bar will be less use to me than tits on a bull if I succumb to the heat along the way. This heat's a bitch!" You could always rely on Rod to tell things the way they were.

We stopped briefly at Moore's Hotel to wash the dust from our throats and then decided to drive straight through to Salisbury some eight hours' drive to the north. On our way out of the town a large white-on-green sign greeted us: 'Welcome to Rhodesia'. Eight hours later in the dying rays of the setting sun we arrived in the capital city of Salisbury.

We were driving down a broad, tree-lined avenue searching for a cheap hotel when a sudden loud clanking noise sounded from the car's engine. The oil warning light on the dashboard flashed on followed by the overheating light. Then the engine died. Rod managed to steer the freewheeling car into a vacant parking bay on the side of the street.

"That's it, mate. This is as far as we go. She's died on us."

I looked up. On the building directly in front of us was a large sign which read, *Le Coq d'Or*.

"Let's arrange for the funeral tomorrow," I suggested to Rod. "But right now might be as good a time as any to hold the wake and this looks like the perfect place to have it."

"Providence comes in small measures," he replied.

Upstairs we found a circular bar thronged with young Rhodesians wearing little more than shorts, T-shirts, slops or 'vellies'—the Rhodesian vernacular for light-colored suede desert shoes. Appropriately it was called the Round

Bar. I looked around. The crowd consisted mainly of lean, suntanned young men in their late teens or early twenties. Behind the bar was an attractive, petite young lady with purple, spiky hair and a blue budgerigar perched on her shoulder. She introduced herself as Tina and asked what we would like to drink. I ordered a beer each for Rod and myself.

"Haven't seen you two in here before. You new in town?" she asked.

"Do we look like it?"

"Well, yes … you're dressed all funny. You're wearing proper shoes and socks. I've never seen regulars in here wearing proper shoes and socks."

I looked around. She was right. The only shoes being worn in the bar were vellies and there wasn't a sock in sight.

"Most of the guys in here are from 3 Commando. They just got back from the bush.

"3 Commando?" I queried.

"Yeah. 3 Commando, Rhodesian Light Infantry. They're based here in town. You'll get to meet some of them just now I'm sure. Hey Piet, got some new recruits for you from out of town," she shouted to some fit young men standing nearby.

Before long Rod and I were surrounded by a group of young soldiers dressed in civilian clothes telling us about their recent escapades in the Zambezi Valley.

"Sounds like a place to avoid. You could develop a thirst for beer in a place like that." Rod was warming up after his second beer. "What were you guys doing hanging around a place like that?"

"Slotting gooks coming cross the river, ek sê … the ones who made it past the flatdogs."

The young man talking to us was obviously the leader. His skin was tanned chocolate brown from the sun and he had piercing, pale blue eyes. I was having difficulty following what he was saying. Just then I felt a hand pat me on my shoulder. I looked around to see a tall, lean, square-jawed man leaning casually against the bar. He looked older than the rest, in his late thirties perhaps.

"Captain Al Boyd-Sutherland is the name." He smiled at Rod and me extending his hand to shake ours. "You're probably having difficulty understanding these guys. It's the unique slang of the Rhodesian Light Infantry, understood only amongst themselves. They've just come off a major operation in the Zambezi Valley. You're talking to some fine, brave young soldiers."

"What's a flatdog?" I asked politely. Capt. Boyd-Sutherland didn't look like the sort of man I would want to pick a fight with in a dark alley.

"A crocodile. Ever seen a dog run over by a truck? That's what a crocodile looks like. Hey, let me buy you young fellows a drink, you look like you need one."

I explained our predicament to the Captain. "We've just arrived from South Africa and our car's engine has seized. We might have to work here a while to earn some money to get it fixed."

"What work do you have in mind?" he asked.

"Haven't thought that far ahead, mate. We're only here on a two-week visitor's permit," interjected Rod. "Got any ideas?"

"Sure. Join a fighting man's army for a year or two and get some marrow in your bones. You'll both leave older and wiser men." He went on to explain that he knew the army recruiting officer, Major Lamprecht, very well. "He can easily arrange for a permanent residence permit for you guys if you think you have it in you to mix it up with guys like this."

He pointed to the group we had just been talking to. They had moved away in deference to an officer who they obviously admired and respected.

Rod and I looked at each other. I could see my position with Stanley & Stanley looking more remote with each passing moment.

"Let's have another drink and think about it," I suggested.

It was well past midnight when Captain Boyd-Sutherland eventually poured us into his car. "Let's collect your belongings and I'll take you to a cheap boarding house on Jameson Avenue."

The next morning I was sound asleep when I heard a loud banging on our door. It was the landlady. She was obviously intent on getting revenge for our having awakened her earlier in the night.

"There's an army gentleman here to see you," she shouted, banging the door with her fist.

I wrapped a towel around my waist and staggered into the foyer.

Before me stood the smartest dressed African soldier I had ever set eyes on. He looked a bit like a soldier from an old British Punjab Regiment doing frontier duty on the Afghan border.

"Corporal Duma, Sah! Compliments of Major Lamprecht, Sah," he shouted, giving me a snappy salute. "I've come to take you to the Army Recruiting Office, Sah." He gave me another salute.

I walked back to our room and shook my snoring Australian friend from a deep slumber. I gave him my most valiant attempt at a salute as my towel slipped from my waist. "Welcome to the Rhodesian Army!"

"Looks like they've already issued you with your rifle, mate," he groaned.

6

Recruit

"As I became older, and a little bolder,
T'was an ambition of mine, to become a soldier. But a recruit now I am, they can
all be damned, I've less in me hand than a remittance man."

—Extract: Off to the Front Line

Dear Mother,
 I have unexpectedly joined the Rhodesian Army. I am a recruit,
but hope to progress.

I have to remain for three years.

Tim

Dear Tim,

I am sending money for you to return to Canada. It's important that you leave immediately.

I think the sun must have got to you.

Mother

Shortly after Rod and I were dropped off at the Army Recruiting Office at the King George VI Barracks we made the acquaintance of Sergeant-Major Paul Coetzer, the resident barber. He didn't possess a single hair on his scalp and saw no reason why anybody else should either. We emerged from our encounter with our heads resembling freshly-plucked turkey breasts.

That afternoon, having spent the entire morning completing volumes of attestation papers, we were deposited outside the front gate of 1st Battalion, the Rhodesian Light Infantry (RLI). The recruiting officer must have chosen to send us to the RLI because we were both classified 'European' and had indicated a preference for joining the infantry. The RLI was the only white Infantry Battalion in the Rhodesian Army.

We must have looked conspicuous loitering around the front gate in our civilian clothes. Soldiers moved purposefully about us in green berets and smart camouflage fatigues. Eventually we were corralled by a stern-looking

114

corporal whose face was badly scarred by acne. Referring to us as "civilian scum-bags," he ordered us to follow him in a "smart and soldier-like manner" to training troop. We stumbled behind him not knowing what smart and soldier-like meant.

The RLI was the primary fighting Regiment of the Rhodesian Army. Its function was to intercept and kill terrorists infiltrating into the country across the Zambezi River. The river formed the country's northern border with Zambia where many of the terrorists were based. The aim of the terrorists was to subjugate and terrorize the indigenous population and murder European farmers. It was the first phase of an insurgency aimed at overthrowing the Rhodesian Government. When the Battalion wasn't actively engaged in operations, it was deployed on a rotating basis with other units of the army, conducting border control operations in the Zambezi Valley.

The RLI comprised mainly white Rhodesians but with a significant number of South Africans of 'Afrikaner' heritage, especially amongst the lower ranks. A sprinkling of Englishmen, Canadians and Australians completed the cosmopolitan makeup of the unit. Of all the nationalities the Battalion embraced, it was the South Africans who gave it its colorful character and out of which was born the special lingo spoken and understood only within the unit.

The RLI was a 'Commando' unit, meaning it was structured and organized at the lowest level into small, elite and self-sufficient sub-units or 'sticks'. A stick was made up of four men who could easily be uplifted by a single troop-carrying Alouette 3 helicopter and deployed independently to operate deep inside hostile territory for extended periods of time. These small sub-units could quickly be re-grouped into larger formations to launch the deadly forays against large terrorist groups for which the Battalion became so well-known and respected.

To increase its flexibility in dealing with the increasing numbers of gangs that were arrayed against it, the RLI later became airborne. Each soldier was required to undertake and pass a parachute training course. During the Second World War it was unusual for members of a parachute regiment to undertake more than four operational jumps during the entire war. It was not unusual for soldiers of the RLI to undertake four operational parachute jumps in a single day.

ભ

The recruit training course wasn't easy. There were days when I thought my body couldn't take another moment of the physical and mental punishment. Thirty-three of us started the course; fifteen of us finished to earn the coveted green beret of the Rhodesian Light Infantry.

Rod absconded from the course midway through the first week. He was unhappy at having been put through the Battalion's Assault Course for the fifth time in one day. The course comprised a rough track approximately a mile long strewn with different obstacles. It had to be completed in full battle gear within a prescribed time; otherwise everyone would have to do it again. One of the obstacles was a wall constructed of logs. It was ten feet high and each man had to clamber over it with the aid of a rope attached to the top. On this particular day we had failed in our first four attempts at completing the course within the prescribed time and were being put through it once again. Rod had arrived at the wall in a state approaching total physical exhaustion and had paused at its base to regain his breath.

"Are you planning on taking a nap, scumbag, or are you planning on getting your arse over that wall?" The instructor was a hard-nosed Brit who had resigned from the Welsh Guards to do service in Rhodesia.

"Neither, mate. I'm trying to decide how much explosives it would take to blow the bitch down. I've already been over it four times today and anyone with an ounce of intelligence would conclude that demolishing it would make a lot more sense than having to climb *over* it."

The instructor had taken exception both to being called 'mate' and to Rod's brilliant flash of tactical wisdom. He rewarded Rod by throwing him off the course which meant he would have to start a new recruit course all over again.

The next morning I found a note taped on my locker. It read, *"I'm returning to Alice, mate. Won't be a dinkem journey without you, but I'll have a cold one for you on the other side of the fence."* It was the last I ever heard from Rod.

❧

During our course we were not allowed to 'walk' anywhere. Everything had to be done in a squad and 'at the double'. This fell somewhere between a jog and a run and was undertaken with our fists clenched firmly against our chest. It must have looked quite comical. It became complicated if we passed an officer. The squad leader would shout something unintelligible and we would have to extend our arms downward and turn our heads in the officer's direction. This meant we couldn't see where we were going and we would each bump into the person ahead and all fall over. The officer would shout something nasty and order us back to where we had started. We never seemed to make much progress getting anywhere.

On our first day we were 'doubled' to the Quartermaster Stores to draw our uniforms and training equipment. I was first in line.

"Number, rank and name?" The Quartermaster Sergeant was a tall, unhappy-looking man with a bushy moustache stained yellow with nicotine. It bristled over his top lip like a stiff nail brush. He wore horn-rimmed spectacles with thick lenses which made his eyes look bulbous.

"5121 Recruit Bax, T.G., Sergeant."

"Q." "What?"

"Q. I'm not a sergeant, I'm a Quartermaster Sergeant. You call me Q, is that understood?"

It wasn't. But I called him Q anyway.

"Yes, Q."

I couldn't imagine why anybody would want to be called Q. It sounded quite absurd. But then I didn't understand most of what I was being asked to do since joining the army. I was quite happy to call him by whatever name he wanted if it made him happy.

"If you don't know what to call someone call them 'Staff', is that understood?" He was beginning to sound like an old schoolmaster. He probably should have been, perhaps it would have made him a little happier. He certainly appeared to be a walking encyclopedia of advice.

The first items of equipment that were issued to me were a large khaki 'kit bag' and sturdy green metal trunk into which I was told to pack the baffling array of kit and equipment that began to rain down on me. The army didn't believe in referring to items of clothing by their normal names, they had to be given army names.

"Drawers cellular, olive green; six pairs for the use of."

Six pairs of drab green underpants were pulled from a large cardboard box on a shelving unit and tossed down to me by a disinterested-looking store man precariously perched atop a long ladder. They floated down looking like little green parachutes.

"Hose-tops, green twill, drill; four pairs for the use of." They looked like long green socks with the bottoms cut off where your feet would normally be.

Everything was suffixed with "for the use of". For the use of *what*, was never explained.

"Anklets, webbing, with brass buckles, left and right; two pairs for the use of."

The equipment kept coming until it formed a small mountain in front of me. I was instructed to pack it into my kit bag and metal trunk and wait for the rest to be issued their kit. I was soon to learn that in the army, 'waiting' was an important activity.

Placing our bulging kit bags under our arms and balancing our metal trunks precariously on our shoulders, we were ordered to double back to the Training Troop Barracks. I wondered what would happen if we passed an officer. Fortunately that unhappy event never occurred and we arrived back at the training barracks resembling a train of disenchanted porters. The barracks consisted of three large inter-joining barrack-rooms each capable of holding twenty recruits. In the front were offices, armories and stores. Inside the barrack-rooms each recruit was allocated just enough floor space in which to fit a small metal bed and two small steel lockers, one on either side of the bed. The green metal trunk was placed at the foot of the bed. Beds had to be immaculately made each morning for inspection. A single crease or wrinkle constituted an unmade bed and would result in punishment being meted out to the entire barrack-room. The only way to achieve making a bed neat enough to pass inspection was to iron the top blanket each morning. As a result few of us ever slept on our beds. It was easier to sleep on the floor to avoid having to make them the following morning.

Before the start of training each morning we would be paraded outside the barracks in the uniform for the day. The Duty Instructor would drill us up and down the road for a few minutes before inspecting our uniforms. The slightest fault would have us doubling to the assault course to better our time of the previous day. Then we would be doubled back to Training Troop and given thirty minutes to clean up our uniforms for another inspection. Some days we would spend the whole day alternating between the assault course and dress inspections. This normally happened if our instructor was feeling hungover from the night before. It saved him from the toil of having to stand on the Parade Square in the hot sun, instructing us on the complexities of forming a 'box' formation at the double. Each evening after supper we would have to sit late into the night laboriously polishing our boots. The Army had another name for them. They were called "boots hobnailed, parade, for the use of" and had to be polished to a mirror finish.

The training course was split into four equal phases of four weeks each.

The first phase was basic drill and weapons, conducted mainly on the Parade Square or somewhere within the perimeter of the Battalion. It was the worst phase, simply because this was the domain of the Regimental Sergeant Major, or RSM. It was his lair and his primary function was to stalk around the Battalion making life as uncomfortable as possible for all within its gated confines. This included young officers who avoided him like the plague. It was not uncommon for the RSM to tell a junior officer that his standard of dress or demeanor was below that expected within the Regiment. This would be followed by a summons to the Adjutant's office for a reprimand.

It was during the third week of training that my first terrifying ordeal occurred of coming face to face with the RSM. It was as if I had come face to face with the devil himself! I had been sent by the Training Officer to deliver a document to the Quartermaster Stores detailing some training equipment needed for the following day. I didn't realize that my route would take me past the hallowed building which was Battalion Headquarters. I was busy doubling along the side of the road as smartly as I could when I heard a low, menacing growl coming from behind a small hedge close by. My first reaction was to run in the opposite direction. Rather than make a spectacle of myself, I stopped and peered nervously around the corner of the hedge. Sitting in a large enclosure snarling at me through sturdy steel bars was a fully grown and very unfriendly-looking cheetah. It was the Regimental mascot which was being temporarily housed near Battalion Headquarters while its permanent home was being renovated. I was busy backing gingerly away from the unfriendly beast when, from somewhere behind me, came a terrifyingly loud noise that sounded like something between a bellow and a menacing bark. I froze.

"Stand still that man. Stand still!" I thought I *had* been standing still, but I must have flinched.

"Stand still, I said! Stand still!" The last "stand still" was barked in an octave so high it would have done justice to a soprano.

I heard the clip of steel-shod drill boots against concrete marching quickly toward me. I held my breath not daring to breathe. Moments later I was staring directly into the face of the sternest-looking individual I had ever cast eyes on. His uniform was so immaculate and flawless that he appeared almost like a statue carved in deathless bronze. Clasped under his left arm was a gleaming silver-tipped pace stick. On his arm was the unmistakable rank insignia of a Regimental Sergeant-Major. I remained rooted where I was, frozen, not daring to move. I would have been less fearful at that moment had the cheetah broken free from its cage and charged.

Regimental Sergeant-Major Robin Tarr was a short powerfully-built man with tanned skin, ramrod straight back, square face and a jaw that looked as if it had been hewn from hardwood. His dark hair was cropped impossibly short above his ears and he had dark eyebrows shaped like an inverted 'V' above piercing eyes. I wondered how he could possibly have gotten through the day without a single crease appearing on his uniform. I thought of asking him but quickly changed my mind. The RSM didn't talk. He communicated by barking in short staccato bursts, like gunfire.

"You idle man. When I tell you to stand still, you stand still. Is that clear?" He barked at me as if shouting at somebody standing twelve hundred yards away. I was standing twelve inches away.

"An idle man who can't obey orders is called a malingerer. What are you?" I didn't know what a malingerer was, but neither did I feel inclined to ask.

"A malingerer, Sir."

"And this malingerer has enough thread hanging from his shirt button to hang himself!"

He grasped his pace stick firmly in his right hand, removed it from under his left arm and prodded its tip at the offending button. I started to look down at the miniscule piece of thread which was barely visible from under one of my buttons.

He unleashed another withering broadside, inches from my face. "If you don't learn to stand still until you are authorized to move soldier, I'll have your guts for garters! Do you understand?"

The velocity of his rapid-fire volley left me quite stunned. With that I was bundled off to the Regimental guardroom for two days' detention to reflect upon the importance of not being a malingerer. I spent the time wondering what bar Rod was drinking in and wishing I was with him. When I was released back to my training course, I was punished again for not having completed the orders that I had been given. I had to spend the next several evenings shining every recruit's stick boots. Double jeopardy was an acceptable doctrine for basic recruits.

❧

On completion of our first month of training we were each issued a pay-book. Everything was done as a *parade* in the Army, even the simple procedure of getting paid. It was called a 'pay parade' and was a rather bizarre event. Each month we would have to form a long line outside the Training Officer's office and when our name was called, march inside to receive our pay. Once inside the office we would have to confirm we were actually who they thought we were.

"5121 Recruit Bax, T.G., give your number, rank and name," somebody would bark.

"5121 Recruit Bax, T.G., Sir."

I was required to shout my name loudly while coming to attention and saluting the officer seated at his desk. I was not allowed to look down, only straight ahead. The first time I did this my knee hit the edge of the desk, jolting it and spilling the piles of coin denominations which had been created on top. This meant the pay parade had to be postponed. In the Army, coin denominations couldn't be mixed during a pay parade. It was against Army regulations!

Half an hour later the pay parade was allowed to resume. The coins had been sorted back into their correct denominations and new piles created which conformed to Army regulations.

"Forty two dollars, twenty eight cents is your pay for the month, Bax. Check that you have the correct amount."

The officer scribbled the amount in my pay-book, signed it, put the money inside the pay-book and slid it across the desk to me. I wasn't allowed to look down at the money, let alone count it.

"Pay checked and found to be correct, Sir." This was the regulation reply each recruit had to give.

A step backwards, another salute, an about turn and I was marched off to the troop administration office to be relieved of half the money I had just received. This was payment for Commando and Regimental funds, though quite what the funds were for nobody seemed to know, nor were we allowed to ask.

෴

The next three training phases, though no less rigorous, were more bearable because they took place outside the Battalion grounds where there was more chance of bumping into a wayward bush pig than the RSM. Phase two involved basic fieldcraft and platoon and section battle drills which we had to do with such monotonous repetition that we could quite easily have done them in our sleep. One day we watched excitedly as the Battalion mobilized for an operational deployment. Soldiers and equipment poured out of every building in the barracks. Rumor had it that as recruits we might be deployed to guard vehicles and stores at a forward base camp to free more operational troops to track down large numbers of terrorist gangs that had reportedly infiltrated the Zambezi Valley. The tracks had been found by game wardens patrolling the area looking for poachers.

Unfortunately we remained behind but the deployment instilled excitement and urgency into our final two training phases. During the third phase we were trained in classical warfare which involved how to fight a conventional war against a neighboring country who might try to invade us. The final and most important phase was counter-insurgency operations or COIN. We were taught how to operate in small, self-contained groups in the bush and the importance of finding and killing the terrorists before they found and killed us. It was all beginning to get terribly exciting.

∾

On 17 June 1970, sixteen weeks after I started my recruit training, those of us who passed were formed up on the Parade Square for the last time as recruits. Then the most unexpected thing happened; I was presented with an award for being 'Best Recruit' of my course. I received an RLI plaque together with a silver-plated bayonet inscribed with my number, rank and name. I was elated!

The first thing I wanted to do was phone the spitting drill sergeant who had tormented my life at the Toronto Armory. The second was to phone my mother. I could do neither. I didn't have the sergeant's number and Mother's I had forgotten in an effort to remember my Army number which I had been told was more important than remembering that I even had a mother.

The reviewing officer was Captain Ronald Reid-Daly who had been the Regimental Sergeant-Major of the Battalion before Robin Tarr, and who was now commanding the Battalion's Base Group. After presenting us with our green berets and stable belts, Captain Reid-Daly presented me with my award. He was a distinguished and highly-decorated soldier who would later go on to command the legendary Selous Scouts.

"Congratulations on receiving this award, Junior." He had penetrating pale blue eyes that seemed to bore into my very soul and a powerful, square-set jaw.

"Serve your country and your regiment with pride, but don't go and get yourself shot. You've been trained to shoot the other guy before he shoots you. Try and remember that."

I had no intention of getting myself shot but was appreciative of his advice. I was now a fully-fledged trooper and I felt terribly proud. My reward for being nominated Best Recruit was being able to choose which commando I preferred to join. I chose 3 Commando, only because it was situated closest to Training Troop and it would be less of an effort to move my kit and equipment.

The following day I was officially inducted as a trooper into 3 Commando, Rhodesian Light Infantry.

I was twenty years old.

7

Trooper

"Let me tune you, ek sê. That gook machine-gunner had me pinned down lekker in the river bed. He was raking the trees above me moi! There was kak falling all around me, ek sê."
"What did you do?"
"I kept my head well down behind a rock!" "You didn't return fire … why?"
"It was my 35th birthday. I skeemed I didn't want to get slotted on my birthday. My mother would have blixemed me!"
—Conversation with George Thorley,
3 Commando, after his return
from operations: 1970

I was pleasantly surprised at how casual life seemed in 3 Commando. It was a dramatic change from the strict discipline which had prevailed at Training Troop. These men were superlatively trained soldiers, blooded in the crucible of war. Their time and privacy within barracks was treated with respect.

The oldest-serving member of the Commando was a soldier named George Thorley. He had been in the Rhodesian Light Infantry for ten years and had never risen above the rank of trooper. He was a tall, gaunt man with blond, unkempt hair and skin tanned walnut brown by the African sun. Pale blue eyes that seemed constantly to dart about gave one a sense that he was always in a state of nervous agitation. He was a self-appointed soldier's friend and barrack-room lawyer, and he happened to sleep in the bed next to mine.

One afternoon shortly after joining the Commando, George asked if I would like to accompany him into town. The Commando was on a period of 'rest and recuperation' which meant that soldiers who hadn't taken home leave could come and go from the barracks as they pleased. I readily agreed and hurriedly dressed into civilian clothes for the first time since joining the RLI. On the way to the main gate to hitch a ride I asked George what it was he was carrying in his top pocket.

"It's the business end of a thunder flash, ek sê. I carry one whenever I johl into town. You never know when you might need one to get out of a difficult situation."

I knew from my recruit training that a thunder flash was a small percussion device about the size of an empty toilet roll designed to replicate the explosion of a hand grenade. Detonated in a confined area it could easily perforate one's eardrum. I couldn't imagine needing one on a friendly excursion into town.

"Where to now?" I asked, as we alighted from our lift.

"I skeem we johl to the Round Bar for a couple of dops, ek sê." We made our way to the same bar in which my destiny with the

Rhodesian Army had been sealed some four months before. Tina was still serving behind the bar with her hair dyed purple—except now it was laced with yellow highlights. On her shoulder was the same blue budgie which had been in attendance the day I had first arrived. We hadn't been at the bar long when it started to fill with patrons, many of whom George knew and I didn't. So when he placed his beer on the bar counter and turned to talk to some new arrivals, I tried to make polite conversation with Tina.

"That's a really tame budgie you have." I didn't know what else to say to somebody whose hair resembled a psychedelic toilet brush.

"His name is Charles. I've had him for three years and he's my best friend. He loves beer but tends to get a bit toasted if he has too much. Look, I'll show you."

She stretched out a finger for Charles to hop on to and moved it in the direction of George's beer. In an instant the bird had jumped on to the rim of the glass and was sipping thirstily at the amber liquid inside. It was still sipping when George, who was still engrossed in conversation with his friends, decided he would like a sip of his own. Reaching behind him for his glass, his hand closed around the feathery form of the budgie which squawked in indignation and sank its sharp beak into one of George's fingers. Swiveling around in his chair he let out a rapid-fire barrage of colorful expletives and flicked the startled bird from his hand directly into his beer.

What happened next was like a pantomime production of *Cat on a Hot Tin Roof*. Tina exploded across the bar like an Exocet missile, slamming into George and knocking him backwards on to the floor. He landed flat on his back with Tina astride him screaming hysterically, her fingers extended like the talons of a falcon. Fearing that she was about to do my friend a fearful injury, I reached down to pull her away but succeeded only in ripping off her blouse amid a flurry of popping buttons. I lost my balance in the process

George Thorley. (Terry Griffin)

and fell backwards into the hands of a distinguished-looking older gentleman standing next to me. He had been standing alone quietly enjoying a pink gin and tonic when the fracas erupted.

"By Jove," he said, while helping me regain my balance. "Better hand me that blouse so I can give it back to the poor woman."

He was smartly dressed with gray hair, a well-manicured moustache and mischievous-looking pale blue eyes that seemed to twinkle as he spoke. I was struck by his kind demeanor and handsome, smiling face.

It was only then that I noticed Tina hadn't been wearing a brassiere. She sprang to her feet and looked around angrily for the person who had relieved her of her blouse. Fixing her eyes firmly on the kindly gentleman next to me she sprang towards him and planted a vicious backhand on his cheek.

"You filthy old man!" she spat angrily, whisking her blouse from his grasp. She gave him another slap for good measure before stalking off to recover her modesty … and her budgie.

"Good riddance," grinned the old man swigging back his gin."Finest pair of dumplings I ever saw. Wouldn't have missed seeing them for the world."

George, still reeling from the ferocity of Tina's attack, decided that discretion was the better part of valor.

"Bliksem, ek sê. I thought I'd been hit by a rocket," he said, staggering to his feet. "I skeem we take the gap quickly before she comes back!"

We sprinted down a long narrow passageway that led from the bar into the relative obscurity of a loud, dark discothèque that adjoined the Round Bar. Shafts of bright light stabbed through the darkness allowing momentary glimpses of throngs of gyrating couples dancing to the raucous beat of Creedence Clearwater Revival. We groped our way slowly to the bar.

George reached into his pocket. "Do you have any start, ek sê?" "Do I have any what?"

'Start' was RLI slang for money. I had very little left from the drinks I had bought in the Round Bar so suggested to George that we call it a day.

"We can't go back without a couple of dops to calm the nerves, ek sê. That chick spooked me more than the gooks."

"Well, we can't hang around here without money. Let's head off back to the barracks."

"Don't worry, my china, in the RLI we always make a plan." George quickly scanned the dark interior of the nightclub before reaching into his top pocket to surreptitiously extract the thunder flash he was carrying.

"You see that table over there with all the civvies? They've just ordered more drinks. Hang around their table and when you hear the thunder flash detonate and the lights go off, grab their beers and meet me back here in a hurry, ek sê."

I looked around. At a table not far from us sat three civilians with half a dozen recently ordered beers.

"What do you have in mind?" I'd had enough of George's shenanigans for one day.

"Normally, I'd just pull the main switch of the electric breaker box. It's situated just outside the men's toilet. But they've become wise now and have put a lock on the cover." Seemingly this was a modus operandi that RLI troopies were quite familiar with when they ran short of money for a drink. "I'm going to place this thunder flash on top of the breaker box. When it explodes it should trip the switches and the place will be plunged into darkness, ek sê. That's when we act."

Before I could say anything George had slipped off in the direction of the toilets. I sighed, wondering whether I should do the right thing and head out the door and back to the barracks, or stick around to do what George was expecting of me. I quickly realized I didn't have any option. Now was not the time to desert a fellow comrade.

I walked toward the table where our free beers were waiting, trying to look inconspicuous. Just as I came close to the table, a thunderous explosion ripped through the nightclub sending concussion waves slamming through the cavernous room. The lights flicked and then died. So did the music. There was a deathly silence followed by the sound of women screaming as the room filled with smoke and the acrid, pungent smell of cordite. Patrons started stumbling towards the exits.

Coming to my senses, I grabbed as many beers as I could and stumbled my way back through the inky blackness to the bar. It wasn't long before the lights flickered back on again and the figure of George emerged from the throngs of people still milling around the entrance. Before long the music started, the throngs returned to their tables, and George and I had enough beer to sustain us through the evening.

At around midnight, having both agreed that we had been involved in enough excitement for one day, we decided to head home. As we walked down the stairs and into the brightly lit street we bumped into the elderly gentleman into whose arms I had fallen earlier that afternoon.

"You two chaps want a lift anywhere? Ron Dick's the name. Superintendent Ron Dick, BSAP."

The Rhodesian Police, or 'British South Africa Police' as they were called, were a legacy from the British South Africa Company that had pioneered the opening of the colony in the early 1900's.

We gladly accepted the Superintendent's offer and he ushered us into the plush leather-bound interior of his old Jaguar. George climbed easily into the front seat as if a ride in such opulence might have been an everyday occurrence. We hadn't travelled far when he asked the Superintendent for permission to light a cigarette. Without waiting for a reply he extracted a cigarette from his pocket and fumbled around for some matches.

"Bliksem, I skeem I left my matches at the disco." It was definitely not turning out to be George's night. "Would you mind catching me a light, ek sê?" he inquired from the kindly man sitting next to him.

"Here, it's a 24 caret, gold-plated Ronson Electrolux Limited Edition. It was given to me by my wife on our thirtieth wedding anniversary." He handed the lighter to George.

George took the lighter, lit his cigarette, wound down the passenger window, exhaled a long blue plume of smoke and unthinkingly tossed the lighter out the window. Then he sat back into his deep leather seat with a sigh of satisfaction.

A number of things happened in very quick succession. The Superintendent, suddenly aware that his cherished lighter had disappeared out the window, threw his foot hard on the break pedal, locking both brakes and wheels. The tyres started burning filling the inside of the car with plumes of choking, foul-smelling smoke. An attempt to double-declutch the car into a lower gear failed. The gear box rattled like gunfire as metal meshed against metal. To add to the confusion, the ageing Jaguar gave two loud backfires that sounded like rockets exploding.

George threw open the passenger door yelling, "Ambush! Ambush! We've been ambushed. De-bus left and follow me."

He propelled himself out of the car whereupon he tripped over the raised pavement next to the road and fell head first into a nearby ditch. Having spent the last sixteen weeks being taught to instinctively follow orders, I followed. We lay low for a few minutes trying to digest what was happening. There was no sign of the Superintendent. The only sound we heard came from a bullfrog on the opposite side of the road. Having got bored with the sudden antics that had interrupted his evening of courtship, the frog had resumed his mating call.

It slowly dawned on us what had happened. We sheepishly got to our feet and made our way back to the Jaguar. As we got close we heard the sound of soft singing. It was the Superintendent crooning a few lines of *Show Me the Way to Go Home*. He had produced a silver hip flask from somewhere and was having a quick nip.

"By Jove, you chaps have quick reflexes. You were out the door before the old chariot had even stopped. Did you find the lighter?" Ever the officer and gentleman he held out his hip flask. "It's good London Dry. Only the best."

"Actually, we're still looking for it," I lied. "We've just come to see if you have a torch we could borrow. It's pretty dark out there."

Thankfully the old man hadn't realized what George was shouting as we leaped from the car; he thought we were eagerly trying to retrieve his lighter. After some time the lighter was found, the old Jaguar was cranked up, and before long we were being deposited outside the RLI main gate.

Thirty minutes later I was eventually able to collapse on to my bed to find solace in sleep from the extraordinary events of the day.

Border Control

"Oh, the stinging tsetse fly and the crocodile eye, This is no place to dally.
There's hunger here, and a thirst for beer,
In the hot Zambezi Valley."
—RLI Troopie's song, Sung to the tune of
Oh, the Buzzing of the Bees in the Cigarette Tree

Six weeks before Christmas, 1970, I deployed with the Commando on my first border control operation. It didn't begin very well. The night before, we had packed our short-wheelbase Land Rovers and the four provision trucks towing fuel and water bowsers and parked them outside the Commando block ready for a first-light deployment. At dawn the next day after receiving final convoy orders, the Commando rolled out of the Battalion main gate in great anticipation of securing Rhodesia's northern border for the next four weeks.

Five minutes later one of the trucks towing the fuel bowser ran out of fuel. A few minutes later the truck towing the water bowser sputtered to a halt. The entire convoy came to an ignominious halt before it was even out of sight of the Battalion main gate. Rhodesia had begun to suffer severe fuel rationing at the time and some enterprising soldier in the Battalion had been busy the night before supplementing his meager supply of gasoline. It wasn't a terribly auspicious start to my first bush trip. I remember thinking how fortunate it was that George Thorley didn't own a car. He would have thought nothing of stealing *all* the fuel and the Commando vehicles wouldn't even have made it past the starting blocks.

Eight hours later we were snaking our way through dense bush along a dirt road winding down the steep Zambezi escarpment. Our destination was an unused fishing camp situated on the banks of the Zambezi, east of Victoria Falls. Deka had once been a remote but popular fishing camp amongst Rhodesians until the first terrorist incursions in 1967. After that, the Army had taken it over as one of a number of base camps dotted along the river from which to deploy patrols looking for signs of terrorist infiltrations. The uninhabited area between the river and the escarpment was a wildlife preserve teeming with animals. It provided a buffer, or no-man's-land, between the river and the European farming areas that lay to the south above the escarpment.

We arrived at the base camp after dark, too late for me to be able to take in any details of my surroundings. It was hot and humid, almost like being inside a steam bath. My shirt clung to me like a wet towel as I began unloading my kit from the open Land Rover into our open-sided makeshift barrack room nearby. My face had been burned red by the sun from spending the entire journey lying in the back of the Land Rover on top of some troop provisions. Sunscreen hadn't yet found its way on to the Army's inventory of necessary combat items. In the still, stifling night lit only by kerosene lamps, the sounds and smells of the bush seemed all-encompassing. Shrieks and screams from within its inky blackness bombarded me from all directions making me feel quite claustrophobic.

I got up before dawn the following day anxious to take in my surroundings. Sitting next to a smoking wood fire he had recently stoked into life from the night before was a fellow soldier, C.J. Skeepers, who was in the same four-man patrol stick as me. Not only was he an excellent bushman, he was also one of the Rhodesian Army's finest trackers. We called him 'CJ' for short.

A three-legged cast iron pot full of steaming coffee stood in the centre of the fire-pit. I reached over to ladle some into my tin mug.

"Wait." CJ waved my arm away and reached for a piece of firewood, one end of which was still burning in the fire. He grasped it and plunged the still-smouldering end into the pot. It steamed and sizzled as he stirred.

"The charcoal improves the flavor."

"Been in the Army long?" I asked. The coffee tasted good.

"Two years. I grew up on my dad's farm in Mangula. The bush was my life. When the first European farmers were killed by the gooks in '66, my dad told me the Army would need people like me to help track down the terrorist gangs. I was only sixteen at the time but as soon as I was old enough, I joined up."

"Been in many contacts?" He had the face of a young boy. Too young I would have thought to have been in any firefights.

"A few. The last was with Sergeant-Major Tourle on 'Op Griffin.' He was the Commando Sergeant-Major before Rockjaw Kirrane. Coolest guy under fire I ever saw. Best shot, too."

"Oh, yeah?" I wanted to hear more.

"We were behind a small rise taking fire from a gang of gooks. Their machine-gunner had us pretty much pinned down so the rest of the gang could make their escape. Sergeant-Major Tourle wasn't worried. He stuck his head over the rise, calculated the distance from where the gooks were firing, adjusted his rear sight, took careful aim and fired one shot. One gook went down. The rest of the gang started running. The Sergeant-Major peered over the rise again, recalculated the distance, adjusted his rear sight, took careful aim and fired another single shot. Another gook went down. He did that six times, killing six gooks."

"What happened to the machine-gunner?"

"Toasted. A fixed-wing aircraft took him out with frantan before the Sergeant-Major could take a bead on him. He wasn't very happy. He wanted that gook machine-gunner to be his seventh kill."

Just then we heard an almost indiscernible sound coming from downstream of the river. CJ rose slowly into a crouch, motioning me to follow. He put his index finger to his lips indicating I should keep quiet.

"It's the bark of an impala. Sshhhh … let's go check it out."

We crouched low on a high bank overlooking the wide expanse of the Zambezi River. Dawn was just beginning to spread its orange glow above the distant trees on the Zambian side of the border. The river looked black and menacing in the gray twilight, the deep water hardly seeming to move. It appeared to brood and ripple, looking like a giant black snake moving slowly down the gorge. Then we saw them, a small herd of impala standing at the water's edge watching, motionless. After a while they bent their heads to drink.

CJ grabbed my arm and pointed, whispering in my ear. "Look, flatdog … not even four feet from them."

Sure enough, two beady eyes barely visible above the dark water and looking like two large translucent bubbles were slowly, indiscernibly, moving toward the impala. There was a sudden, furious explosion of water and foam and the large crocodile had the snout of an impala clamped firmly in its long powerful jaws. It lay still for a moment, the impala kicking its hind legs in a vain attempt at escape. The rest of the herd vanished quickly from sight. Suddenly and with incredible force, the crocodile flung the impala first one way then the other, instantly snapping the animal's neck.

"It'll drag it underwater and wedge it under a root of a tree or a rock. When the meat decomposes the crocodile will eat it."

Just then reveille sounded from the direction of the camp. A wood dove announced its presence from somewhere deep in the bush. A fish eagle gave its haunting, high-pitched call further up river. We walked quickly back toward the camp. The thick, oppressive tropical heat was already making its presence felt as the sun stabbed its first glowing rays over the distant horizon.

We received our deployment orders later that morning. I was to form part of a four-man patrol to be lifted by helicopter down stream from our base.

We were to conduct a two-week patrol along the river searching for signs of recent terrorist incursions. The members of the patrol were Sergeant Smith, C.J. Skeepers, a machine-gunner named Hodgson and myself.

We spent the rest of the day preparing our equipment. Rifles had to be cleaned and inspected, radio communications checked, rations packed into backpacks, maps marked with up-to-date information and ammunition issued. Each member of the patrol carried four additional magazines for their rifle plus a spare belt of ammunition for the machine gun. A phosphorous grenade, high-explosive grenade, smoke grenade and a small claymore completed each soldier's personal ammunition holding. We needed to be light and mobile enough to move quickly and stealthily, but with sufficient equipment to be self-sufficient for fourteen days.

We wore typical RLI bush gear; shorts, sleeveless camouflage shirts, head coverings (or bandanas to act as sweat-bands) and canvas tackies with no socks. We wouldn't have won any competitions in the 'Who's Who of Best Dressed Combat Soldiers', but our dress was ideally suited for the harsh, uncompromising conditions of the African bush. Lightweight sleeping bags made from parachute silk were preferred to the more conventional sleeping gear. Each member of the patrol carried a morphine capsule and a field dressing to treat gunshot wounds. These would sustain us and keep us alive in the event of being wounded until we were evacuated by helicopter to the nearest hospital. A single saline drip was carried by the patrol.

An hour before we were due to deploy, the pit fire was stoked with freshly chopped wood. We sat in its billowing smoke wearing our deployment gear so that our skin and clothes would become impregnated with the odor of burning wood. Being a natural smell of the bush, it would disguise our human smell from the wild animals and locals. An indigenous person can smell a European's body odor two hundred yards away, but not if it's disguised by the smell of woodsmoke.

❧

We lifted off from the base at 4 o'clock that afternoon. The Alouette helicopter was at maximum weight as it lifted sluggishly into the air, turbine engines screaming. It hovered momentarily at 100 feet, turned 90°, dipped its nose slightly and clattered along the river line at treetop level looking like an oversized dragonfly. Below us, the landscape alternated between thick, impregnable bush and more open mopani scrubland. Occasionally we flew over the deep gorge of a river or tributary snaking its way down from the escarpment before spilling into the Zambezi River. Game trails criss-crossed everywhere.

We had been flying for some thirty minutes when the helicopter suddenly banked into a sharp left-hand orbit, its blades clattering noisily. The pilot pointed to a small open watercourse below us which would act as a suitable landing zone (LZ). Moments later the pilot flared the aircraft's nose, hovered momentarily, and then settled gently into the LZ with the blades thrashing the air like a paddle beating against water.

We quickly deplaned into all-round defence and waited as the aircraft rose in a swirling dust cloud, hovered, and then disappeared above the treetops. Moments later we shook ourselves into a single file formation and departed the LZ. The helicopter might attract unwelcome attention from anyone nearby with hostile intentions. CJ took the lead as the point man looking for tracks, followed by the patrol commander and the MAG gunner. I brought up the rear.

We walked slowly, stopping often to listen, letting our senses become accustomed to the sounds and smells of the bush. Just

before twilight there was a sudden clap of thunder followed by a streak of lightening that stabbed earthward. Storm clouds began rolling towards us with the speed and sound of an approaching avalanche. The sky quickly darkened. Sharp volleys of thunder sounding like a rolling artillery barrage boomed above us accompanied by blinding flashes of lightning that illuminated the surrounding bush in stark detail. The valley was known for its sudden, violent thunderstorms. We had been walking along a large game trail that meandered along the bank of a river when the rain came. It fell in torrents.

"Let's get off the trail and into a defensive position until nightfall; eat some cold rations, and after it gets dark we'll walk another 100 yards, split up and lie low for the rest of the night. And remember, keep your muskets dry." Sergeant Smith wasn't a typical regimental NCO. He disliked parades and barrack life as much as any. But he was an excellent soldier, a good leader and had an intimate knowledge of the bush.

We spent the night huddled under our ponchos, trying to snatch what little sleep we could. I had been assailed earlier that afternoon by squadrons of mopani and tsetse flies, followed later in the day by the stinging 'chewore buzzards'—large brown flies that stabbed their painful sting into our exposed skin. Now with the rain continuing to fall, I was plagued by swarms of mosquitoes. Their incessant high-pitched buzzing and the shrill chirping of the

Arriving at Deka Base Camp at night, Zambezi Valley. (Terry Griffin)

cicadas were the only sounds I could hear above the rain falling on my poncho. I awoke from a fitful sleep shortly after midnight. The rain had stopped and the soft orange glow of moonlight filtered fleetingly through the scurrying clouds. I instinctively knew I was not alone. Slowly, cautiously, I peeled back the corner of my dripping poncho clutching my rifle and slipping off the safety lever. Initially, I was unable to focus on anything in the speckled glow of the moonlight. Then I realized that I was looking directly into the large gray mass of something right next to me. It was the foot of an elephant not even two feet from where I lay!

An entire herd was moving noiselessly past like ghostly sentinels. Large fleshy pads on the bottom of their feet smothered the sound of breaking twigs or branches. Their trunks swayed from side to side in front of them, occasionally rising to snatch a succulent leafy branch from above their heads. They were obviously aware of my presence but were not alarmed by it. The smoke from the wood fire had worked its magic. The herd moved slowly past and melted unseen into the night.

The next morning we regrouped, and after brewing a hot cup of tea on our small gas stoves and wiping down our rifles with a slick of oil, we moved out to continue our patrol. It was around 9 o'clock when CJ suddenly raised his arm and crouched, indicating danger. He had come across human tracks leading from the river heading south in the direction of the escarpment.

Sergeant Smith conferred quickly with his tracker. "How many?"

"Five. They're travelling light and not too fast, probably about three hours ahead of us." CJ studied the tracks closely, making full use of the shadow cast by the oblique angle of the sun on each set of footprints. Each footprint told a story and CJ was able to give an accurate assessment of who had made them, their speed and how far ahead they were. He was also able to tell us the approximate weight of the load each person was carrying.

Sergeant Smith looked at his map. We were 500 yards from the river. He radioed a situation report, or SITREP, back to Commando H.Q. and instantly made a decision as to what to do next.

"Backtrack to the river," he ordered CJ. "I want to see if they crossed by boat. If they did and we can find it, it might give us some clues as to who we're dealing with."

We shook out into follow-up formation with CJ following the tracks. Sergeant Smith positioned himself directly behind CJ, with Hodgson and myself deploying forward of the tracker on each flank to provide him with a protective screen. It didn't take us long to reach the river. It took us even less time to locate the two dugout canoes pulled up on to the riverbank. They were hidden under the overhanging branches of a tree. While the rest of us stood guard, Sergeant Smith and CJ searched the canoes for clues as to what the purpose of the occupants might be. They were hoping to find a piece of webbing, or a stray round of 7.62 intermediate ammunition, all standard equipment carried by terrorists ... anything that might link them to being part of a terrorist group. There was nothing, just some rusty pieces of baling wire and old nylon fishing line.

"Looks like poachers coming across the river looking for ivory or rhino horn."

An updated SITREP was radioed through to Commando H.Q.

The radio crackled with static. The calm, modulated voice of the Commando Commander came through.

"34B, this is 3 Sunray speaking. Destroy the dug-outs and commence an immediate follow-up. Let me know if there is any change to the situation."

Major Barrett-Hamilton was unflappable in any situation and would always be trying to second-guess possible scenarios so as to be able to support his men on the ground if and when needed.

We punched holes in the bottom of the dug-outs and pushed them into the river, watching them slowly sink below the surface as the current carried them downstream.

"3, this is 34B, commencing follow-up."

We got back into formation and started following the tracks at a brisk pace. Sergeant Smith pumped his hand back and forth in the air indicating he wanted us to move fast.

"Come on ouens," he whispered. "Let's catch these guys before nightfall."

The sun beat down on us mercilessly the whole morning as we followed the tracks. It was a sweltering hot day and the sweat poured from our bodies. Nothing moved in the valley; not a single bird in the sky or animal on the ground. Every living creature had scurried for shelter from the baking sun. The heat reflected off the cracked, dry ground around us distorting our vision. Only the swarms of mopani and tsetse flies continued their relentless torment. Eventually we came to the bank of a river where thick vegetation offered a welcome and shady reprieve from the sun. It was here that the group we were following had stopped for a break. It was here, too, that CJ was able to glean more information about them.

"They stopped for a meal here," he said, pointing to a tiny morsel of smoked fish. "They have no idea they're being followed. No sentry was posted."

Then he whistled softly to himself, indicating for Sergeant Smith to join him. He softened his voice into a whisper.

"At least one of them is armed with a rifle." He pointed to a small scuff mark on the tree one of them had been resting against.

"Probably made by the front sight of the rifle he is carrying. Look," he said pointing to the ground, "you can see the faint imprint of the rifle butt."

"AK, SKS?" queried Sergeant Smith, referring to the standard weaponry carried by terrorists.

"Neither, this weapon is longer, probably some sort of blunderbuss."

The discovery confirmed we were following a group of poachers. The fact that one of them was armed added some flavor to the situation but was no cause for alarm. The old blunderbuss rifles used by the poachers were as inclined to kill the person firing them as they were to kill the animal being fired at and its range was limited. But they were still deadly weapons.

CJ scouted ahead to locate the tracks. He told us we were now an hour behind the poachers.

"Quick brew, ouens. Fifteen minutes, then we're off. I want these guys caught today."

It was late afternoon during one of our pauses to look and listen, that CJ made a shallow up and down motion with the palm of his hand. It was a cautionary signal indicating that he had heard, seen or smelled something. He then put a finger to his nose indicating that it was the latter.

"Wood burning, maybe seven hundred yards ahead."

The bush had thinned out into rolling mopani scrub. Sergeant Smith motioned us into an extended line and we moved forward cautiously.

We hadn't gone far when we heard the sound of wood being chopped, a hollow sound which carried loudly through the silence of the bush. We paused to listen. Nothing moved. It was as though nature herself might be holding her breath in anticipation of what might follow. Ahead of us the ground sloped uphill into a shallow crest covered in thorn scrub and long grass. We crept forward cautiously and peered silently through the grass. Below and 100 yards to our front, five poachers were in the process of building a fire. The leader was loading his blunderbuss. Behind them was an old rhinoceros, its hind leg caught in an old rusty wire snare which had almost cut through to the bone of the poor animal. Sergeant Smith was infuriated. He motioned us back to the base of the fold.

"CJ, when we crawl back up there I want you to shout to those bastards that each and every one of them has a rifle aimed at them. One false move and they will be sent to the land of their forefathers. As you start talking, we'll all stand with our rifles aimed in their direction so they know we mean business." CJ spoke the vernacular as well as the Africans themselves.

We crawled back up to the shallow crest and positioned ourselves. CJ called out to the poachers. As he spoke we rose as one on the crest of the hill, our rifles aimed. The armed poacher whirled, took quick aim with his weapon and fired a shot. The lead ball whistled just a few inches over our heads, dangerously close. Before he had released his finger from the trigger to re-load, he was dead. The rest threw up their hands in surrender. A helicopter was called to uplift the dead poacher and take the rest to a Parks and Wildlife camp. There they would be interrogated and the remains of their leader returned to his family for burial. A decision was made to shoot the rhino to put it out of its misery.

The remainder of our trip was uneventful. We spent days patrolling the border finding no sign of terrorist incursions. It became a matter of trying to survive the heat and the tsetse flies until it was time to go home. I was struck by the harshness of the Zambezi Valley. Death could come in an instant; it was kill or be killed.

But it would get much, much worse.

∽

Two weeks after the Commando's return to Salisbury I was lying on my bed in the barrack-room. It was early Christmas morning. I was summoned downstairs together with a handful of other soldiers who had remained in the barracks, the rest of the Commando having gone home to spend Christmas with their families. We were told to bring our tin mugs with us. Downstairs, Captain Ron Reid-Daly and the Commando medic, Jimmy May, were waiting for us, standing in front of a huge urn of steaming tea.

"It's a Rhodesian Army tradition borrowed from the British Army, Gentlemen. Those troopers without homes to go to at Christmas are issued 'Gunfire' on Christmas morning, served by officers of the Regiment."

With that he ladled steaming tea into each of our mugs. "Happy Christmas, ouens."

I took a sip from my steaming mug and almost choked. Ron Reid-Daly looked at me and smiled.

"It's one part sweet tea and two parts Scotch whisky, Junior." He raised his mug in salute. "It's a soldier's drink … a soldier's Christmas drink. Merry Christmas!"

Gunfire on Christmas morning is a tradition I have never missed
since.

∽

Two days later, everybody returned from their break and the Commando commenced an intensive two-week period of retraining. On 29 December the Commando set out on a twenty-mile timed "forced march" in full battle gear. It was an exercise to test both our physical fitness and endurance. We marched in a squad and as we were completing the exercise, I suddenly realized what day it was: my 21st birthday and I hadn't even remembered! I was so exhausted after the run that all I could do was summon the energy to have a hot shower and crawl into bed.

The next morning I was feeling depressed that such a special day had come and gone without celebration or acknowledgment when I was summoned by the Sergeant-Major. He told me I was to appear before Major Barrett-Hamilton on orders. That made me even more miserable. I was quite sure he didn't want to wish me a "Happy Birthday" and I couldn't imagine what I might have done

WO2 Trevor Kirrane. (Jacqui Kirrane)

wrong.

Sergeant-Major Kirrane marched me into the office as though I was appearing on a court-martial.

"Quick ... march! Left, right, left, right. Halt!"

I found myself standing in front of an extremely stern-looking Major Barrett-Hamilton.

"Bax, I have some interesting news for you." His features softened suddenly and he smiled.

"You're one of only two candidates from the Battalion to have been chosen to attend an Officers' Selection Board. The other is Sergeant Walker from 1 Commando. The process starts next month. If you pass selection, you will attend a formal Officers' Training Course at the School of Infantry in Gwelo which will commence in February. If you pass you will be commissioned as a Second Lieutenant. Congratulations." He reached out and shook my hand.

I was speechless. The waiting Sergeant-Major wasn't.

"Left, right, left, right, left, right. Halt! Bring yourself towards yourself, soldier," he ordered, marching me out of the office.

"You're not a damned officer yet!"

8

An Officer I Wanted to Become

"To suggest that the General was the architect of the victory would be a perverse distortion of the truth. His success was attributable to the Army War College, whose ability it was to select the right men to become his Lieutenants. With the young officers at the guns, he was able to retire to the Mess tent and the solitude of the bottle; victory was thus assured."
—Army Staff College, "The Importance of Junior Leadership",
Lessons from the Crimea: 1976

S even months' soldiering with the Rhodesian Light Infantry hadn't left me flush with cash. My instructions from Army Headquarters were to present myself at the guard room of the Llewellyn Barracks at 8:00 a.m. sharp with, among other items, a suit and pajamas. I owned neither. I managed to secure a loan from the Standard Bank to buy a dapper-looking suit with flared trouser bottoms and a pair of very military-looking tartan pajamas. The bank manager suggested that I might wish to consider increasing the size of my loan.

"You might wish to consider investing in some shirts, shoes and socks?" Almost as an afterthought he added, "And what about a tie or two?"

I caught the overnight train to Bulawayo and arrived at the Llewellyn Barracks guard room at the appointed time, suitcase in hand. I felt rather important, like an executive arriving for a business meeting. A Corporal guarding the gate didn't think I looked important at all. He looked me up and down as though I might be a lost clown looking for his circus.

"Are you lost?"

"I'm here to attend the Officers' Selection Board." I replied sanctimoniously.

"God help us. Name?"

"Bax." I didn't tell him I was *Trooper* Bax. I was feeling too important to be a trooper.

"Hop in and I'll take you to where they're meeting." He pointed toward the back of an extremely dirty and rather dilapidated-looking open Land Rover.

"I'll sit in the front if you don't mind."

"Suit yourself, but you might be a bit uncomfortable."

The Corporal pointed to a large tear in the front passenger seat from which protruded a broken seat spring. I was glad he had pointed it out. I didn't relish attending my first interview with the crotch of my expensive new suit ripped open. I picked up my suitcase and climbed into the back. Not wanting to get my new suit dirty, I was trying to decide the least dusty spot on which to sit when, without warning, we roared off. I was knocked completely off balance and ended up with my bottom firmly wedged inside the well of a spare wheel lying on the floor of the vehicle.

A few hair-raising minutes later we arrived outside a large building at the entrance of which stood a rather motley collection of individuals. They were milling around in civilian clothes looking somewhat bemused at the antics of a short, unfriendly-looking Sergeant-Major who was circling them like a sheep dog around a flock of bewildered sheep. I jumped off the Land Rover just as the Sergeant-Major started barking orders for everyone to get inside the building. Next to me was standing an extremely tall and debonair-looking fellow wearing a loud green jacket and yellow checkered trousers that barely covered his ankles.

"My word, what an extremely unpleasant fellow." He spoke with a frightfully British accent.

Inside the hall were 35 desks and chairs, one for each candidate on selection, arranged with military precision in neat, orderly rows. On top of each desk was a card printed in bold black lettering identifying the name of the candidate to whom the desk had been assigned. At the front of the hall was a large lectern next to which stood an old wooden table piled high with large bundles of paper. Gathered around the table were a number of important-looking officers who, except for their immaculate uniforms, looked like they might be a group of schoolmasters plotting against a new intake of pupils. The 'headmaster' of the group was an older and very weathered Colonel who looked like he had been through just about everything that life had to offer. He introduced himself as Lt. Col. Sandy Maclean, officer commanding the Selection Board.

"Good morning, Gentlemen." He spoke in a low, authoritative growl. "Take your assigned seats, please."

After introducing himself and the other officers on the Board, the Colonel informed us that they were henceforth to be referred to as Directing Staff, or 'DS'. He went on to explain that the Board would be conducting the selection process in two phases. The first phase, to be held at Llewellyn, would last four days after which those who passed would be transported to the Rhodesian School of Infantry in Gwelo for phase two. The second phase would be of two weeks' duration.

After a light finger-lunch during which the officers circled us like victors around the vanquished, scrutinizing our every move, we re-assembled in the hall for the first of our scheduled tasks. We were called up one at a time and given three minutes to prepare a fifteen minute speech on a topic given to us by the DS. Each candidate was required to introduce himself and explain where he was from before launching into his presentation.

The first candidate called was a very serious-looking young man who introduced himself as Martin Pearse, the only child of a well-to-do family from Johannesburg, South Africa. Martin would later be destined to command a squadron of the Rhodesian Special Air Service Regiment (SAS), one of the world's most elite Special Forces Units. Right now he was a very nervous young candidate who had to give a fifteen minute speech on 'organisms'.

"Orgasms are an important part of the reproduction of animals and plants."

Martin began speaking with great authority, trying to impress the DS both with his knowledge of organisms and his skills as an orator. Laughter rippled through the room at his unfortunate misuse of the word 'orgasm'.

Concerned that we were not taking his presentation seriously enough, Martin adopted a more serious and authoritative posture, raising his voice by an octave. The more he spoke of the importance of 'orgasms', the more the rest of us spilled into laughter. Ten minutes into his speech he realized that something must be amiss. He wasn't sure what, but if nobody else was going to take his presentation seriously, neither was he. He stepped off the lectern and broke into a wide grin. The rest of us burst into peels of laughter. So did Martin. The laughter didn't stop until his remaining five minutes of allocated time had elapsed.

"By Jove," said the tall Englishman sitting next to me, clearly caught up in the exuberance of the occasion. He was trying to uncoil himself from his desk to give Martin a standing ovation, but only succeeded in tipping both himself and the desk on to the floor.

"Good show, jolly good show, bravo," he chortled from the tangled mass of arms, legs and steel tubing lying at my feet.

Martin returned to his seat looking sheepish.

"Do organisms have orgasms?" asked Lt. Col. Maclean.

Martin looked perplexed. So did the dour-faced Sergeant-Major who hadn't the faintest idea what all the fuss was about.

༄

The following day we were trooped off to an outside area where a number of odd-looking structures had been constructed. It looked rather like an amusement park in which some avant-garde artist had been let loose to build a series of abstract forms. When we arrived we were told that each structure represented an 'obstacle' that would have to be crossed, climbed, or in some way overcome.

We were split up into seven syndicates of five, with each syndicate being allocated a DS. The DS carefully explained what each obstacle represented and painted a rather improbable sounding 'battle picture' of what we were required to do. Within each group, a leader was then appointed and given five minutes to formulate a plan on how best to overcome the obstacle. The syndicate leader would have to explain his plan to the DS before getting the rest of us to help him put his plan into action. I was in the same syndicate as the tall English fellow next to whom I had sat the previous day. His name was the Honorable Mark Wrottesley whose aristocratic lineage, he took pains to explain, extended far back into British history. At a smidgen under 7 feet tall, Mark towered over everybody else.

Our first obstacle was a complex series of poles, ropes and planks which we were told represented a demolished bridge. Blue chalk dust sprinkled on the ground depicted a deep, wide river over which the bridge had once stood. A 44-gallon drum full of concrete stood on the side of the 'river' on which we were standing. The DS assigned to our syndicate was a tall, rangy, infantry Captain named Charlie Aust who would later go on to become one of the most respected commanding officers of the Rhodesian Light Infantry.

"Right, Gentlemen, the blue chalk dust represents a deep, fast-flowing river which is full of crocodiles. This syndicate represents a patrol that has to get to the opposite side of the river taking the 44-gallon drum with them. You have to act quickly because you are being chased by the enemy who are a few minutes behind you."

None of us had a clue as to how to go about crossing the river, let alone how to get the heavy drum across with us. We each tried to make ourselves inconspicuous so as to avoid being nominated syndicate leader. Mark Wrottesley's height made it extremely hard for him to escape attention.

"Wrottesley, you're the syndicate leader. You have three minutes to explain your plan of action. Now get on with it."

I detected an audible groan from poor Wrottesley. He decided that his best course of action would be to play for time.

"I say, what did you say was in the river, Captain?" "Crocodiles, Wrottesley, *hungry* crocodiles."

Wrottesley took a nimble step backwards from the chalk river, as if a real crocodile might suddenly leap from the sand to snap off his leg. He scratched his head looking at the structure as if it might be a bad dream. He blinked, hoping it might miraculously melt away before his eyes.

"I say, Captain. It's a rather improbable scenario don't you think? After all, why the devil would anybody want to spend time getting a drum full of concrete across a crocodile-infested river with the enemy breathing down his neck?"

This prompted the unhappy Sergeant-Major who had been hovering nearby to leap into action. He began swatting at Wrottesley with a leafy branch he was carrying.

"Come on, come on, the enemy isn't far behind! What are you going to do? What *are* you going to do? Think, *think*!"

The Sergeant-Major's task was obviously to distract the syndicate leader as much as possible while he was busy trying to formulate a plan. This was evidently to simulate battlefield distractions. He hovered around Wrottesley like an annoying horsefly.

"Look, the enemy's right behind you! *What are you going to do*?" Wrottesley glanced quickly behind him as if to reassure himself that a column of austere German storm troopers weren't indeed bearing down on him. All he saw was a line of smartly dressed native waiters from the Officers' Mess. They were carrying trays of tea and cucumber sandwiches in preparation for the serving of morning tea.

"I think I'm going to have a cup of tea, Sergeant-Major. Would you care to join me?"

By the end of the fourth day only 25 of the original 35 candidates who had started the selection course remained. By an astonishing stroke of luck I was amongst them; so were Martin Pearse and Mark Wrottesley. I hadn't expected Wrottesley to survive his leisurely morning tea break on the banks of the crocodile-infested 'river', nor had he.

'I don't think I've got any chance of passing,' he told me the evening before. He seemed rather sad. 'It's going to be tough explaining it to my dad.'

School of Infantry. (Terry Griffin)

'Just tell him you were outnumbered by Germans as you tried to finish your afternoon tea,' I consoled. Fortunately, Capt. Aust decided that humor and an ability to remain cool, calm and collected under pressure were desirable traits for someone aspiring to become an officer and Wrottesley remained with us for the next phase.

☙

On the morning of the fifth day we were driven to the Rhodesian School of Infantry in Gwelo to begin phase two of the selection process. On arrival we were deposited on the edge of a square where an important parade was in progress. We must have looked a bit out of place milling around in our civilian clothes with our suitcases in hand: rather like a bunch of confused tourists suddenly disgorged from their tour bus waiting for the appearance of their tour guide. Wrottesley's extraordinary height made us look terribly conspicuous. He towered above the rest of us like an unwelcome giraffe amongst a herd of skittish impala intent on making themselves less noticeable to a pride of nearby lions.

I was standing next to a fellow with whom I had become friends at

Llewellyn. His name was Colin Willis and he was a short, stocky, self-assured man with the build and doggedness of a bullterrier. He too would later join the Rhodesian SAS and become one of their most decorated squadron commanders.

Suddenly, a loud bellow issued from the direction of the Parade Square.

'Who's that idiot shouting at?' asked Colin looking in the direction of a Sergeant marching purposely towards us.

'I rather think it's us,' I replied. 'He doesn't look terribly happy.'

'Who are you scumbags standing around my parade making the place look untidy?' bawled the Sergeant. I was beginning to think that sergeants were incapable of holding a civilized conversation.

'We're on Officer Selection Course,' responded Colin, with an air of self-righteous indignation.

'Officer Selection my ass, you're nothing but shark shit. And for those of you unlucky enough to pass selection and become officer cadets at this school remember this: you will be treated as shark shit for the duration of your course.'

I had been wondering what our status would be as officer cadets.

Now I had been informed in no uncertain terms. I wasn't too sure what being treated like shark shit meant but it didn't sound terribly promising. Having made his point, the Drill Sergeant executed a snappy about turn and rejoined his parade. Deciding that perhaps we weren't quite as important as we thought, we scuttled away from the parade ground like crabs from an incoming tide. A short while later we were rounded up by another extremely unfriendly-looking Sergeant who marched us to a dilapidated barrack-room with the unlikely name of 'Alanbrooke'.

Shortly after getting settled in, we were herded off to the Quartermaster Store to be issued with fatigues, boots, hats and webbing, including backpacks. The issuing of this field equipment indicated to us that we were about to be deployed into the bush. This was a most unexpected development. After all, even with our newfound status of 'shark shit', we were still aspiring to become officers and gentlemen. Surely we weren't going to be subjected to the rigors and hardships of the African bush without the proper training? With that thought still haunting us we were finally allowed to turn in for the night.

The following morning we were rudely awakened by the deafening explosion of a thunder flash thrown inside the barrack-room. An eerie silence followed. It was broken by the bemused sounding voice of Wrottesley.

"I say, was that you old chap?" He was speaking to the person lying on the bed next to his.

"No, but it could have been. Damn near shat myself." Terry Griffin was a young Kenyan, who two years after leaving the South African Navy had decided to attempt officer selection with the Rhodesian Army. By a quirk of coincidence, Terry was destined to become an expert on explosives as the commander of one of Rhodesia's military engineer squadrons.

Moments later the barrack-room erupted into a crescendo of noise and confusion. The lights flickered on and from out of the choking plumes of acrid smoke appeared the chilling face of the unfriendly Sergeant-Major from Llewellyn. It was as if Lucifer himself might have descended on a cloud of foul-smelling cordite to make our lives miserable.

"Up, up! Get yourselves dressed into field training kit … up, *up!*" We were given barely enough time to get dressed and into our gear before being herded on to the back of a truck and driven into the night. As dawn broke the truck stopped and we found ourselves in the middle of an extremely inhospitable and desolate piece of countryside. Standing on the side of the road was the same group of officers who had taken us for our first phase at Llewellyn. They were sipping steaming mugs of hot tea as they watched us tumble out the back of the truck.

We were each issued two days' water and rations and told to conserve what we had because we were about to embark on a strenuous march through the bush for an undetermined number of days. Into each of our backpacks was placed an absurdly heavy load of rocks, each numbered in bold red paint. A record was made of which rocks were placed into which packs, and it was explained that if any went missing it would result in automatic expulsion for the person involved. Then we set off into the sweltering heat like a caravan of reluctant camels heading for some remote desert wadi.

On the fourth day of the march I was appointed group leader. We had finished the last of our food and water earlier that morning and were now close to complete mental and physical exhaustion. We had stopped next to a dusty, dry track for a short break in the late afternoon having no idea how much further we would have to walk. I was sitting with my back against the trunk of a tall acacia tree trying to suck moisture from a stalk of grass while swatting angrily at an annoying fly, when a welcome shadow moved over me affording temporary relief from the boiling sun. I looked up to see the officer who had been accompanying us silhouetted against the afternoon sun. Captain Trevor Desfountain was a lean, rangy RLI officer who knew the bush like he knew his own backyard. He had an irrepressible sense of humor which he would disguise by masking his face in deep concentration.

"Tell me, Bax, what's a Canadian lumberjack doing out in the middle of the African bush dying of thirst and wondering where his next meal is coming from?" He was referring to the prepared speech I had given a few days earlier when each candidate had been required to give a brief synopsis of his life to the Selection Board.

I took the withered stalk out of my mouth and contemplated it for a while.

"I don't know, Sir. But if I should die of dehydration and hunger before this is over, would you be so kind as to inform my mother that I have a small clothing debt payable to the Standard Bank?" Just then I heard the distant sounds of a coughing engine.

"I think you might have to repay that loan yourself. It looks like the cavalry has arrived just in time to save you."

A few minutes later the 'cavalry' arrived in the form of a tired-looking Bedford truck which sputtered into view through a parting screen of dry acacia. It was being driven by an equally tired-looking African. As it drew alongside, its engine clanked to a stop with an ominous sound of finality. Scrawled on its side in bold white chalk were the words, 'Cadet Pick-up Express'. I wasn't particularly confident of the express vehicle's ability to go anywhere, let alone get us home. We crawled aboard the back of the truck using our last reserves of energy and waited while the driver tried to crank its engine back to life. Like a stubborn mule it refused to start. After a few minutes of coaxing, it must have decided that the inhospitable African bush might not be a place to linger. The engine coughed, backfired, coughed again and belched a plume of blue smoke before clattering noisily to life. The relieved driver turned the belching truck, and we lurched precariously down the bumpy track.

We spent the following week undertaking more grueling tests and interviews to ascertain our suitability for commissioned rank. On the last day of selection, Lt. Col. Maclean called us individually into his office for our final interview. It was the moment of reckoning when we would be told whether we had passed or failed. Col. Maclean was a man of few words who didn't believe in waffling. He stood up and shook my hand.

"Congratulations, Bax. You've passed the selection and will commence your officer cadet training on 1 February. Good luck." That was it.

Our initial group of 35 had been whittled down to 13. Unfortunately, Wrottesley or 'Wrotters' as he had fondly become known was not among the successful candidates. At the end of the selection he joined the ranks of the

Trevor Desfountain. (Jacqui Kirrane)

Rhodesian Light Infantry where he served with great honour and distinction. Years later he was tragically killed. He never realized his dream of becoming a commissioned officer, but he was born a gentleman and remained a gentleman until the day he died. I was honored to have been acquainted with him, even for a brief period of his short life.

I left the School of Infantry the next day to collect my belongings from the RLI and returned the following week. I thought it best to get another letter off to Mother to tell her where I would be for the next twelve months.

Dear Mother,

I have been accepted to attend an officers' course at the Rhodesian School of Infantry in Gwelo. The course lasts for twelve months.

P.S. Preparing for the course has left me financially embarrassed. Please, could you lend me some money to repay the Standard Bank a small loan I had to take to pay for a suit and pajamas?

9

An Officer I Became

"I'm sure that some of my fellow officers are quite normal.
Some have even managed to avoid falling off the edge of propriety. Thankfully,
none of my associates are amongst them."

—Major 'Spike' Powell to the author,
RLI Officers' Mess: June, 1974

"You will be groomed over the next twelve months to become officers and gentlemen. The highest standards of honor, integrity and chivalry will be expected of you at all times. These values are not negotiable. Compromise on any of them and you will be removed from the course."

I was sitting in a lecture room with the rest of Officer Cadet Course Inf 25/14 listening intently to the opening address by our senior course officer, Major Dick Lockley. I was forming my first impressions of the man who would be the chief architect of my fate over the next twelve months.

Three weeks later the entire course came close to being removed *en masse*. We were caught cheating. Each of us had been required to submit a written paper about *The Influence of Communism on African Nationalism*. One of the cadets had managed to acquire an answer sheet used by the Directing Staff, or DS, for grading assignments. The fact that we had each listed identical points for discussion was bad enough. That we had presented identical arguments was worse. That each cadet's paper was identical to the illegally-procured DS answer sheet was considered a scandalous breach of honor and integrity. We were saved from expulsion only because an entire course of officer cadets had never before been dismissed from the school. It wasn't a precedent for which Major Dick Lockley cared to be remembered. Had he been presiding over a group of cadets from the Imperial Japanese Army he might well have had to fall on his sword. Being a good Rhodesian he was able to restore his honor and dignity by adjourning to the Officers' Mess for a pink gin.

A Rhodesian by birth, Major Lockley was a product of Britain's Royal Military Academy, Sandhurst. A tall, blond, broadly-built man with a square face and jaw, his proudest achievement at the Academy was becoming

champion heavyweight boxer. It was an accomplishment he was seldom prone
to allow us to forget. Boxing was considered a 'gentleman's' sport in the British
Army, especially amongst the Officer Corps. Its purpose was to instill a sense
of aggression tempered by an appreciation for the rules of fair play. Fighting by
the 'Queensberry Rules' was an important facet of British military culture, one
that Major Lockley wanted incorporated into the Cadet Wing of the school.

As he frequently reminded us, "You must not fight simply to win. No holds
barred is not the way. You must win by the rules."

However, it seemed that an inability to knock an opponent out in the
ring might cast doubts upon a potential officer's ability to knock a foe out in
the field of battle. My own suitability for commissioned rank must have been
thrown into question the first time I entered the boxing ring. I took a wild
swing at my opponent, missed, pirouetted to the far corner and fell out of the
ring. It was a spectacle that was adversely commented upon during my first
mid-term report. "Cadet Bax needs to concentrate harder on improving his
abilities in the sporting arena."

Major Lockley was a Regimental Officer, more at home amongst the elite
of the *haute société* in the Officers' Mess than cooking over an open fire with
his troops in the field. But he was forthright and upright, and he had little
patience for those who did not aspire to his own high standards of excellence.
Later in his career he would be invested as a Member of the Legion of Merit
for his operational exploits.

By contrast, our assistant course officer was the epitome of the dashing,
fearless young officers who made up the *haute bohèmia* of Rhodesia's elite
fighting units. If the *Charge of the Light Brigade* had taken place 117 years
later, Lieutenant Jeremy Treadwell Strong would have been found with saber
in hand leading the charge of the six hundred, and there would *"nere have
been a man dismayed."* He was a tall, dark, handsome Rhodesian who projected
an aura of quiet, almost shy confidence. Also a product of the Royal Military
Academy, Lieutenant Strong was a recipient of the Academy's Sword of Honor.
He was the personification of the pioneering Rhodesian spirit, happiest in
the bush leading his men from the front rather than being back in barracks
immersed in the pomp and ceremony of Regimental duties. Lieutenant Strong
had joined the School of Infantry from the RLI where he was considered one
of the Battalion's most outstanding Troop Commanders. It was during his
time with the RLI that he was awarded Rhodesia's Bronze Cross for bravery
following a series of ferocious skirmishes with terrorists in the Zambezi Valley.

He believed in leading from the front, and like Major Lockley, would later be invested as a Member of the Legion of Merit for operational leadership.

It was as a young officer recently returned from operations that the *sine qua non* of Lieutenant Strong's contribution to the history of the RLI was made. He was at a party in the Officers' Mess when, having consumed a beer too many, he sneaked back into his room feeling slightly the worse for wear. Stripping off his clothes he fell naked on to his bed and into a deep slumber. His fellow officers sneaked into his room shortly after and carried both him and his bed on to the middle of the Battalion's Parade Square. There the unfortunate Lieutenant was left to sleep all night minus his bed sheets. He was rudely awakened early the following morning by the sounds of recruits marching back and forth at the foot of his bed. Realizing that he wasn't merely having a bad dream he sprang into action. His naked half-mile sprint through the phalanx of recruits back to the Officers' Mess was the first 'streak' ever recorded in the Regiment.

&

The first phase of the Cadet Course was three months of basic drill and weapons. We were tied each morning to the Parade Square like an unborn baby to its umbilical cord. We were tied each afternoon to the butt-end of a machine gun until we were able to squirt a burst of automatic fire through a target the size of a halfpenny. Having recently completed my sixteen-week recruit course in the RLI, I found having to march up and down the Parade Square each morning like a mechanical robot to be infinitely tedious. Ironically, the only relief from the monotony of the parades was provided by our drill instructor. He was a tough, battle-hardened SAS Sergeant-Major who, by his own admission, had long forgotten what little he had ever known about drill. He had been posted to the School of Infantry to qualify for future promotion, but like many operational soldiers in front line units, would have preferred to forego promotion and remain in the bush rather than be posted to the School of Infantry. The Army had other ideas.

Giving a word of command on the correct foot is crucial if a drill movement is to be executed with any degree of fluency. Our instructor clearly had no idea on which foot to give any commands and he cared even less. In his book, giving a word of command on the correct foot was of infinitely less importance than being able to calculate the distance of an enemy and adjust one's sight before squeezing the trigger. But like it or not, drill instruction is what he had to teach and every time he gave a word of command it happened to be on the

Major Dick Lockley, Officer Cadet Course, Course Officer. (Dick Lockley)

wrong foot. The result was that our squad would end up dispersed around the Parade Square like confetti in the wind. Eventually in an effort to cause less of a spectacle, the unfortunate Sergeant-Major would give us precautionary warnings as to what he intended telling us to do, then ask in a loud whisper if anybody knew on which foot the command had to be given. Invariably he would receive conflicting answers. Rather than risk another embarrassing fiasco he would simply forego issuing any command at all. We would be left to continue marching in the direction we were going until we stumbled off the Parade Square like a train off its tracks.

His efforts at rebuking us and getting us to reform on the Square would be cut short by somebody asking, "Hey, Sergeant-Major, tell us what it's like on operations?"

This was all he needed to call for a smoke break, whereupon he would regain his prestige by relating stories of his operational exploits. He would tell harrowing stories of long-range reconnaissance patrols conducted into neighboring countries and of free-falling into areas to locate terrorist base camps at night so they could be attacked the following morning.

"But how could you find terrorist base camps at night?" asked one of our group, looking bewildered. He had left his job as a senior bank clerk to undergo officer training.

Jerry Strong receiving the Sword of Honour, Sandhurst. (Jerry Strong)

Jerry Strong, Officer Cadet Course Instructor (Jerry Strong)

"By the smell," glowered the Sergeant-Major.

"The smell?"

"The smell. Do you know what 50 unwashed backsides perched over an open latrine smells like?" The bank clerk, soon to become a commissioned officer, didn't know nor did he feel inclined to ask.

By some remarkable stroke of good fortune, by the time we started doing sword drill the Sergeant-Major had been replaced as our drill instructor and was using his vast operational knowledge teaching fieldcraft and tactics. Otherwise, we might all have ended up impaled on our swords.

✌

During the first phase of the Cadet Course we were quartered in the same barrack-room we had stayed in during our selection. Every morning after physical training we would shower, then dress in parade uniform for a barrack-room inspection. We would stand rigidly to attention at the end of our beds while every square inch of the room was meticulously inspected by a course instructor wearing white gloves. A single speck of dust or less-than-perfect uniform would result in the entire course being punished.

One day a fly was found on the end of one cadet's bed. David Rawlins was a young Rhodesian whose father, Brigadier Rawlins, had fought in the Malayan Campaign and who now commanded one of Rhodesia's three operational Brigades.

"A pet?" trumpeted the instructor triumphantly, as if having unmasked a great conspiracy within the barrack-room.

It was as if his find might equal in epic proportion the finding of the entrance to the tunnel in the *Great Escape*. He walked silently up and down the barrack-room, glowering at us. I wondered vaguely whether such a heinous crime might result in the disbandment of the entire course.

"Keeping pets in the barrack-room is a breach of Army regulations," he growled, his voice barely audible. "It is contrary to the Code of Military Discipline, section 42(13)a. You will all report to the Duty Officer at 18:00 hours to receive your punishment. Is that clear?"

He lingered momentarily in case any of us dared challenge his interpretation of military law. We didn't.

That evening the entire course paraded outside the office of the Duty Officer to await our fate. The standard punishment was to put us through a series of rapid 'change parades'. The Army had a different uniform for every possible occasion; as officer cadets we had been issued with most. Change parades entailed forming-up in front of the Duty Officer in one particular uniform, being inspected, and being ordered to return fifteen minutes later dressed in a completely different uniform. Each time we returned we would be closely inspected. A less-than-immaculate uniform would result in further punishment being levied. On this particular evening, the Duty Officer was ensconced in his room watching a TV replay of a rugby test match he had missed the previous weekend.

"Course Inf 25/14 ready and awaiting your inspection in Office Dress, Sir," shouted the duty student diligently.

"Right, be back in fifteen minutes in Parade Order," came the disinterested voice from behind the closed door of the Duty office.

"Course Inf 25/14 ready and awaiting your inspection in Parade Order, Sir," shouted the duty student fifteen minutes later.

"Right, be back in fifteen minutes in Battle Fatigues," came the same bored response from behind the closed door.

"This is a crock of shit," muttered Dave Rawlins as we frantically ran back to our barrack-room to get changed into our camouflage fatigues. "We could

3 Commando boxing team. (Jacqui Kirrane)

be dressed in our birthday suits for all he cares. Let's just stay in our Parade Order and save ourselves the trouble of getting changed."

Fifteen minutes later we were once again outside the door of the Duty Officer.

"Course Inf 25/14 ready and awaiting your inspection in Battle Fatigues, Sir."

The door of the office slowly creaked open. Out stepped the Duty Officer. We froze in trepidation. We were still in our Parade Order.

"Right, Gentlemen, seeing that you have been so diligent in putting on your Battle Fatigues, and given that Battle Fatigues are an appropriate dress to run to the top of the 'kopje', that's where you will all go. The last five back will run to the top again—Go!"

The kopje was a steep-sided rock-strewn hill situated behind the school up which we often had to run as a form of punishment. To have to run to the top at night in our mirror-finished hobnail boots and starched parade uniform was the cruelest form of retribution. We staggered back forty-five minutes later looking as if we had been set upon by an impi of Zulus. Our parade uniforms were unrecognizable and we had an early morning drill parade scheduled for 8 o'clock the following morning.

We wouldn't be getting any sleep that night.

◥◣

The focus on the second phase of our training was 'conventional' warfare. We began to see less of our NCO instructors during this phase and more of our course officers. It was the start of our formal officer training.

The prevailing wisdom in the Army was that in order to fight a successful counter-insurgency war, an officer had to be well grounded in the principles of fighting a conventional war. There was also a lingering concern that a protracted and successful insurgency could evolve into a phase, whereby insurgents might mount conventional attacks using tanks and armor against government forces, such as had been the case during the dying weeks of the Vietnam War.

The problem was that no army existed anywhere in Africa capable of mounting a conventional attack against Rhodesia that we could use as a model to train against. So the School of Infantry invented its own hostile army. A fictitious army was drawn up on paper with the imaginative name of 'Anti South African Army', or ANTISAN. It consisted of three battle groups, each comprising mechanized and armored infantry, artillery, tank regiments and anti-aircraft batteries; everything we needed to train against in a conventional setting.

But there was another problem we had to contend with—outdated weapons and equipment. The only conventional weapons the Rhodesian Army possessed were a handful of expired scout cars and a scattering of 25-pounder field guns, relics of the opening salvos that had heralded the start of Montgomery's advance into El Alamein during the Second World War. We possessed no tanks or heavy artillery and no anti-aircraft batteries … all vital assets needed for training in conventional warfare.

Given that the equipment we needed to train with simply didn't exist, we had to rely solely on our vivid imaginations. The result was that it was sometimes difficult to capture the enthusiasm of the moment during the frequent 'war games', or exercises we engaged in. During one such exercise I was appointed a Platoon Commander and was told by Major Lockley to expect the arrival of a Russian battle tank that was apparently clattering towards my position. I wondered where Major Lockley could possibly have acquired a Russian battle tank for the exercise, and began to get quite excited at the prospect of seeing one. I didn't have long to wait. Major Lockley began shouting at me animatedly.

"Here comes the tank, Bax. What are you going to do now? Think boy, *think*!

I peered over the rim of my trench in great anticipation of seeing my first ever battle tank. Instead of the large mechanical monster I was expecting to see churning towards me with dust spewing furiously from its clanking tracks and belching a covering screen of smoke, I was confronted by the sight of a tired-looking Bedford truck wheezing laboriously up the hill in first gear, farting plumes of oily gray smoke. It looked ominously like the 'Cadet Pick-up Express' from our selection phase. Balanced precariously on the back was a disinterested native steward who had been commandeered from the Officers' Mess. He was sweating profusely under the weight of a sawn-off 44-gallon drum out of which protruded a broom handle. The contraption was supposed to replicate a tank turret. The steward had been told that he was now a Russian tank gunner, a position he had accepted with great reluctance.

"Come on, Bax! It's almost on top of you. It could decimate your entire platoon! How *do* you intend dealing with it? *Think, boy!*"

Just then the old Bedford gave a loud backfire, lurched forward a couple of yards and came to an abrupt and permanent stop, steam spewing from its overheated engine. The mess-steward-turned-Russian-tank-gunner lost his balance and fell off the truck in an undignified heap. He was still wearing his red steward's fez making him look uncannily like the figure of General

Cadet course, air operations. (Terry Griffin)

Gordon from Khartoum wearing his 'tarboosh'. He certainly didn't look like a Russian gunner. I almost burst out laughing.

"I think the tank has broken down, Sir."

"That doesn't matter! It could still bring its gun to bear on you, Bax. Where's your anti-tank gun?"

Just then there was a loud clank. The sawn-off 44-gallon drum which had been precariously teetering on the back of the Bedford also fell to the ground, almost impaling the mess steward with its protruding broom handle.

"I think the gun has fallen off the truck, I mean the tank, Sir." I found it increasingly difficult to refrain from laughing at the spectacle that was unfolding before me.

Major Lockley was becoming exasperated. His well-planned and coordinated tank attack was not going as planned. In fact, it seemed to be unraveling before his very eyes without a shot having been fired.

"I want you to pretend it's a real tank and that it is about to engage your platoon position with its gun! Where's your anti-tank gun?"

A fellow cadet, Athol Gillespie, had been appointed my anti-tank gunner for this exercise and I knew he had purposely left the anti-tank weapon behind hoping that nobody would notice … it was simply too heavy and cumbersome to carry. The 3.5 shoulder-fired rocket launcher was the only anti-tank weapon the Rhodesian Army possessed. It was a large weapon and when fired spewed a frightening blast of flame from the rear of its firing tube which would incinerate anyone standing in its path. Unfortunately, for the luckless Athol Gillespie, Major Lockley was more than aware of the missing anti-tank gun and it was toward the unfortunate Gillespie that he now turned his attention.

"Gillespie," he shouted, appearing more caught up in the exuberance of the occasion than were his cadets. "The gun on that Russian tank is about to fire at you! You're the anti-tank gunner, what are you going to do?"

"I don't see a gun, Sir," replied Gillespie peering over his trench toward the broken down Bedford.

"There, you fool, *there!*" exclaimed Major Lockley, pointing excitedly toward the broom handle that was impaled firmly in the ground behind the Bedford.

"But that's a broom handle, Sir, and I think it's broken!"

"It's a *notional* Russian tank gun you fool, use your imagination!" "Then I'm going to shoot at it with my rocket launcher, Sir." "What rocket launcher?" Major Lockley thought he had

Gillespie in a corner.

"With my *notional* rocket launcher, Sir."

Major Lockley gave Gillespie a thwack across his back with a walking stick he called his 'Cadet Beater' which he was never without on field exercises.

Notional (imaginary) weapons were the exclusive preserve of the Directing Staff.

৩

What our course officers lacked in equipment to make our conventional war training realistic, they more than made up for in imagination. Countless hours were spent in lecture rooms learning the principles of advance, attack, defence and withdrawal. We spent days in a large auditorium split into groups of opposing forces huddled around a meticulously-detailed 'cloth model'. These were made from large sheets of linen laid out on the floor which were scaled and contoured to depict a 'battlefield'. Epic battles of grand proportion would be fought on the cloth model with whole brigades of troops and squadrons of

Officer Cadet Course. Standing from left: Martin Pearse, Tim Bax, Deon Kriel, Athol Gillespie, Terry Griffin. Seated from left: Theo Williams, David Rawlins, Andy Chait, Colin Willis. (Terry Griffin)

armor being moved between its creases and folds … all with the deft movement of a hand. The misguided placement of a foot by one of us stepping on to the model to move a battalion of infantry might result in an entire squadron of tanks being squashed underfoot. It was like playing a giant game of chess. A move by one side would precipitate a counter move by the other, with one side trying to maneuver into an unassailable position to inflict a crushing defeat on the other. The only rules we had to follow were the principles we had previously been taught. Dominating 'high ground' would become a precarious endeavor when a mountain where troops had been deployed one minute might suddenly be transformed into a flat plain by someone inadvertently stepping on it.

Later, we would be driven into the field to spend the day sitting on a remote hilltop overlooking a road, our map boards clutched diligently in our hands as we listened intently to Lieutenant Strong relate a battle picture of an imaginary enemy advancing along the road towards us.

"Advancing along the road is a mechanized infantry company with a screen of armored cars. You are Major I. C. Trouble, Company Commander Bravo Company, 1st Alpine Regiment. You have two hours to plan the defensive position of your company and stop the enemy long enough to allow the Battalion Commander time to organize a counter attack." Lieutenant Strong spoke with great conviction, as though by straining our eyes hard enough, we might actually see the formations of enemy vehicles churning slowly towards us.

This form of exercise was called a TEWT or a 'Tactical Exercise Without Troops'. It involved complex battles and maneuvers between opposing formations of troops, except the troops were all imaginary. Having been given the 'battle picture' we would have to scuttle away and individually plan our defensive positions and draft our detailed orders. One of us would then be nominated to issue the orders to the rest of the group.

One particular afternoon I was sitting close to Cadet Theo Williams who had left the South African Parachute Regiment wanting to become an officer in the Rhodesian Army. Not long after I had started drafting my orders, I heard a noise coming from his direction which sounded like the rancorous idling of a Harley-Davidson. I wasn't sure what it was and wondered for a moment if it might be a *real* enemy scout car that had mysteriously been procured from somewhere to outflank our position. Looking towards Theo to warn him of the impending danger, I noticed him sitting against a rock fast asleep with his legs stretched out looking like a giant iguana basking in the sun. The sound

I had heard was snoring. I threw a pebble at him and whispered in a voice as loud as I dared, "Have you finished your orders already?"

He woke with a start. "I'm not even going to bother," he yawned. "I had to give the last set of orders, so I won't be asked again." With that he settled back into a deep sleep and it wasn't long before the Harley-Davidson resumed its rhythmic snoring.

Two hours later Lieutenant Strong summoned us back to his position. He was sitting in a green camping chair smoking one of his trademark Madison cigarettes.

"Right, are you all ready?" We waited in breathless anticipation to see who the poor person was who would have to give their orders.

"Williams, give us your outline plan and detailed set of orders." Lieutenant Strong flicked some ash from his cigarette, exhaled a long plume of blue smoke and settled comfortably into his chair to listen to Williams' orders.

Williams looked startled, "Me, Sir?"

"Yes. I think your name is Williams?"

"Yes, Sir. Williams, Sir."

"Good. Now that we have established who you are, let's get on with your plan and orders."

Williams looked gob smacked—utterly crestfallen. He looked pleadingly around at the rest of us as if hoping that somebody might rise to his defence and offer to give the orders in his place. No one did. Realizing he had been caught out, he did what soldiers throughout the ages have always done when confronted with impossible odds—he resorted to humor.

"Well, as a matter of fact, Sir, I was busy scouting out a defensive position like you told us to when I was captured by the enemy. They were good enough to tell me that they had overstretched their lines of communication and would soon be withdrawing down the road they had just come along. Luckily, I managed to escape a few minutes ago and am very pleased to be able to tell you, Sir, that there is now no need to give any orders at all."

Humor is in the mind of the beholder. Jerry Strong was not amused. Neither was Theo Williams later that night as he continued doing a series of change parades that would last almost until dawn.

꒰꒱

Phase two of our training brought with it a considerable elevation to our status. We were moved out of the barrack-room and into the cadet accommodation wing of the school. These were quite salubrious lodgings by comparison. Each cadet had his own private bedroom/study. Adjacent were a well-appointed lounge, bar, anteroom and dining room, complete with its own kitchen and catering staff. We even had our own full-time barman. The accommodation rooms were known as 'the stables' because each had a stable door accessing a long open-sided verandah that ran the length of one side of the wing. To add a touch of glamour to our newfound status, we were given white 'gorget' tabs to wear on our uniform lapels and a broad white band to wear around our peak caps. We began to feel quite lofty. So much so, that a week after we had been moved out of our barrack-room, we were almost moved back in for having an overinflated opinion of our own importance. With our change of quarters didn't come a change in status; we were to remain as 'shark shit' for some time to come.

It wasn't all beer and skittles. With our move into the Cadets Mess came new responsibilities. A 'Mess Committee' had to be elected, and meetings held to manage the affairs of the Mess. Major Lockley insisted on being present during the meetings, primarily to keep tabs on the bar stocks and hence our consumption of alcohol. Some momentous and far-reaching discussions took place at the meetings. Minutes of one such meeting held on Feb 15, 1972, records the following:

1. Item 5: The bar's tot measure has mysteriously gone missing and the Rhodesian Breweries refuse to supply another.

2. Item 6: The garden member reports the astonishing news that a hole has appeared in the garden hose pipe. The grounds man doesn't know how to fix it. Nor does anyone else.

3. Item 7: The house member reports that the ablutions are in an appalling state: one of the basin plugs has gone missing and a portable wooden toilet used on field exercises has become in-fested with white ants. Considerable debate ensued as to whether or not funds could be expropriated from the 'enter-tainment fund' to buy a new one. It was decided that this would be permissible so long as it was recorded in the asset register as a 'musical box' and not a 'thunder box'.

4. Item 13: Major Lockley proposed a vote of thanks to himself for the good work he has done for the Mess throughout the year; motion seconded by Major Lockley.

It wasn't very often that we were able to leave the school and travel into town. When we did, our civilian attire had to conform to the 'Standing Orders for Civilian Dress as Worn by Officer Cadets of the Rhodesian Army'. In typical army fashion the title of the standing orders was almost as long and perplexing as its content. We were required to wear regulation grey flannel trousers, white shirts, dark jackets, black lace-up shoes and a *"conservative slim-line tie, which tie will be tied with a regulation half Windsor knot, not to exceed a width of one and a quarter inches."* The *pièce de resistance* was a grey or black Trilby hat which was to be worn with its band situated *"two inches above the top of the eyebrow."* The intention of the dress code was to make us look like English squires and gentleman. What we actually looked like was a mob of Mafiosi that had descended on the town to extract murderous retribution for having been stiffed out of a questionable consignment of Chianti. Pedestrians seeing us walking towards them would duck through the doors of nearby shops or cross to the opposite side of the street.

Regardless of whether we looked like squires or mobsters we were distinctly unsuccessful in our endeavors at attracting the attention of the opposite sex, so we concentrated our efforts toward the one source of women that seemed reasonably available—the Nurses' Home. All previous efforts at enticing them from their lodgings had failed. This was primarily because we had never been able to get past a very buxom and dour-looking matron who guarded the inside foyer as if it were the cloistered entrance to a sheik's bordello. She had even confounded the most strenuous efforts of our most accomplished Casanova and self-appointed 'ladies' man' in being able to sneak past her. Terry Griffin boasted he could talk his way into the Bernadette Nunnery at Lourdes. Perhaps he could, but every attempt he had made thus far at trying to talk his way into the Nurses' Home in Gwelo had met with abject failure. It didn't take us long to realize that it was going to take a lot more than white gorgets and Trilby hats to impress our way past the vigilant matron. Another plan would have to be hatched.

One evening about a month after we had moved into the stables, I accompanied Colin Willis and Terry Griffin on yet another foray to gain entry into the Nurses' Home. We had decided the only way to circumvent the matron and gain direct access to the nurses was by climbing a drainpipe attached to the exterior wall at the front of the building which led directly into the nurses' second-floor bathroom. Our plan was for Terry to shimmy up the drainpipe and climb through the bathroom window whereupon he would announce his presence like a Prince Charming to damsels in distress. Colin and I would remain as lookouts below and distract the matron's attention should she come to investigate. Having gained access to the dormitory, Terry would then use his great charm to convince the nurses to allow Colin and me to climb the drainpipe to join them for a party.

"Perhaps we should send Terry up with a bottle of champagne," suggested Colin before leaving the Mess. "He can't go knocking on their bathroom window empty-handed." We procured a bottle of champagne from the cadet's bar and set off on our mission.

After making sure the coast was clear, Terry started his long climb up the drainpipe. He was halfway up before I realized he had left the champagne behind.

"Pssst, Terry," I hissed in as loud a voice as I dared. "Come back down—*quickly*!" Terry paused momentarily in his climb. He looked quite breathless and I worried that he might lose his grip and fall.

"What?" he gasped, looking down in agitation. "Get back down here quickly!"

He came slithering down the drainpipe as quickly as he could, thinking that the whole operation had been compromised. He landed amidst a tangled heap of thorny bougainvillea, ripped from the wall during his descent.

"What's happened?" he stammered breathlessly.

"You forgot the champagne," I whispered thrusting the bottle into his hand. "Now, hurry back up before the matron gets wind of us."

Terry was momentarily undecided as to whether he should crack the bottle over my head or resume his climb, but the lure of what lay ahead proved too great. He untangled himself from the bougainvilleas, tucked the bottle under his armpit and began his ascent back up the drainpipe.

I was preoccupied with my lookout duties and didn't see Terry precariously clinging to the pipe with one hand while trying to lever the bathroom window open with the other. I did hear the shriek of indignation that came from inside the bathroom moments later. A nurse happened to be sitting on the toilet beneath the window just as Terry managed to pry it open and poke his head through. She didn't even allow him the courtesy of introducing himself. Leaping up, she armed herself with a toilet brush and proceeded to beat the hapless 'Prince Charming' over the head with it. Then all hell broke loose.

Terry dropped the bottle of champagne and slithered down the drainpipe a lot faster than he had gone up. He landed in a crumpled heap with his bottom impaled on a piece of glass from the broken champagne bottle. The humorless matron flew out the front entrance and started raining blows on the poor man with a mop handle. Colin and I, in our haste to escape, forgot all we had been taught about the need to vacate a position in an *orderly* manner during a withdrawal. We simply turned on our heels and bolted. A 'retreat' is not a phase of war taught at military colleges because it is never suppose to happen.

It happened that night outside the Nurses' Home.

ↄ

It was during phase two of our training that we lost five members from the course. Four were found to be unsuitable for continued officer training. They were all fine men in their own right; commissioned rank was just not their calling. The fifth had joined the course from the Rhodesian SAS and had become one of my closest friends. He was removed from the course, not because of any lack of leadership ability or officer potential. He had all of that and more. Andy Chait was a tough, good-looking young Rhodesian who was seldom without a disarming smile. During his service in the SAS he had developed a reputation as an outstanding soldier. He was a man's man and knew more about soldiering in the African bush than most. He was good at what he did and wasn't shy to voice a dissenting opinion if something was said with which he didn't agree, even if it was from one of our instructors. It was for this reason he was removed from the course … he was simply too outspoken. He and I would talk for hours about my lumberjack days in Canada. He seemed enchanted by the thought of living in a log cabin with just a burning wood stove as protection against the deep winter nights.

"Tim, if we get thrown off the course let's pack our bags and go to Canada," he would say, his dimpled face breaking into a disarming smile. We would shake hands and pledge to become lumberjacks together. Unfortunately it was not to be. The day he left he gave me a mocking salute and a wide smile; then we embraced and said our goodbyes. I never saw Andy again. He was a proud man and I knew that he was bitterly disappointed at having been removed from the course. But I also knew he would be glad to get back to his beloved SAS and the bush he loved so much. Some time after rejoining the SAS Andy was mortally wounded while leading his men in a daring raid against terrorists in Mozambique; his death was well avenged.

ↄ

Phase three of the Cadet Course was by far the most important and interesting ... counter-insurgency warfare. I knew that on completion of the course some of us would be lucky enough to be posted as officers to the Rhodesian Light Infantry. I also knew that the RLI soldier, unlike his British counterpart, was not easily impressed or intimidated by rank, social status or reputation. An officer had to earn respect in the Rhodesian Light Infantry. The only way he could do this was by doing everything a soldier could do—only better and faster. Those of us who aspired to join the Regiment would have to excel during this phase.

As a trooper in the RLI, I had served briefly under a flamboyant Portuguese paratroop officer who had joined the unit as a Captain from the elite Paraquedistas. He had arrived with a reputation for being an outstanding commander; a 'reputation' quickly unmasked by Rhodesian soldiers. It had been a tradition of his in the Portuguese Army to don a pair of white gloves whenever contact with the enemy seemed imminent.

"It's important that an officer be correctly dressed when he intends to engage in the noble art of killing his enemy," he said to us one day.

Some months later during his first contact, he ordered us to hold back while he put on his white gloves. Not bothered with the trivia of having to wait for anything while terrorists were shooting at us, least of all being correctly dressed, we threw ourselves into the fray.

By the time the hapless Portuguese Captain eventually caught up with us we had already dispatched most of the gang, consolidated the contact area, and set off through the thick bush in hot pursuit of the rest. That night when the unfortunate Captain asked one of us to clean his rifle he was surprised and appalled at the reaction.

"In the RLI officers clean their own gats, ek sê. Clean it yourself or stick it where a monkey sticks his peanuts."

The Captain was flown out the next day and replaced by a homegrown Rhodesian.

❧

The final months of the course seemed to come and go in a blaze of frenzied activities. We travelled to the bleak, inhospitable mountains of the Eastern Highlands to take part in a three-week Escape and Evasion exercise. Split into small groups, we trudged for endless miles through narrow mountain passes attempting to avoid capture by battle-hardened soldiers acting as the enemy.

But we were all captured, thrown into cells, blindfolded, interrogated and subjected to sleep deprivation for days.

We attended a tracking and bush survival course on the shores of Lake Kariba in the country's far northwest. Here we learned the art of tracking human quarry through the bush. More important, we learned the art of anti-tracking to prevent terrorists from tracking and killing us.

We did a bus tour of military installations in South Africa to gain firsthand knowledge of weapons and equipment we had previously seen only as cardboard cutouts on cloth models and in sand pits. We even operated for a while with a squadron of South African battle tanks. They looked infinitely more lethal than the old Bedford truck.

We took part in exercises with regular troops so that our ability to hold command appointments could be tested. Our final counter-insurgency exercise was held with a Commando of RLI troops near Kariba, in the Zambezi Valley. Although it was only an exercise, a sense of realism and excitement was added as there was always the possibility of coming across a real terrorist gang infiltrating the escarpment. In the event of this happening we carried magazines of live rounds in addition to the blank rounds that were used for exercise purposes. In order to avoid any fatal mishaps the magazines containing live rounds were

Andy Chait. (Carol Doughty)   Andy Chait's final resting place. (Carol Doughty)

Colin Willis, SCR, C Squadron, SAS. (Colin Willis)

taped over.

During the fourth day of this exercise I was leading a troop of twelve men through a flat, sparse and extremely dry flood plain below the Zambezi escarpment. The earth had been baked by the scorching sun to the consistency of hard clay. The ground was so parched that deep cracks large enough to slip your hand into had opened on the surface. They snaked in all directions and had become home to a veritable selection of insects and reptiles seeking shelter from the intense heat. We had been out of water for the entire day and thirst was becoming a serious problem. The sun blazed above us like a globe of molten metal. Shimmering heat waves reflected off the hard dry surface distorting the view of everything more than a few yards away. Cresting a slight rise in the ground we were confronted by a herd of elephants. They were guarding a small watering hole just ahead of us. It was the only water for miles around and we needed some of that water desperately.

I knew the RLI soldiers would be watching my every move with keen interest. From the tracking course I had previously attended, I knew that any metallic noise is alien to wild animals and will normally scare them off. Very gingerly I walked as close as I dared to the herd extracting a spare rifle

Relaxing whilst on an officers' course. (Terry Griffin)

magazine from my pouch and tapped it against my rifle. Nothing happened.

"Better take the blank firing attachment off your gat, ek sê. You may have to do some culling," I heard one of the troopies say behind me.

I looked around. The RLI soldiers had already unscrewed the blank firing attachments from their rifles and were busy loading magazines of live rounds. They were letting me take charge, but they were going to be in a position to back me if I needed help. I quickly unscrewed my own blank firing attachment, slipped it inside my shirt pocket and walked a little closer to the herd. This time I tapped harder on my rifle. Surely that would scare the elephants off. Standing closest to me was a large bull elephant who decided that two could play the 'scare' game. His method was less subtle than mine. Waving his trunk high above his head and bellowing a loud scream of indignation, he flared his huge ears out from his head and charged.

It was only while I was frantically trying to load my own rifle with a magazine of live rounds that I looked up and noticed that he had stopped his charge amidst a cloud of churning dust about ten yards from where I stood. I had been told about the 'mock' charges that elephants often make as a precursor to the real thing. I glanced quickly behind me as I started inching slowly backwards. This had been no mock charge. Standing in an extended line directly behind me were twelve RLI soldiers. Without me realizing, they had silently made their way off the crest and were now just a foot behind me in their trademark shorts, sleeveless shirts and 'vellies'. Their rifle butts were tucked firmly into their shoulders and each one was peering down the barrel of his rifle with a bead on the elephant's forehead. The old bull must have thought twice about pressing home his attack.

"You didn't think we were going to let you take the flak on your own did you, ek sê?"

The Troop Sergeant spoke softly and evenly, without a trace of emotion. Even as he spoke he continued peering directly down the barrel of his rifle at the slowly retreating elephant.

"Another foot and he would have been dead meat before his tusks even scratched your nose, Sir."

That was the moment I knew I wanted more than anything to be posted back to the RLI.

❧

With only a month remaining of our course, I had written to Mother to invite her to attend the final commissioning parade. She wrote back saying that she would be delighted to attend and would be bringing my twin sister, Janet, who was on assignment for the Canadian government in Belgium. I was elated.

During the final week of our training we seldom left the Parade Square. We spent endless hours rehearsing over and over the intricate parade order for the final commissioning parade. Two days before the course ended we were summoned by Major Lockley to be told where we would to be posted. I was more than a little nervous. I didn't relish the thought of telling Mother that she had come all the way from Canada just to see her son commissioned as an officer with the Rhodesian Army Services Corps.

"Bax. You joined the course as a trooper from 3 Commando, RLI."

"Yes, Sir." I hardly dared imagine that I would be posted back to the RLI. Everyone who was anyone wanted to be posted there. The Battalion only had limited vacancies.

"Congratulations. You're being posted back to 3 Commando Troop Commander, 14 Troop." He shook my hand firmly. "It's an unusual thing to happen. I can't think of a situation where anyone from the ranks of the Army has been posted back to his original sub-unit on completion of officer training." I felt terribly proud.

Confrontation with an Elephant at the watering hole. (Dennis Croukamp)

The long-awaited day of our commissioning finally arrived. It was the culmination of a grueling twelve months of emotional, physical and mental endeavor. Eight cadets were formed up on the School of Infantry Parade Square in the company of a contingent of troops from each of the units in the Rhodesian Army to which we were being posted. They included detachments from every Infantry Regiment in the Army. We were particularly honored by the presence of a detachment of SAS. Little was it known at the time that two of the cadets on parade would one day become troop commanders with that elite unit. One would later be killed in action heroically leading his men from the front.

But today it was our parade. The only persons who seemed to be missing were my mother and sister. I didn't know what could possibly have happened to them. I was devastated that they should have missed such a proud moment in my life.

Martin Pearse was called forward by the Reviewing Officer and presented with the Sword of Honor for being Most Outstanding Cadet. We had marched on to the Parade Square to the tunes of *Marche des Parachutistes* and *The Saints*. Having won the Sword of Honor, Martin had the privilege of marching us off to the tunes of *Auld Lang Syne* and *Jellalabad* played by the band of the Rhodesian African Rifles.

Officer Cadet Course Passing-Out Parade. (Terry Griffin)

Officer Cadet Course, course photo. (Terry Griffin)

As we marched past the reviewing stand, Martin gave us the command "Eyes left" in a salute to the Reviewing Officer, General Keith Coster, General Officer Commanding the Rhodesian Army. It was then I caught sight of Mother waving frantically from amongst the throngs of guests. With her was Janet. Unbeknownst to me they had arrived at the school just as the parade was starting.

I ended the parade as Second Lieutenant Timothy Bax, proudly wearing the rank insignia of a commissioned officer of the Rhodesian Light Infantry.

At the age of 22, it was the proudest moment of my life.

10
Subaltern Officer

"The Portuguese Officer was stengah'd." "Stengah'd?"
"He was drunk."
"During a firefight?"
"Yes."
"How shameful!"
"Greater than his shame was his amazement at having found the enemy!"
—Major Peter Rich, RLI Officers' Mess:
September, 1972

Mukumbura

My first operational trip with the Rhodesian Light Infantry wasn't very eventful. Neither would have been my second, had it not been for the intervention of the British South Africa Police (BSAP).

I had been deployed with my troop to Mukumbura; a small, dusty outpost on the Mozambique border. It consisted of a handful of dilapidated single-storey buildings made of brick and stucco. The roofs were of corrugated metal which radiated the heat downwards, so that inside they became like miniature furnaces. The gleaming white paint they had once sported had faded to a dirty, dull gray. Most of the buildings had been taken over by the Army. Layers of sandbags reaching as high as the windows were stacked around each building as protection against mortars and small arms. They looked like layers of green mould that had sprouted from the walls. The only building not occupied by the Army was the Police Station. It was a squat, oblong structure built over a deep underground bunker. The bunker had conveniently been converted into a well-stocked bar with a sign outside that proudly proclaimed it to be the 'Mukumbura Surf Club'. Interestingly, the nearest surf was three hundred miles to the east.

Not far from the outpost flowed the Mukumbura River which formed the border between Rhodesia and Mozambique. It was a shallow river with sandy riverbed across from which sprawled a Portuguese garrison town. Years before,

Two officers from our course, Colin Willis and Martin Pearse, joined the Rhodesian
SAS. Martin, seated seventh from left, was later killed in action. (Carol Doughty)

a dirt road had linked the two towns together necessitating the establishment
of a police station on the Rhodesian side to monitor border crossings. The
border had since been closed and what the Police Station's function was now,
nobody seemed to know. They cared even less.

The Police Station's only occupant and long-term resident was a Special
Branch Detective named Winston Hart. He had been there for as long as
anybody, including himself, could remember. He was a tanned, medium-built
man whose main features were a blond beard, a shock of sandy-colored hair, a
permanent smile and twinkling, pale blue eyes. The only uniform he seemed
to posses was a pair of tattered shorts, vellies, a khaki shirt and an old briefcase.
He was never without his briefcase. He looked like he would be more at home
on the sea than in this hot, desolate outpost.

Upon my arrival I had converted one of the buildings into my 'operations
room', a rather grandiose name for a room that comprised nothing more than
a metal trestle table, a steel chair, two radios and a map board. I was sitting in
the room one morning watching in bored fascination as a large green bottle-fly
walked purposefully across my map board toward a pin which indicated the
position of one of my patrols. It was a green pin. Green indicated friendly forces.
The fly didn't look very friendly; in fact it looked intent on trying to devour

the pin. I thought it rather ironic that the fly should be green. I wondered if I should impale it with a red pin.

Red indicated the enemy. I didn't have any red pins on my map at the time because I didn't know where the enemy was. My thoughts were suddenly interrupted by a knock on the screen door. It was Winston.

"Thought I'd drive across the river and pay a social visit to Captain Dos Santos."

"Dos who?" I asked, my attention momentarily distracted from the fly.

"Dos Santos. He's in charge of the Portuguese garrison on the Mozambique side. Care to come along?"

I had been ordered not to cross the river into Mozambique unless in hot pursuit of terrorists fleeing across the border. A social visit to the Portuguese garrison Commander seemed to be stretching even the most liberal meaning of 'hot pursuit'.

"Give him my best regards," I replied, turning my attention back to the fly. Unable to devour the map pin, the fly had decided to deposit a blob of black excrement on it. I wondered if this might be a bad omen for the patrol and considered contacting them to find out if they were alright.

"I think you should give him some advice on what to do about the increasing FRELIMO activity in his area. They've just about taken over control of his whole province." FRELIMO, or the *Frente de Libertação de Moçambique* was the terrorist organization fighting to overthrow Portuguese colonial rule in Mozambique. "If the two of you can coordinate your patrol activities, it might make his job a little easier."

I wondered vaguely if Dos Santos was being plagued by the same flies as I was. "Fair enough, anything to help our Portuguese allies. Give me a few minutes and I'll join you."

"You'd better take those rank epaulettes off your shoulders. He might not appreciate being given advice from a Second Lieutenant. I'll introduce you as Captain Bax."

"That's all I need, disobeying orders by crossing into Mozambique and impersonating an officer of superior rank. That should do my promotion prospects a lot of good."

"Don't worry, no one will be the wiser. Come along, let's go."

I grabbed my rifle and walked with Winston to his Land Rover. We snaked slowly down a sandy track towards the dry riverbed, the center of which marked the border between the two countries. Drifts of gleaming white sand made it

Winston Hart. (Winston Hart)

Winston Hart and the Land Rover destroyed by a landmine. (Winston Hart)

impossible to cross in anything other than four-wheel drive.

"Look out for landmines," warned Winston. "I got blown up here last month."

I instinctively jerked my feet off the sandbagged floor of the vehicle. "Shouldn't we be walking?" I asked. The Portuguese garrison was situated just north of the town, certainly within easy walking distance.

"Too much trouble. Besides, Dos Santos isn't getting our advice for free. We have enough room in the front for at least two cases of Macieira brandy. Perhaps even a case or two of Laurentina beer."

"We have enough room in the back to stock your bar for an entire month," I suggested dryly.

"We have to put it in the front. The back isn't mine-protected. Would hate to hit a landmine on the way back and waste all that good liquor."

A few minutes later we had churned our way out of the river bed and were driving slowly through the little border town on the Mozambique side. It looked like a rundown movie set from a long-forgotten western. Suddenly a volley of automatic rifle fire erupted from the front porch of a single-storey building to our left. I ducked, reaching for my rifle. A shirtless Portuguese soldier was slouched on a knee-high wall swigging a bottle of beer and brandishing a G3 automatic rifle.

"Should I return fire?" I asked, bemused by the soldier's antics. He hardly looked capable of shooting his way out of a brothel, let alone a firefight with FRELIMO.

"Don't worry," calmed Winston. "He's just cleaning his weapon."

"By firing it?"

"Yeah … that way they know it's still working."

We eventually arrived at a grayish building that looked like it might once have been the town hall. It was now the headquarters of the Portuguese military garrison in Mukumbura. The stucco was badly cracked and pockmarked by bullet holes. It looked like it had been used for target practice by somebody who clearly needed a whole lot more.

Inside we were met by Captain Dos Santos. He escorted us into what he referred to as his 'Military Headquarters'. It was an oblong room with a large table in the centre around which were scattered four or five wooden chairs. The only activity in the room was from squadrons of flies that dive-bombed us from all directions. Taped on to the wall at the far end of the room was a small-scale road map of the region. The only discernable markings on the map were bloodied splotches where flies must once have been swatted and killed. With the arrival of the sweltering summer heat, the killing of flies must now have become too much of an effort and they swarmed everywhere. At the other end of the room was a large window, its glass shattered by bullet holes. Heaped against a side wall were dozens of crates of empty Laurentina beer bottles. Above us a dusty ceiling fan hung precariously by its exposed electrical wires. It wasn't turning. There was no electricity. There hadn't been for the past eight months. An overpowering smell of stale beer, garlic and cigarette smoke permeated everything in the room.

"Welcome, welcome to the headquarters of the *Exército Português Intervento Brigado.*" Captain José Dos Santos was a flamboyant, slim, olive-skinned man in his mid-thirties who looked more like a matador than a soldier. His jet black hair was slicked back over his head and he wore a slim black moustache, twisted at each end into a sharp point. He had dark eyes that looked like black olives and around his neck he wore a red silk bandana. He was wearing the immaculate uniform of the Portuguese *Grupos Especiais Pára-Quedistas*, an elite parachute brigade. He didn't look like the sort of man to venture out into the bush very often. I learned later he *never* ventured out.

With the preliminary niceties of formal introductions dispensed with, the Captain sat us around the wooden table.

"A Laurentina for my friends," he smiled, flipping the cap of the first bottle and passing it to Winston. "It's my last crate. We hope for a re-supply soon … very soon."

I looked at Winston. It was only 10:30 in the morning. Winston raised his beer and winked at me before taking a swig of the tepid liquid. It was better not to offend our Portuguese friends by turning down their hospitality.

"Let me introduce you to the glorious exploits of the Intervento Brigado." Dos Santos launched into a glowing account of the Brigade's heroic interventions during Portugal's past colonial wars. He seemed somewhat more reticent about explaining the Brigade's contribution to the Mozambique War.

Putting down my beer, I asked if I might have a look at his operations map so I could compare his troop dispositions with my own.

Taking another swig of beer, he gestured vaguely toward the fly-spattered map on the far wall.

"No troop dispositions," he said emphatically. "But where are your patrols located?"

"No, no. No patrols. It's too dangerous. I send out patrols and they get ambushed. I bring them back here. It's safer in the base."

"You mean you have no patrols out looking for FRELIMO?" "Only one patrol. It's been out for a week."

"Where is it?" I asked hopefully.

The Captain shrugged. He walked over to the map and drew an imaginary circle with his half-empty beer bottle around an area north of the garrison's position.

"Somewhere here. We've had no communications for a week.

Who knows?" He shrugged again as if the matter was of no great importance.

"Why don't you send patrols out to find them … an aircraft perhaps?"

"Too dangerous, too dangerous, they would get killed," he said with finality.

"So you don't know where the enemy is?" I was beginning to feel decidedly despondent.

"Tomorrow. We will know tomorrow."

"How?" Maybe there was more to Captain Dos Santos than I had initially imagined.

"Tomorrow the ration convoy is arriving from Chicoa. The convoy will get ambushed. Then we will know the location of the enemy!"

"What happens if the convoy doesn't get through?"

The Captain shrugged his shoulders. "It must get through. We are out of brandy and beer."

I looked at Winston. With the exception of the lost patrol and the shirtless soldier we had seen drinking beer and cleaning his rifle, there were no troop dispositions to learn of and seemingly, no brandy. We had little reason to remain. We made our way back to the Land Rover and headed back toward the river. Along the way we came across the same Portuguese soldier we had met on our way in. He was making his way slowly across the road to a rectangular building which I hadn't noticed before; its once pristine coat of red paint now faded to a dirty pink. Of particular interest was the lack of a single bullet hole on its exterior walls. A garish sign above the front door with 'Erma's House' painted in bright red beckoned visitors into its sleazy-looking interior.

"He seems to have misplaced his recently-cleaned rifled," I observed to Winston.

"Erma's house is the local bar and bordello. The Madame prefers that weapons not be brought inside. The rule applies to both Portuguese soldiers and FRELIMO alike. It's never once been attacked or hit."

"You mean Portuguese soldiers *and* FRELIMO terrorists share the same facilities at Erma's?" It sounded almost inconceivable.

"Welcome to Mozambique," replied Winston with a smile. "Would you care to pop in?"

Having already disobeyed orders by crossing the border into Mozambique and impersonating a senior officer to a foreign official, I didn't think that I should be adding "visiting a Portuguese brothel while deployed on operations" to my litany of potential charges. This was only my second bush trip.

As it turned out, I *was* charged on my eventual return to the RLI Barracks in Salisbury. I had travelled with a canvas water cooler hanging from the wing mirror of my Land Rover. The cooler had left a small scuff mark on the vehicle's camouflage paint. The Battalion Transport Officer, a craggy-faced and very dour Major called Keith Dyers, charged me with 'Malicious Damage to Government Property'. I was banned from driving a military vehicle for two weeks and had to spend my first seven nights back from the bush doing duty as the Battalion Orderly Officer.

I thought I had escaped rather lightly.

A Girl in my Soup

"Did you hear about the new Lieutenant's lady friend?"
"No!"
"She passed out."
"Where?"
"In her soup."
"How scandalous!"

—Discussion, Officers' wives tea party:
November, 1972

Back in the RLI Barracks, I was looking forward with trepidation to attending my first formal 'Dining-In Night'. My anxiety turned to disappointment when I was told that it would be a *Ladies* Dining-In Night. I didn't know any ladies to invite. I decided to approach my good friend Martin Pearse who had been on Cadet Course with me. He and I had been posted to the RLI at the same time. Martin was extremely good-looking and his closet was seldom bare of available women.

"Don't worry; I have just the person for you. She happens to be a friend of the girl I'm taking. I'll collect them both and bring them to the Mess on the evening of the function."

I was rather pleased with this arrangement, as the only transport I possessed at the time was a small motorcycle.

"There's only one problem I should warn you about," continued Martin.

"Oh, what's that?" I asked suspiciously.

"She tends to drink rather a lot. But I'm sure you'll be able to take care of that."

"Well, at least she'll be in good company," I responded.

The junior officers of the Regiment were collectively known as 'Skid Row'. We even had our own charter proudly displayed in the Officers' Mess.

The evening of the function, I carefully dressed in my green and scarlet Mess tunic and waited anxiously at the entrance to the Mess for the arrival of my partner. Mary was an attractive and petite lady whose appearance reminded me of the English nanny portrayed by Julie Andrews in *Mary Poppins*. I asked her if she had ever been to a formal function at an Officers' Mess.

"I can't say that I have but I've been told they are terribly stuffy, darling. Just give me enough to drink and I'll try to remain with the programme."

"Well, that's just the problem," I replied nervously. "The evening entails rather a lot of drinking. You might want to, uhm … pace yourself a little."

"Don't be so boring, darling. Now, are we going to stand out here talking all night or go in for a drink?"

I guided her through to the bar where most of the other guests had already gathered and dutifully introduced her to the senior officers and their wives. Leaving her with a small group of my peers I went to the bar to buy a round of drinks. Mary had ordered a double vodka on ice which I took to her before returning to the bar for the remainder of the order. By the time I returned she had already thrown back her drink and nonchalantly demanded another. By the time we adjourned to the anteroom for sherry she had consumed four double vodkas and was feeling rather gay. I had warned her previously that there would be only sufficient glasses of sherry on the trays being circulated by the Mess stewards for each guest to have a single glass. Unperturbed by this minor detail of decorum she picked up a sherry, slugged it back, and scooped up another before the startled waiter could stop her. Then she walked unsteadily towards the band of the Rhodesian African Rifles which was playing a medley of pre-dinner marches in a corner of the room. There she asked a startled band member if she could blow on his flute! By the time we walked into the

Resting beneath a parachute canopy during an external operation. (Winston Hart)

formally-set dining room, she was plonked.

After being seated at the table, the wine steward looked moderately surprised when, after filling Mary's wine glass from a decanter of *Saint Chinian Château Bousquette*, she tossed it back and demanded another. Ten minutes later I was engrossed in conversation with the lady on my left when I felt a discreet tap on my shoulder. I looked up to see the Mess caterer superciliously peering down his nose at me.

"Yes, Sergeant?"

He coughed slightly, as if wanting to clear his throat before making an important proclamation. "Your lady is asleep, Sir," he announced with an air of sanctimonious snobbery.

"Asleep … where, Sergeant?" "In her soup, Sir."

As he spoke I sensed a hush envelope the room. I glanced to my right. Sure enough, Mary had passed out face down in her bowl of *Bisque de Langoustine* with her nose firmly wedged between the claws of a crustacean. The lobsters had been specially flown in from Mozambique, courtesy of our Portuguese allies.

The following morning I was summoned to the Adjutant's office. Captain

Bruce Snelgar was not amused.

"Lieutenant Bax, the Officers' Mess of the Rhodesian Light Infantry demands a high standard of behavior and decorum at all times from officers of the Regiment *and their guests*. The presence of a drunk and disorderly lady at a formal dinner evening will not be tolerated. Do I make myself clear?" He sounded quite breathless.

"Yes, Sir!" I wasn't too sure what else to say.

"What upsets me even more is this Parade Order I have in my hand. It's for the Opening of Parliament next week and you, Lieutenant Bax, *you* are appointed Ensign to the Colour."

He stood up to emphasize his displeasure. "Of all the officers in this Battalion, it is you, Lieutenant Bax, who will have the distinct honor of Parading the Colours! Do you know how much it pains me to have to tell you that?" He didn't even wait for a response. "You'll report to the Parade Square tomorrow morning at 10:30 for rehearsals in Colour Drill. Dismissed."

I walked straight down to 2 Commando to find Martin Pearse. I found him sitting in the Troop Commander's office with his feet resting casually on his desk and reading a recent addition of *Scope* magazine.

"Martin, how could you have fixed me up with such a lush last night? I just had my ass chewed off by the Adjutant."

Martin looked up at me with his feet still on the desk and gave me his trademark whimsical smile.

"My dear chap, don't concern yourself with such trivial matters. Only one thing matters, did you get laid?"

෴

After tea the following morning the Regimental Colours were hastily produced together with the required escort. At the actual Opening of Parliament I would be required to march at the head of the Battalion directly behind a mounted police escort. In order to make the rehearsal as realistic as possible, and to get me accustomed to marching behind a horse, somebody had produced an old nag from somewhere. Sitting unsteadily on top the horse was Trooper Van Schalkwyk from the Quartermaster stores representing the police escort. The problem was that Trooper Van Schalkwyk had never been on a horse, and the horse had never been on a parade!

At the appointed time, I formed up with the Colours directly behind the restless animal. Flanking me on either side was an armed escort of smartly-dressed non-commissioned officers. We braced to attention as the RSM gave us a preliminary word of command.

"Colour Party … Colour Party … Shun!"

We sprang smartly to attention. I was a bit concerned about the lack of reaction from Trooper Van Schalkwyk who was beginning to look distinctly uncomfortable. Looking even more uncomfortable was the nag he was sitting upon.

"Colour Party … March on the Colours."

For a second nothing happened. Then the nag farted loudly. A moment later, amid another loud grumble of flatulence, a mountain of manure belched from its rear end. I stumbled backwards, grimly holding on to the Colours. The stench was unbelievable. The horse, rejuvenated after its call of nature, decided to gallop on to the Parade Square with Trooper Van Schalkwyk grimly hanging on to its mane.

My first rehearsal at marching on the Colours had not been a spectacular success. After suggesting to the RSM that it might be an idea to requisition another horse before attempting any further rehearsals, I returned to the Officers' Mess with the Colours. On the way I chanced upon Captain Ron Reid-Daly. He had been standing some way off watching the proceedings with some amusement.

"Let me give you some advice, Junior." Ron fixed me with his piercing blue eyes. "There's a lot of tradition attached to the carrying of those Colours and from what I've seen, not many have been adhered to this morning."

I felt somewhat embarrassed. It was not a good idea to get on the wrong side of Ron Reid-Daly. He continued, "However, there's one tradition that you can still conform with to save the day."

"What's that, Sir?" It was tradition for lieutenants to call captains by their first name, but Ron was so highly regarded I decided to address him more formally.

"It's traditional that the Ensign to the Colour be served a tot of sherry before the Colours are furled. I suggest you hasten yourself to the bar and order a double tot of sherry on me."

I did. In fact I ordered two.

It was the start of a long and close association that I would share with that legendary officer over a period of many years.

A Walk in the Dark

"The Lieutenant told me we're walking into Mozambique tonight." "Tonight?"
"Tonight, my china. He said we'd be walking into thousands of
gooks." "Thousands?"
"He told me thousands, I tune you." "Bliksem, we'd better set our gats on sing!"
—Conversation between RLI troopers,
Nyamasoto Airfield: September, 1972

In May of 1972, taking advantage of an unexpected lull in terrorist activities, the Battalion took part in a Brigade conventional war exercise. Few could recall the last time the Battalion had been involved in such an exercise and fewer still could remember any of the drills involved. It got off to a rocky start. An early morning 'advance to contact' the Battalion was to spearhead was held up because somebody had stolen the Battalion Motor Transport Officer's red striped pajamas. He stood in front of the leading screen of scout cars dressed in white long johns refusing to let the advance commence until his pajamas were returned. I eventually had to own up to being the culprit, not through any moral conscience, but because they happened to be flying from the top of my Land Rover's radio aerial. I had sneaked into the crabby old Major's tent earlier that morning while he was engaged in a noisy ablution, and taken them from his camp bed. I did so in retaliation for him having unnecessarily disciplined me some months before for carrying a water cooler on the outside mirror of my Land Rover. With the pajamas now returned to their rightful owner, the advance was able to continue and the exercise got underway.

The only other bit of excitement was at the conclusion of the exercise when a group of us decided to steal a 25-pounder gun from an artillery battery parked close to our Battalion Headquarters. It was late at night and we were in the Officers' Mess tent drinking in celebration of the conclusion of the exercise. It was the only time during the entire exercise that anybody had shown any real enthusiasm. With our thoughts well-honed by some fine Johnny Walker, five of us jumped into a Ford F250 and drove to the gun lines where the 25-pounders were parked for the night. Hitching a gun to the back of our vehicle we beat a hasty retreat, being pursued by an extremely irate Artillery Squadron Commander in a Land Rover. Unfortunately, we ran out of fuel before we could get back to our Battalion lines. The vehicle sputtered to a stop just as we crested a steep rise. Showing extraordinary bravery, we abandoned both vehicle and gun in the middle of the road and absconded into the bush. The Squadron Commander, roaring up the hill in hot pursuit behind us had to swerve violently into a ditch to avoid colliding with the gun, and sustained considerable damage to his vehicle. We later learned that we had caused irreparable damage to the gun by not securing the barrel before driving off. Rhodesia did not have many field guns and the loss of just one was sufficient to diminish the functionality of the entire Artillery Regiment. At the time, this was of less concern to me than where I was going to find the money to pay for my portion of the damage to both gun and Land Rover.

Not long after the exercise ended, the entire Battalion moved to the Umfurudzi Wildlife area northeast of Salisbury, ostensibly to take part in a two-week training exercise in counter-insurgency. The exercise was actually a ploy to group the Battalion in preparation for an imminent large-scale incursion into Mozambique.

During the late afternoon on the second day of the exercise, officers were told to gather by the Officers' Mess tent to be addressed by the Second-in-Command, Major Peter Rich. He had joined the RLI from the SAS, and in the finest British tradition, was imbued with an unending capacity for dry wit and fine brandy. Standing on the tailboard of an open Land Rover with his trademark glass of Bolls Brandy already in hand, he gave an inspiring address which, while not rising to the level of Lincoln's speech at Gettysburg, was just what we had been waiting to hear.

"Gentlemen, as most of you are aware, the Portuguese soldiers fighting in Mozambique have not been blessed with the tracking skills of Daniel van der Boone, nor the musketry skills of Davie van der Crockett. The only skill they seem to have been able to master, and master rather well, are the sleeping skills of Piet Van Winkle. If any of you want to get to the bottom of the *Myth of the Long Distance Runner*, I might suggest you pay a visit to your nearest Portuguese garrison when the bullets start flying. You will find that it is not a myth at all."

He went on to tell us that the Battalion was to deploy en masse thirty kilometers inside Mozambique to sever the stranglehold that FRELIMO terrorists had on the Portuguese Army, and to disrupt the supply lines of Rhodesia's own ZANLA terrorists based in Mozambique. In order to achieve the element of surprise and secrecy, the Battalion would walk in under cover of darkness. The deployment would take place over two nights, with the Battalion lying up under cover of thick bush during the day.

3 Commando being briefed for operations in the Zambezi Valley. (D. Scott-Donelan)

Deploying along the Zambezi. (Dennis Croukamp)

The Portuguese had been given details of the impending operation in an effort to get them to remain in their barracks during the period of our deployment. Letting them in on the plan was a bad mistake. Word tended to spread among Portuguese soldiers and the indigenous population quicker than forked lighting through an electrically-charged sky. It wasn't long before details of the operation where posted on every bedpost at Erma's Bordello in Mukumbura.

∽

A battalion of two hundred men marching through enemy-infested bush at night, loaded with two weeks' supply of food, ammunition and water, is no stroll in the park. Add to this mix, thick impenetrable bush liberally laced with steep ravines and gorges, and it becomes a recipe for chaos.

The first night we hacked and slashed our way through the bush in single file with the line of soldiers bunching up and then spreading out like a troop of monkeys climbing an elasticized vine. One minute we would be up each other's backsides; the next, stretched so far behind the man in front we couldn't hear, much less see him. To make it easier to see the person in front in the pitch dark, each man had a piece of white cloth tied to his back.

My good friend Colin Willis, with whom I had been on Cadet Course, was the 'point man' for the Battalion. Major Rod Tarr, Commander of 3 Commando, was the overall ground commander. Bringing up the rear of the unwieldy column was tall former British Army officer who, like most Brits, was not averse to making his shrill voice heard when it came to complaining. Lieutenant Steve Cary could land an 81mm mortar bomb into a trash can from 4,000 meters. Make him walk at night behind a long column of men expanding and contracting through the bush like a flexing bungee cord and he became a veritable choirmaster of discontent.

Two hours into the march, Major Tarr called a short break to give the lead troops a rest from the exertion of having to hack their way with machetes through the dense, tangled bush. Thirty minutes later his voice crackled over the radio.

"OK, let's not fall asleep; we still have a long way to go. We're moving out in five minutes."

Steve Cary's voice crackling back in response was almost as shrill as it was instant. "Bloody Hell. I haven't even stopped yet! I have men strung out behind me like ships in a North Atlantic gale and you want to press on? It'll take me another fifteen minutes just to catch up with the rest of the column!"

It was the beginning of a long chorus of bleats that would keep us entertained for the rest of the night.

Walking directly behind me was an older, rather portly and bespectacled Lieutenant to whom fitness had long ago taken a back seat to the lure of a bottle of fine malt. Lieutenant Ian Robinson was one of the Battalion's best-loved officers, more at home sitting behind a desk doing administrative duties than hacking his way through a foreign jungle at night. I had been hacking my way through some particularly thick thorn scrub trying to keep up with the man in front, when the piece of white cloth on the back of my bergen ripped off and got snagged on a thorn bush. Ian, seeing the stationery piece of cloth in the darkness thought I must have stopped for another break. With a thankful grunt of relief he collapsed on to the ground and lay back against his bergen. So did everyone behind him. Then he fell asleep.

I had just climbed out of a particularly steep ravine when I realized that nobody was behind me. By that time we were already half a mile from where Ian and the rest of the column had been left behind. I managed to get the front of the column to stop while I made contact with Ian on the radio. Eventually, through a series of shouts and wolf whistles, which must have alerted every terrorist within a radius of ten miles, he was able to ascertain roughly where we were and make his way toward us. Stumbling through the night like a snorting, blindfolded rhinoceros with a bee up its backside, Ian suddenly appeared out of the steep ravine behind me. He looked as though he had just emerged from a frightful skirmish with a band of marauding Apaches.

"Jesse, jesse, jesse. Gullies, gullies, gullies. Who's driving this bloody bus anyway?" He flopped down next to me and promptly dozed off again.

Eventually dawn broke and the Battalion lay low in a defensive position in some thick bush at the bend of a large river. Major Tarr was busy sending a situation report to Battalion Headquarters situated on an airfield just inside the Rhodesian border, when the Commando medic handed him a mug of boiling tea. Somehow the tea slipped from Major Tarr's grasp and spilled inside his boot, scalding him badly. A helicopter had to be requested to casevac him back to base. That was the second major mistake of the operation. The helicopter gave FRELIMO confirmation of what they had already gleaned from 'Erma's House' … that the Rhodesians were indeed on their way.

The third mistake occurred the following night. The Battalion was laagered for the night in an all-round defensive position on a small hilltop some five

General Coster, Lt Col MacIntyre and WO1 Tarr. (Jacqui Kirrane)

miles south of a Portuguese military base. Just after midnight the sky to our north erupted in a kaleidoscope of exploding mortars, rockets and machine gun fire. Green tracer bullets arced through the night sky in all directions. Our Portuguese friends were being attacked by FRELIMO. The firing eventually subsided and we lay low hoping that we might be next. We were itching for a fight. A couple of hours later we had just about given up hope of a good scrap when I heard the tense voice of Martin Pearse whispering into his radio.

"This is call sign 22, I have the sound of movement to the front of my position."

This was it. This was the moment we had all been waiting for … a good set-to with FRELIMO. Everyone in the Battalion was either listening to Martin's voice on the radio or was being kept informed as to what was happening. Two hundred fingers started curling expectantly around the triggers of two hundred weapons.

With the medical evacuation of Major Rod Tarr earlier that morning, Captain Charlie Aust of 2 Commando had taken over as Column Commander.

"Steady Martin, steady. Hold your fire till you can see what you're shooting at."

"They're creeping closer toward my position." Martin's voice was breathless

A break during early border control operations. (D. Scott-Donelan)

Deploying into Mozambique. (Dennis Croukamp)

with excitement. Two hundred fingers began slowly tightening around two hundred triggers.

"I can see them," Martin's voice was tense and barely audible. Only a cat's whisker was stopping two hundred breach blocks

with exposed firing pins from slamming forward into the percussion caps of two hundred 7.62mm NATO rounds to start a tidal wave of lead smashing into the unseen enemy.

"They're almost on top of me … ."

He didn't have time to finish. An eruption of fire spewed from every weapon in the Battalion. The deep, rhythmic, chatter of a medium machine gun positioned close to me started spitting tongues of death in a wide arc to my front. The firing continued unabated for a few minutes before anyone realized that there didn't appear to be any return fire. When the realization finally dawned and the firing stopped, we wondered what had become of the enemy. Could they all have been killed in our initial volley of fire?

We waited impatiently for dawn to break.

As darkness began lifting its shadowy veil and a diluted light began to filter through the eastern skies, we looked expectantly down the slope in front of Martin's position. We were expecting it to be reminiscent of the Indian slaughter portrayed in *Death on the Western Prairie*. There was no sign of any terrorist bodies. Instead, four stray cows which had been grazing in the night close to Martin's position lay riddled with bullet holes in the grass some fifty yards away. The Battalion had expended its entire first-line holdings of ball ammunition without a terrorist yet having been seen.

It wasn't the start we were hoping for. It didn't take long before the slogan *Rhodesia soldados estão vindo, Rhodesia soldados estão vindo* was being yodeled from the treetops of every FRELIMO base within a three-hundred mile radius. *The Rhodesians are coming, the Rhodesians are coming*. The terrorists were like hares running from the hounds.

All that remained for us to do over the next few weeks was destroy the vast network of camps and arms caches left behind by the fleeing terrorists.

Early border control operation. (Doug Lambert)

A Lady in the Attic

"I say, I'm going to have to ask you to preside over another Board."
"Another! What's it this time?"
"Another lady reported in the barracks."
"Hasn't that become rather routine?" *"Not this one."*
"Oh?"
"She's reported to have taken up permanent residence!"
—Captain Colin Dace talking with the author,
RLI HQ: December, 1972

Back in barracks, I became reluctantly caught up in the tedious routine of
regimental duties. A short time would be spent on retraining and re-equipping
after which the troops would be stood-down for some rest and recuperation.
As officers we weren't quite so lucky. There was always the prickly question of
'administrative duties' to be disposed of. The Army saw little sense in resolving
matters with a minimum of fuss when it could just as easily tie down officers
for days on end conducting internal investigations. The weapon of choice was
the Board of Inquiry; its chief architect, the Battalion Administration Officer.

In the Rhodesian Light Infantry, the Administration Officer was a well-liked Captain named Colin Dace. He was a pleasant, dark-haired individual who was seldom without a cigarette in his mouth, another in his hand and yet another in an ashtray precariously balanced on top of a mountain of paperwork on his desk. One morning he called me into his office.

"Tim, there are some disturbing rumors of a lady of questionable repute having taken up residence in the 3 Commando attic."

It sounded rather intriguing. I couldn't understand why, as an officer in that Commando, I hadn't previously become aware of her presence.

"In the attic? I say, it must be a bit uncomfortable for the poor lady!"

"She is reputed to be entertaining some of the men up there in consideration for a small sum of money."

I had visions of the attic having been transformed into a lavish boudoir reminiscent of the *Delectable Delights of the Mistress of Delhi.*

"What do you have in mind, Colin … having a portion of her takings made payable to the Commando funds?"

"I want you to convene a Board of Inquiry on the matter." "A Board of Inquiry?"

"Yes, Tim. A Board of Inquiry."

"Surely a better idea would be for me to stick my head into the attic and see if there is anybody up there?"

"It's not a matter that the Army would care to dispose of without the calling of witnesses," replied Colin sanctimoniously. "You will convene a Board of Inquiry to investigate the circumstances surrounding the reported presence of a bordello existing in the 3 Commando attic, contrary to the good order of military discipline. You will call witnesses to give evidence, which witnesses may be cross-examined. You will state your findings, give opinions and make recommendations to the Commanding Officer. The typed proceedings of the Board will be submitted to the Adjutant's office in quadruplicate with each copy being neatly bound and annotated."

"You must be joking! It'll take me five minutes to walk down to the Commando to take a look and you'll have your answer before tea."

"The Commanding Officer would prefer to see a dossier of all the available evidence," replied Colin, reaching down to shake another Peter Stuyvesant from a box on his desk. He already had two burning in his ashtray.

That afternoon I borrowed a stepladder from the Quartermaster Stores and with great trepidation poked my head through the trapdoor leading into the 3

Commando attic. I was petrified that I might be confronted by the sight of a row of white tutus dangling from the rafters. Even worse, that I might become entangled in the frilly yellow drawers of the resident Madame standing over the entrance waiting to ensnare me in her web of sin. Thankfully, the only web I became entangled in was that of a very large and unfriendly-looking black spider. It had large luminous pink eyes which glowed in the dark. It hissed at me from the centre of its silky home. After ascertaining that the spider was the only resident of the musty attic, I retreated down the ladder with a sigh of relief.

The following day I commenced the laborious task of convening the Board of Inquiry and calling witnesses. I was not allowed to subpoena myself to give evidence and I suspected that the Army would not wish to stake its reputation solely on the evidence of an unfriendly spider.

The only witness I called was a trooper reputed to have been responsible for bringing the mysterious lady into the barracks. He didn't even know of the attic's existence. I believed him and concluded the Inquiry with the recommendation that "attics be included in the weekly barrack-room inspections for any evidence of women's lingerie."

Some months later I was asked to convene a similar Board to inquire into the presence of a woman reported to have taken up permanent residence inside the barrack-room. There appeared to be compelling evidence that this was the case. Thankfully, she absconded before I commenced my inquiry, reportedly because the young rascals she was entertaining had fallen behind in their payments.

෬

I was living in the Officers' Mess single quarters which were wedged between the Mess and some adjacent tennis courts. Walking in for lunch one day I sat next to Steve Cary who had recently been appointed Senior Subaltern responsible to the Adjutant for the behavior of junior officers. He was still smarting from his long walk into Mozambique. A waiter presented him with the lunch menu, the main course of which was *Rôti de Canard á l'Orange*.

"How the hell am I supposed to know what's for lunch when the bloody menu's printed in French?" bleated Steve in his high-pitched shrill voice. The waiter wasn't much help, so the Mess caterer was summoned. "This is supposed to be a menu, not a book of French poetry! What are we having for lunch?"

"*Rôti de Canard á l'Orange*," offered the Mess caterer in his most fluent French. He gave Steve a smug look as if to suggest that if he didn't understand

French, he might want to consider eating in the troopers' canteen rather than in the Officers' Mess.

"What the hell does that mean!" screeched Steve in annoyance. "Roast duck, Sir," the caterer responded with a look of holier-than-thou righteousness.

"Well, whatever it is, give me some cooked the English way and print a proper menu next time. You're the Mess caterer, not a French poet!"

Later that afternoon Steve summoned all the lieutenants living in barracks to a meeting at the Mess. There had been a complaint from some of the senior officers' wives whose custom it was to walk past the officers' single quarters each day on their way to play tennis. Evidently they had taken umbrage at the large number of condoms that were being flicked like rubber bands out the windows of the single quarters. Some of these had landed on a pink hibiscus hedge that separated the quarters from the tennis courts. The ladies had found them dangling from the hedge looking like deflated balloons from yesterday's garden party.

"Condoms are not to be disposed of outside your windows. It upsets the married ladies who find the sight of them objectionable and distasteful," sighed Steve. The following morning a notice to that effect appeared on the single quarters' notice board. It had been expanded to include 'condom wrappings'.

❧

Frolics in the officers' mess. The author with Colin Willis. (Phee Fletcher)

It seemed that I was always in trouble for something. One evening I had been having a night on the town with some fellow officers. One of them was Ian Robinson who had dozed off during our night excursion into Mozambique. The other two were Lieutenants Dave Hopwood and Keith 'Fingers' Noble. Keith had acquired his nickname for his ability to divest a lady of her brassiere quicker than a Turkish trader could relieve an English tourist of his money. We had returned to the Officers' Mess for a nightcap and were feeling quite peckish. Dave Hopwood suggested we raid the cold-room in the kitchen for something to eat. We found a quantity of sirloin steaks, but the alcohol we had consumed robbed us of our ability of fathoming out how the stove worked.

"Sirloin steaks are best barbequed anyway," announced Dave, as if he might once have been the head chef at an expensive restaurant. "Let's take the meat into the bar and cook it there."

"What do you have in mind? Building a roaring fire in the middle of the bar-room floor?" asked Ian. "That should gain you a free pass to the Adjutant's office."

"Might cause a few raised eyebrows," conceded Dave.

"But what about if we build the fire on a grate," I suggested. A few whiskies tended to stir my thought process; an entire bottle tended to inhibit it altogether. "There's a coal grate in the anteroom.

We could fill it up with coal and place it in the middle of the Mess floor."

It was the second bottle of Scotch that night that proved our undoing. Having cooked and eaten the steaks, we left the burning grate in the bar and staggered off to bed. It was only the following morning that I realized something was amiss. I was intercepted on my way to the dining room for breakfast by a very upset-looking barman. Percy was an African who had been the Officers' Mess barman for as long as he or anyone else could remember. He was a salubrious gentleman who didn't take kindly to the antics of junior officers. In fact, he looked down at us as if he might not be the barman at all, but rather the Honorary Colonel of the Regiment. He took me into the bar and pointed to a blackened hole that was still smoldering through the linoleum tiles in the middle of the floor.

"Who did this?" he asked, looking at me with grave suspicion. Later that morning the 'Firesome Four', as we later became known, were summoned by Captain Ron Reid-Daly into his office. Ron happened to be the President of the Mess Committee and was not looking particularly happy.

"I don't take kindly to being shrieked at by the Commanding Officer

RLI officers (author back row centre). (Terry Griffin)

because of the lunatic antics of young officers. I enjoy even less being shrieked at in language reminiscent to that used by Scottish soldiers fighting against the ancient Roman Legions."

The Commanding Officer was a tall, lean Scotsman to whom flowery language was as alien as a parade without bagpipes. Lieutenant Colonel Derry MacIntyre had once floated the idea of having the Regiment wear kilts. He had changed his mind only when told that a kilt was as alien to an Afrikaner as leopard skin 'trews' to a Scots Guardsman.

Ian Robinson tried to calm Ron down. "Don't worry, Ron. We've already made arrangements to have the burnt tiles replaced. Should all be tidied up in a day or two."

"Now, listen to what I have to say, Gentlemen, and listen very carefully." Obviously Ian's remarks had done little to abate Captain Reid-Daly's anger. "The entire bar-room floor—and I mean the *entire* bar-room floor, will be replaced—and it will be replaced by the time the bar opens this evening. Is that clear?"

Luckily, the manager of the tiling company we immediately went to see took pity on four young officers who were about to face possible court-martial. He agreed to have the flooring replaced the same day. In fact, he was quite amused by our dilemma and even donated a silver plaque on which was engraved:

"This floor was kindly donated by Lieutenants Bax, Hopwood, Noble and Robinson."

Later that day we bumped into the Commanding Officer at tea. He had obviously calmed down somewhat. He addressed us in his broad Scottish brogue, "Make surre the entirre floorr of the barr is rrreplaced by t'night, ya hear. Now fook off 'n get some sense into y'rrr woolly heads, yerrr damn idiots!"

I thought we had got off rather lightly. We were not so lucky later that evening. Percy, the barman threatened to stop any further credit on our bar accounts. His anger with us hadn't abated in the least, even with his spiffy new floor. The following day I had to pay another visit to my bank manager. The cost of a new floor was well beyond the meager means of four young lieutenants.

I was extremely glad the following week to be told that the Commando would be deploying back into the bush.

11

Mozambique

"The enemy is behind us.
The enemy is in front of us.
The enemy is to the right of us and to the left of us. They can't get away from us
now!"

—Rhodesian Minister of Defense,
P.K. van der Byl ,
Mount Darwin: 1974

A year after I was commissioned into the Rhodesian Light Infantry the war began to intensify. Major Rod Tarr had relinquished command of 3 Commando to a young major fresh out of Staff College. Major Doug Lambert was a born Rhodesian of medium build and dark complexion. His firm but calm demeanor made him an outstanding field commander. They were leadership skills that would be sorely needed as the Commando, and the entire RLI, edged inextricably on a collision course with a ruthless enemy who sought to subjugate an entire country through force of arms. In the resulting battles, the result would never be in doubt.

The Commando had been ordered to deploy into neighboring Mozambique to locate and destroy a large terrorist base camp that had been reported by a captured terrorist, and to interdict terrorist movement across the Rhodesian border. A headquarters was established just inside the Rhodesian border from which the Commando would launch its cross-border forays. I was to deploy with 14 troop fifty miles inside Mozambique to the confluence of two large rivers where the terrorist base camp was thought to be.

Colin Willis, commanding 11 Troop, was to deploy some three miles to my east. Both troops would be inserted by helicopter ten miles south of our target area so that our presence wouldn't immediately be detected.

"How many gooks are reported to be in the camp?" I asked Major Lambert.

"There could be as many as 150 terrorists. We can't pinpoint the camp by air because of the dense foliage. It's up to you guys to find and destroy it."

My troop comprised 15 men. Some 15 RLI soldiers against 150 terrorists

Ian Smith reviews a parade. (Jacqui Kirrane)

might be overcooking it a little, but with the hint of air support, a gentleman might wager a bet on a successful outcome.

"Air support?" I asked.

"One Trojan fixed-wing aircraft based at an airfield twenty miles south of here."

The Italian-manufactured Aeromacchi AL-60 B Trojan was a chunky and clumsy-looking aeroplane that could barely flap itself off the ground in ideal conditions, let alone with bombs and rockets slung under its high wings. When taking off, the ungainly-looking plane would lurch down the runway looking like a clumsy Emu with the pilot deliberately aiming for bumps in the airfield to bounce the plane off the ground and into the air. Once airborne, the noise made by its underpowered engines was out of all proportion to its performance. It sounded like a souped-up Lamborghini sports car minus exhaust manifolds. Its performance was that of an overloaded Zeppelin still tied to its mooring mast.

"A Trojan?" I replied, worried. "I thought I saw a Provost flying about earlier."

The Provost was a much more powerfully built, propeller-driven ground attack aircraft capable of carrying a formidable array of weapons. Fearless young pilots had used them to great effect in earlier operations in the Zambezi Valley swooping low into the steep gorges to strafe and bomb terrorists hiding in the rocky outcrops below.

"Don't worry," said Major Lambert. "If you find yourself with your feet to the fire, I'll fly out by helicopter with some of the reserve troop."

In later engagements, Major Lambert was to prove himself as good as his word. He was one of the bravest, calmest commanders under fire that I ever served under.

༄

Later in the war the quality of our air cover would improve dramatically. So would the effectiveness of its firepower. A frantic call of "Send top-cover!" would have a pair of silver-winged Hawker Hunter ground attack jets slashing through the sky at mach 0.94 to give immediate assistance.

One day I was pinned down in a rocky field taking heavy fire from a 14.5 anti-aircraft gun situated on a hill some 500 yards from my position. The gun crew had cranked the barrel of the large gun down to its minimum elevation to fire at my patrol. Two of my soldiers had already been hit and were badly wounded. Fifteen minutes after calling for top cover, two Hawker Hunter jets streaked overhead awaiting my instructions, eager to sweep like falcons on to their prey.

"Give me a ground description of where the gun is located, Tim."

The lead pilot's voice was so casual he might have been asking how I would like my steak cooked. I gave him a quick target description of where the enemy was, as well as the position of my own troops.

"Hurry up, Peter. I have two men down. We're taking heavy flack." Less than a minute later came the same calm, modulated reply, "Roger-D. Keep your heads down ... we are live in the dive."

The first I saw of the two jets was when they were pulling out of their steep dive, engines burning at maximum thrust with their tail pipes glowing like orange infernos.

The 14.5 gun emplacement and crew had ceased to exist.

'Live in the Dive' became the battle cry of the Hunter Squadron. But that was then. Now, I had other things on my mind.

༄

Major Doug Lambert. (Doug Lambert)

Members of JOC Hurricane. (Terry Griffin)

Having finalized his briefing, Major Lambert wished us good luck and we emplaned into the helicopters to be airlifted across the Mozambique border. Once on the ground I moved some way off before stopping for a tea break about seven miles from where the terrorist camp was reported to be. My machine-gunner, a large beefy Afrikaner called Marius Marais, was keeping a lookout next to a game trail where we had stopped, when he spotted a lone terrorist walking towards our position carrying an AK-47 assault rifle. Not wanting to compromise our position, Marius decided not to shoot. He waited until the terrorist was almost alongside him then deftly stepped from his hiding place and flattened him with an uppercut to his jaw. At 250 lbs, Marius was born when meat was cheap and the terrorist was knocked unconscious. It was the troop's first capture under my command. We relieved the terrorist of his weapon and I informed him that his immediate well-being would depend on his guiding us to the terrorist base camp. He readily agreed. He would have been happy to guide us to hell and back if it meant keeping out of reach of the hefty machine-gunner.

The following day we made an early start and around mid-morning arrived at a bend in a river in which there were a few muddy pools of brackish water. I told my Troop Sergeant, Bruce Fitzsimons, that we would stop to refill our water bottles and have a quick brew before moving on. Bruce was a gruff, no-nonsense Sergeant with a hairstyle like Elvis Presley and a temperament like Attila the Hun. We were sitting together on the bank of the river enjoying the civilized routine of a cup of tea when the thick foliage on the far bank erupted into a calamitous explosion of gunfire. Rounds began tearing into the clearing in which Bruce and I were sitting. The small gas cylinder attached to the stove on which our tea was brewing got struck by a round and exploded into the air like a malfunctioning rocket. Two rounds went through the mess-tin I was holding, transforming it into a sieve. To add insult to injury, a rocket slammed into the riverbank below us causing it to partially collapse almost toppling us into the riverbed.

"I say, Bruce. They could at least have waited until we had finished our tea … " I realized I was talking to myself. Bruce had already leapt to his feet, his rifle chattering angrily. With a loud shout of profanity, he ordered some of his men to follow him and together they sprinted across the river in pursuit of the terrorists. Within a short span of time he had reported back on the radio that he had killed two, but was taking fire from a terrorist machine gun on his left flank. Thinking that we might inadvertently have come across the camp we were looking for I immediately called for air support.

"03 this is 34. Contact, contact! Require air support."

I thought if I could get an aircraft overhead quickly it would keep the rest of the terrorists pinned down while we outflanked their position.

"34 this is 03. An aircraft is on its way. Talk to pilot overhead when you have him visual."

I heard the aircraft about twenty minutes before I could see it. So did the rest of the terrorists. They fled through the thick bush like chickens from a fox. Even the best efforts of Bruce Fitzsimons running after them spraying a mixture of bullets and blasphemy failed to stop them. Eventually, the Trojan arrived high above our position looking like a square cigarette box suspended from a wing. The noise made by its engine as it lurched around our position was so extreme that we couldn't even hear if we were taking any further fire. There was little chance of the pilot being able to assist as a spotter, let alone put in a ground strike; he was too busy struggling to keep his kite in the air. The plane was making such a racket that I was eventually forced to ask the pilot to leave. He was only too happy to oblige and after making two further orbits, lurched back from whence he had come. I resolved never to use a Trojan for close air support again.

We didn't have any trouble finding the camp the following day. It was just a matter of following the tracks of the fleeing terrorists. One of the gang had been wounded and his blood trail made the tracker's job easy. The tracks eventually linked up with a well-worn path leading through dense vegetation. The thick bush on either side of the path made it impossible for us to fan out into a proper patrol formation so I took the lead with the rest following. Thick impenetrable undergrowth and a tangle of trees limited my visibility. It was reduced even further by a light misty rain that had begun to fall. I knew we were close to the camp by the smell of wood fires. I didn't realize just how close. Rounding a sharp bend in the path I suddenly found myself in an area completely devoid of undergrowth. Vast numbers of pole and thatch 'bashas' spread before me as far as I could see. Automatic rifle-fire started spitting towards us shredding the leaves and branches above our heads.

We swept through the camp pouring rifle fire into the structures and surrounding bush like pre-programmed automated robots. My machine-gunner, Marius Marais, was walking next to me, his gun chewing through hundred-round belts of ammunition like hay through a harvester. We didn't stop firing until we had swept through the camp and into the thick tree-line

Mr Smith and his staff, Lushoto School. (Tim Bax)

Pupils on a hike at Lushoto School. (Tim Bax)

Trevor Kirrane. (Jacqui Kirrane)

Officer selection. (Terry Griffin)

Officer selection tracking course at Kariba. (Terry Griffin)

Selous Scouts Tracking Wing, Kariba. (Noel Robey)

Rehearsing for Passing Out Parade. (Terry Griffin)

The author carrying the colours. (Terry Griffin)

The author carrying the colours in the RLI. (Terry Griffin)

Part of my Troop. (John van Zyl)

RLI soldiers testing weapons before deployment. (Dennis Croukamp)

A view of a K Car. (Dennis Croukamp)

Early SAS border control operations. (Carol Doughty)

A Fire Force deploys. (Dennis Croukamp)

Sergeant Major Peter McNeilage, SCR. (Selous Scouts Association c/o Tom Thomas)

Members of the Selous Scouts Reconnaisance Team. (Dennis Croukamp)

Selous Scouts preparing to deploy into Mozambique. (Dennis Croukamp)

Bax and Collett on parade after being wounded. (Tim Bax)

Lt. (later Captain) Dale Collett. (Selous Scouts Association c/o Tom Thomas)

Neil Kriel, Ron Reid-Daly and Jerry Strong in the Selous
Scouts Officers' Mess. (Phee Fletcher)

The author home from the bush on R&R. (Tim Bax)

Tim Bax, Tom Thomas and Keith Samler. (Selous Scouts Association c/o Tom Thomas)

11

Captain Athol Gillespie. (Selous Scouts Association c/o Tom Thomas)

Bob Wishart, in wheelchair. (Selous Scouts Association c/o Tom Thomas)

Selous Scouts standard being paraded at 5 Reconnaisance Regiment. (Noel Robey)

Peter Donelly, Selous Scouts soldier extraordinaire. (Pete Donelly)

Author with Pete Donelly on his farm. (Pete Donelly)

COIN formal dinner. (Debbie Patching)

COIN Security Group managers. The author is seated at the centre. (Debbie Patching)

Para drop during Fire Force deployment. (Dennis Croukamp)

RLI deploying on operations inside Mozambique. (D. Scott-Donelan)

beyond. That night I was joined by Colin Willis, who was operating with his troop in an area adjacent to mine.

Thankfully none of my men were killed or wounded, but the smell of death from dead terrorists hung over the area like a sickly cloak. Occasionally, the staccato chatter of AK-47 fire would rudely interrupt the still, wet night as the remaining terrorists probed our position. It would be answered immediately by the heavy thump-thump-thump of Marius's machine-gun, its heavy rounds travelling at twice the speed of sound mowing down huge swaths of vegetation and, more often than not, silencing the terrorist fire. Closer to dawn the firing stopped. The terrorists knew that we would be hot on their trail as soon as the sun came up.

Early that morning I was sitting with Colin on the perimeter of the camp waiting for the trackers to establish a 'line of flight' when two terrorists made a sudden appearance ahead of us. Seeing us, they fired a burst of automatic fire in our direction, turned and fled.

Colin was after them faster than a sprinter out of the starting block.

Not waiting for me or anyone else, he chased the two terrorists through the bush like a hound after a hare. I ran after him as fast as I could, but he was faster. Emerging out of the cover of the forest, I saw Colin sprinting a hundred yards ahead making ground on the fleeing terrorists. I watched as he chased them across a river and up the far bank, closing on them rapidly. The two stopped, turned, and took aim at Colin. Colin was quicker. With a short burst from his assault rifle, he ensured that the two terrorists would take no further part in the war. It was his determination to close with and engage the enemy that would eventually earn Colin both the Silver Cross and Bronze Cross of Rhodesia.

❧

When I was eventually pulled out of Mozambique with my troop, I thought that my excitement for one bush trip would be over. I was the last to be uplifted in an Alouette helicopter together with three of my men. The aircraft was piloted by a slim, red-headed 'chopper jockey' called 'Baldy' Baldwin. About ten miles from the Rhodesian border we started taking ground fire and a bullet went through the helicopter's fuel line. Baldy managed to put the disabled aircraft down in a small clearing and switched off its turbine engines. The whirling rotor blades slowly came to a stop and we looked at each other bewildered.

"What do we do now?" I asked in the ensuing silence.

RLI patrol resting up. (D. Scott-Donelan)

"I don't know. I was about to ask you the same question," replied Baldy. "We're on the ground with an incapacitated aircraft; that means you're in charge."

"Well, in that case, I suggest we deplane into all-round defence and brew a cup of tea while we wait for assistance."

Thirty minutes later, much to my horror, the same Trojan that had come to my assistance earlier lurched overhead looking like a giant bumblebee. It lumbered around in a tight orbit making a frightful noise, scaring everything away within a fifty-mile radius, including the terrorist who had shot us down. Thankfully, another helicopter arrived an hour later with an extra technician and a new fuel line.

I had been glad to get away from the barracks four weeks earlier. Now I was glad to be returning.

A Port Too Many

One of the first things I did on my return to the barracks was get in touch with

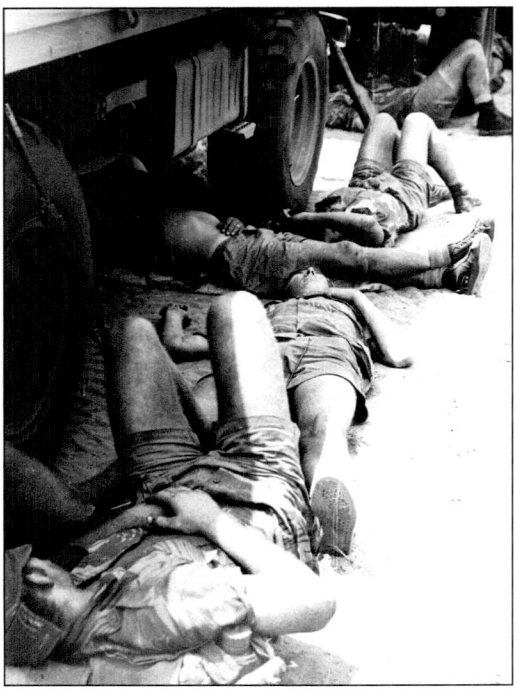

RLI soldiers resting during a vehicle-borne raid into Mozambique. (D. Scott-Donelan)

a young lady called Carol Grant to whom I had been introduced some months earlier. Carol's father was the Headmaster of the Rhodes Estate Preparatory School in Bulawayo, arguably one of Rhodesia's most highly-regarded junior boarding schools. Her mother was a teacher at the same school. When I first met Carol, she was attending a business college in Salisbury and was living in a girls' residence in the centre of town. We had discussed plans for moving into a flat together and I thought now would be as good a time as any to make the move. It would be four weeks before I would have to return to the bush, giving us enough time to get settled. We had no difficulty finding a comfortable one-bedroom flat which suited our needs and moved in soon after.

We had been in our new home for some three weeks and were preparing to go out for dinner one evening when there was a knock at the front door. It was Martin Pearse.

"Hi Martin, we're about to go out for dinner … would you care to join us?" asked Carol.

"I'd love to, but I don't have a date. I'd feel a bit foolish coming on my own."

I had never known Martin to be without an attractive lady and wondered why he was now without one. Later I learned that he had ended his most recent relationship after receiving an irate call from the lady's angry husband!

"Don't worry," said Carol. "I have a friend called Mandy who is working in a pharmacy down the road. She finishes work in a few minutes. Why don't I call her and ask if she would like to join us? I'm sure she would be thrilled."

A phone call later it was arranged that Martin would drive with us to the pharmacy to meet his new date. We explained to him that once we arrived, Carol and I would wait in the car while he went in and introduced himself. Then we would drive off together for dinner.

When we arrived, Martin jumped out of the car and walked nervously into the pharmacy. He browsed around a bit before walking up to the counter.

"May I help you, sir?" asked Mandy from behind the counter. "Yes, please. I'd like to buy some French letters."

"French what?" asked Mandy, innocently.

"French letters."

"This is a pharmacy, sir. There's a stationery store around the corner."

"No, no—I mean … condoms. I'd like to buy some condoms." Rhodesia practiced strict censorship at the time and such things were kept discreetly out of sight in back storerooms. There was a prevailing thought amongst the junior officers in the RLI that the Commanding Officer's wife might have had

RLI soldiers taking a break during external operations. (D. Scott-Donelan)

RLI soldiers troop for a fire-force deployment. (Dennis Croukamp)

a hand in this particular censorship rule. She had walked into the Officers' Mess one afternoon just prior to a Regimental Ball and found a group of us in the bar enjoying lunchtime drinks. Thinking we should be more gainfully employed, she told us to make ourselves useful by blowing up balloons for the Ball. Taking umbrage at having our afternoon of drinking interrupted, we inflated some condoms instead. The Commanding Officer's wife seemed quite pleased with our efforts until somebody pointed out to her what they were. Then she thought they were rather disgusting, especially hanging from the ceiling at a Regimental Ball.

Mandy thought she might have misunderstood. "I beg your pardon?"

"Do you sell any condoms, please?"

Mandy blushed. "Well, yes. I think so. They're kept in the back.

May I ask how many you would like?"

"A gross, please."

"A gross? I don't think we have that many."

Mandy disappeared into a back room and returned a few minutes later looking red and flustered. In her hand was a large cardboard box containing the pharmacy's entire supply of prophylactics.

"Will there be anything else for you tonight, sir?" "Yes, please. Could you tell me who Mandy is?" "Mandy? I'm Mandy."

Martin extended his hand. "Hi, I'm Martin Pearse. We have a date tonight."

Carol and I watched Martin walk dejectedly out of the pharmacy … alone.
"Where's Mandy?" we asked, as he climbed into the car.
"I think I asked for a condom too many."

❧

Prior to my deployment back into the bush, I attended another formal dinner evening at the Officers' Mess. It was the Regiment's farewell to Lt. Col. MacIntyre. He was being replaced as the Commanding Officer of the RLI by Lt. Col. Dave Parker.

During these formal dinners, it was customary after the serving of dessert for waiters to place decanters of Port strategically around the table. These would then be circulated around the table like gourds of 'chibuku' (a local beer) at a native wedding for everyone to fill their glasses prior to the formality of the 'Loyal Toast'. It was traditional for the toast to be given by the junior subaltern, who on this occasion was a young officer who had recently joined the Regiment and who was clearly nervous at the prospect of saying anything, let alone proposing a toast. To steady his nerves he had consumed a few glasses of Port beforehand, discreetly supplied by one of the waiters. Unfortunately, he must have consumed a Port too many. When the time came to give the toast he got unsteadily to his feet, stammered out the toast and slugged back the contents of his glass. However, his aim deserted him … as did the wisdom of retaining a firm grip on his glass. Both glass and Port went flying through the air almost hitting the Regimental Colours on display nearby. Not so lucky was a frumpy older lady trying to sneak out for a call of nature. The glass struck her like a rocket, spilling Port down the front of her dress. She leaned forward to wipe the offending mess from her blouse, but succeeded only in displaying more bosom to the startled guests than they cared to witness.

After the formalities of dinner, it was customary for the Commanding Officer to lead the officers and their guests back into the bar for after-dinner drinks. It was then that the evening's frivolities would really begin. In the RLI, they were usually led by the Regimental Quartermaster, an ex-Irish Guardsman named Major George Walsh. An older, portly and distinguished-looking gentleman, he was legendary for his antics in the Mess and would delight in leading fellow officers and guests in singing a rendition of *Maggie May* that was so salty, it would have the ladies blushing into their handkerchiefs.

Later in the evening and well fortified with ale, Major Walsh would kneel precariously on top of a low table and face everyone in the bar like the impervious conductor of a badly-choreographed choir. Raising his hands into the air he would give a rousing performance of an extraordinary recital he called *The Old Bazaar of Baghdad*. This was somewhere between a wail and a chant and must have been learned in some questionable establishment on the banks of the Euphrates during his service in the Middle East. On the completion of each verse, he would prostrate his upper body on the table with his bottom in the air and give a loud wail that would have everyone thinking he had done himself a grievous injury. This was the signal for everyone else in the bar to join in the chant … "Yes, Dad! No, Dad! Three bags full, Dad!"

The *real* festivities in the Mess would begin after the departure of the Commanding Officer and other senior dignitaries. I owned a motorcycle at the time and on this particular evening I rode it into the bar for a competition to see who could ride through each room in the Mess without falling off or hitting any furniture. Most of us tipped over before even making it out of the bar. The winner was adjudged to be a fearless young Lieutenant called Johan DuPloy who had joined the RLI from the South African Army. He at least made it out of the bar and on to the front veranda before veering out of control and plunging with the bike into an ornate fish pond on the front lawn. There he remained until found by his batman early the following morning. The batman had been anxiously searching for the young officer in order to serve him his early morning tea.

My own claim to fame on the motorcycle was transporting four of my very drunk colleagues back to the barracks one afternoon after a session of heavy drinking in Salisbury. A policeman we passed was so shocked at the sight of five drunken officers on a motorcycle singing at the top of their voices that he took some time in collecting his wits before giving chase. We weaved off as quickly as we could and by the time he caught up with us, we had managed to slip through the Battalion main gate into the sanctuary of the barracks. Much to the policeman's annoyance, the gate guards refused to allow him in.

The following morning Carol insisted I get rid of the bike.

Brush with Fire

It was a welcome relief to get back to the sanity of the bush. For the next year, 3 Commando alternated between conducting external operations inside Mozambique and Zambia and carrying out internal operations inside Rhodesia.

The internal deployments invariably involved Fire-Force operations wherein the entire Commando would deploy to a forward airfield accompanied by a section of five or six troop-carrying Alouette 111 helicopters, a helicopter gunship, a fixed-wing ground attack aircraft and a paratrooper deployment aircraft. This powerful, mobile strike force would remain on full alert at the airfield waiting for a report of a terrorist presence to be radioed in by one of the numerous clandestine observations posts (OP's) or Army patrols deployed throughout the area. Once a presence was established, the Commando would immediately be airlifted by helicopter to the target area accompanied by the helicopter gunship in which the Commando Commander would be positioned. This was to enable the Commando Commander to exercise control over the battle while having a three-dimensional birds-eye view of the battleground. The arrival of the helicopters over the target area would be precisely timed to coincide with the arrival of the fixed-wing attack aircraft and paratroopers.

The attack would invariably be initiated by the fixed-wing ground attack aircraft, followed immediately by high-volume, steep-angled fire from the helicopter gunship. At the same time, the helicopter-borne troops would vertically envelop the target area thereby preventing any terrorists from escaping. Unable to flee, the terrorists would be forced into a decisive confrontation with the soldiers while being subjected to withering fire from the air.

When we weren't engaged in actual fighting, we would linger next to our helicopters all day … reading, playing cards or doing something … anything to relieve the monotony of waiting for a report of a terrorist presence to be radioed in. The monotony of waiting must have been similar to that experienced by Battle of Britain pilots during the Second World War. They would wait around their Spitfires all day for a report of enemy aircraft. When it came, they would scramble to intercept and engage the incoming German squadrons over the English Channel. Then they would return to the airfield to refuel and re-arm their aircraft ready for the next call-out. Similarly, once we had concluded our attack, we would return to the airfield where we would re-equip, re-arm and refuel the aircraft and wait for the next call-out. Sometimes we would be engaged in up to three or four call-outs in a single day.

During mid-1975, the Commando was on Fire-Force duty in the small farming town of Mount Darwin in the northeast of the country. The town also happened to be the Regimental Field Headquarters of the Rhodesian Light Infantry. I was lying on my bed one morning reading James Jones's *From Here to Eternity,* when I heard the siren heralding another call-out begin its long, mournful wail. Quickly grabbing my rifle and gear I rushed into the operations room for a briefing. A gang of six terrorists had been sighted in what was thought to be a camp situated in thick bush along a riverbed some forty miles to our north. Major Lambert gave his normal precise and detailed orders and we were airborne in less than ten minutes.

Twenty minutes later we were orbiting around dense bush along the bank of a shallow river where the gang had last been seen. I was deployed with my stick by helicopter into a clearing some distance away. We quickly shook out into an extended line and began a sweep towards the river. My trusted machine-gunner, Marius Marias, was walking on my left and slightly behind me as we disappeared into the thick blanket of foliage close to the river. Branches and creepers tugged at my webbing as I inched my way forward. Above me clattered the gunship carrying Major Lambert. He was already taking control with his calm, unhurried voice, telling each sweep line where to go and what to look for. He didn't use call-signs; he preferred calling each stick-commander by name. Visibility was about two feet. We walked slowly … *very* slowly, our senses attuned to the slightest indication of a terrorist presence.

I had just stepped around a thick, low-growing tangle of brush when automatic rifle fire erupted all around me. Immediately I felt a searing pain through my right leg. It felt as if somebody had simultaneously thrust a white hot poker through my leg and hit it with a sledge hammer. Then I heard the deeper, heavier, rhythmic chatter of friendly machine-gun fire. I turned to see Marius holding his weapon waist-high in his huge, beefy hands, firing half a belt of ammunition into the thick bush I had just walked around. It all happened so quickly that I instinctively thought I had been hit by a round from my own machine-gunner.

"Marais, you bloody idiot!" I yelled. When the guns start firing, yelling is the only way to make oneself heard. "You just shot me through the leg!"

"No, Sir. It was a fucking gook that shot you." He pointed indignantly at a bush that lay between us, the business end of his machine gun still aimed menacingly towards it. "I culled him before he could fire another burst at you."

"Well, thank you. That's terribly decent of you, Marius."

I looked down. Lying well-camouflaged inside the tangled bush was a dead terrorist. On the ground in front of him, still pointed in my direction, was his AK-47 rifle. He had been hiding in the bush and fired at me as I walked past, not realizing that behind him was 250 lbs. of angry Afrikaner carrying a medium machine-gun who hadn't taken kindly to seeing his Troop Commander being

An RLI Fire-Force waiting to be called out. (Dennis Croukamp)

A Fire Force helicopter refuelling in the bush (Dennis Croukamp)

K Car. (Dennis Croukamp)

shot. I was jolted from further thought of pain by more gunfire erupting all around us. We had walked into the perimeter of a terrorist base camp. To add to the confusion, the camp was being engaged by the helicopter gunship orbiting overhead, its 20mm Hispano cannon spitting a deadly volley of steep-angled fire into the camp.

We swept into the camp, killing two more terrorists. I must have told Major Lambert that I had been wounded because I suddenly became aware of his voice over my radio telling me to prepare for a helicopter evacuation.

"Don't worry about me," I replied. "We still have more gooks shooting at us down here."

My leg was hurting badly and I was beginning to feel like I could do with a stiff tot of gin. Since gin was not prescribed medication carried in our troop medical pack, and since it was not a commodity one might expect to find in a dead terrorist's backpack, I thought I may as well carry on and get the job finished.

About thirty minutes later we had accounted for the entire gang.

I was busy consolidating the area when I heard Major Lambert's voice over my radio.

"Tim, get yourself to an LZ now. There's a chopper on its way to uplift you."

I looked down at my leg. It was bleeding badly and I desperately wanted that slug of gin. I heard the sound of an approaching helicopter and shouted to two of my troopies to assist me to an open landing zone nearby. The chopper descended slowly through the trees, its rotor blades thrashing at the thin, hot air, and landed with a hard bump. The pilot looked at me through the visor of his helmet and smiled, giving me a 'thumbs up'. I half stumbled and was half carried into the aircraft's welcoming interior. The pilot tugged on his collective lever, the rotor blades dug into the air and I felt myself being yanked vertically up through the trees. We hovered momentarily, turned and flew back toward Mt Darwin.

The next thing I remember was lying in the Army sickbay at Mount Darwin looking up into the face of the Regimental doctor. The Rhodesian Army was blessed with a large pool of talented young doctors of extraordinary ability. Dr. Charlee Griffiths was among the best. Of slight build and fair complexion, he had a shock of blond hair that looked as if it had seldom, if ever, seen a hair brush.

"I was told somebody had been shot but I didn't expect to see you here, Tim. How are you feeling?"

"Desperately in need of a sip of gin, Doctor."

"Well, I should think that a vial or two of morphine would help you more. But on second thoughts, a sip of gin might not do you any harm. Might thin

Helicopter deployment into Mozambique. (Dennis Croukamp)

Issuing orders – RLI soldiers in Mozambique. (D. Scott-Donelan)

your blood out a bit and make the morphine work quicker." He picked up the telephone and contacted the Officers' Mess. "Get a bottle of gin down to the sickbay immediately—for medicinal purposes—Doctor's orders."

The person who took the call was Captain Andrew Samuels, a good friend of mine. "OK, Doc. I'll bring it down myself. Who's the guy that's been shot?"

"Tim," replied the Doctor.

"Tim Bax? The bloody fool, tell him I'll be right down."

A few minutes later Andrew barged into the sickbay. He was a big, dark complexioned man with a barrel chest and thinning dark hair.

"Bax, you damn fool. You need to be more careful where you walk." He unscrewed the top from the gin bottle and took a swig before passing me the bottle. "There's no better excuse for a drink than seeing your buddy down."

I took the bottle from Andy and took a *long* sip. I hadn't realized just how thirsty I was.

"I'll have a sip, too, if you don't mind," said the Doctor, reaching for the bottle. He took a hefty swig before returning his attention to stabilizing my leg.

An hour later I was being driven by ambulance to the nearby airfield where a fixed-wing aircraft was already waiting, its engines running and propeller spinning. The Doctor helped me into the cockpit, bade me farewell and closed the door. The pilot opened up the throttles, released the brakes and we were rolling down the runway. As we started moving, I noticed a Land Rover speeding towards us. It stopped just ahead of us and I saw the figure of Andrew Samuels get out. He started running toward the moving aircraft waving for us to stop. We were already half way down the airfield by the time the pilot managed to bring the plane to a stop. Andrew ran breathlessly to the pilot's window holding up a brown paper bag.

"What's in there?" shouted the pilot above the roar of the engines.

"A bottle of gin! Tim might need a sip on the flight back," shouted Andrew, thrusting the bottle through the cockpit window.

The pilot reached down for the bottle and gave Andrew a salute before closing the window, then turned and looked at me.

"We're half-way down the runway," he shouted. "Do you think we have enough to get airborne?"

"Looks good enough to me," I shrugged, taking another nip from the bottle. I was definitely beginning to feel a lot better.

The pilot winked and gave me a mocking salute.

"OK, I'll give her full throttle. It's going to be tight, so hang on. Here we go!"

The engines roared back into life as we gathered speed down what remained of the runway. We hit a pothole which bounced the plane into the air just before reaching a low line of thorn trees that marked the end of the airfield. The plane's wheels clipped the tops of the branches and we banked south towards Salisbury.

I was beginning to feel rather good. It had been a good day, overall. An entire terrorist gang accounted for, a gunshot wound in my leg to guarantee me time off with Carol and an almost-full bottle of gin to see me on my way.

Yes, I was definitely beginning to feel *really* good.

Early Bird Catches the Worm

After spending three weeks in the hospital recovering from my leg wound, I was posted back to Mount Darwin as the RLI's Intelligence Officer. I had been there a week when a company of South African Police (SAP) arrived at the base, having journeyed all the way from Pretoria.

Dr Charlee Griffiths. (Dr Charlee Griffiths)

The South African Government, anxious to assist Rhodesia's war effort and thereby avoid having to fight an insurgency war on their own border, had deployed a number of their paramilitary-trained police companies to Rhodesia to assist in border control operations. This freed Rhodesian Army units to concentrate on areas where there was a known terrorist presence and to conduct cross-border raids against terrorist base camps in neighboring countries. Sending South African 'policemen' to assist in Rhodesia's war effort was seen as politically more 'palatable' than deploying South African Army units which might have led to international condemnation.

We always looked forward to the arrival of the SAP companies with great anticipation. This wasn't so much for their operational contribution (although this was appreciable), but mainly because they would bring with them a tantalizing array of equipment, the likes of which we had never seen. It was so highly sought after that they had to put as much effort into guarding it from the equipment-strapped Rhodesian soldiers as they did having to defend themselves against terrorist attacks. The Company that arrived in Mount Darwin was no exception.

It was mid-afternoon when the Company arrived giving them ample time

Dr Charlee Griffiths – my first sip of gin! (Dr Charlee Griffiths)

to unpack their vehicles, check stores and do an inventory of equipment. I was sitting in the Battalion Operations room with the Commanding Officer, Lt. Col. Parker, a few hours later when the SAP Company Commander walked in.

"Good evening, Colonel. Major Viljoen is my name." He spoke in a guttural Afrikaans accent. "I wish to inform you that all our logistics stores have been unpacked on the front lawn for an inventory check before we move to the border in a couple of days. I know you 'Rhodesias', ja, so I have posted guards for the night, ja. I have even issued them with a clever password, ja. So please, tell your 'Rhodesias' to stay away from my stores tonight."

The Major seemed well pleased with himself for having had the presence of mind to issue his guards a password. He had obviously been well briefed before leaving South Africa. He would show these thieving Rhodesians a lesson or two.

"Jolly good idea," replied Lt. Col. Parker.

"Ya, Colonel. I thought so myself. The password the guard will use tonight is 'Wilhelm'."

"And what's the response?" asked Lt. Col. Parker.

This seemed to confuse the Major immensely. He had been taught at his 'pre-deployment battle school' in Pretoria not to give the enemy the response to a password. Weren't the 'Rhodesias' the 'enemy'?

"Goot, Colonel. I have to protect my stores from you 'Rhodesias', ja. I can't

give you the response. I know you 'Rhodesias', ja! You will steal me sterk, ek sê."
The Major looked satisfied with his retort. These 'Rhodesias' thought that they were going to outsmart him … he would show them a lesson or two.

"Major, I don't want my soldiers walking around your stores tonight not knowing what the response is to the password. It could end up in a shooting match and I wouldn't want to wager any bets on your policemen winning."

Mention of a shooting incident seemed to worry the Major. Were these 'Rhodesias' about to outsmart him after all? He started to feel a little out of his depth. To make matters worse, English wasn't a language that he felt comfortable conversing in. He looked around, as if hoping to see one of his officers with whom he could consult. There were none. This was a command decision he would have to make on his own.

"OK, Colonel," he whispered, his voice barely audible. "The reply to the password is *Wilhelm*!"

As he said it, our African steward walked in from the Officers

Mess carrying a tray of drinks. The Major glared at him as though he might be Judas Iscariot about to betray his cleverly thought out security plan for the protection of his stores. Afrikaners, especially those in the SAP, had an inherent distrust of all blacks.

"A drink, Major?" asked Lt. Col. Parker. The SAP Major appeared shocked that we should be drinking alcohol at a field headquarters.

"My orders from Pretoria are that no alcohol will be taken while we are inside Rhodesia, Colonel. It is not good for discipline, ja!"

"Well, in that case, I might suggest that you keep out of the Mess tonight. You might get the impression that, not only are we a bunch of thieves, but ill-disciplined drunks as well. Now then, might I suggest that it is not a good idea to have a response to a password which is the same as the password itself? You might want to think of changing the reply to something else."

"Ah, don't worry, Colonel, because tomorrow the password is *Piet*!" The Major was beginning to feel back on top of his game.

Rhodesian Army-issue raincoats were flimsy green synthetic garments that did little to keep the water out and everything to keep the heat in. They were like mobile sauna suits. The SAP on the other hand was issued magnificent full-length, ventilated, brown nylon raincoats which kept the rain out in even the fiercest tropical storm. They were considered an extremely attractive item by Rhodesian soldiers. Aware that their arrival in Rhodesia had coincided with the annual rainy season, this particular SAP Company had brought with them an entire truck load of raincoats.

Throughout that night, the SAP constable guarding the stores was constantly bombarded by ceaseless calls of *Wilhelm … Wilhelm* as RLI troopies helped themselves to armfuls of SAP raincoats from the quickly-diminishing piles. The following morning I was having tea in the Operations Room, discussing with Lt. Col. Parker where best to deploy the SAP Company, when in walked a very upset Major Viljoen. A light rain had begun to fall.

"Colonel, Colonel! I have had some terrible news from my Quartermaster. Last night we had two hundred raincoats stacked on the front lawn. This morning only twenty are left."

I looked at Lt. Col. Parker and he looked at me. We were both wearing brand new SAP raincoats. Just then there was a knock on the door and the Mess steward arrived with more tea, wearing a new SAP raincoat!

"Now, Major. We have far more important things to discuss than one or two raincoats having gone missing in the night. Sit down and let's talk about your deployment orders for tomorrow morning. You'll have to be extremely vigilant, I'm afraid. There's a lot of terrorist activity in the area."

Nobody in the SAP Company had ever seen combat; neither had Major Viljoen. He forgot all about his missing raincoats. By the time I had completed the intelligence briefing, he was looking quite pale. Missing raincoats were suddenly the last thing on his mind.

"When were you thinking of moving out tomorrow?" asked Lt. Col. Parker.

"I plan on leaving at 04:00 in the morning, ja," replied the Major, still looking shocked at the prospect of being deployed into such a hotbed of terrorist activity.

"04:00 in the morning? There's no need to leave *that* early."

"Ja, Colonel. But as we say in the South African Police, the early bird always catches the worm."

The poor Major certainly caught the worm all right. It came in the form of a double anti-tank landmine his truck hit as he was leading his convoy into his deployment area. He had to be casevaced (Casualty Evacuation) back to South Africa and never returned to Rhodesia again.

The Doctor and the Cane Rat

One day a Situation Report (SITREP) came across my desk about an incident involving Doctor Charlee Griffiths who had attended to me when I had been wounded. The report was headed, 'Doctor in Long Range Contact with Cane Rat'. I couldn't imagine what the report meant but knew that with Charlee, anything was possible. It contained an account of an incident related in Charlee's own words:

I was returning to the operational area in a Land Rover driven by a medical orderly. Suddenly we heard the sound of gunfire at close quarters and I wondered vaguely whether we had been ambushed! The orderly immediately stopped the vehicle in the middle of the road. He hadn't been shot, but he might just as well have been; he didn't seem to know what to do! My own training as a Medical Doctor had not covered in any great detail what to do when caught inside an enemy ambush. The orderly remained frozen at the wheel in the middle of the killing zone. I decided that this was probably not a good place to stop and that I had better do something, so I dragged him out of the vehicle and into a ditch on the side of the road. As we were lying there I thought I saw movement at the base of an anthill some distance away.

All I had for protection was my Medical Corps 9mm Browning pistol. I didn't know if it worked, as I hadn't used it before. Beginning to feel a bit nervous about the movement around the anthill, I decided to shoot at it to see if the pistol actually worked. Taking careful aim, I fired at its base. I had the great satisfaction of seeing a puff of dirt fly up about fifty yards short of the target. An indignant cane rat scurried from its base and sat looking at us preening its whiskers. I heard two more rifle shots and took aim at the anthill again. Once again my shots fell short, so much so that the cane rat didn't even flinch. In fact, it looked quite bemused. I heard yet another shot and began to think we might be surrounded. Then I heard the engine of the Land Rover, which had been left running, cough, splutter and stall. Thankfully, the firing seemed to stop.

Just then a police vehicle arrived and we were able to radio for support. A helicopter with some RLI reaction troops arrived shortly after to scour the area. They couldn't find any trace of a terrorist presence or of any firing positions. The frightened orderly decided to clamber back inside the Land Rover, anxious to leave the area as quickly as possible. As he started the engine, two more shots rang out. The orderly decided he wasn't going to hang around and wait for me, so he did a quick u-turn and sped back toward Salisbury with all of my kit, including cigarettes, money and hat still in the vehicle. Another volley of gunfire seemed to follow the vehicle.

"There it is again!" I shouted to the RLI stick commander. He laughed at me.

"Don't you know the difference between the sound of a vehicle backfiring and gunfire?"

I got a lift to the RLI Headquarters feeling rather silly. I was thankful for the Officers' Mess credit system; the drinks in the Mess were on my account for the rest of the week.

❧

The following morning feeling rather sheepish, Doctor Charlee asked me if I would take him to the range for some target practice.

The first thing I suggested was that he rid himself of his pistol and learn how to handle a rifle. To my amazement he proved quite adept with one. He looked quite pleased with himself but asked, "Isn't it against the Geneva Convention for a doctor to carry an assault weapon?"

"Probably, but I don't think anyone's going to worry about that out here, Doc. A rifle is what you need and besides, it makes a very handy club if you happen to run out of ammunition." As usual, the good doctor adhered to my advice.

Dr. Charlee Griffiths might not have had the musketry skills of Daniel Boone, and it would be a foolhardy man who would wager a bet on his being a better tactician than Akbar the Arab, but as a medical doctor, he was a class act. I had the opportunity of watching him work during the three months it took for my leg to recover.

One night I was assisting him with a cluster of casualties who had been brought into the field hospital with gunshot wounds. A vehicle had been ambushed on a road north of us and the wounded had been brought into our camp for treatment at the field hospital. There was a power failure at the time and Dr. Charlee had temporarily moved his operating equipment outside so he could work using the headlights from his Land Rover.

"Find me a hacksaw, quickly!" he told me midway through one critical surgery."

"A hacksaw?"

"A hacksaw. This arm has to come off—and quickly."

I found a hacksaw … and a bottle of whisky to steady my nerves. M.A.S.H. wasn't far off the mark in its portrayal of the chaos of a Mobile Army Surgical Hospital. In *real* life it seemed much worse.

About a week later, still at the RLI field headquarters in Mount Darwin, I was sitting in the Officers' Mess one evening enjoying a quiet drink when Dr. Charlee made a dramatic entrance through the door. He was covered in blood from head to toe and his eyes betrayed a look of shocked indignation, rather as a soccer captain might look on finding out that his goalkeeper had deserted mid-game.

"Have you come in for a drink or to get cleaned up?" asked the Commanding Officer.

"I need some help. My medical orderly has thrown in the towel and I want to know if Tim can come and assist me. I'm working on a woman who has lost a portion of her face in a grenade explosion."

I threw back my whisky, ordered another for both myself and the doctor, and followed him outside. The medical orderly had been overcome by the sight of blood and gore and was busy throwing up outside the hospital. I helped the doctor as much as I was able, watching him skillfully stabilize the woman and perform complex surgery on her shattered face. I learned many months later the woman had made a remarkable recovery.

Later that same night the doctor and I were back in the Officers' Mess soothing our nerves over a few more drinks.

"Tim, you know I've been doing a lot of work for the Selous Scouts."

"That's quite an honor, Charlee. Wow, the *Selous Scouts!*"

The Scouts was the most highly-trained airborne Special Forces unit in the Rhodesian Army with a fearful worldwide reputation for hunting down terrorists.

"Major Reid-Daly asked me the other day if I knew of any good officers in the RLI who might have the aptitude to join the Selous Scouts. I told him I knew of only one. I gave him your name, Tim. And you know that Major Reid-Daly never takes 'no' for an answer. You're going to be on your way to Inkomo Barracks quicker than you might think."

He reached for his old six-string guitar which he kept in the corner of the Mess and started strumming the tune to his favorite song, Bobby Picket's *Monster Mash*. It was a song he and I had sung together on many an evening in the Officers' Mess.

Dr Charlee Griffiths and his newly-issued rifle. (Dr Charlee Griffiths)

Two days later I found myself summoned to Inkomo Barracks outside Salisbury for an interview with Major Ron Reid-Daly, Commanding Officer of the Selous Scouts. I knew the unit specialized in tracking terrorist gangs using superbly-trained 'hunter killer' groups, and in conducting 'small group' long-range reconnaissance patrols. That was its *official* function as far as public knowledge was concerned. What the public did not know at the time was that the Selous Scouts were involved in a far more secretive and clandestine war, the success of which was to dramatically turn the tide of the war in Rhodesia's favor. It was pseudo-operations; the shadowy war of terrorist gangs and counter-gangs.

The secretive Headquarters of the Selous Scouts looked more like a Chindit base camp in the Burmese Jungle than a formal barracks. It consisted of a number of corrugated, galvanized iron buildings cloistered together under the trees of a forest plantation. The Parade Square, unlike a formal barracks, was tucked away to one side of the camp. Excelling in drill was not considered a high priority in the training of a Selous Scout. The centerpiece of the camp was a large rectangular Operations Room surrounded by a veritable forest of tall aerials which towered upward through the trees like the electric pylons of a national power grid. I was hustled into its bright interior by an Intelligence Sergeant with long hair and a beard who looked like he might just have emerged from an extended stay in the Burmese jungle.

The bustle inside the Operations Room resembled the floor of the New York Stock Exchange on a busy day of trading. Map clerks hustled about with SITREPS in their hands moving numbered pins marking the location of Selous Scout call-signs on giant maps that covered every inch of wall. A large radio console at one end of the room looked like a replica of the flight deck of the space shuttle. Banks of high frequency and very high frequency radios spat out a continuous crackle of chatter that had clerks reaching to and from handsets like jugglers in a circus. Every now and then, the low, modulated dots and dashes of a Morse code message would probe through the static, making the radio operator scramble for a signal pad. On each side of the console, rows of different-colored telephones linked the Headquarters to everyone who was anyone.

I sat at the end of a long table in the centre of the Operations Room watching in fascination. Eventually Major, soon to be Colonel, Ron Reid-Daly emerged from the chaos of the business end of the busy room. He sat down next to me and smiled. He looked older and grayer than when I had seen him a year before. He shook my hand.

"Thanks for coming, Tim. Now, let's get straight to the point." He was obviously a busy man. "I know you have worked well leading white troops in the past. What do you know about working with black troops?"

"You mean the Rhodesian African Rifles?" I asked.

"Them and others," responded the Major. He looked at me, moving a little closer and dropping his voice slightly. "Terrorists, Tim. You'll be working with gangs of captured terrorists operating *against* real terrorist gangs in the bush. Essentially, you will be required to live and operate in the bush for an extended period of time acting as a terrorist yourself." I wondered what time the bar might open, or whether a bar even existed in the camp. I felt badly in need of a drink.

"I'm willing to give it my best shot," I replied.

"Good. There's a Selous Scouts Selection Course which starts at Wafa-Wafa, Kariba, in two weeks. Make sure you're on it. If you pass you'll become a member of the Selous Scouts."

"Wafa-Wafa?" I asked.

Helicopter deployment of a Selous Scouts reconnaissance team. (Dennis Croukamp)

"It means '*You're Dead – You're Dead*' in Shona. It's the name of our selection camp." I definitely felt in need of that drink.

"Won't I have to ask Army Headquarters for a posting out of the RLI?" I asked.

"Leave that to me, Junior. Just be here in two weeks to catch the transport to Kariba."

He got up and shook my hand. "Good luck. Now, you look like you need a drink. It's almost lunchtime. Come and meet some of the chaps over a beer and some lunch."

ↄ

I returned to the RLI the following day to say my final goodbyes. Before I left, Major Lambert called me into his office.

"Tim, I'll be sorry to see you go. I want to be the first to congratulate you!"

"But I haven't been accepted yet. I still have to pass the Selous Scouts Selection Course."

Major Lambert smiled and patted me on my shoulder. He handed me a citation from Army Headquarters.

"No, it's not the Scouts, Tim. I want to be the first to congratulate you on your award of the Military Forces Commendation."

I thanked him, feeling quite emotional. Then I saluted, shook his hand, about-turned and walked towards the Officers' Mess. Percy, the barman, was the only one in the bar. It was 10:30 in the morning.

"Give me a gin and tonic, Percy. On second thoughts, make that a double.

12

An Unconventional Wisdom

It takes a thief to catch a thief; a pickpocket to catch a pickpocket.
There is only one way to find a snake; you must send another snake.
But you Boers, you think you can send a lion to find a hyena. You are wrong.
You must send a hyena to find a hyena.

—Lecture from a captured terrorist,
Selous Scouts Selection Course: 1976

Selection

I was wondering what I was doing sitting on a log inside a terrorist base camp along the thickly-wooded banks of the Nyaodza River. I felt distinctly out of place, rather like a Rabbi at a Hindu convention. I had already been through two selection courses in my short Army career; I must be stark raving mad to be trying another.

It was six-thirty in the morning and the temperature in the shade had already clawed its way upwards of 100 degrees Fahrenheit. Before me lay a small circle of flat, fire-blackened stones in the center of which still smouldered indiscernible shapes of gray charcoal. It was all that remained of last night's cooking fire. A wisp of white smoke rose lazily from a solitary, flickering ember. I knelt down on hands and knees to light my last remaining cigarette before the flame died, the smoke burning my eyes. Returning to my seat, I stared vacantly at the smoke as it curled upwards into the hot still air, my mind in a trance. The shrill mournful call of a fish eagle jolted me momentarily from my lethargy. It was perched on a tall fossilized stump in the shallow waters of Lake Kariba, just visible through the trees. Its piercing call heralded the awakening of yet another sweltering dawn. Nothing moved; it was too hot to move. It was stifling. My attention drifted back to the slowly rising smoke.

The camp wasn't a real terrorist base camp. It had been created to replicate one. I inhaled deeply on my cigarette. A tsetse fly hovered menacingly close to my right forearm. I watched it in pensive fascination, waiting for it to impale its long painful sting into my flesh. It was still early but I was too fatigued from heat, hunger and exhaustion to slap it away. Above anything, I wanted a cup of hot, sweet tea.

⁊

I had arrived at the 'Wafa-Wafa' training camp on the shores of Lake Kariba a month earlier. It had been named by the first African soldiers to attempt a Selous Scouts selection. *You're Dead-You're Dead* was an apt name for a camp in which the limits of human endurance were pushed to the extreme. A Sergeant-Major with whom I had operated in the Rhodesian Light Infantry two years before and who was now running the Selection Course, met me as I climbed off the truck. I hardly recognized him. Charlie Krause looked as though he had been plucked from the jungles of Borneo after living with a tribe of pagan headhunters. His long straggly hair looked badly in need of a wash and the bushy black beard he sported was streaked with gray. He wore shorts, a T-shirt and a pair of improvised sandals made from the bark of a tree. He showed me to a crude grass basha in which a family of scorpions had already taken up residence.

"What's this?" I asked, thinking it might be the shelter for a pet mongoose I had noticed tethered to a nearby tree.

"It's your sleeping quarters for the next three weeks," replied the Sergeant-Major dryly.

"I say old fellow, don't you have anything a little more salubrious; I'm an officer after all."

"There's no rank or special status on a Selous Scouts Selection Course," replied the Sergeant-Major impassively. "Everyone gets treated the same."

I wondered vaguely whether this might not be in breach of some Army regulation. If it wasn't, it should have been.

As an afterthought he added, "You'll be sharing it with a couple of corporals." The basha hardly looked big enough for one.

I dragged my bergen into the cramped basha under the watchful eyes of the scorpions. Opening it, I was horrified to discover my scarlet and green Mess uniform, complete with white shirt, bow tie and jodhpurs! I had spent the evening before my departure from the Rhodesian Light Infantry in the Officers' Mess attending a farewell party that had been held in my honour. In true RLI tradition, my fellow officers had decided they knew better than me what to take on a Selous Scouts selection. They had found my carefully-packed bergen and divested it of most of the equipment I had painstakingly packed. A few bottles of whisky had convinced them that I would find my Mess uniform far more useful in the African bush than my lightweight camping kit. One of the scorpions reared its tail angrily at the sight of such an obtrusive piece of apparel. It was probably the first Officers' Mess uniform it had ever seen. It probably hoped it would be the last. I could just imagine myself dressed in a scarlet uniform swinging through the trees like a pirate of the Caribbean might swing through the rigging of a three-masted barkentine. Any illusions I might have harbored of being a modern day Tarzan were soon dispelled.

Each morning one of us would have to climb a rope attached to the branch of a tall tree and clang on a metal ploughshare that was attached to the branch. Being the only officer on the course, I stupidly volunteered to climb the rope on the first morning. Having clawed my way to the top to clang the ploughshare, my strength deserted me and I began slithering back down a lot quicker than I had gone up. I tried breaking my speed by clutching the rope tightly in my hands but only succeeded in peeling the skin off my palms. I spent the next two weeks with my hands bandaged in strips of white dress shirt, courtesy of Harrods of London.

There were twelve of us on the course: six European soldiers from the Rhodesian Light Infantry and six African soldiers from the Rhodesian African Rifles. I was the only officer. For those of us who passed would come the privilege of wearing the beret and badge of the Selous Scouts, a unique Special Forces unit unlike any other in the world.

I can only imagine that the syllabus for the course must have been drawn up by a rancorous fanatic after watching *Death in the Amazon*, a rather morbid account of an Englishman dying of starvation and fatigue after becoming lost in the Amazon jungle.

For the first two days we were given no food. On the third day we were each given a small piece of fishing line and a single hook and told that if we were hungry, to "Get on with it." Fishing had never been a speciality of mine nor it seemed, had it been a speciality of the others. By the end of the third day the sum total of our catch was two tiny fish. We eventually decided that we might have more luck praying than fishing. As it turned out we weren't very successful at that either. For reasons best known unto the Great Messiah, He didn't show us the same compassion as He showed the five thousand on Galilee's shores two thousand years before. Our two pitiful fish remained two pitiful fish regardless of how hard we prayed. All each of us got out of the meager catch were a couple of scales and a bone, which we ate carefully

The first group of Selous Scouts instructors. (Noel Robey)

wrapped in a wild spinach leaf.

On the fourth day, our instructors shot a baboon and strung it in a tree next to our camp. We were told this would be our next meal. Two days later the flesh had become so rotten in the heat that it seethed with maggots. The stench was indescribable. On the fifth day, the carcass was cut down and thrown into a large pot of boiling water. It was left to simmer for a day over an open fire after which we were allowed to eat it. It was the first food we were given in six days.

The one stroke of genius that had been displayed by my fellow officers in reorganizing my kit prior to my departure from Salisbury, was in emptying my water canteens and filling them with gin. It was to prove my salvation throughout the selection. Man's ability to withstand fatigue when starved of food is not without limits. With a nip of gin to sustain him, his endurance is considerably enhanced. It certainly gave me the courage to consume a few mouthfuls of rotten baboon flesh. It also gave me the fortitude to sustain me through what was arguably the worst three weeks of my life!

Five men out of the initial twelve made it to the final phase of the Selection Course; the remaining seven were returned to their original units. This phase was called the 'Dark Phase'. It was less of a selection process and more a teaching exercise to give us detailed insight into the shadowy world of terrorist gangs. Just as important, we were taught the modus operandi of counter-gangs, or 'pseudo-gangs'. Our instructors were all seasoned Selous Scouts operators who had been involved in a number of successful pseudo-operations in the past. One of the instructors was a captured terrorist who had held the rank of 'Political Commissar' in the hierarchy of his gang. He had adopted the rather bizarre name of Moses. I asked him one day if he knew of the existence of his biblical namesake.

"Definitely I know of Moses," replied the former terrorist. "He's the one who was hiding inside the bushes to save his life."

"Well, in the bulrushes actually … not the bushes," I corrected. "It's the same with me. I was always hiding in the bushes. I was hiding in the bushes the day the soldiers found me. That's why my name is Moses."

Eventually the course came to an end. It was just as well as my stock of gin had run perilously low. My status as an officer having been restored, I was about to climb into the front of a Land Rover for the journey back to the Selous Scouts Barracks in Salisbury when Moses called me aside.

"Old man." I was only a few years his senior but his calling me "old man" was a mark of respect. "Don't be foolish and think you'll be able go unnoticed if you meet up with a gang of terrorists, even at night with your disguise."

Captured weapons after a Selous Scouts raid. (Dennis Croukamp)

"Why? You have taught me well. I might be a European, but at night with my disguise who will know?"

"There's something about you, old man … your mannerisms. I have been watching you. You might look like a hyena at night but you have not yet learned to act like one. Take my advice, old man, and stay well hidden in the shadows if you should come into contact with a gang of terrorists."

We shook hands. Much later when I was doing my first pseudo-operation, I was extremely pleased to have Moses by my side.

The Regiment

The Selous Scouts was an interracial Special Forces unit whose members specialized in musketry, bushcraft and tracking. It was a lethal combination. A Scout was as much at home in the African bush as Davy Crockett was in the wilds of Tennessee … and it would be a brave man who would wager a bet on who could shoot faster or straighter. The unit specialized in reconnaissance missions and in providing tracker-combat groups to hunt down terrorist gangs in the vast tracts of wilderness that formed much of Rhodesia's northern border. In 1972, Rhodesia started introducing limited numbers of highly-specialized pseudo-terrorists into areas where a terrorist presence was either known or suspected. These counter-gangs proved so successful at being able to root out real terrorist gangs that their numbers were increased. But a place had to be found for these unconventional specialist soldiers. The Selous Scouts Regiment provided an ideal home. Pseudo-operations became the unit's primary function. Later it pioneered the use of long-range mechanized raids to strike at terrorist camps located deep inside neighboring countries.

The Regiment was named after Captain Fredrick Courtney Selous, D.S.O., a salubrious English gentleman educated at Rugby School in England. At the age of nineteen he travelled to Africa where he quickly established a reputation for being a fine officer, frontiersman, explorer and hunter. In the late 1880s he was appointed by the famous English explorer, Cecil John Rhodes, to act as a lead scout and guide for the British East India Company in its quest to wrest control of Southern Rhodesia from the warlike Matabele tribe.

Selous had taken to the African bush like a Greek swindler to a group of unsuspecting tourists. Unfortunately, as many an early English explorer could testify, celibacy in the loneliness of the African bush can be a virtue as fleeting as the mists on the Matabele plains. That the 'gentleman scout' took a Matabele wife and fathered a child with her might have been forgiven as an unfortunate lapse brought about by the heat of the noonday sun. That he took two further wives fathering children with both of them, could only have been attributable to his great stamina … or to a case of too much 'mampoer', the potent homemade brandy distilled by Afrikaners. It had proven the downfall of many a noble and unwitting Englishman in the past. But first and foremost, Selous was a great scout and tracker and like Davy Crockett before him, was killed in the service of his country. He was shot by a German sniper bullet on the banks of the Rufiji River in 1917, at the site of what is now known as the Selous Game Reserve in Tanzania.

It didn't take me long to appreciate the extraordinary uniqueness of the individuals who made up the Regiment. Some had acquired 'folklore' status, both within the Army and amongst the general civilian population as well.

One afternoon I was having a pink gin in the Salisbury Sports Club with a friend of mine who used to play cricket for Rhodesia. He was busy drowning his sorrows having recently been caught under the Club's billiard table with the wife of a well-known attorney. The attorney, in a very unsporting gesture, was in the process of having him blackballed from the Club. My friend asked me how individuals in the unit might best be described.

"Different and extremely unpredictable," I responded.

"Ah yes, rather like the batting crease at the Rawalpindi Cricket Club," he replied, ordering another round of drinks. "They serve the best damn stengahs west of Singapore."

I had never been to Rawalpindi, let alone to its Cricket Club, so I let the comparison go unchallenged.

"Isn't that fellow Schulenburg in the Scouts?" asked the cricketer, stirring a few drops of Angostura bitters into his gin.

"Yeah. Bravest man I ever met."

Christophel Ferdinand Schulenburg was a tall, rugged and powerfully-built Afrikaner to whom bravery was as normal as doing up his bootstraps each morning. He was Rhodesia's most-decorated soldier and his particular speciality was long-range reconnaissance missions. There was nothing particularly unique about this, except that Chris, or 'Schulie', as he liked to be known, liked to operate alone. His simple philosophy was that it was easier for one man to remain undetected than two.

"Tell me about some of his exploits," pressed my friend. Schulie's exploits were so secret that only a handful of people within the unit knew of their details. But when he wasn't parachuting into some remote terrorist camp deep inside a hostile neighboring country, he was the scourge of the Scouts camp with his mischievous pranks. His latest involved some female clerks who had recently been posted to the Selous Scouts Headquarters.

"Just the other day he carried out one of the bravest acts I have ever witnessed," I replied with an air of great secrecy.

"Really, what happened?"

"It was just before lunch right inside our camp. Three female clerks were at the camp hospital for their annual tetanus injections. While they were there Schulie slipped into the women's toilets, unraveled the toilet rolls in each stall, sprinkled buffalo-bean on the toilet paper and rolled them up again."

Buffalo-bean was every Rhodesian soldier's worst nightmare. It was a plant that grows wild in the African bush and is similar to an English stinging nettle, except much worse. Get some of the tiny, barbed hairs that grow on the leaves on to your skin, and the resulting itch will drive any man crazy for hours. Scratching only served to spread the hairs over a greater area making the itching worse.

"Good heavens, what happened?"

"When the girls came out of the hospital they went straight into the toilets. By the time they arrived in the dining room, they were wriggling their bottoms around like they had fire ants in their pants. They were so mad they started shouting at the doctor thinking that he might have been responsible … you know, some allergic reaction to their injections."

"Must have been quite a sight?"

"It was. After being told by the doctor that it couldn't have been anything to do with the tetanus shots, the girls started to smell a rat. They started ranting at the guys who had just returned from the bush. There were Scouts tumbling out of the windows in their haste to get away from the wrath of those women.

"And Schulie?"

"He stood his ground like a real trooper. He kept the women at bay until the last Scout had left the dining room before abandoning his position. It was bravery of the highest order.

Chris Schulenburg, GCV. (Dennis Croukamp)

Moses

*"Those Selous Scouts, ek sé. They have eyes like owls and they can
see in the dark."*
"What do you mean?"
*"They are voodoo, I tell you. You can't see them but they're eyeing you out all the
time from the shadows."*
"Are they dangerous?"
*"I tune you, don't get too close to those okes or your mother will
never see you again. They are ruthless, ek sé."*
—Rhodesian soldiers of mixed race talking amongst themselves
about the Selous Scouts,
Mount Darwin: August, 1977

My first pseudo-operation with the Selous Scouts was into a remote area below
the Zambezi Escarpment. I was deployed with my old friend Sergeant Bruce
Fitzsimmons who had left the Rhodesian Light Infantry to join the Selous

Scouts some time before me. He was one of the most successful pseudo-operators in the unit and his troop had recently come off a number of successful operations. It was Bruce's job to teach me the ropes. The area we were deployed into consisted of flat woodland plains interspersed with small, rocky outcrops or koppies. African villages, or kraals, lay scattered throughout the area with the villagers eking out a meager existence as subsistence farmers and tending their cattle. Intelligence reports had indicated the area was being used as a transit route for terrorist gangs traveling to and from Rhodesia from their supply bases in Mozambique. Terrorists often based close to kraals on their journey inland in order to obtain food and water and to glean information on the whereabouts of Rhodesian Security Forces.

The plan was for Bruce and me to covertly base on a hill close to one of the kraals. From there we would control our six-man pseudo-group who would try to establish themselves with the locals as the 'resident' gang of *real* terrorists. In this way, if and when a gang of real terrorists passed, our pseudo-group would be informed by the local village headman who would then try to arrange a meeting between our group and the terrorist gang.

It was extremely tedious and uncomfortable work for the two of us. We had to lie up for days wedged between large rocks barely able to move. Although we were dressed in terrorist garb with our skin dyed black, we couldn't risk being seen by anybody and compromised as Europeans. If we were, it would certainly mean the end of our pseudo-operation and might jeopardize the lives of our operators. We remained hidden and virtually motionless all day. Only at night would we cautiously move around to stretch our legs and cook a meal on the small butane stoves we carried. The locals never moved outside their villages at night; they were too afraid of leopards. I would try and encourage Bruce to sleep during the day because his persistent low gurgling snore sounded remarkably like the growl of a leopard. It would be a brave local who would come snooping around the koppie by day to investigate the sound of a leopard. Bravery and leopards were not synonymous to villagers in the Zambezi Valley.

Once every two nights, Bruce and I would slip down from our hidden base into the inky blackness of the night to meet up with our pseudo-operators at a prearranged rendezvous. There we would debrief them on information they might have gleaned on terrorist activity in the area and issue further orders. They were having a much easier time of it than Bruce and I.

"Have you been accepted by the villagers as a legitimate gang?" asked Bruce brusquely at the first meeting.

"Yes, Sir. They can't do enough for us. Every night they bring us cooked chicken with sadza. 'Sadza' is maize ground to the consistency of meal and when cooked looks like thick porridge. It is the indigenous staple food in much of sub-Saharan Africa.

"They even send young women into our camp at night."

My selection course instructor, Moses, was the leader of the pseudo-group. He talked effusively about how well they were being treated. While we never encouraged our operators to fraternize with local women, we couldn't prevent it. Our gang members had to do what the terrorists did, and female company was always first on their list of demands.

"You bloody fools, you'd better be careful your penises don't fall off," chastised Bruce gruffly. He could always be relied upon to tell it like it was. "If any of you bloody fools catch a disease I'll chop your penis off and dock you a week's pay when we get back to base."

Moses laughed. They loved Bruce and treated him as their father. After spending time gleaning whatever intelligence we could, the group would slink back into the night and Bruce and I would return silently to our hill, making sure to anti-track the whole way.

We had been lying up for a week when Moses informed us that a terrorist gang was due to pass through the village below us the following evening.

"The headman says it's a gang of four on their way back to Mozambique. They're going to collect supplies and bring new recruits back with them. We're to meet with the gang in the headman's village."

Because the meeting was to take place at night, Bruce suggested that I might want to join our pseudo-group for the meeting. "It'll be good experience for you and nobody will be able to say you're still wet behind the ears. Besides, if the shooting starts you'll be there to take control."

I wondered who was in command of the operation, Bruce or me. I didn't really want to go, not after what Moses had told me on my selection course. But I didn't want to appear timid either and besides, Moses would be there to help out if things became unstuck.

We decided that if everything went according to plan we would try to avoid having a shoot-out with the gang. If we did our cover would immediately be compromised and we would be unable to operate in the area again. The loss was not worth the gain of killing four terrorists. A far better plan would be to arrange to meet the gang on their way back from Mozambique when the pickings would be greater. We could then have a Commando of RLI standing by to attack the terrorists without our pseudo-team being compromised.

While I accompanied the pseudo-group into the village, Bruce would remain behind on the hill to communicate with our

Headquarters in case things went wrong and we needed assistance. That night I carefully re-applied my black skin dye and checked my equipment before waving goodbye to Bruce. Then I slipped into the night to rendezvous with our group. Before long we arrived at the village to await the arrival of the terrorist gang.

"Don't forget what I told you on your selection, Ishe," whispered Moses. "You must stay well hidden behind a hut. I'll tell them that you have become deaf and dumb from losing your nerve in a contact with the Security Forces. If they come to you, keep your head down and say nothing." I wondered again who was giving the orders tonight, perhaps it was Moses!

I sat alone on a bench leaning back against the cold mud wall of a hut. It was pitch dark and I was freezing. I was wearing a grimy overcoat that I had picked up in a terrorist camp some months before. It reeked of woodsmoke and stale tobacco. On my head I wore a floppy hat pulled down just above my eyes. I waited impatiently, wondering just what my role for the night might be. The rest of the pseudo-group waited with the villagers around a small fire which burned in the centre of the kraal.

Some time after 9 o'clock, I heard unfamiliar voices whispering on the other side of the hut. I knew that the terrorist gang had arrived. I slowly released the safety catch on my AK and curled my finger gently around the trigger keeping the barrel pointed in the direction of the voices. I might not have been sure what my role was to be, but if shooting started, I wouldn't be found wanting.

A short while later I heard the sound of voices raised in anger. It didn't sound very promising and I kept my finger lightly curled around the trigger of my AK. I was beginning to wonder whether I should sneak off into the night when from around the side of the kraal appeared Moses followed by a gang of four very scruffy-looking terrorists. One of them, who obviously was the leader, had a bushy black beard and unkempt hair that might once have been an attempt at an afro-cut. Right now it looked like a tangled jesse bush on top of his head. His face was a mass of suppurating sores and I wondered if this might have been the result of a lack of personal hygiene. They stood in front of me arguing for a while with their weapons held loosely by their side. I figured that whatever had given rise to the argument couldn't be too serious or they would have their weapons at the ready. Before long they were called back to the centre of the kraal by the headman who had apparently produced a large gourd of beer.

It wasn't long before the sounds of singing and clapping indicated that whatever the altercation between Moses and the terrorist gang had been about, it must had been resolved. I cautiously peeked around the side of the hut. Logs had been thrown on to the fire and I watched motionless from the silence of the shadows as the two groups sat around the dancing flames singing revolutionary songs and drinking large quantities of native beer from a communal gourd.

I returned cautiously to my bench behind the hut and was beginning to wonder when the party might end, when from around the corner of the kraal lurched Blackbeard himself. He had obviously consumed a beer more than the limited capacity his brain could contend with. He stumbled toward me in the company of an equally unstable-looking native girl whom he kept calling 'Raspberry'. Either her mother must have been imbued with a keen sense of humor at the time of her christening, or Blackbeard was more of a romantic than I was giving him credit for. She looked more like a pear than a raspberry. After pausing unsteadily in front of me, they fell into some bushes directly opposite where I sat. What followed was not a sight I cared to behold or remember.

After completing his business with the woman, Blackbeard staggered to his feet and lurched toward me. He wasn't a pretty sight. His shirt was hanging out of his trousers which were undone at the waist and his penis was hanging from his open fly like a swollen Italian sausage in an advanced state of decay. Leaves had caught up in the thick mass of his hair giving it the appearance of an autumn potpourri arrangement. He certainly didn't look like the sort of person a girl might want to bring home for mother to meet.

He must suddenly have realized that he had left his AK on the ground next to his mistress, so he staggered back to retrieve it. As he bent down his trousers started to fall and he appeared to become confused as to what to do first … hold on to his trousers or retrieve his AK. Thankfully, modesty prevailed and he chose the former.

Blackbeard swayed before me as if trying to make up his mind who I really might be. The large quantity of beer he had imbibed wasn't helping his thought processes very much. He started talking loudly while at the same time pointing to where Raspberry still lay sprawled on the ground advertising more flesh than I dared look at. I remained impassive, sitting with my back to the wall, head down. This seemed to annoy Blackbeard and he became angry. I thought I might have to shoot him. I wondered what he might have done had he realized he was talking to a white Rhodesian Army officer. I slowly, very slowly, pointed my AK in Blackbeard's direction with my finger tightening around the trigger.

Luckily for Blackbeard, Moses sprang into action just in time to prevent his untimely death. He started reasoning with the terrorist leader with the skill and panache of a seasoned negotiator. He pointed towards my crotch which made me extremely uncomfortable and I began to wonder if I had left my fly undone. If I had I was pretty certain I hadn't bothered to apply any skin dye down there! I didn't dare look. Eventually after a burp and a loud burst of flatulence, Blackbeard seemed to calm down and staggered back to rejoin his gang, muttering under his breath. He had apparently forgotten about the luckless Raspberry, who remained sprawled in the bushes before me. Thankfully, it wasn't too long before the terrorist gang left and I was able to extricate myself from a situation in which I felt distinctly uncomfortable. Shortly after, I was able to rejoin Moses and the rest of his team.

"What on earth was all that about?" I asked, when we were safely out of hearing distance of the village.

"First, the terrorist leader wanted to take you back to Mozambique," replied Moses, laughing quietly to himself. "He said it was pointless for you to remain behind if you were deaf and dumb. Then he became angry that you rejected his offer to go with the woman. I told him that you had your testicles shot away in a contact with the Security Forces and that they should have pity on you."

Soon after the incident we left the area. Our pseudo-group had gleaned valuable information from Blackbeard about the location of a number of other terrorist gangs south of our location. Moses and his team would have to return to the barracks to be debriefed so that other pseudo-groups could be deployed into those areas. Our team would have an opportunity to get some R&R before returning to the same area to meet Blackbeard and his gang on their return from Mozambique. This time a Fire-Force of the RLI would be waiting for them. They would be very happy to meet Blackbeard and would show him little mercy.

I hoped that they might be a little more lenient towards Raspberry.

❧

The first Regimental duty I performed on my return to Inkomo Barracks wasn't particularly glamorous, nor was it particularly successful. I was called

Lt Col Ron Reid-Daly. (Phee Fletcher)

into Major Reid-Daly's office shortly after my return from the bush.

"Tim, as you know one of our chaps was killed two days ago. He's to be buried here on the base. I want you and Sergeant-Major Bruce Antonowitz to supervise the burial arrangements."

The Selous Scouts had consecrated a parcel of ground within the barracks to bury its fallen African soldiers. It had become extremely dangerous to bury them in their rural villages. On more than one occasion, terrorists had attacked Security Force funerals in remote areas, indiscriminately killing both family and mourners alike.

If a Selous Scout was as different and unpredictable as the batting crease at the Rawalpindi Cricket Club, Sergeant-Major Bruce Antonowitz was one of its most flamboyant batsmen. He was a tall and lean, dark-complexioned individual who always seemed to know a better way of doing things than the Army way. For this reason he was ideally suited to being a Scout. Some time previously he had requisitioned an Army Land Rover to use as his personal runabout within the barracks. When told that one wasn't available, he had taken umbrage and acquired an old horse to carry him to and fro. Thereafter, he refused to travel on any form of motorized transport contending that his old nag was more reliable. "It doesn't use oil and petrol and farts less!"

Selous Scouts pseudo-team with their command element. (Dennis Croukamp)

I found the Sergeant-Major lurking near the Quartermaster Stores with his horse.

"Bruce, I'm afraid that you and I have to make the funeral arrangements for Corporal Ndweni. The funeral is in two days."

He didn't blink an eye at my troubling news, as though he might be an old hand at arranging funerals.

"The first thing we have to do is dig a grave," he said, as a matter of fact.

I hadn't thought of this very important detail. Neither could I recall ever having been taught on my officers' course what dimensions a grave should be. All I remembered being taught was how to calculate the size of a latrine pit based upon a given number of men making two calls of nature per day.

"Is there an Army Manual we could consult about the dimensions of a grave?" I asked hopefully. There seemed to be a manual for everything in the Army. There was even an Aide Memoire on *Personal Hygiene in the Bush*. It had been written by an Army doctor who had never been into the bush. The need to "wash one's hands with soap and warm running water before eating" was apparently vital for one's chances of survival in the bush … never mind terrorist bullets. I had never heard of anybody carrying soap into the bush, nor had I ever come across any warm running water.

"Sir, the first thing you must learn in the Army is never to do anything the

Army way," replied Bruce airily. "We'll just keep digging till we think it's large enough."

The next day the Sergeant-Major grandly announced that the grave had been completed. "You might want to check it yourself to make sure you are happy with it, Sir. You're the guy who is ultimately in charge."

Feeling rather important, I walked towards the grave site not really knowing what I was supposed to be checking. It didn't look quite as large as I had imagined and I wondered if perhaps I shouldn't jump in and try it out for size. But I was a bit worried that I might not be able to climb out again, so decided against the idea.

On the day of the funeral the burial party duly formed up at the freshly-dug gravesite. Major Reid-Daly stood at the head of the open grave, the Regimental Sergeant-Major stood next to the coffin to supervise its lowering into the ground, and the family of the deceased soldier and mourners stood in a group on the opposite side. The Guard of Honour was formed up nearby. On the command from Major Reid-Daly everybody gave a snappy salute, the Guard of Honour presented arms and the Regimental Sergeant-Major ordered the coffin lowered into the ground.

I heaved a sigh of relief as I watched the casket slowly disappear below the surface. Then came a pause for concern as halfway down it became stuck. It wouldn't move. The intrepid RSM started prodding at it with his pace stick. It still wouldn't budge. Everyone held their breath wondering what to do. The RSM pushed a little harder with his pace stick and then gingerly placed a foot on the coffin trying to force it down. It still wouldn't budge. He pushed a little harder with his foot, whereupon the coffin suddenly freed itself, crashing to the bottom with the unfortunate RSM sprawled on top like a rag doll. There was a gasp of horror from the assembled crowd. Slowly … very slowly, the Sergeant-Major reappeared out of the grave, large white eyeballs contrasting vividly with his black face. Somebody at least had the forethought to rush to the bar to get the poor man a drink.

Later that morning I suggested to Bruce Antonowitz that he might want to revise his method of calculating the dimensions of a grave.

"It wasn't the dimensions that we got wrong," replied Bruce, with the authority of a Harvard professor. "I had them calculated correctly. It was the handles that did us in. You can't lower a coffin with the handles still attached into a grave situated any closer than six feet from a tree. The handles have a tendency to get caught on the protruding roots."

On a previous visit to Arlington Military Cemetery in Virginia, I had witnessed the burial of a soldier in a grave nestle peacefully under the shade of a beautiful large oak tree and hadn't noticed the handles having been removed.

I wondered what the Americans were aware of that might have escaped Bruce's attention.

Mechanized Raids

The Long Range Desert Group caused us more problems than any other unit of comparable size. The mechanized patrols of British, Rhodesian and New Zealand soldiers operating deep behind our lines tied up large numbers of our troops which could otherwise have been utilized in our desert offensives.
—Field Marshal Erwin Rommel: January, 1942

After my second bush trip, I was deployed on a number of external raids into Mozambique. I was rather happy about this as I was beginning to think that perhaps Moses was right. Perhaps I wasn't cut out to be a pseudo-terrorist after all. The Portuguese had recently capitulated in Mozambique and handed over power to FRELIMO, the Mozambique Liberation Movement. Yesterday's terrorists had become today's Mozambique Government soldiers.

Rhodesia already had a hostile neighbor on its northern border and now found itself with a hostile neighbor on its eastern border as well. FRELIMO was more than willing to provide sanctuary and sustenance to terrorists operating within Rhodesia, especially the Zimbabwe African National Liberation Army (ZANLA) which now found itself with a safe haven in Mozambique. It was time to show ZANLA that they were anything but safe in Mozambique … or anywhere else for that matter.

My first raid was to destroy a terrorist complex thirty miles inside Mozambique in what was called the Gaza Province. We found it on the banks of a large river confluence, and after a number of fierce skirmishes managed to destroy it. We hadn't realized that FRELIMO had placed an anti-aircraft gun position on a high ridge overlooking the complex to protect it from just such an attack. It was from the ridge that they opened fire on us with their 14.5 anti-aircraft gun, wounding two of my men. Two Hawker Hunter jets of the Rhodesian Air Force streaking in at mach 0.94 put an end to their shenanigans.

My second external operation was commanding a vehicle-borne raid some hundred miles into Mozambique. The raiding party consisted of twenty Selous Scouts driving in four recently-acquired German Unimog vehicles. Our aim was to pay the large FRELIMO base at Chigamane a visit, destroy their vehicles, blow up their fuel depot and render unserviceable any other military hardware we happened to come across. On our way back we would attack and destroy any ZANLA terrorist transit bases we came across. It was the first vehicle-borne raid ever to be mounted by the Rhodesian Security Forces into a neighboring country, and its success or failure would set the tone for similar operations to come.

The overall coordinator of the operation was Major 'Butch' Duncan, operating from a mobile command vehicle situated just inside the Rhodesian border. He was a meticulous and rather fastidious officer who, when planning an operation, would cover every probable contingency—and most improbable ones as well. If all General George Patton ever wanted to know was whether sufficient fuel would be available for his tanks at the end of each day, Major Duncan would want to know who was delivering it, what octane it was and how much it was going to cost.

Our Unimog vehicles were similar to those that had been used by the Portuguese in Mozambique and which were now being used by FRELIMO. We had stripped the vehicles down, removing back canopies, cab roofs and windscreens, so that machine guns could be mounted on to the front passenger dashboards. A further machine gun was mounted centrally on a tripod on the back. We painted the vehicles to look like those being used by FRELIMO and replaced the Rhodesian license plates with those that had previously been used by the Portuguese. Then we blackened our exposed skin, donned FRELIMO uniforms and were ready to go.

We were to operate in a similar manner to those intrepid Rhodesians who had distinguished themselves serving with Major Bagnold's Long Range Desert Group in Libya during the Second World War. Just as they had set off through the desert in their Willy's Jeeps to cause havoc to Luftwaffe airfields behind German lines, we were about to do to FRELIMO and ZANLA deep inside Mozambique. Not that irregular African forces or guerillas could be compared by any stretch of the imagination to the disciplined soldiers of Rommel's Afrika Korps. But the concept was the same.

I was driving the lead vehicle. Sitting next to me behind his mounted machine gun was arguably the most frightening-looking individual I had ever set eyes on. He scared me; I could only imagine what he did to the enemy.

Selous Scouts pseudo-team. (Noel Robey)

Selous Scouts pig blown up in a landmine. (Dennis Croukamp)

Sergeant-Major Pete McNeilage was a short, powerfully-built Rhodesian with balding head, thick black beard and piercing black eyes. Had he been seen on the streets of Russia in the early 1900s, he might well have been mistaken for Rasputin. The protective eye goggles and black head scarf he wore gave him the appearance of an apparition from hell. He was scared of nothing and would quite happily have chased Satan through his own gates with his machine-gun blazing.

We set off early in the evening, crossing the Rhodesian/ Mozambique border and making our way on to the Mozambique road system for the hundred-mile trip inland to the FRELIMO garrison at Chigamane. Because we planned to return along the same route as we had entered, I decided not to cause any major chaos during the drive in. We would drive the hundred miles to Chigamane, destroy the FRELIMO base there, then retrace our route back paying social visits to any terrorist bases we had passed on the way in.

As it happened, the entire raid was relatively uneventful. Having destroyed the garrison at Chigamane, we returned slowly along the road meeting little resistance. Everyone had fled into the bush at the first sign of firing. This didn't make Sergeant-Major McNeilage very happy. He was all for abandoning our initial mission and driving straight through to the main Mozambiquean port

Selous Scouts column refuelling before launching attack
in Mozambique. (Dennis Croukamp)

Selous Scouts operator. (Dennis Croukamp)

city of Beira. Not happy with a visit to FRELIMO's backyard, he wanted to drive into their front yard too and while we were at it, into the neighboring yards as well.

"We may as well make this a worthwhile trip and take out the whole FRELIMO High Command while we're already halfway to Beira," muttered Pete into his beard. "I've only fired three belts of ammunition. It's pointless taking all this ammo back to Rhodesia."

"What do you have in mind, Pete—shooting up the FRELIMO High Command in Beira then driving through Tanzania to take out the Morogoro terrorist training facility before returning through Zambia and destroying their army as well?" I chided.

"Sounds like a plan to me," grunted Pete. "We have enough ammunition and we could commandeer some fuel along the way."

Had I asked Pete to drive his Unimog north through Africa to lay siege to the Egyptian pyramids, he would merely have replied, "Just show me the way, Sir." As it was, I placated him by allowing him to lay some TM-46 Russian anti-tank landmines behind us to dissuade FRELIMO from using the road to deploy ZANLA terrorists being infiltrated into Rhodesia.

Sergeant Major Peter McNeilage, SCR. (Selous Scouts Association, c/o Tom Thomas)

Pete McNeilage. (Selous Scouts Association, c/o Tom Thomas)

We arrived back at the border just as the sun was coming up. Although the raid had been uneventful, it showed the ease and usefulness of being able to drive armed mechanized columns deep into hostile countries to disrupt lines of communication and destroy terrorist facilities.

I was unaware at the time that I was soon to take part in a much bigger and bolder raid into Mozambique.

13

Passage of Fire

"Are you taking part in the Mapai raid?"
"Yes."
"What's your role?" "I'm riding a bicycle." *"A what?"*
"A bicycle."
"Where?"
"Along the railway tracks." *"Are you mad?"*
"Probably!"

—Conversation between the author
and Lt. Ian Gillespie, Selous Scouts
Officers' Mess: June 1976

After a short stint of R&R, I was called into the Selous Scouts Operations Room by Ron Reid-Daly who had recently been promoted to the rank of Lieutenant Colonel. Surprisingly enough, I had just been promoted to Captain in spite of several skirmishes with the Military Disciplinary Code. Shortly before leaving the Rhodesian Light Infantry, I had hurled a bottle of beer at a friend of mine while attending a function at the Army Headquarters Mess. It was a farewell party for General Keith Coster, the General Officer Commanding the Army, who was leaving on retirement. The bottle had missed my friend and hit a gruff old Colonel squarely on his forehead. It was deemed to be 'conduct unbecoming an Officer and a Gentleman' and I was given a serious reprimand. I might have been cashiered from the Army had the old Colonel not come unexpectedly to my defense. "Best damn party this stuffy Mess has ever seen," he stated at my disciplinary hearing.

Gathered in the Operations Room was a team of some of the finest operators in the Regiment. We were briefed that we were to take part in a vehicle-borne raid on a town called Mapai, about 120 miles inside Mozambique. It was a large transit and supply base for approximately a hundred ZANLA terrorists. In addition, there was a company of Mozambique FRELIMO soldiers in residence. Our vehicle column would comprise fifty-eight officers and men travelling in four Unimog vehicles similar to the ones used during my recent incursion into Mozambique. Fifty-eight Rhodesian soldiers against a combined force of two hundred FRELIMO and ZANLA were certainly odds well within our favor. I was trying to decide whether two Second World War scout cars which Colonel Reid-Daly said would accompany us for added firepower would help or hinder our chances of success, when he fixed me with his steely eyes.

"And you, Junior, will lead a reconnaissance team in prior to the raid. But don't think you're getting out of a good fight. On completion of your reconnaissance you'll link up with the column so you can take part in the assault."

I was about to inform the Colonel that reconnaissance wasn't really my speciality when he continued.

"There's a railway line travelling from the border almost directly into the town of Mapai. You and Sergeant-Major Piet van der Riet, together with two handpicked men of your choice, will deploy into the area on a specially-designed quadcycle that our workshops have designed to travel along the railway line. That way you won't leave any tracks to compromise your presence."

I had no idea what a 'quadcycle' was but it sounded uncomfortably like a bicycle. I had been singularly inept at riding bicycles in my youth and had fallen and hurt myself more times than I cared to remember. I didn't think my skills would have improved with age.

"I don't think I know what a quadcycle is, Sir?" I said, feeling rather foolish.

"Don't jump ahead of me, Junior. I'm about to tell you."

Col. Reid-Daly went on to explain that it was two tandem bicycles secured side-by-side at precisely the same distance apart as the tracks of a railway line. This would enable the contraption to be pedaled along the railway lines. The two tandems were secured together with metal struts, with the handlebars of each locked in place as steering was not required. Small guide wheels projecting down from the wheel supports of both tandems would run against the inside of each track to keep the tyres firmly on the railway lines.

"The British Army used them to patrol the railway lines during the Boer War. It prevented the Boers from being able to blow up the tracks. All your kit and equipment can be placed on a platform rigged between the two tandems. If each man pedals hard enough, a speed of thirty miles an hour can be maintained."

It all sounded rather romantic, but I was aghast at having to fall back to a level of technology that had been developed by the British over a hundred years before.

"Why don't we just parachute in and be done with it?" If I had to go on a reconnaissance mission, I would prefer not to do it on a bicycle.

"Because, Junior, there's a secondary FRELIMO base situated halfway along the route to Mapai and I want you to reconnoiter that base before you continue on to the main target. The column will be attacking it on its return from Mapai."

"How many FRELIMO are in the secondary base?" It was beginning to sound more interesting by the minute.

"About a hundred or so."

It was beginning to look like we would definitely have a fight on our hands.

૯ಾ

Three weeks later, the column together with my reconnaissance team positioned at a railroad siding just inside the Rhodesian border. The commander of the operation was Major 'Butch' Duncan, the officer who had commanded the first external raid I had been on. Unlike the previous raid, he would accompany the column into Mozambique as the ground commander. While the men making up the column busied themselves preparing for the raid, my team conducted final rehearsals for the reconnaissance. We were all to go dressed as ZANLA terrorists; our pseudo-uniforms had to be checked, the captured terrorist weapons we were using cleaned and the lengthy process started of dying our skin black.

Two days after we arrived at the siding the four of us slipped out of the base under cover of darkness to begin our task. The quadcycle had been broken down into four manageable pieces so we could easily manhandle it through the thick bush. We crossed the border into Mozambique without mishap and arrived at their side of the railway line just before midnight. There we quickly set about re-assembling the quadcycle. Every now and then a FRELIMO vehicle would drive down a dirt road that ran parallel with the tracks causing us to scramble into the bush for cover. We had almost completed the assembly when we were interrupted by a FRELIMO foot patrol that came plodding down the road. We had no time to move off the tracks so lay motionless where we were. We each carried a silenced sub-machine gun and had we been seen we would probably have been able to take out the patrol without compromising ourselves. By the time their bodies were found the following day we would be many miles away. Luckily for the patrol they continued along their way without seeing us and we were able to continue our task. Eventually we were ready. We mounted the quadcycle and set off like intrepid cavalrymen into the night.

We were just beginning to pick up speed when the machine came to a sudden, jarring halt. Piet and I riding in the front were sent tumbling over the handlebars like two clowns from a Cossack Circus. Behind us lay the mangled remains of the quadcycle. We had failed to notice in the dark that some of the cast iron bolts attaching the tracks to the wooden sleepers had come loose and were protruding almost as high as the tracks themselves. This had resulted in the small guide wheels being ripped off the wheel supports of the quadcycle. With nothing to keep the tyres on the tracks, the machine had spread-eagled like a novice skater on an ice rink. My luck on bicycles didn't seem to be improving. The shattered remains of the quadcycle looked incapable of travelling another inch, let alone the hundred and twenty miles we still had to travel.

"It's less use to us now than tits on a bull," said Piet, looking dejectedly at the ruined machine.

A closer inspection of the tracks also revealed that some of the wooden sleepers had been removed, probably stolen for a better purpose. This had caused the steel tracks to sink into the ballast. The Mozambique railway system had deteriorated to the extent that it could no longer handle an 80 lb. quadcycle, let alone a 180-ton diesel locomotive.

Tim Callow, Selous Scouts Reconnaissance expert. (Tim Callow)

Tim Callow on a reconnaissance. (Tim Callow)

Six hours later we arrived back at our base carrying the remains of the ill-fated contraption. It had been a great idea … undone by the state of disrepair of the Mozambique railways. The evening's endeavors wouldn't be remembered as one of the most successful Selous Scouts reconnaissance missions ever undertaken, and I doubted it would fall into the category of modern military endeavors.

I made a cup of tea and found a camp bed to fall into for a few hours' sleep. I was awakened two hours later by Major Duncan.

"Tim, it's important that we get some sort of confirmation on the intelligence we have on those two camps. What do you think about taking a 'snatch party' across the border and capturing a prisoner?"

"When?" I asked, rubbing the sleep from my eyes.

"Tonight," he responded, sounding surprised I would find it necessary to ask something so obvious.

That night I found myself once again crossing the border, this time with a larger body of men to capture a prisoner. With us was a tall, lean Sergeant-Major who had been in the Selous Scouts since its inception. Jannie Nel was a man of few words and quiet demeanor but he had an aura about him that commanded respect. His hair and beard were jet black and his skin had been burned the color of dark ochre.

Snatching a prisoner isn't like your average walk in the park. It isn't simply a matter of walking into a FRELIMO or ZANLA base camp, knocking on the front door and snatching the first person who pokes his head around the corner. It would be easier trying to catch an angry wildcat than a frightened man intent on avoiding capture. We decided to lay an ambush along the road which ran parallel to the railway tracks where we had seen so much traffic the night before. We planned to stop the first vehicle that came our way on the pretence that we were ZANLA terrorists wanting a ride. Once the vehicle came to a halt we would apprehend whoever happened to be inside, commandeer the vehicle and drive it back across the border together with our reluctant prisoners.

We hadn't been at the road very long when a Land Rover sped toward us, headlights probing through the black night. Jannie Nel stepped out into the road and brazenly waved the vehicle down. Piet van der Riet and I crouched in the shadow of some nearby bushes to give immediate assistance. The vehicle braked hard and its sole occupant began yelling out the driver's window, berating Jannie for having had the audacity to stop a senior ZANLA commander. I could only imagine his surprise when he found himself confronted not by a lowly terrorist cadre, but by a tall, bearded and very unfriendly-looking individual with distinctly Corsican features.

We had previously received radio intercepts from FRELIMO that they were expecting a delegation of Cuban officials to pay them a visit for discussions on military assistance. The driver might have been forgiven for thinking he had come across Fidel Castro waiting on the side of the road for a lift. His surprise must have turned to terror when his door was suddenly jerked open and he felt himself being unceremoniously yanked out of the Land Rover by his shirt collar with the barrel of an AK pressed firmly against his belly.

Our prisoner turned out to be more than we had bargained for.

He was Gabriel, the senior ZANLA Commander in the area, who was on his way to visit his local FRELIMO counterpart in the border town of Malvernia. I felt elated. Even better, once Gabriel became aware of his precarious situation, he started singing to us like a canary. He told us all we needed to know about the two base camps we intended attacking, plus a whole lot more. He even volunteered information about the FRELIMO base in Malvernia which he had been on his way to visit before being so rudely stopped. I had initially planned to deviate around the town, driving the captured Land Rover through the bush back to our base in Rhodesia. With Gabriel eagerly stammering out details of the FRELIMO base in Malvernia, Jannie and I looked at each other with the same thought ... this was an opportunity too good to miss. We decided to recce the base on our way back using Gabriel as a guide.

After detailing one of my men to drive the Land Rover, the rest of us bundled into the back, with Jannie and I sitting on either side of our still-stammering prisoner. We drove brazenly into Malvernia with Gabriel giving us a guided tour of the FRELIMO establishments including the residence of the local camp commander. However, there was one thing that Gabriel failed to tell us ... that he had no intention of accompanying us back to Rhodesia. We were almost in the town when he suddenly sprang from the Land Rover like a hare from a trampoline. He was running as his feet hit the ground. There is nobody who dislikes the horrors of war more than a soldier. Gabriel was aware of the fact that we were going to attack the combined FRELIMO and ZANLA base camp in Mapai. Being outnumbered, we were relying on stealth and surprise to deliver a knockout blow to the enemy. Had Gabriel managed to escape, we would have had to call off the operation or be prepared to suffer serious casualties.

With one well-aimed burst from his Kalashnikov rifle, Jannie Nel ensured that the raid could continue.

❧

Two nights later, on 25 June 1976, our column crossed the border headed southeast along a cutline, then turned due east along some power lines before intercepting the road that ran parallel to the railway line. There we regrouped and headed southeast toward Mapai. We were wearing an assortment of FRELIMO and ZANLA uniforms and carrying communist-made weapons.

I was travelling in the last Unimog with eight others including my old friend Bruce Fitzsimmons. Thirty miles down the road the column was stopped by a lone ZANLA sentry close to the secondary camp we intended attacking on our return. He was either a very plucky individual to be stopping a heavily-armed column or very stupid. Perhaps he thought we were a FRELIMO supply column. The sentry was joined by three others who materialized from the darkness. We couldn't risk a firefight as we were too close to the ZANLA camp and we would lose the element of surprise when attacking our primary target in Mapai.

I was carrying the only silenced sub-machine gun in the column. I received

A mechanized raid into Mozambique. (Dennis Croukamp)

a whispered message over my radio from Dale Collett, a fellow officer who was travelling in the column's lead vehicle.

"Tim, we need you up here with your silenced weapon to take care of these guys before the whole operation is compromised. They're becoming suspicious of who we are."

I jumped out of my Unimog and ran to the front of the column just as the four ZANLA terrorists were raising their automatic weapons in Dale's direction. Seeing me, the leader swung his AK toward me, barrel leveled towards my chest. I didn't feel inclined to wait and see how good his aim was. I squeezed the trigger of my silenced sub-machine gun and swung it round in a shallow arc killing three of the terrorists instantly. The fourth managed to turn and bolt into the darkness shouting at the top of his lungs. He sprang through the bushes like a startled gazelle with Dale lunging after him like a marauding lion. The shouting suddenly stopped and shortly after, Dale reappeared from out of the inky blackness carrying the unfortunate terrorist's AK. After a brief pause to make sure that we hadn't unsettled the FRELIMO base, the column resumed its journey.

Just before dawn we stopped to refuel the vehicles from a bowser we were towing and prepare our kit before the last few miles into Mapai. It was freezing cold and I donned two pairs of nylon tracksuit bottoms under my fatigues and exchanged my silenced sub-machine gun for a folding-butt AK. Each vehicle had been allocated a specific target in the town to attack, and at first light we roared into the town with each Unimog peeling off to its assigned task.

My target was a single-storey residence that was alleged to accommodate the senior ZANLA hierarchy in the town. At the appointed time I dismounted from the vehicle, arranged my squad into an assault formation and stormed the house. We smashed our way through a large plate glass window and were met by a burst of automatic fire from two ZANLA terrorists who had been sleeping in the well-appointed lounge. A brief firefight ensued during which the two terrorists were killed and a fine mahogany liquor cabinet standing in the corner of the lounge, damaged. Miraculously none of the numerous bottles of fine port and brandy, including a bottle of Bombay Sapphire gin, were damaged. Either the terrorist hierarchy had a penchant for fine wines or we had come knocking at the wrong door. We started making our way cautiously through the rest of the house which was beginning to look more and more like a single family dwelling. The only other occupants we came across were a young Portuguese couple crouching in the corner of the master bedroom. Clearly this was not the target we had thought it to be, though Sergeant Bruce Fitzsimons had different feelings.

"They're probably part of the Cuban delegation here to help FRELIMO," he growled, eyeing them suspiciously. "They must be pretty important having two gooks guarding them. If we don't cull them, let's bundle them on to the vehicle and take them prisoner."

"Well, the two gooks are now dead and these two certainly don't look like combatants; neither of them is armed. In fact, they looked frightened out of their lives so let's leave them alone."

I calmed the couple down as best I could, telling them that we had no intention of harming them and apologizing for the mess we had made of their home. They were shaking in fear so I pulled a blanket from their bed to cover them and suggested to Bruce that he fetch them a tumbler of brandy from the lounge to soothe their nerves. I had been considering repatriating the contents of the liquor cabinet back to Rhodesia where it would have made a welcome addition to the bar stocks of the Officers' Mess. The spoils of war are as synonymous to a soldier as corruption and graft to a politician. However, I didn't feel inclined to make the young Portuguese couple more uncomfortable than they already were by stealing their supply of expensive liquor. Much to the protestations of the rest, I decided to leave it behind. The couple would be

A mechanized raid into Mozambique. (Dennis Croukamp)

more in need of the liquor once this was all over than us … orsoI thought.

I was busy searching the house for anything of intelligence value when I received a message over the radio that Lieutenant Dale Collett had been badly wounded. I left the rest of my group to secure the house, told Bruce to follow me and sprinted down to where I knew Dale's target to be.

It was a large double-storey building in the centre of the town which might once have been a hall or a sporting arena during the days of the Portuguese rule. It comprised an enclosed area large enough for an indoor basketball court. At one end was an upper floor balcony accessible only from an external stairway. To the rear of the balcony, accessible from the same stairway, were a series of passages and offices. Intelligence reports had indicated the building was being used as an armory for weapons being infiltrated into Rhodesia from Mozambique.

Dale had run up the exterior staircase to investigate what was in the upper-level rooms. He had been moving cautiously along a passage when a burst of fire cut him down. He had managed to drag himself back along the passage and down the stairs using only his arms. We didn't realize at the time that Dale had been shot through his spinal cord and would never walk again. It was a terrible injury and a stunning loss not only to the operation, but to the unit as a whole.

I was furious. After Dale had been placed under the care of our medic, we fired volleys of rocket-propelled grenades through the open windows and door of the upper level in an effort to flush out whoever was inside. Nobody appeared. Telling Bruce Fitzsimmons and Jannie Nel to follow, I sprinted up the stairs. If whoever had injured Dale wasn't going to come out willingly we would go in and force them out. Inside the door was a ten-foot long passageway, at the end of which were additional passages leading left and right. Taking the passageway on the right, I was about to throw a grenade into the first room I came to when there was a loud burst of gunfire behind me. I turned and saw Jannie Nel wheel around and start staggering back along the passage. His back was a bloody mess of gunshot wounds. Bruce and I followed Jannie, firing long bursts of automatic fire down the corridor as we withdrew. As soon as Jannie got to the head of the staircase he collapsed, using his last remaining strength to drag himself down the stairs. He was dead as he reached the bottom, falling into the arms of his shocked comrades waiting below.

Emotion is never a good thing, especially in combat. It clouds one's ability to act rationally and inhibits a logical thought process. I was stunned. In a matter of moments two of our most experienced operators and two good friends of mine had been cut down. I noticed one of our open-backed Unimog trucks parked some hundred yards in front of the staircase. On the back stood an African Corporal who I recognized as being from Jannie Nel's troop. Corporal Burundu was standing stoically behind a medium machine-gun mounted on the back of the vehicle. I ran to where the vehicle was parked, lit a cigarette and handed it up to the Corporal. Then lit one for myself.

"Ishe?" Ishe was a term of respect used by Africans … almost of reverence. "Why don't you stand behind the gun and cover me while I run up those stairs into the building. I want to be the one to avenge Sergeant-Major Nel's death. He was like a father to me."

"No, Corporal Burundu, you're better with that machine-gun than I am. Let me be the one to avenge his death. You cover me as I go back inside the building."

I had barely finished talking when a camouflage-clad figure suddenly burst out the door at the top of the staircase, fire stammering from his AK-47. Corporal Burundu's machine-gun barked back instantaneously in response, cutting the terrorist down. He tumbled off the top landing and lay sprawled at the bottom of the stairs, dead.

"Cover me, Corporal Burundu, while I go and see if there's anyone else up there." I sucked hard at what remained of my cigarette, inhaled the smoke into my lungs and started running back toward the stairs.

I heard Corporal Burundu shouting behind me. "Ishe, be careful. I sense there is death still in that building."

Without a second thought I found myself bounding up the stairs for the second time that morning. Halfway up I realized the stupidity of my actions in not having someone follow to cover me. By then it was too late. My momentum had already carried me up the stairs and through the door. This time I decided to take the passageway on the left. It was from there that the firing had come that killed Jannie. I walked about ten paces down the passage and was cautiously approaching the first room on my right when I felt a searing pain in both my legs and at the same time heard the deafening sound of an automatic weapon being fired in a confined space at close range. My legs felt as though they were being pulled through a giant grinding machine. The burning smell of cordite assailed my nostrils. I staggered against the wall of the passage as another long burst of fire tore into my legs and I felt myself begin to buckle. Somehow I found the strength to stagger down the passage and into the room to my right. I half staggered and half fell across the room toward a bed positioned against a low wall at the far side. I collapsed on to it and lay still for a minute, listening for the sound of following footsteps. Thankfully, there was only a deathly silence after the cacophony of sound of a moment ago.

I quickly took stock of my situation. It wasn't looking particularly good. I had dropped my AK in the passageway as I stumbled away. Luckily I was carrying a Russian-made Tokarev pistol holstered on my belt. I unholstered it and cocked it. If whoever had shot me intended coming in to administer the *coup de grâce*, I would be ready. I was determined not to go alone.

I looked at my legs. The bullets had almost severed my right leg just below the knee. The two halves were attached only by pieces of skin and sinew. Jagged shards of smashed bone protruded from the tattered material of my fatigues. It looked as if somebody had removed the bottom part of my leg and tried to re-attach it backwards. I began to get morbidly amused by the fact that I seemed able to move my big toe and thought I must be hallucinating. My left leg had fared slightly better; all the skin, flesh and muscle had been shot away from the back of my knee together with a good portion of bone. I started to get a blinding headache. This worried me more than the pain in my legs. I have always hated headaches and found the pain extremely difficult to tolerate. I reached into my shirt pocket where I usually kept a supply of aspirin, but could find none. My girlfriend, Carol, had forgotten to send me away with some and I resolved to chastise her for her forgetfulness if I ever got out of this mess.

I became surprised at the bright color of the mattress I was lying on. Bright red was not a particularly clever color for a military base. Then I realized it was blood. It was spurting from the severed arteries in both my legs and I realized that if I was going to survive for much longer, I had better start doing something about trying to get myself rescued. I found a small notebook in my shirt pocket. Feverishly, I began scribbling a note to fling over the half wall I was lying against. Hopefully, somebody in the hall below might see it and realize that I was still alive.

"Upstairs behind the half wall. Both legs out of commission. Need help urgently." I was about to toss the note over the wall when I decided to add one last thing. "Got an excruciating headache—please hurry!" I wrapped the note around a bullet I extracted from my Tokarev magazine and tossed it over the wall.

I began to wonder how I could possibly have gotten to where I was lying, from where I had been shot. Effectively, I had no legs and I knew that even if my life depended on it, I could not move another yard. My thoughts were interrupted by something landing near my bed. It was a piece of paper wrapped around a stone and by a stroke of good luck, it landed within easy reach.

"We're holding a mattress up. Get over the wall and we'll catch you." It was signed by Sergeant-Major Piet van der Riet.

I didn't know where I was going to find the strength to heave myself off the bed, let alone over the half wall! As to how I was going to do it without leaving my right leg behind was another matter. Quickly I decided that saving my life was more important than saving my leg, so with my last reserves of strength I pulled myself on to the top of the half wall and pushed myself over. I felt myself plunging into space like a rag doll. I lost consciousness momentarily but came to immediately upon hitting the mattress. I looked up to see four of the grimiest-looking individuals I could ever recall seeing in my life. They were holding the mattress and smiling down at me, their whiskered faces blackened and streaked with blood and sweat.

"You guys certainly wouldn't win any beauty contests," I groaned through clenched teeth.

"And you look like you've just been pulled through the business end of an abattoir," replied one of the four who had caught me. He was our medic, Bruce Laing, arguably one of the finest medical NCOs in the Rhodesian Army.

"Is my right leg still attached?" I asked.

"Only just, though I'm not sure how," replied Bruce. "It must have been reluctant to remain behind, so it followed you over the wall like a loyal dog."

It was not unusual for our Army medics to perform functions in the field that under normal circumstances would be executed only by experienced surgeons. Bruce took one look at my legs and gave me his considered prognosis.

"Your right leg will have to be amputated below the knee and your left leg will have to have extensive reconstructive surgery. If you want, I can chop the right one off now and be done with it?"

"Leave it on for the time being, Doc. I've grown quite attached to it over the past twenty seven-years."

"OK. I'll patch you up as best I can and let the surgeons at the hospital make the call. The good news is that if I get to work on you now and fill you up with some saline fluid, there's a chance you might survive. There's a chopper on its way to uplift you, Dale and Jannie. It should be here in the next thirty minutes."

With that I was carried outside to a shady and more secure spot on the side of the building and lowered gently to the ground. Bruce Laing rolled up his sleeves, administered a couple of ampoules of morphine and got to work stabilizing my injuries. I later learned from surgeons in Salisbury that it was only through his exceptional treatment that my right leg was eventually saved from immediate amputation.

I began to get concerned a few minutes later when I heard someone talking urgently on the radio to the pilot of the approaching helicopter. "How far out are you?" Whoever was talking was standing just outside my field of vision.

"About twenty minutes from your location," came the flat, hollow response from the pilot. "How many casualties can I expect?"

"Two critically wounded and one KIA." There was a slight pause and the voice added, "If you don't hurry-up it will be one critically wounded and two KIA."

My concern deepened when I saw the familiar figure of Bruce Fitzsimmons looming over my mattress. He looked pale and gaunt even through the dark mask of his camouflage. His face was streaked with grime, sweat and blood. He appeared to be on the verge of exhaustion.

"Mr. Bax, we've been through a lot together, good times and bad. I'm going to miss you." He spoke gruffly trying to hide his emotion. "I've got to go and ambush the road leading into the town. Is there anything I can do for you before I go?" He spoke with an air of finality, as though not expecting to see me again.

"Bruce, the house we attacked this morning, the one with the liquor cabinet?" I croaked in a whisper. "Would you run up there quickly and ask the Portuguese lady if she would spare me a nip of her Bombay gin?"

If I was going to die on the way home, a sip of gin would at least add some ceremony to the austere occasion. It seemed like a civilized thing to do.

"I'll be right back." Bruce abruptly turned and walked quickly up the rise toward the house.

He returned a short while later just as I began to hear the first, faint sounds of a helicopter approaching. In his hand was a porcelain cup he must have found. He knelt down next to me, gently lifting my head in his right arm and poured a long sip of gin down my parched throat. It burned, but it tasted good … it tasted *very* good.

Then I lost consciousness.

14

Matriarchic Matron

"Who assisted you out of the passage?"
"Nobody."
"But that would have been impossible with your wounds!"
"Then perhaps I was assisted."
"By whom?"
"I don't know!"

—Mr. Nangle, Orthopedic Surgeon,
talking with the author, Andrew Fleming Hospital: July, 1976

Shirley Tucker was the Senior Matron and self-appointed matriarch of the Andrew Fleming Hospital in Salisbury. Her authority extended to nursing staff and physicians alike. She presided over them like a puritanical stage manager overseeing a cast of freewheeling actors in a stage production of *No Sex, Please ... We're British*. It was a brave surgeon who would act against her will. She also happened to be the aunt of my girlfriend, Carol, and by a stroke of good fortune she was on duty the day I was rushed into the operating theatre.

After being helicoptered out of Mapai to the nearest military airfield in Rhodesia, Dale and I had been loaded into a fixed-wing aircraft for the flight back to Salisbury. It was an uneventful flight except for the pale young English doctor who accompanied us. He threw up at the sight of my mangled legs. He had recently arrived from England hoping to utilize his talents in the peaceful, if not always tranquil, atmosphere of a local city hospital. He hadn't been very happy when the Army called him up to do duty at a forward military field hospital. War wounds were not his speciality. I wished that I had asked Bruce Fitzsimmons for the entire bottle of gin before leaving Mapai. After treating my legs in the airplane, the doctor looked badly in need of a drink.

On landing in Salisbury we were met at the airport by a military ambulance and rushed to Andrew Fleming Hospital in the company of a noisy police escort. I was immediately taken into an emergency operating room where a surgeon was already waiting. Mr. Nangle was Rhodesia's leading orthopedic surgeon. He made the decision to amputate my leg at just about the same time

Matron Shirley Tucker recognized who I was through the dirt and grime of my camouflage. She was aware that Carol and I planned to get engaged soon and that Carol had been authorized to make medical decisions on my behalf in the event of my being incapacitated.

"I'm going to amputate just below the right knee," announced the surgeon, with the casual demeanor of a butcher about to chop the leg off a sheep's carcass.

"No, you're not. Not before I phone my niece for permission," replied the Matron firmly.

"Your niece, what's she got to do with it?" inquired the surgeon, not too happy with the turn of events.

"I know this patient; he and my niece are to be engaged soon. I'm not going to be a party to you lopping off his leg without getting her permission. She has authorization to make medical decisions on his behalf."

"Well, you better hurry up," responded the surgeon irritably. "I'm not going to stand around here and wait all day for your niece to make up her mind on what is essentially a foregone medical conclusion."

Five minutes later Shirley Tucker strode back into the theatre. "My niece is adamant. No amputation until a second opinion is obtained."

"We don't have time for a second opinion and if you want the leg saved it's not me you should be talking to but a magician."

"I must insist that you make every endeavor to save his leg, Mr. Nangle." The Matron was adamant.

The surgeon sighed. "OK, but I must warn you, it's a long shot." It's a credit to the doctor's work, to Matron Shirley Tucker and to Carol's insistence that my leg not be amputated that a few years later I was chosen to be a member of the Selous Scouts' soccer team.

We were playing against an African schoolboys' side. It was with *that* leg I scored the winning goal.

Shortly after the operation to save my right leg, I underwent reconstructive surgery to my left leg. I woke up from the operation to find myself in a ward lying next to a Colonel who I recognized as being from Army Headquarters. His name was Colonel Stokes and I wondered whether he was in the ward as a patient or whether he had been sent specifically to keep an eye on me. I tried to sit up and make polite conversation with him but found myself being severely chastised.

"You can't sit up. You must lie down."

"Why?" I responded groggily, trying to hoist myself into a sitting position. "You're still listed as critical." "What does that mean?"

"It means you might die at any moment so lie down and behave yourself!" replied the Colonel with the authority of someone who had recently graduated from the Royal College of Surgeons.

"Well, I don't feel very critical."

"How *you* feel isn't important. It's how the doctors *think* you should feel that's important. Apparently, they think you should not be feeling very well."

Just then an attractive nurse walked briskly into the ward. I learned later that she was the sister of the tracker I had been deployed with on my first operational tour with the Rhodesian Light Infantry.

"What are you doing sitting up like that?" she fussed, easing me on to my back. "You must remain flat on your back without moving."

"Well, nobody told me that and besides, I feel perfectly all right, thank you very much."

"You've just had an operation to remove part of your thigh which has been grafted behind your knee. You'll have to remain flat on your back for at least three weeks." She started clucking over me like a mother hen over a recalcitrant chick. "Don't even think about wandering out of my sight for the next few weeks." I didn't feel capable of wandering out of anyone's sight, least of all this attractive nurse's.

It was during one of the many visits by Mr. Nangle to check on my progress that he questioned me on how I had managed to get from the upstairs passage in which I had been shot into a side room and on to a bed lying against a far wall. He remained adamant that with the wounds I had sustained, I could not have done so on my own.

"At the outside," he said, "I might be inclined to accept that you managed to crawl away, but even that is highly improbable given your condition. You must have been assisted by somebody." I knew perfectly well that I hadn't been assisted by anyone, so we left the matter unresolved.

The answer came to me many years later after I had moved to the United States with the kind assistance of my sister, Shelagh, a successful homebuilder in Florida. I was living in a small town called Lake Placid and had become friendly with an American called Mark Fortier who owned a small business in the town. Tragically, Mark's young son, Todd, was killed in a vehicle accident shortly after I arrived and I was privileged to attend the service held in celebration of the young man's full and bountiful life. Todd held the

Colonel MacIntyre and Ian Smith. (Jacqui Kirrane)

distinction of becoming one of the youngest Americans ever to qualify as an Eagle Scout. The service was one of the most moving I had ever attended and left an indelible impression upon me. It was as a result of that service that I resolved to join a church of my own Anglican faith, and shortly thereafter became a member of the St. Francis of Assisi Anglican/Episcopal Church in Lake Placid.

One Easter the Rector, Reverend Elizabeth Myers, asked if I would take part in an Easter Vigil. I found myself sitting alone inside the peaceful tranquility of the church at midnight on Good Friday. It was cold and dark, the only light coming from a flickering candle set in one corner of the nave. The altar had been stripped of all linens. Only a crown of thorns lay on its stark, bare surface. The tabernacle had been emptied and lay open, with the sacrament laid to rest on a small 'table of repose' to one side of the communion rail. It was discreetly covered with a white purificator. On the floor in front of the chancel lay a life-sized cross hewn from rough timbers. Not a breath of air moved. The silence was as deep as it was moving.

I had never previously thought back to the events in Mapai, choosing to erase them forever from my mind. But in the peace and solitude of that church on the night of Good Friday, what happened on 26 June 1976 replayed in my mind with a clarity and detail that was so stark, so real, that I could almost smell the cordite; almost feel the bullets tearing into my flesh and smashing my bones. It was as if I was re-living the incident in slow motion replay. I shivered. Then I realized … it was all so vivid, so clear. Mr. Nangle had been right all along. I had indeed been assisted by a strong, helping hand as I stumbled down that passage of infamy. I wished the good doctor was still alive for me to unravel the mystery for him.

The Mess

"What's on the luncheon menu?" "Oxtail, Sir."
"Oxtail!"
"Yes, Sir, oxtail. Served with a rich burgundy sauce, Sir."
"The whole bloody ox to choose from and you have to serve us the tail?"
—Major Duncan talking with the
Officers' Mess caterer, Selous Scouts: 1978

After my release from the hospital, and an extensive period of recuperation at home, I returned to work at the Selous Scouts Headquarters at Inkomo Barracks just outside Salisbury. The unit had moved out of its secluded galvanized-iron camp into a modern new facility adjacent to an existing airfield. The new barracks was named after Sergeant Andre Rabie, one of the unit's original pseudo-operators who had been tragically killed by a patrol of Rhodesia Light Infantry in a dreadful case of mistaken identity. Sergeant Rabie had been leading a team of pseudo-terrorists trying to make contact with a gang of real terrorists when his group was spotted by the RLI patrol. Thinking that Sergeant Rabie's group was a real gang of terrorists, the RLI patrol fired on the group. In the ensuing firefight, Sergeant Rabie was killed. At the time of its completion, the Andre Rabie Barracks was the most modern military facility in Africa.

I was delighted to learn that my old friend, Superintendent Ron Dick, had been recruited into the Selous Scouts during my absence. He was the kindly old gentleman who had given George Thorley and me a lift from the Round Bar in the Le Coq d'Or when I was a trooper in the RLI. He had retired from the British South Africa Police and had been enjoying semi-retirement as Chief of Security at the Andrew Fleming when Col. Reid-Daly approached him to join the Selous Scouts to be commander of the unit's Base Group. 'Major' Dick as he became known, was a thorough gentleman with impeccable manners whose presence presiding over the Regimental Headquarters added a sense of 'dignified decorum' to the otherwise unconventional unit.

"I'd like you to smooth some of the rough edges off these helter-skelter young officers when they return from the bush and instill in them a sense of propriety and deportment … if that's at all possible," said Colonel Reid-Daly, enjoying a drink with his newly-acquired Base Group Commander in the solitude of the Officers' Mess.

At that moment in walked a well-known operator in the unit, Major Neil Kriel, who had just returned from a long bush deployment. His dirty hair was long and shaggy and he sported a long, matted black beard. It was difficult to determine where his hair ended and his beard began. On his feet he wore a pair of homemade rubber sandals cut from an old car tyre. Exceptionally long hands that seemed to extend past his thighs gave him the rather absurd appearance of an orang-utan. The Rhodesian press had interviewed him once and dubbed him the 'walking armpit'.

"I think that's going to be easier said than done," replied Major Dick, rubbing a finger through his impeccably-manicured moustache. He was watching in mild amusement as Neil slouched over the bar threatening grievous bodily harm to the barman if he didn't immediately produce a cold beer.

Ron Dick took to his new appointment like a keen master to a prestigious boys' college. Although married with a home in Salisbury, he chose to reside in a house made available to him directly across from the Officers' Mess. The Mess was his pride and joy and he presided over it as if it was an exclusive gentlemen's club. This was often at odds with the younger officers who preferred to treat the Mess as a venue for uninhibited, freewheeling parties to whom anyone, especially ladies, could be invited.

One Saturday afternoon a group of us had remained in the bar drinking gin slings after lunch. A wall at the far end of the bar was festooned with Regimental plaques that had been presented to the unit from time to time by visiting military dignitaries. Prominent in the center was an Army Headquarters plaque. Army Headquarters was not our favorite establishment. Placing a large ice bucket at the opposite end of the bar from where the plaques were hanging, we decided to have a competition to see who could dislodge the offending plaque with a well-aimed ice cube. The gin slings we had been consuming must have had a detrimental effect on our aim. Almost an hour later in spite of our best endeavors, every plaque had been dislodged from the wall with the exception of the one we were aiming for.

Into this arena of hooliganism walked Major Dick. He looked aghast at the clutter of plaques and ice strewn about the floor of his beloved Mess, and at the chipped plaster on the wall. It was beginning to look as if it had been used for shotgun practice. Greater than his anger at our behavior was his shame at the standard of our aim.

"If we have to rely on you chaps to win the war we are in mortal danger! Sometimes it takes an old soldier to teach a young Turk new tricks."

With that the Major picked up a large ice cube, took careful aim and hurled it at the Army Headquarters plaque. At that precise moment, into the bar walked the Commanding Officer, Lieutenant Colonel Reid-Daly. The ice cube struck the plaque squarely in the middle dislodging it from the wall and leaving another large gouge in the plaster.

"I guess that wins me the competition," glowed the old Major proudly.

"Ron, it's lucky I saw you hit that plaque. It's the only thing that would lead me to believe that you haven't been drinking with these young hooligans all afternoon. I think they need to spend a day or two on the range to improve their aim." With that, Lieutenant Colonel Reid-Daly turned to the rest of us with a stern eye.

"Chaps, some high jinks among young officers in the Regiment are a good thing. It builds spirit and is good for the *esprit de corps* of the Regiment. But you know the rules on causing damage in the Mess. That wall will be re-plastered and painted by the time the bar opens this evening, with the plaques re-hung—including the Army Headquarters plaque." He turned to leave, then paused.

"Ron," he said, turning to Major Dick. "I'd like you to arrange with the Regimental Sergeant-Major to take these young officers to the rifle range tomorrow. It seems they could all sharpen up on their shooting skills a little."

છે

Not long after the incident with the ice cubes, it was decided to hold a formal 'Dining-In' night in the Officers' Mess. The Regiment's reputation, both inside Rhodesia and abroad, as one of the world's most effective counter-insurgency forces was hardly in dispute. However, we had begun to acquire a rather unsavory reputation for being wild and unruly; undisciplined fighters who lived in the bush eating rats and baboons as we mercilessly hunted down the enemy. We needed to show that while we were best adapted to life in the bush, we were as capable of organizing a formal dinner evening as any other unit in the Army, and with just as much pomp and ceremony. However, unlike the rest of the Army whose kitchen staff and waiters were drawn from qualified personnel from the Army Services Corps, the Selous Scouts employed a motley combination of locally-recruited Africans and captured terrorists to run its various Messes. Trying to teach a former terrorist how to become a suave waiter in a Regimental Officers' Mess was not without its problems, especially a former terrorist whose culinary skills and dining etiquette had hitherto been restricted to sitting under a tree eating sadza with his fingers. It was an unenviable task that fell squarely on the shoulders of a somewhat reluctant Major Ron Dick.

In the Officers' Mess dining room there were two swinging doors, one at either end of the wall that separated the dining room from the kitchen. The problem was that the doors swung both ways. To avoid the potential for accidents, one door was designated for *entering* the kitchen and the other for *leaving*. It seemed like a simple enough solution, but not to the unsophisticated African. To their uncluttered and uncomplicated minds, a door was a door. If the Europeans wanted to complicate matters by putting two doors in the same room serving the same function, that was fine. It just meant more doors to

Neil Kriel, Ron Dick and Jerry Strong in the Selous Scouts Officers' Mess. (Phee Fletcher)

Ron Reid-Daly and his wife Jean with Philippa Fletcher. (Phee Fletcher)

move in and out of in either direction.

The Dining-In night began relatively smoothly with only a few minor mishaps. One happened earlier in the evening: there was a loud scream of indignation from a lady dignitary who was attending to a call of nature when into the stall she was occupying walked a bearded officer unzipping his fly. Somebody had neglected to inform him that the men's room had been temporarily taken over as a lady's powder room!

After aperitifs in the bar, dinner guests were shown to the anteroom for a customary glass of sherry before dinner. Upon an announcement being made by the President of the Mess Committee, guests were escorted to their assigned seats in the elaborately-set dining room. They bowed their heads reverently as the Regimental Chaplain said grace, and then sat in expectation of the first course to be served. That's when the *real* trouble began.

The serving of the first course, an elegant *Velouté aux Artichaux et aux 'Epinards,* had almost been completed when there was a loud clatter from the kitchen, followed instantly by the sounds of china plates smashing on the floor. A waiter hurrying out of the dining room had thrown the door open against a waiter hurrying in carrying a tray laden with soup. There was a startled silence broken by a sudden burst of profanity from inside the kitchen as the African waiters started blaming each other for the accident. In African culture, the person who is the most vocal in an argument is deemed to have won the day. Finally the clamor subsided and we waited expectantly for the remaining bowls of soup to arrive. Instead, a sullen-looking waiter emerged from the kitchen empty handed and stood with his back firmly against the wall, arms tightly folded across his chest. A splash of green soup which had spilled down his white tunic made him look as though he was wearing a sash of some order of British chivalry.

"I say, old chap, we seem to be short a bowl or two of soup. Would you mind bringing more so we can start?" The debonair Major Dick was the hallmark of polite sophistication.

"Sheet, Suh. The soup—she is finished, Suh!" Waiter Rishidi, ex-comrade Rishidi of a gang of terrorists from the Pungwe Tribal Trust Land, was the epitome of unrefined impropriety.

Luckily it was only the junior officers at the end of the table who found themselves without soup. They made up for it by imbibing in substantially more wine than would normally have been tolerated of junior officers.

It was the wine that caused Waiter Rishidi's second undoing of the evening. He had been requested by a guest to bring another bottle of red *Quinta do Espirito Santo*. Standing close to the head table he inserted a corkscrew into the bottle and with great determination attempted to yank out the cork. He succeeded only in ripping the corkscrew out, showering the table with fragments of the broken cork, with the remaining cork still in the bottle. Unperturbed by this minor setback, the innovative waiter extended his index finger into the neck of the bottle and pushed the cork firmly into the wine, spewing ruby red liquid all over his already soup-stained tunic. With an engaging smile he attempted to pour wine into the glass of a snobbish-looking woman who happened to be the wife of an Army Headquarters Brigadier. The cork inside the bottle blocked anything other than a slight trickle from being poured into her glass. Without hesitating, Rishidi inserted his finger into the neck of the bottle to dislodge the cork as he continued pouring. The wine gushed out with such force that some splashed on to the unfortunate lady's bosom. She was wearing a white floral dress decorated with prints of red roses. Had the waiter left things as they were, it would have looked as if a new rose had suddenly bloomed from her ample cleavage. As it was, Rishidi whipped a soiled cloth from his trouser pocket and attempted to wipe away the offending spillage. He told me later that his experience of being captured by the Selous Scouts had been a far less traumatizing ordeal than his skirmish with the Brigadier's wife.

The final mishap of the evening occurred much later. Dale Collett, who had been wounded with me in Mapai and was now confined to a wheelchair, had not allowed his predicament to interfere with his reputation as an imbiber of considerable renown and a firebrand on the dance floor. He and his wife, Cilla, lived in a house across the road from the Officers' Mess. They were usually the last to leave a party. This night was no exception. However, eventually Cilla decided enough was enough for one evening and made her way home, leaving Dale doing wheelchair pirouettes on the dance floor.

The following morning an urgent call was received by the Duty Officer reporting that a body had been found lying motionless in some shallow water in a ditch adjacent to the Officers' Mess.

"Who is it?" asked the startled Duty Officer.

"I don't know, Suh," replied the equally startled African who had made the discovery. "It must be someone important, Suh. He is wearing a red tunic, Suh."

The Duty Officer rushed to the scene fearing some dreadful skullduggery and found Dale, still in his Mess uniform slumped in the watery ditch sleeping off a hangover. He had been trying to get himself home in the early hours of the dawn with his internal compass malfunctioning from an excessive intake of port and had ended up falling out of his wheelchair as it plunged into the ditch. Deciding that this was probably as good a place as any to spend what remained of the night he had fallen asleep.

When the Duty Officer made a call to his wife suggesting that she might want to come and retrieve him she replied, "Serves him right. It will teach him a lesson. Leave him there until he sobers up and he can make his own way home."

"But Cilla, he's lying in a pool of water and he could drown!"

"It'll teach him to wear a lifebelt next time he stays out for a frolic on his own."

A Rocky Engagement

"I've decided to get married, Mother."
"Good. Does that mean you'll settle down and stop chasing after those
horrible people?"
"Probably not. Will you come to the wedding?"
"Might you still be alive?"
—Telephone conversation with the author's mother: September, 1977

It was during my long recuperation that I decided it might be a good idea to start living a more sedentary life. I was 27 years old and middle age was already beginning to look ominously out of my reach. Mother, who was still living in Canada, had written to tell me she was getting tired of receiving phone calls at all hours informing her that her son had once again been admitted to the hospital.

"You need to stay at home more and try to lead a more genteel life, dear," she pleaded in her most recent letter. That was when I decided to get married. Carol and I had been living together for two years and it was time to take the plunge. I secretly purchased an engagement ring and told Carol one evening that we were going out for dinner to her favorite restaurant in Salisbury, the *El Castilian*. Piling into my Volkswagen Beetle we set out for what I planned to be an engagement dinner. Carol was driving because my right foot was still in plaster. Along the way I heard a dreadful roaring noise which sounded as if it was coming from an aeroplane in distress.

"Wind down your window and see if you can see anything," I said in alarm. "I think an aeroplane might be about to crash into us."

"It doesn't sound like an aeroplane at all," responded Carol calmly. "It sounds like a noise coming from the engine."

I wound down my window to try to establish the source of the racket and the inside of the car immediately started filling with black, oily smoke. The engine sputtered to a stop with a loud 'clunk' and the car abruptly stopped. Carol tried cranking the engine a few times but nothing happened.

"It doesn't sound very promising," I said. "Hang on, let me hop out and see what's wrong."

I clambered out of the car and peered into the engine compartment. The workings of an internal combustion engine were as alien to me then as they remain today; even a Volkswagen engine the size of a sewing machine. I was busy tinkering with it when Carol joined me.

"When was the last time you checked the oil?" She nonchalantly asked.

"Checked the oil? I've only had the car eleven months!"

"Well, it smells like burning oil to me so you might want to see if there's any left."

Carol was as clueless about engines as I was but made up for it with an abundance of commonsense. Eventually I found what looked like the dipstick and pulled it out. It was glowing red hot.

"I think we'd better wave down a taxi to take us to the restaurant," I suggested.

"Don't you think we should rather wave down a taxi to get us home?" responded Carol calmly. "We need to make arrangements to have the car towed to a garage."

"No. We have to make it to the restaurant. I have something important to ask you." The evening wasn't going as I had planned.

"What?"

"If you will marry me?"

"Oh! Well, in that case we had better make it to the restaurant after all. I'd like to be asked in a more romantic setting than on the side of a road next to a broken-down car."

❧

A week later we drove to Bulawayo where Carol's parents lived to tell them the happy news. To my surprise they expressed delight that I would be taking Carol off their hands. I had rather been expecting them to ask what a beaten-up officer in the Rhodesian Army could possibly offer their daughter … a sentiment with which I might well have been inclined to agree.

The following day dawned cold and wet. Carol and I made arrangements to drive out to the nearby Maleme Dam to spend the day with my good friend Doctor Charlee Griffiths and his wife, Anne. It was arranged that Carol's mom and dad would join us later in the day. We headed for the Matopos National Park in which the dam was situated, arriving just before midday. A slight drizzle was falling and visibility had been reduced by a damp, gray mist that hung over the dam like a wet cloak. As we arrived at the visitors' bungalows above the dam, we saw Charlee and Anne about to set off fishing. Carol and I asked if we might join them. It was decided we would travel together, so the four of us piled into my car with Carol at the wheel and set off slowly down the narrow, winding dirt road toward the dam.

"There's a large rock on the edge of the water about seven hundred yards further along. It's quite deep at that point. I caught some good bream there yesterday. It's the best spot around," said Charlee, enthusiastically.

We arrived at the water's edge and took a right turn toward the area Charlee had indicated. Almost immediately we passed a small Army pup-tent pitched close to the water next to which was sitting a young, neatly dressed soldier in uniform. His army-issue FN rifle was lying on the ground next to him.

"He's a National Serviceman studying klipspringers in the park," remarked Charlee, as we drove slowly past. I felt comforted by the soldier's presence. I was seldom without my Selous Scouts-issued folding-butt AK-47, but on this occasion had left it at the home of Carol's parents.

Ahead of us just visible in the thick mist and light drizzle was the rock which Charlee had mentioned. As we drew nearer we saw it was already occupied by a group of six Indians. They were standing on its edge with their fishing lines already in the water. Large reeds growing in the water gave excellent cover for the shy bass.

"Drive on another thirty yards. There's another good spot we can try," suggested Charlee.

Fifty yards further along Carol stopped the car and I had just begun to clamber out when we heard the loud stammer of an automatic rifle being fired at close range.

"Who the hell is firing an automatic weapon in a National Park?" I asked. The firing seemed uncomfortably close.

"Don't worry," said Charlee. "It must be that Army chap we just passed."

"Well, in that case I'm going to give him a piece of my mind. This is a National Park, not a military firing range!"

I hadn't gone a couple of yards in the serviceman's direction, when through the soupy, wet mist I saw the outline of somebody walking toward the Indians. As he got closer to them he discharged another burst of gunfire into the ground. I froze. Something was not right. Then I heard him speak.

"You know who I am?" he said to the Indians, his voice low and menacing. He had his weapon pointed in their direction.

"You're a terrorist," came back the frightened response. I was now able to see the outline of the figure's Chinese chest webbing and the distinctive curved magazine of the AK-47 assault rifle he was carrying. My blood froze. This wasn't the National Serviceman we had passed moments earlier. This was a dirty, shaggy-haired and very mean-looking terrorist.

"I'm a freedom fighter," he snapped back. "Throw me your watches, jewelry and wallets—*quickly!*"

There is one thing that Indians are extremely reluctant to part with even under the direst of circumstances and that is their wallets.

For a moment nothing happened—no one moved. Then without warning, the air erupted with yet another volley of automatic fire. The terrorist raked the group of defenseless Indians with a deadly stream of lead from his assault weapon. It was cold-blooded murder. Four of them were killed instantly, the impact of bullets tearing into their bodies and throwing them backwards into the water. I was vaguely aware of Charlee and Anne plunging into the dam as I whirled around to grab Carol. We stumbled toward the cover of a ridge of rocks close by. It was impossible for me to run with my right foot still in a cast. As we started clambering clumsily up the ridge, well-aimed rounds starting impacting around us, showering us with pieces of rock. We collapsed behind a large boulder with shots pinging all around. I felt more helpless than I had ever felt in my life. It was only a matter of time before the terrorist came looking for us and then it would all be over. I lay over Carol's body waiting for what seemed like the inevitable.

As rounds continued to be fired in our direction I started to become aware that the sound of the weapon seemed too loud, too heavy for an AK. It seemed more consistent with the sound of the heavier caliber FN NATO assault rifle favored by the Rhodesian Army.

"Perhaps the terrorist was killed by the National Serviceman." I whispered hopefully in Carol's ear. "Perhaps he saw us running up here and thought we were part of the same gang."

"Well, can't you shout at him to stop?" urged Carol. "I don't know who's going to kill me first, you lying on top of me with that cast or him shooting at us."

Just then we heard the sound of vehicles speeding down the road and police sirens wailing. Then we heard the voice of Carol's father calling out to us. I shouted back that we were lying behind a rock and that if the person shooting at us would care to stop for a minute, we would stand up and show ourselves. After a minute or two during which time no more shots were fired, I carefully peered out from behind our cover. Thirty yards away, standing at the base of the rock upon which the Indians had been murdered, were a handful of armed policemen. With them was the National Serviceman we had seen earlier. Lying sprawled on the ground close by was the body of the dead terrorist.

It was exactly as I had thought. Hearing the sound of shots being fired, the National Serviceman had grabbed his rifle and killed the terrorist with two well-aimed shots. In the mist, seeing the indistinct figures of Carol and me stumbling towards the rocky ridge, he had thought we were part of the same gang and had started shooting at us.

I looked around for Charlee and Anne. I had seen them plunge into the dam when the shooting started and wondered what could have become of them.

"Look," said Carol pointing to the water close to where we were standing. "Isn't that reed moving?"

Sure enough, two large, hollow reeds were sticking out of the water, one of which appeared to be moving slowly but surely towards the area where the dead bodies were floating. It looked like a periscope from a toy submarine. A short while later it stopped. As we watched, the unmistakable shape of Charlee's head emerged slowly from the water until just his eyes were visible above the surface. His hair was covered in green slime.

After watching us for a moment like a half-submerged crocodile,

Charlee must have realized that the coast was now clear. He rose from the water like a latter day King Neptune from the deep, smothered in green algae and weed, with the end of a large reed dangling from his mouth. His sudden emergence from the dam startled some of the African policemen standing nearby. They must have thought he was a terrible monster rising from the dam to wreak vengeance for the slaughter of the innocent. Two of them turned and fled in terror.

As soon as Charlee had clambered out of the dam and satisfied himself that the two wounded Indians had sustained only minor wounds, he set about doing a postmortem on the dead terrorist. The sight of a slime-covered figure emerging from the water to slit open the dead terrorist's stomach proved too much for the superstitious African policemen who had remained. They fled into the bush, screaming for their lives. The sounds of moaning from one of the wounded Indians prompted Charlee to stop his postmortem and fetch his fishing bag from my car. From it he triumphantly produced a bottle of Johnnie Walker Red Label Scotch whisky.

"It's the only medicine you're going to get for a while, but there's nothing better than good Scotch to numb the pain," he said to the wounded man before pouring a good quantity down his throat. He passed the bottle around for the rest of us to take a swig before having one himself.

"Let the dispatches record that the day was saved by a bottle of fine Scotch whisky," exclaimed Charlee. With that, the good doctor drained the remainder of the bottle.

"For goodness sake, Charlee, spit that filthy reed out of your mouth. Can't you see it's scaring the natives? It looks disgusting, like a piece of drool hanging down your chin. What's it doing there anyway?" asked Carol.

"I was using it as a snorkel to breathe through," replied Charlee, as though breathing through a reed while submerged under water was a perfectly natural thing for anyone to be doing. "But I started to get starved of air, so I thought I would move as close as possible to the bodies, then float to the surface and pretend to be dead myself."

Bending down to retrieve the dead terrorist's AK, Charlee announced that where there was one terrorist there were likely to be more. He turned to the National Serviceman.

"Let's go and scout around to make sure there aren't others lurking about the bush before I tell Anne she can get out of the water." It was only then that we realized Anne was still missing.

"Where did you leave her?" asked Carol, sounding concerned. She's still in the water breathing through that reed over there," said Charlee pointing in the direction of the moving reeds we had noticed earlier. I don't want her to come out until the coast is clear."

Eventually a senior policeman arrived to take charge of the carnage. Having finally coaxed Anne out of the water, the four of us climbed back into my car and beat a hasty retreat up the hill to where Charlee and Anne were staying.

"Would you like to come back to Bulawayo with us?" asked Carol, still concerned. "You never know whether there might be more terrorists out there."

"Oh, it's perfectly alright, thank you," replied the doctor. "We still have the bungalow booked for another two nights. Anne and I will remain here and try our luck at fishing again tomorrow."

"Well, choose a safer place than where we were today," cautioned Carol.

"You can't beat that rock for catching bass," replied Charlee. "We'll be back there tomorrow morning. The fish will be feeding like crazy after what happened today!"

15

Interlude

"Have you seen our Squadron mascot?"
"What is it?"
"A spotted Dalmatian."
"Yes, he was in our camp last night." *"May we have him back, please?"*
"I'm afraid not."
"Why?"
"We ate him!"

—Air Force pilot speaking with a
Selous Scouts officer, Chiredzi: April, 1977

By 1977 the insurgency war in Rhodesia had spilled into most of its rural areas. A number of 'Joint Operation Centers' or JOCs, had been set up throughout the country to coordinate and manage the escalating insurgency. These were military bases established close to airfields and which comprised senior members of the Army, Air Force, Police Special Branch and other civil authorities. The JOCs reported to their respective Brigade Headquarters which in turn reported to a Combined Operations Headquarters (COMOPS) situated in Salisbury. COMOPS Headquarters was responsible to the Prime Minister for the co-ordination of the national war effort.

A Selous Scouts base had been established in close proximity to most of the JOCs. This was because pseudo-operations had become such a crucial component to the national counter-insurgency strategy. The bases were called 'forts' because that is precisely what they were intended to be. From the outside they looked like something an Apache raiding party might have expected to come across as they sought to rid the Dakota plains of American settlements in the late 1800s. The only difference was that the Selous Scouts forts were constructed not of logs, but of high-tensile corrugated iron.

Each fort covered an area about the size of a football field and comprised living and sleeping quarters, kitchens, messes and an operations room, all situated around an open parade square which substituted as a vehicle park and helicopter landing zone. The outside walls were 10 feet high and made from corrugated iron with a gate to allow for the passage of covered vehicles transporting pseudo-teams to and from their deployment areas. Pseudo-operations were classified top-secret and the forts were off-limits to anyone who was not a member of the Selous Scouts.

It had become policy that all terrorists captured during the war be immediately taken to the nearest fort and placed into the custody of a Police Special Branch Officer permanently attached to the Selous Scouts. More often than not these terrorists would be suffering from wounds requiring immediate medical treatment. They couldn't be treated at civilian hospitals as it was important their identities not be compromised. It was for this reason that each fort was also equipped with a modern, fully-equipped surgery capable of treating most major wounds. Adjacent to the operating room was a small recovery ward. Once the terrorists had recovered from their wounds they would be inserted back into the field to join our pseudo-teams. There was only one downside to this arrangement. The Regiment seldom had sufficient doctors to post at every fort. The result was that treatment of wounded terrorists was often left in the hands of soldiers in the fort who had little or no medical experience.

In command of each fort was a Selous Scouts Liaison Officer whose function was to oversee and coordinate the unit's operations with other arms of the Security Forces. The insertion of pseudo-teams into areas in which regular Security Forces were active necessitated an extremely high level of planning and coordination. The immediate area in which the teams were operating had to be cleared of regular troops in order that the sort of fatal mishap that had resulted in the death of Sergeant Andre Rabie some years before did not happen again. High levels of map reading skills were required, both from the pseudo-teams and the Security Force patrol commanders. Often these men were of no higher rank than junior NCOs.

It was as a Liaison Officer that I was appointed during the latter part of 1977 after recovering from my leg wounds. My first posting was to a fort adjacent to a JOC located on the side of an airfield near the small agricultural town of Chiredzi in the southeast of the country. This fort was normally under the command of a flamboyant, red-headed Major called Bert Sachse who had attended the Sandhurst Military Academy in England. Bert was on leave at the time and the fort was under the temporary command of Captain Athol Gillespie, a colleague of mine with whom I had been on Cadet Course. I was to spend a month understudying Athol before being given my own fort to command.

Pre-deployment briefing at a Selous Scouts' fort. (Dennis Croukamp)

"I'm afraid the war isn't going too well at the moment," warned Athol the day I arrived.

"Oh, why is that?" I inquired.

"Whenever we ask the Air Force for a helicopter to deploy our teams, they tell us there isn't one available, the lying bastards!"

"That's odd. Why wouldn't they want to allocate us helicopters?"

"It might have something to do with the fact that we ate their mascot a few nights ago. Bloody blue-jobs, they have no sense of humor."

"You ate what?"

"Their mascot. Cut it up into steaks for a BBQ we were having."

"You ate their mascot … what was it?" I asked horrified.

"A spotted Dalmatian called Spotty. It had been the Air Force mascot for three years."

"Well, I'm not surprised they won't assist you with helicopters. It's not every day somebody eats your mascot, especially when the mascot happens to be a spotted Dalmatian!"

"To hell with them, it's not as though we didn't offer them any of the meat. We even invited them to the BBQ but they declined. They asked me this morning if we could provide some additional men to help guard their aircraft tonight. There's a reported gook presence close by and they're afraid of being hit. I told them to go screw themselves."

It appeared that the war effort in the Chiredzi area was certainly headed in the wrong direction.

I had been at the fort a week when one of our pseudo-teams pinpointed the location of a large gang of terrorists who had taken up residence close to a nearby farming area. They had been making life extremely uncomfortable for the European farmers in the area and had already ransacked two farms, killing the farm labourers and torching the homesteads. Luckily, the farmers had been enjoying sundowners with their family at the Chiredzi Club at the time of the attacks. A young farmer's wife on a third farm whose husband had been called up for National Service had single-handedly repelled an attack on her farmhouse killing one terrorist and sending the rest scurrying into the bush to lick their wounds.

The camp in which the terrorists were living had secretly been under observation by one of our pseudo-teams for a few days. Once it was established the camp was occupied, a Fire-Force of Rhodesian Light Infantry were deployed to attack it. In the ensuing firefight eight terrorists were killed and one captured, wounded. Athol and I had both been monitoring the contact over the radio in the Selous Scouts operations room and knew that the wounded terrorist had received a gunshot wound to the stomach.

"The captured gook is being choppered here for treatment," shouted Athol running from the operations room towards the surgery. "Quickly, help me clean out the operating room."

"What's there to clean?" I asked, sprinting after him. The operating rooms in previous forts I had been in had always been kept spotlessly clean and sterile.

"Chickens," panted Athol breathlessly. "I put twenty chickens in there the other day. There'll be shit all over the place. We'll have to move them into the recovery ward."

"Chickens! Why do you have chickens in the surgery?" I asked in astonishment.

"Best place to keep them. The operating lights keep them warm at night. They keep us in fresh eggs and supplement our army rations."

Thirty minutes later an Alouette helicopter clattered noisily into the fort, turbines screaming and rotor blades spewing clouds of dust everywhere. Lying on a stretcher inside was a badly wounded terrorist with what looked to be a large portion of his intestines spilling from his stomach. Athol and I helped carry him into the hastily-cleaned surgery and on to the operating table. We glanced at each other across the table, our senses temporarily numbed by the deafening noise of the helicopter lifting clumsily out of the fort.

"This looks a bit out of our medical expertise," said Athol, probing around at the wounded man's intestines.

"I say, don't you think you should wash your hands before you go delving into his stomach?" I asked.

"Don't worry about trivial things like that. Concern yourself with the bigger picture." I was learning fast. "Get on the phone to the Chiredzi Hospital and tell them to send a doctor over quickly!"

The doctor I eventually contacted was the same English gentleman who had attended to my wounds while flying out of Chiredzi some months before. His name was Alexander Rothschild, a rather grandiose name for a timid little man who always appeared as if life had dealt him a cruel blow. He was extremely reluctant to venture anywhere near the fort, suggesting instead that we bring the wounded man to the hospital.

"I'm sure we have far better facilities for treating stomach wounds at the hospital than you have in your camp. I'm certainly not convinced it would be in the patient's best interests to treat him over there."

He remained unconvinced even after I explained to him that it would not be possible to treat the wounded terrorist at the hospital for security considerations. He changed his mind only after I told him it would be in *his* best interest to come over as quickly as possible, otherwise I would have him arrested by the Police Special Branch.

By the time the doctor arrived, Athol and I had done a respectable enough job cleaning up most of the evidence of chickens having been kept in the operating room. We had sterilized the instruments we thought might be needed to patch up our wounded friend and had even anesthetized the fellow by pouring a tumbler of Scotch whisky down his throat. The only problem was that, try as we might, we were unable to get rid of the overpowering smell of chicken manure that hung over the surgery like a pungent cloud.

"There's a terrible odour of chickens in here," remarked the doctor as he walked in. "It's a most unusual smell to be associated with any sort of surgery."

He looked around suspiciously, sniffing the air like a bloodhound, as if hoping to uncover some heinous medical malpractice.

"You're obviously not very familiar with war wounds, Doctor. It's the smell coming from that gook's spilled guts," replied Athol, sounding like a professor of emergency medicine. "He must have eaten more chicken than was good for him before being wounded. Now get on with it and sew him up before the stench overpowers us all."

"I think I might need an assistant to help me," replied the doctor taking a closer look at the protruding intestines.

"You already have two," I replied, pointing at myself and Athol. "A third person would just get in the way."

The doctor glanced dubiously at Athol and me then shook his head, rolled up his sleeves and got to work. Halfway through suturing the man's stomach, he asked Athol to prepare to pass him some forceps. Athol retrieved the forceps from the sterilization tray and calmly began using them to clean his fingernails.

"Forceps, please," said the doctor holding out his hand.

"Hang on, Doc … I'm on my last fingernail." I looked up. Athol was busy extracting some dirt from one of his fingernails using the pointed end of the forceps.

It was at that moment one of the roosters decided to indicate his displeasure at being penned in the recovery ward by giving a loud and rancorous crow.

The doctor looked up, an inaudible sound coming from his quivering lips. I was afraid his heart might have stopped because his face turned a deathly white. He methodically placed his instruments down and began slowly to remove his surgical gloves. Then he appeared to become completely unhinged. He started shouting, scolding Athol and me as if he might be a schoolmaster who had caught us peeping up a schoolmarm's dress.

"Keep your voice down, Doctor; you'll frighten the poor prisoner." Athol seemed as surprised at the doctor's outburst as I was.

"I will not take any further responsibility for this poor man's life!" he screamed. I was shocked. He had always appeared so timid and afraid. "You will very likely be responsible for his imminent death. I have a good mind to report you both to the Special Branch." With that he strode out of the surgery and was gone.

I didn't have the heart to tell him that the only Special Branch Officer in the area happened to be Detective Section Officer Peter Dew who was himself attached to the Selous Scouts. Peter's personal hygiene was probably worse than our own.

"Well, I suppose we'd better finish up where he left off," remarked Athol, retrieving the doctor's instruments.

"I guess so. At least your fingernails are clean," I replied. Remarkably, Comrade Simon Chipete, late of the Zimbabwe African Liberation Army, made a full recovery and later joined the Selous Scouts, fighting with distinction against his former comrades. He was killed in action just before the war ended.

Honeymoon

"What on earth is that noise?" "It sounds like mortars!"
"Are they dangerous?" "Very."
"Well, for heaven's sake tell them to stop! This is your honeymoon after all."
—Conversation with my twin sister,
Kariba Breezes Hotel: September, 1977

After leaving Chiredzi and before being posted to a fort of my own, I decided to take a few weeks' leave to get married. Carol and I had moved into the married quarters at Andre Rabie Barracks at the request of Lt. Col. Reid-Daly so that I could be more conveniently utilized for base duties. Carol, together with a number of other wives living at the barracks, was working some 60 kilometers away in Salisbury. One of the 'perks' offered to entice families to move into a married quarters situated so far out of town was the provision of a bus service to take them to and from work each day. International sanctions had been applied against Rhodesia for unilaterally declaring independence from Britain. This had resulted in a critical fuel shortage necessitating the introduction of strict fuel rationing.

One morning I was asked to man the Selous Scouts Operations Room because the duty officer had reported sick. Even though I was technically still on leave recovering from my wounds, I readily accepted. It was late in the afternoon and there were a number of contacts taking place throughout the country necessitating my immediate attention. Troop movements had to be arranged and coordinated, requests submitted for helicopter and fixed-wing aircraft and situation reports (SITREPS) sent to Army Headquarters. I had just finished speaking on the radio to one of our forward bases when my thoughts were interrupted by the shrill ringing of one of the many telephones arrayed before me. The female voice at the other end sounded extremely angry.

"Is this the Army?" she demanded. It was a very broad question so I gave an equally broad answer.

"Yes, Madame, this is the Army."

"I want to speak with the man in charge, please."

This put an entirely new perspective on matters. Impersonating the Commander of the Army could land me in a lot of trouble. Not wanting to disappoint the woman by telling her she was talking to a lowly Captain, I decided to continue the charade.

"You're speaking with him, Madame." I was beginning to feel rather important.

"I have one of your natives apprehended in my house."

"You mean one of our soldiers, Madame? Why do you have one of our soldiers apprehended in your house?"

"Soldier!" she screeched in indignation. "If that's what you call him, God help us!"

"Why do you have one of my native soldiers apprehended in your house, Madame?" I didn't particularly like the direction the conversation was taking.

"I caught him on my bed this afternoon," she hissed.

"On your bed, Madame? Was he sleeping?" The conversation seemed to be going from bad to worse.

"No. He was having *sex*." She whispered as if it were too vulgar a word to say out loud.

"Sex! Sex with whom, Madame?"

"With my housemaid. It's disgusting!" She spat out the last sentence with such vitriol that I could almost feel the spittle in my ear.

"Did he perhaps give you his name, Madame?"

"His name is 'Duma'. It's sewn on to his shirt. It's the only thing he was wearing, the *disgusting* man."

I didn't know whether she was referring to me or the lusty romeo she had evidently caught in the act. I did know that Corporal Duma was the driver of the bus which transported the wives into town each weekday. I could just imagine them impatiently waiting to be collected from their places of work while their randy driver was trying to formulate an escape plan from the clutches of this angry woman. I decided to bring the matter to a quick conclusion.

"Madame. Please, would you release the man immediately? He's to pick up some ladies from town and is already behind schedule."

"Pick up more ladies! What are you running, a brothel?" she screeched.

"These are married ladies, Madame."

"You're using married ladies? That's disgusting!" The phone went dead. I didn't know whether she had slammed it down or fainted.

I was rather happy to hand the whole sordid affair over to Major Dick the following morning. After all, I was on leave and had an important marriage to attend.

❧

Carol and I were extremely excited. My mother and twin sister had both agreed to attend our wedding. The plan was for Mother to fly from Canada to Brussels where she would meet up with Janet who was working with the United Nations. They would fly together to Rhodesia via Portugal, arriving in the country a day before the wedding.

On the day of their expected arrival I received a call from Mother who was with Janet at Lisbon Airport. "I'm afraid we won't be able to make the wedding, dear. The Portuguese pilots seem to have gone on strike."

"Mother, you didn't really book your flight with Air Portugal, did you?"

"Yes, we did, dear. I've heard very good reports about their service. It's just that their pilots are having a bit of a gripe at the moment."

"For goodness sake Mother, the last time anyone relied on the Portuguese for anything other than a bottle of Port was in the days of Vasco da Gama."

"Now don't be nasty, dear. They are being as helpful as they can. It's just that we will only be arriving a day after your wedding.

The wedding service, minus Mother and Janet, took place at the Rhodesian Light Infantry chapel in Salisbury and was officiated by the Reverend Peter Grant, Chaplain to the Selous Scouts.

The following morning Carol and I drove out to Salisbury Airport to collect Mother and Janet. They had agreed to join us on our honeymoon at Lake Kariba, a huge inland body of water which forms Rhodesia's northwest border with Zambia. It was quite a squeeze with four of us plus luggage crammed into my recently-refurbished Volkswagen Beetle. It wasn't helped by the fact that I was wielding an automatic carbine through my passenger window while Carol, who was driving, had a folding-butt AK across her lap. I wasn't about to be caught in the same predicament as we had found ourselves in at Maleme Dam.

"I thought we were coming on a civilized holiday," remarked Janet, looking aghast at the array of weaponry sprouting from the car. "I feel as if I'm about to embark on a stagecoach journey through some outlaw-infested part of the

Wild West."

Her sense of unease grew when about an hour out of Salisbury we had to wait to join an armed convoy before proceeding on our journey. The convoy was being escorted by two armored cars and a detachment of troops.

"Now I feel as if I'm taking part in Patton's charge to Berlin," sighed Janet.

We were speeding around a tight corner at the top of the Zambezi escarpment trying to keep up with the fast-moving convoy. In the event of an ambush, speed was crucial in getting through the killing zone as quickly as possible. In such an eventuality, drivers of civilian cars had been instructed to race ahead at high speed leaving the armored cars to repel the attack. Janet was not impressed.

"Don't you think this is all rather exaggerated?"

"Not really," I replied. "There's not much you can do by yourself if you round a corner to be confronted by twenty gooks peering at you from behind their machine guns. I'm prepared to bet that none of them would have heard of the Geneva Convention, much less cared about it."

We arrived at the small resort town of Kariba just before lunch and checked into the Kariba Breezes Hotel. We were greeted at reception by a tall, suave-looking gentleman in a white tunic who introduced himself as James. He stood behind the Reception desk looking down his nose at us as if he might not be the Receptionist at all, but rather the General Manager of the group of hotels to which this one belonged.

"May I be of assistance?" he asked, sounding rather bored. He must have worked hard at his accent which seemed borrowed from some English aristocrat who might previously have stayed at the hotel.

"Mr. and Mrs. Bax, Mrs. Bax, and Ms. Bax. We have a booking," I replied.

"I beg your pardon, Sir?" He took a nimble step backward as if I had just announced I had a contagious disease.

"The Baxs. Mr. and Mrs. Bax, Mrs. Bax, and Ms. Bax. We'd like two inter-connecting rooms overlooking the lake, please."

"Inter-connecting rooms?" He gave us a scandalous look as though we were a group of polygamists making an unwelcome arrival at the hotel.

Another group of tourists had arrived and were waiting impatiently behind us so James thought it best to get us out of sight as quickly as possible. Hastily completing the register, he handed us the keys.

"The rules for the hotel are printed behind the door. May I suggest that you read them carefully?"

Leaving our luggage in our rooms, we made our way to the well-appointed dining room for lunch. A number of families were already seated. Most of the men and some of the women had rifles leaning against starched linen tablecloths which had been imported from Messr. John Finlay of Bridge Street in London.

"This is absurd," said Janet. "The very least they could do is leave their guns outside. It's enough to give anybody indigestion."

"That wouldn't help if some fleet-footed terrorists came bounding through the dining room door spraying machine gun fire in all directions," I replied, ordering some mulligatawny soup.

"That is *such* an exaggeration," responded Janet. This is a holiday resort and besides, there is a police station just up the road. We passed it on the way in. The terrorists wouldn't dare come near here." I let the remark go unchallenged.

We had just finished lunch and were enjoying coffee on the veranda overlooking the lake when we heard the first "crump" of a mortar bomb exploding behind us. Windows rattled and tables shook as successive bombs whistled overhead, exploding in an area of bush some half mile away.

"What on earth is that noise?" demanded Janet.

"Mortar bombs. It's terrorists firing at us from about two thousand yards away."

Declining Janet's suggestion to go and tell them to stop, I herded the family into a large, secure-looking bar with walls constructed of natural stone.

"I think you should order each of us a double martini to calm our nerves, dear," suggested Mother.

As I walked up to the bar counter to order the drinks, another bomb exploded harmlessly in the distance. The barman was standing stoically at his post behind the bar, seemingly unruffled by the sound of bombs whistling overhead.

"Four double martinis please."

"Will that be with one olive or two, Sir?"

∾

The rest of our honeymoon was relatively uneventful and a week later Carol and I were able to deposit Mother and Janet safely back at Salisbury Airport for their flight home.

An Angry Brigadier

"Where have you set up camp?"
"At the airfield."
"The airfield! Will you have guards?" "Why do you ask?"
"It gets rather busy there at night." "Busy?"
"It's where couples mix after dark."

—Conversation in the Balfour Hotel bar,
Rusape: March, 1978

In October of 1977 shortly after my return from leave, I was asked by Lt. Col. Ron Reid-Daly to establish a Selous Scouts presence in the small agricultural town of Rusape in the northeast part of the country. There had been a significant increase in terrorist activities in the adjoining tribal areas so a JOC had been established in the town to coordinate a Security Force response. Because it was a new operational area and because the building of a fully-fledged fort took a lot of planning, time and money, it was decided initially to establish a temporary tented base from which to deploy our pseudo-teams. The Police Special Branch Officer detailed to join me was Detective Inspector Keith Samler. Keith had joined the British South Africa Police from the ranks of the London Metropolitan Police many years before.

There was a small airfield situated just outside Rusape and it was there that I decided to locate our base. It was an ideal location, close enough to town to allow for easy liaison with the JOC, but secluded enough to allow for the secure deployment of our pseudo-teams.

Like most small Rhodesian towns during the war, social activity in Rusape centered mainly around the bar. It was there that locals would congregate each evening to mix with off-duty policemen and soldiers to get an update on the prevailing security situation. The most popular bar in Rusape was the Balfour Hotel and it was there that Keith and I decided to go one evening to become acquainted with the locals.

The initial excitement and relief of the patrons when they heard there would be a Selous Scouts presence in the area soon turned into a clamor of concern when they learned that our base was being established on the side of the airfield. It quickly became apparent that the airfield had become the accepted *emplacement préféré'* for discreet liaisons amongst a population starved of any other form of evening entertainment. The only person who appeared pleased with the arrangement was a crusty old farmer named Major Bellingham to whom age had lent an abundance of wisdom. He looked upon our presence at the airfield with some relief and even asked if I could arrange a 'preferred parking space' for himself and his mistress under a large umbrella tree close to the camp entrance. He was apparently involved in a liaison with a policeman's wife who was prone to pneumonia, a condition aggravated by her exposure to dampness.

"It's the only place you can spread a blanket on the airfield and be free from the evening dew," he said to me through a haze of Cavendish smoke exhaled from his meerschaum pipe. "But it's a popular spot and more often than not it's already occupied by the time we arrive."

"How do you propose I keep it reserved for you?" I asked, shocked by his bold revelation.

"Quite easy young man," growled the Major through billowing clouds of tobacco smoke. He looked at me as though I might still have a lot to learn. "You simply put a sign under the tree 'Danger: Claymores'. If you see any vehicle parked there other than my blue Land Rover, you simply detonate a small explosive charge nearby. That'll keep the rascals away."

I learned later that he had earned his spurs, and an MBE, fighting the Mau Mau while serving with the Royal Inniskilling Fusiliers in Kenya.

Later that night and many beers later, Keith and I poured ourselves back into my camouflaged Army Land Rover to return to our base. On our arrival at the airfield we were shocked to see an assortment of cars strung along its length looking like a flotilla of small craft at anchor in a darkened harbor. I decided to switch off my vehicle headlights and take a slow drive up the airfield to see the extent of what was obviously a nightly phenomenon. We had just about reached the far end when a car with no headlights emerged from behind the cover of some thick trees heading in our direction. By an extraordinary bizarre quirk of fate, we both ended up turning in the same way to avoid a collision. The next moment there was a jarring crunch as the winch on the front of my Land Rover impaled itself into the radiator of the oncoming car. Inside was an extremely embarrassed young couple who seemed more concerned at not having their identities compromised than with the formalities of dealing with the accident. In spite of our strenuous efforts at separating the two vehicles, they remained firmly meshed together, like two male antelope locked together in mortal combat. We agreed to meet the following morning to have the wreckage removed, and walked our separate ways.

Keith Samler. (Keith Samler)

I was at the scene of the accident early the next morning waiting for a recovery vehicle to tow the vehicles off the runway when a military Cessna aircraft made an unexpected appearance overhead. It began orbiting the airfield like an angry bee, occasionally making a low pass over the wreckage below. Inside was an angry Brigadier who was unable to land because of the obstruction. The plane swooped low over me, banked, and swooped again like an angry magpie. Then it turned and headed home. I extended my middle finger in a salute of good riddance at its departure.

I decided to inform Col. Reid-Daly of the unfortunate events as I suspected this would not be the last I would hear of it. There was no one more loyal to his recalcitrant subordinates than the Commanding Officer of the Selous Scouts … providing he heard about their misdemeanors directly from them and not from someone else. I didn't have long to wait for the repercussions. The following day I was summoned by my Commanding Officer to Andre Rabie Barracks.

"Junior, it's just as well you told me what happened when you did. The Brigadier wants your guts for garters. You're to appear on orders at Army Headquarters tomorrow morning charged with malicious damage to Government property and for the reckless endangerment of an aircraft."

The Colonel's jaw was firmly set as he looked at me through his piercing blue eyes. Then his features softened into a wry smile.

"Apparently a third charge of scandalous behavior has been dropped. I must say I couldn't help myself from smiling when I heard you had given the Brigadier the bird as he flew over. Luckily the charge can't be proven. It's a good thing the Colonel who's taking you on orders is an old soldier and a man's man and who knows we have more important things to worry about than the frolics of a young officer. I've already told him I can't afford to lose you from Rusape."

The next morning I appeared before Colonel Vic Walker at Army Headquarters to attend the second disciplinary hearing of my Army career. Unlike the other crusty-looking senior officers who occupied the Headquarters, Colonel Walker was a pleasant-faced officer whose own Army career was as distinguished as it was long.

"Captain Bax, I have a statement from your Commanding Officer, Lt. Col. Ron Reid-Daly. He states that you had just returned from a dangerous night deployment at the time of the accident and were probably exhausted. Because of these extenuating circumstances I have decided to reduce the charges against you to a single charge of negligence. You are sentenced to a reprimand. Dismissed."

I was delighted, but not surprised, at the support I had received from my Commanding Officer. It was the reason he enjoyed such enormous popularity in the unit. I was lucky to have got away with a light rebuke, but it was not a terribly auspicious start to my first command as a Selous Scouts Liaison Officer.

I remained at Rusape for a year. It was the height of the insurgency and perversely the beginning of the peace. International negotiations were being brokered to reach a political accommodation between the African Nationalists and the Rhodesian Government. At the same time, the so called 'liberation armies' were being urged by their Russian and Chinese masters to increase the momentum of the insurgency to gain leverage at the negotiation table. It was a chaotic game of cat and mouse being played out in the remoteness of the African bush; of gangs and counter-gangs operating secretly in the silence of the shadows. Sometimes the war would emerge from the shadows with the scrapping adversaries trying to bludgeon each other through sheer force of numbers and firepower. This invariably resulted in overwhelming casualties being inflicted on the terrorist forces and those that survived would slink back into the bush melting once more into the shadows. Then the deadly game of hide-and-seek would repeat itself. It was Africa's war fought with the predatory instincts of the animals that prowled its untamed wilderness, unseen, watching, waiting.

The Selous Scouts achieved some astonishing successes in the Rusape area. To a large extent we neutralized the insurgency in that region. I didn't have as much luck stemming the nocturnal frolics on the airfield. On many a moonlit night Major Bellingham, MBE, and his partner could be seen lying on a blanket under the umbrella tree grateful for the proximity of the Selous Scouts camp in ensuring the security of their coital bliss. I never did put up the claymore sign he wanted. It wasn't needed. Arriving at his favorite spot one evening, the testosterone-fueled Major found a car already parked there. In a fit of pique he fired a round from his .45 caliber revolver at the offending vehicle. The bullet ricocheted off the engine and almost castrated the poor romeo lying next to it. It was the last time anyone ever challenged the lustful Major for his favorite spot and it thereafter became his personal domain. It didn't surprise me that the Mau Mau had thrown in the towel with the likes of Major Bellingham, MBE, chasing them through the Aberdares.

෧ඁ

Just before leaving I was delighted to be told by Col. Reid-Daly that he had recommended my investiture as a Member of the Order of the Legion of Merit.

16

Melting Pot

"We have some business." "Business?"
"Yes. To make an example of the Chief."
"Which Chief?"
"The one who has sold us out."
"What will you do?"
"Give him the machete."

—Pseudo-team talking with
terrorist gang leader, Karoi Tribal District: April, 1978

Shortly after Christmas in 1977, I was called into Lt. Col. Ron Reid-Daly's office at Andre Rabie Barracks. He told me that peace talks had started between the Rhodesian Government and a group of moderate Black Nationalists which, if successful, might lead to political power sharing. This was encouraging news, as some of the leaders claimed the support of a substantial number of terrorist gangs inside the country.

"If they could be convinced to lay down their arms or even to change sides and fight on the side of the Security Forces, it could deal a lethal blow to the insurgency," said Ron with a trace of skepticism. He was an ideal Special Forces soldier, always looking beyond the conventional paradigms of prevailing military wisdom towards a more unorthodox approach. If the views of senior commanders pointed in one direction, Ron Reid-Daly would confound them by doing something completely different.

"Badly-trained guerrillas in bed with the Rhodesian Army sounds like a mismatch of partners to me," I remarked. I hadn't been imbued with Ron's great capacity for looking beyond localized issues towards a grander prize. He chose to ignore my remark and press on with his thoughts.

"The problem is that the radical Nationalist leaders living outside the country, like Mugabe and Nkomo, are afraid of being marginalized by the talks. Mugabe is pouring hundreds of ZANLA terrorists across the border into Rhodesia from his camps in Mozambique with orders to kill anyone involved in negotiations with the Government. They've also been told to intimidate the

307

locals into supporting a continuation of the armed struggle. One of the areas involved happens to be adjacent to one of our most important tobacco farming regions."

Ron walked toward a large map of Rhodesia which hung on his office wall. He pointed out an area in the north of the country that included the fertile Doma/Mangula tobacco farming area on the edge of the Zambezi Escarpment. He paused before continuing.

"A number of moderate blacks have already been killed and the gooks have begun attacking European tobacco farmers in the area to try and drive them off their farms. If that happens it will affect not only our tobacco exports but the economy of the entire country."

Ron went on to explain that a JOC had been set up in Sinoia to coordinate a military response to the incursions. Sinoia was a small farming town situated on the main road to Kariba and was the focal point of tobacco-growing activities in the area. A Fire-Force of the Rhodesian Light Infantry had been deployed there, but the terrorists first had to be found before they could be engaged. I was beginning to wonder what part I might play in this unfolding drama when Ron fixed me with his piercing blue eyes.

"This is where you come in, Junior. I want you to establish a Selous Scouts fort near Sinoia from which to deploy our pseudo-teams. Once they locate the gangs, you can leave the rest up to the RLI Fire-Force." Ron walked back towards his desk and sat down before continuing. "But you'll have to be quick. Time is of the essence. I've promised the RLI they'll have their first target within a fortnight."

I had no doubt as to the outcome of an engagement between a Commando of the RLI and a gang of ZANLA terrorists. What I was less sure of was being able to find the terrorists at such short notice.

"What about terrorists loyal to the parties involved in peace talks? What's going to happen to them?" With so many different warring factions involved, it sounded like I was being asked to sail into a confused sea.

"If you'd just shut up for a minute and listen instead of talking, I'll tell you." Ron paused to let his remark take effect. "That's the trouble with the training they give young officers these days. They teach you to start flapping your gums before you've finished listening."

It was impossible to take offense at the Colonel's remarks. Commissioned from the ranks, Lt. Col. Ron Reid-Daly was a man's man who believed that leadership and grit were borne out of the crucible of battle and not something that could be learned in frilly lecture rooms at a military college. There were no limits to the lengths he would go in supporting his men, including the issuing of some "old soldier's" advice when needed.

"We expect significant numbers of terrorists to surrender once they've received word that their leaders will be accommodated in a new government. We need to find an area where they can be concentrated so we can exercise some sort of command and control over them while we figure out how best to utilize them. I want you to look for some suitable areas and come back to me with suggestions."

A week later I had established a temporary Selous Scouts fort on a remote farm a few miles east of Sinoia. A disused farm manager's house provided ideal accommodation for my headquarters staff and would provide sufficient electricity to power a mobile operations room which I had parked nearby. The Police Special Branch officer attached to my headquarters, Detective Chief Inspector Bob Wishart, was a well-known personality who had earned his reputation and spurs coming up through the ranks of the British South Africa Police. He was a tall, lean, dark-haired and dark-complexioned Englishman with a keen investigative mind and a vast knowledge of the terrorist organizations operating inside Rhodesia.

"It sounds confusing enough to me having so many terrorist factions running around," I said to Bob as we settled into our base. "Imagine how confusing it's going to be for our pseudo-teams. They're going to feel like undercover agents walking around the woods at a bootlegger's convention."

We inserted our first pseudo-group into a tribal area whose Chief was a firebrand of discontent and a well-known ZANLA supporter. Our group gave out the cover story that they were ZANLA terrorists anxious to make contact with other gangs in the area. Ironically, some five miles to the south lay another tribal area whose Chief was opposed to prolonging the insurgency and had expressed open support for peace talks. The two Chiefs fervently disliked each other and it was only a matter of time before the tension between them boiled over into open hostility.

It wasn't long before our pseudo-group was approached by a village contact person with information that a resident ZANLA gang in the area wanted to meet them. A meeting was duly arranged but unfortunately it took place some distance from where the team's European controller, my old friend Sergeant-Major Bruce Antonowitz, was based. This would mean that he would be unable to deploy the Fire-Force once our pseudo-group had the terrorist gang visual. Bruce was the salty individual who had miscalculated the dimensions of the grave shortly after I joined the Selous Scouts. At the meeting, the ZANLA gang indicated their intention to confront the tribal Chief who was supportive of the peace talks and make an example of him by murdering both he and his family. They wanted our pseudo-group to join them in their grisly undertaking, so it was arranged that the two groups would meet up again at a prearranged location closer to the Chief's village. The meeting was set to take place in two days' time. This was ideal as it would allow Bruce time to relocate his position to where he would have sight of the meeting place and be able to call in the Fire-Force once the real terrorist gang arrived.

As luck would have it on the day before the meeting, Bruce reported that he was running low on radio batteries. This presented a serious problem because without radio communications he would have no way of contacting either his pseudo-team or the RLI Fire-Force. To make matters worse, my colleague Bob Wishart had left two days earlier to attend a Special Branch meeting in Salisbury. Bob was a vital cog in my operational planning and I was loath to act without him. But time was now of the essence, so I decided to take in a re-supply of batteries myself. This would not only solve the communications problem but would give me an excellent opportunity to be present to help coordinate the next day's Fire-Force deployment.

That night I donned my kit, checked my weapon and blackened my exposed skin. Weighed down by an ample supply of batteries, I was dropped off in thick bush about four miles from where Bruce and his team were based for the night. After walking alone through the bush for some three hours I eventually linked up with them. It was just past midnight. Bruce was based with his pseudo-team on top of a rocky hill overlooking a thick ravine close to the village of the Chief who the ZANLA gang intended murdering the following morning. It was in the ravine that the meeting between our pseudo-group and the gang of terrorists was to take place. Even with Bruce's presence it was a weird feeling being amongst a group of scruffy, armed Africans, most of whom were captured terrorists who only a short while ago had been intent on killing Rhodesian soldiers. They looked and smelled like a gang of Mau Mau who had been lurking in the depths of the Aberdare Forest for the past six months. The leader of the pseudo-group, Corporal Chidomo, wore a scruffy beard and matted hair that made him a splitting image of Dedan Kamathi, the infamous Mau Mau leader. I almost gagged at his smell as I huddled next to him to be briefed on the plan for the next day.

"We're to meet in the ravine below us around midday tomorrow," he whispered in the still, chilly night air. "They want us to accompany them in rounding up the villagers in the Chief's village and force them to watch as they torture the Chief for being a sell-out."

"What do they intend doing to him?" I whispered back.

"First they will flog him in front of his people. Then they will hack off his ears so that he cannot listen to any more negotiations with the Government. After that they will slice off his lips so he cannot talk about peace."

"With all the villagers being forced to watch?" It sounded too grisly to imagine.

"Yes, but that's not all, *Ishe*. Then they will take a machete and hack off his arms, then his legs. They will leave him to die while they rape his wife in front of him."

This would certainly be a gang worthy of the attentions of the Rhodesian Light Infantry.

The next day dawned cold and misty with low cloud cover. I was worried the weather might not lift in time to allow the Fire-Force to deploy when we had the gang visual. An hour before midday it began to clear, leaving the ravine below in bright, clear sunlight.

Just before midday, Corporal Chidomo touched me lightly on my shoulder. He pointed towards a narrow path in the distance which followed the overgrown banks of a shallow river meandering into the ravine.

"There, *Ishe*," he whispered. "There they are."

I made out a gang of twelve scruffy individuals in the distance, dressed in filthy denims and armed with AK-47's and RPD machine guns. They were heading directly towards the ravine. Our target was in sight. I quickly got on the radio to deploy the RLI Fire-Force.

"Two nine this is five one Alpha. Target visual. Twelve armed CTs at grid reference US312652." This was just what the RLI Fire-Force had been waiting for. The report would unleash a sequence of events that would culminate in a battleground tactic that had proved to be the most successful counter-insurgency strategy in the world. There were none better at executing it than the young soldiers of the Rhodesian Light Infantry.

At the Sinoia airfield the crew of an Alouette helicopter gunship were waiting expectantly inside the cockpit of their aircraft. When my report of a terrorist sighting came through, they sprang immediately into action. With a low whine which increased steadily into a high-pitched scream, the helicopter's powerful turbine motor roared into life. A minute later with engine screaming at full throttle, torque to the aircraft's main rotor was engaged and the three massive blades began turning, quickly picking up speed until they were spinning so fast the aircraft began to shake. Seated behind his 20mm cannon, the gunner cocked his weapon sending an explosive-head round slamming into the breach of his weapon. He looked at his pilot giving him the 'thumbs up'.

Nearby, three troop-carrying Alouette helicopters, each with a stick of four fearless young RLI troopers, shook and vibrated under the strain of their own spinning rotor blades; their pilots anxiously waiting for the thumbs up from their section leader to get airborne. When it came, the four helicopters clattered noisily into the air, hovered momentarily, turned and headed north for a rendezvous with the twelve murderous terrorists. The helicopters became airborne at about the same time as the terrorists, whose destiny the RLI Fire-Force would seal, were beginning to get settled into the ravine, sharpening their machetes in preparation for the afternoon's slaughter.

Twenty minutes after my call, the helicopters appeared as four tiny dots on the horizon flying fast at treetop level. The pilots had no fancy navigation equipment to assist them to their target. They relied solely on a compass and their skill at reading a 1:50,000 scaled map. At a distance of 1,000 yards from the ravine, the gunship began to climb steeply, its rotor blades clattering noisily in the thin air as it gained altitude and started circling the target below in a tight orbit. Almost immediately the gunner started laying a withering stream of 20mm cannon fire into the thick foliage inside the ravine. The three troop-carrying Alouette's orbited once and then descended heavily into a nearby cornfield amidst clouds of flying dust and debris, quickly disgorging their cargo of RLI troopers.

There were no thoughts by the young soldiers of taking cover and waiting for the gunship to inflict maximum damage before their assault. Without waiting for any orders they fanned out into an extended line and advanced quickly toward the ravine. They started taking heavy fire from the terrorists' position even as they started skirmishing quickly and inextricably towards their prey, deadly streams of lead spitting from their assault rifles.

The soldiers were all in their late teens or early twenties, some barely out of school uniform. They wore no helmets, no body armor, no heavy boots. They were not weighed down by layers of heavy equipment or by heavy weapons. Their uniforms were black running shoes, military green shorts, T-shirts and camouflaged sweat bands around their heads. Their exposed skin was tanned a deep brown by the African sun. Around their waists they wore webbing with enough water, food and ammunition to sustain them through the day. Each carried a Fabrique Nationale NATO issue 7.62 automatic assault rifle. Every fourth soldier carried a general purpose medium machine-gun. They were light, mobile, fearless—and they were unstoppable. They had only one thought: to close with and kill a murderous enemy who sought to take their country through force of arms.

Modern military doctrine is never to engage an enemy unless with overwhelming force of numbers. The Rhodesian soldier enjoyed no such luxury. From my vantage point on the hill I heard a vicious firefight taking place inside the ravine below me. It was twelve RLI soldiers against twelve terrorists who enjoyed the advantage of fighting from a prepared defensive position. Fighting would be at close quarters and victory would belong to the bravest and the best trained. RLI soldiers were the bravest of the brave and they were superbly trained.

The outcome was never in doubt. It was over almost as quickly as it had begun. Thirty minutes after they had disappeared into the ravine, the young troopers emerged from the other side. Nine terrorists had been killed and three captured. One Rhodesian soldier had suffered a minor flesh wound to the shoulder. It would quickly be patched up and he would be fighting alongside his comrades later the same day in yet another firefight, at yet another location.

Leaving my team behind on the hill, I slithered down to congratulate the RLI soldiers on their incredible effort. One of them was holding a .45 revolver in his hand with a beautifully carved pistol grip made out of ivory.

"The leader of the gooks had this tucked into the waistband of his trousers," said the RLI Corporal, handing me the revolver. "Probably stolen from some European farmer he's recently murdered. You might want to take it back with you and have Special Branch do a trace on it."

Not only were RLI soldiers some of the most aggressive and best trained in the world, they were also the most highly disciplined. It wasn't for nothing that the Prime Minister of Rhodesia, Ian Douglas Smith, had referred to them as 'The Incredible RLI'. Thereafter, they were known simply as the 'Incredibles'.

It had been a good start to our deployment but we still had lots more work to do. The information from our pseudo-team was that there were still a few more ZANLA groups in the area that would need our attention … and that of the Incredible Rhodesian Light Infantry.

Third Sip of Gin

"Where are you headed?"
"Innisfree Farm."
"It's very remote and there are reports of terrorists." "We have guns."
"What if I hear shooting?"
"Don't worry. It will be us testing our weapons."
"Should I be worried?" "No."

—Farmer talking with Detective Inspector
Bob Wishart and the author,
Doma/Mangula Farming area: May, 1978

Two months after we had arrived in Sinoia, Bob and I were enjoying evening cocktails at the headquarters of the town's social activities, the Sinoia Sports Club. Ron Reid-Daly had been putting pressure on me to find a suitable location to assemble the increasing number of terrorists who had indicated a willingness to cease hostilities when the black leaders they supported were included in a new Government of National Unity. At the Club I met a grizzled old tobacco farmer who owned a farm on the fringes of the Doma/ Mangula farming area where it borders the Wildlife Reserve of the Zambezi Escarpment. His farm had been attacked four times in the past month, the last of which had resulted in the terrorists ransacking his tobacco barns and outlying buildings. He had finally decided to abandon the farm and move with his family into the relative safety of Sinoia.

"Bloody bastards stole my .45 revolver with hand-carved ivory pistol grip. It was given to me by my dad for my 21st birthday."

"You'll be pleased to know we have it. The terrorist who stole it, and most off his gang, were killed. The pistol is now with the Special Branch but I'll make sure you get it back." The old man was elated.

"My farm's the last one in the area before you get to the escarpment. I think it must be located on a transit route for terrorists coming in and out of the country. If you want to use it as an assembly area to house your tame gooks, be my guest. You won't catch me going back till the bloody war is over."

"What's the farm's name?" I asked. "Innisfree."

I thanked him for his offer and told him I would reconnoiter it
the following day. If we could occupy the farm with armed groups supporting the peace talks, they might be able to drive off the ZANLA gangs

that were making life so uncomfortable for the remaining tobacco farmers. Ron Reid-Daly's unconventional wisdom was finally beginning to rub off on me.

The next morning Bob and I climbed into an armored, open-topped Unimog for the fifty-mile trip to the farm. It was armed with an imposing .50mm machine gun mounted centrally in the back. The vehicle had been specially designed and engineered in our workshops to provide maximum protection from landmine blasts. The sides were armor-plated to provide protection from small arms for those seated inside as well as for the machine-gunner. The squat, specially-designed vehicle had been given the rather unglamorous designation of 'The Pig', because that is precisely what it looked like.

Traveling with us was a black signalman, Geoffrey, who I asked to accompany us so that I could maintain communications with my base in Sinoia. Remaining behind to assume command during my absence was a young Special Branch officer named Tom Thomas who had joined us some weeks before. Tom was a short, stocky young Rhodesian with the temperament of a bloodhound whose job it was to help interrogate captured terrorists. He was an extremely capable young police detective and I was glad to have somebody of his caliber remaining behind in case anything went wrong during my absence.

As we were about to leave I suggested to Bob that I do the driving and he operate the gun. "It's quite a difficult vehicle to drive, Bob. Let me drive and you handle the machine gun." Bob was quite happy to man the heavy machine gun. With his rugged features and windswept black hair and beard, he must have looked like a modern-day pirate about to lay siege to the surrounding seas. He certainly elicited a lot of waves from the admiring young women as we drove through the town.

Three hours later we were driving through the last occupied farm before reaching our destination. We paused to speak to a farmer who was talking to some of his farm workers on the edge of a cornfield. His name was Johan van Rooyen, an easygoing giant of a man, wearing shorts, an open-necked khaki shirt and large sun hat. Slung over his shoulder was an army-issue FN automatic rifle. Like many farmers in the area he was often called upon to do active military service. When this happened his wife would take over management of the farm and when necessary, defend it and her children against terrorist attacks. In spite of the deteriorating security situation, van Rooyen had a permanent smile etched into his weathered face. When he spoke it was with a guttural Afrikaans accent. He offered to accompany us to Innisfree Farm as he knew the area intimately. I declined, not wanting to have to explain to him what my plans were for the unoccupied farm.

"My workers say there are reports of a terrorist presence in the area," he cautioned. "If I hear any shooting, I'll drive out to assist."

It was typical of Rhodesian farmers. They were scared of nothing and would think nothing of single-handedly following the tracks of a terrorist gang which they might find on their farm … and engaging them once they had caught up with them.

"Don't worry," replied Bob tapping the breach of his .50mm machine gun. "We intend doing a bit of target practice when we get there. If you hear any firing, don't pay any attention."

The farmer waved us goodbye and was quickly lost to view behind the rolling clouds of thick red dust left behind as we sped along our way.

The last mile was along a narrow, winding dirt road that snaked through thick bush along the edge of the Zambezi Escarpment. Bob had to frequently duck to avoid the thorn-covered creepers that hung like tentacles from branches extending across the road. They scraped the top of the Unimog as we cautiously drove the final few hundred yards to the deserted farm. I wondered whether I should stop and change places with Bob behind the gun. I was beginning to get a premonition that we were not alone in this desolate and remote part of the Zambezi Escarpment and if the shooting started, it was behind the gun that I belonged. I was about to stop when, driving around a bend in the road, Innisfree Farm suddenly came into view. Its once well-manicured lawns and gardens had given way to an invasion of weeds and creeping undergrowth. The windows and doors of the homestead had been smashed open and nothing moved except for the open front door banging softly in the breeze. Planking had been stripped from the surrounding tobacco barns and there was a prevailing pungent smell of fresh wood-smoke.

Leaving Geoffrey behind in the Unimog, Bob and I climbed out and cautiously began to look around. We were both armed with AK-47 rifles. We had only gone a few hundred feet when we stopped, both with an overwhelming sense that we were not alone. We were being watched. The hair on my arms and the back of my neck raised in a primal reaction to danger. I looked at Bob; neither of us said a word. We both sensed that if we didn't get back to the security of the Unimog quickly, we would be lucky to leave the farm alive. Peering intently into the surrounding bush, trying to seek out the dangers we knew lurked within its secret shadows, we edged our way back to the vehicle.

Our every sense was fine-tuned to take immediate evasive action if we were fired on.

After what seemed like an eternity but could only have been a minute, we made it back to the relative safety of the armored vehicle. I told Bob to get into the driver's seat and start driving as I scrambled quickly behind the machine gun. Cocking the weapon, I lost no time in aiming into the surrounding bush and squeezing the trigger. A steady stream of fire spewed from the gun's heavy barrel, the .50mm caliber rounds shredding the foliage at the base of the trees and bushes in a wide arc to my front. Hot empty casings clattered on to the metal floor of the vehicle from the spent rounds being ejected from the rapidly firing gun. They began to form a large pile at my feet as I fed belt after belt through the hungry weapon. A grey lourie shrieked in righteous indignation as it flapped its way out of the tangle of undergrowth to my right. I continued firing until Bob had reversed the vehicle and we were heading back toward the road. Attaching another full box of ammunition to the gun and feeding in another belt, I re-cocked the weapon keeping my finger loosely curled around the trigger as we turned and headed back down the road we had just come in on.

It was as Bob was turning out of the second bend in the road that we hit the landmine. It was two Russian anti-tank mines placed one on top of the other and they detonated the instant the front driver's side wheel hit them. The landmines had obviously been laid while we were reconnoitering the farm.

The resulting explosion completely severed Bob's right leg just below the knee and mangled his left foot, almost severing his big toe. The bones in my left arm were snapped in two and my fingers were split open at the ends by the force of the machine gun being ripped off its mounting. The noise of the explosion numbed my senses. I was flung against the rear steel door of the vehicle and became vaguely aware of bullets impacting into my chest and legs. I felt oddly at peace with how little pain I felt and wondered how long it would take to die. Then I realized it was unexpended rounds from the box of ammunition attached to the machine gun that were hitting me. The force of the explosion had ripped the bullets from their belts sending them flying into the air. They were now raining back down on me as I lay sprawled in the vehicle.

A deathly silence followed. Thick clouds of cordite-filled smoke and dust billowed inside the vehicle. Through it I made out the figure of Bob. The force of the explosion had swiveled him around on his seat so that he now sat facing me. The stump of his severed leg was propped upright against the back of the seat and all I could see was a bleeding, mangled, fleshy mess.

"Bob—you've lost your leg!" It sounded so inane … so pathetic, but it was all I could think of to say. I had to say something if only to assure myself that this was not a terrible dream.

"No, I haven't. There it is over there." Bob pointed to where the bottom portion of his leg lay resting on the floor of the Unimog. "I wonder how the shoelace became undone."

It is impossible to imagine the indescribable brutal agony Bob must have been feeling at that moment. That he was able to make light of his appalling situation is testimony to the irrepressible humor and grit that Englishmen have shown throughout the ages in the face of such terrible adversity. He didn't grimace, nor flinch, nor utter a solitary groan of pain.

"Timmy, do you think you could manage to light me a cigarette, my pack seems to have gone missing."

I saw Bob's open packet of cigarettes with lighter still inside lying on the cluttered floor of the vehicle. It was within reach so I leaned over and extracted one with my uninjured right hand. I lit it and inhaled the smoke into my lungs before shuffling towards Bob. The nicotine seemed to dull the pain in my shattered left arm as it dragged behind me. Bob took the cigarette from my outstretched hand and placed it between his dry lips, his fingers beginning to shake badly. Taking a long, slow drag he inhaled deeply, keeping the smoke in his lungs for what seemed like forever.

"I wonder where Geoffrey got to," he wondered aloud. "We're going to die of thirst if we don't get help soon."

There was no sign of the signaler. The back door of the Unimog was still latched, so the force of the explosion must have thrown him and his radio out of the vehicle.

We managed as best we could to put a tourniquet around Bob's leg to stem the bleeding. Then we sat and waited. I had managed to retrieve my AK which I kept pointed towards the rear door in case the terrorists decided to return to admire their handiwork. I was petrified they might lob a grenade into the back. That would have been messy.

I knew I would have to leave to find help if we were to survive but was loath to leave Bob alone. He was still plucky and jocular but I knew his life was quickly draining away. He seemed to sense my dilemma.

"Don't worry about me, Timmy. Go and find help, I'll be fine. Just leave me another cigarette and lock the door behind you when you leave."

Just then, miraculously, we heard the distant sound of a vehicle. It seemed to be speeding in our direction. Some minutes later a Land Rover pulled up behind us. It was van Rooyen. He had heard the shooting and initially thought nothing of it knowing that we intended doing some live firing. But he knew we must be in terrible trouble the minute he heard the explosion. Without any regard for his own safety he had shouted to one of his farm workers to join him and had sped off to find us. Along the way he came across Geoffrey running down the road who breathlessly explained what had happened.

Together with his farm worker and with some help from the still shell-shocked Geoffrey, the burly van Rooyen managed to extract Bob from the carnage in the front of the Unimog and lay him gently in the back of his Land Rover. I climbed in beside him and we were about to set off for the Mangula Hospital some five miles away when Bob told us to wait.

"Could somebody fetch my leg, please? I'd like to bring it along. My wife brought me these veldskoens last week and they're still brand new. She'd kill me if she knew I'd left one behind!"

Geoffrey climbed back inside the Unimog to retrieve Bob's leg with the veldskoen still attached. Then we sped off along the bumpy road to Mangula. Upon our arrival at the hospital, Bob was wheeled directly into surgery while I waited on a stretcher in an adjoining room. The pain in my shattered arm had become intense. Even worse was the pain in my fingers. They felt is if they were on fire. The motherly Matron who fussed over me was unimpressed when I asked her to go in search of a sip of gin … even when I explained how thirsty I was. She remained unimpressed when I explained that it had been a sip of that fiery liquid that had sustained me on the two previous times I had been wounded.

"Well, you won't get any gin in this hospital. What you and your friend both need is an infusion of blood, not alcohol!"

The blood transfusions Bob and I eventually received were from a donor who had neglected to disclose the rather important information that he had recently been diagnosed with malaria. Later that afternoon I managed to place a call to my wife with news of what had happened.

"Wounded! Not again, darling. She was becoming accustomed to being phoned at odd hours with news that I was back in the hospital. I suggested that she and Bob's wife, Wendy, travel up together to see us. A family who lived close to the hospital had kindly offered to accommodate them.

"We'll travel up this evening. Is there anything I can bring … some underwear or a toothbrush perhaps?"

"As a matter of fact there is one thing, dear. They seem to be averse to a spot of alcohol in this hospital. Perhaps you could bring me a nip of gin."

Carol and Wendy arrived later that evening and were shown directly into our ward. The first thing Carol did as she took a seat next to my bed was hand me my hipflask. I was about to take a swig when the Matron walked in to announce the rather depressing news of the contaminated blood transfusions.

"The malaria is going to complicate your recovery and you will both have to be transferred to the Andrew Fleming Hospital in Salisbury as soon as the physician says you are well enough to travel. A nurse will be coming in shortly to administer doses of quinine."

This seemed as good an excuse as any to have my sip of gin. "Don't worry about me, Matron, I have my own supply."

I placed the hipflask to my lips and poured the burning contents down my throat. It was the first time since the explosion that I began to feel remotely human.

℘

Two days after being admitted to the Mangula Hospital, the physician attending to Bob and me confirmed the news that we had both been diagnosed with a particularly virulent strain of malaria. This was not good news, especially for Bob who had just been told he would have to have further amputation to his leg. He went on to say that we would be transferred to the much larger and better-equipped Andrew Fleming Hospital in Salisbury the following day. An ambulance had already been requested from Army Headquarters to make the transfer.

That night Bob expressed concern about being transported in a military ambulance. "The only ones I've ever seen have looked like rejects from early episodes of MASH. Can't something be done about getting us a decent civilian ambulance?"

"Don't worry, Bob. The Army has recently acquired a whole new fleet of ambulances from South Africa. They're the most modern available. I can assure you we'll be travelling to Salisbury in style.

The ambulance that pulled up in front of the hospital the following morning certainly wasn't the pristine chariot I had led Bob to believe would be collecting us. In fact, it looked as if it had just emerged out of a time warp from a Second World War campaign in the Libyan Desert. It was pouring with rain and the first thing I noticed was that the windows in the rear patient compartment were missing. I was tempted to demand a different ambulance but was talked out of it by the physician who was waiting to see us off. He suggested that Bob's chances of survival would be better served if we got to the Andrew Fleming sooner rather than later, even it was at the expense of a comfortable ride.

The arrangements were that Carol and Wendy would ride behind us in Wendy's car. Tom Thomas, who had arrived from Sinoia earlier that morning, would provide an armed escort in his police Land Rover. We had only been on the road a short while when the rain that had been falling intensified and started blowing in through the missing window above Bob's stretcher. It didn't take long for the dressings on his amputated leg to become completely soaked. Then to make matters worse, his stretcher became unlocked from its tracks and started jolting backwards and forwards between the front bulkhead and the double doors at the rear of the vehicle. Having his broken toe propelled against the back door every few minutes was definitely not in the best interest of its healing process. But the worse was yet to come.

Speeding along the highway at sixty miles an hour, the double rear doors of the ambulance started to swing open and Bob's free-wheeling stretcher began rolling out. He was already a third of the way out by the time I managed to get my good hand on his stretcher to prevent him from completely disappearing out the door. The shock of tumbling out of an ambulance travelling at 60 miles an hour might, at the very least, have given him a sore head. The indignity of subsequently being run over by his wife's car could quite possibly have driven him to drink. For Wendy and Carol, the unfolding drama must have appeared like something out of a terrible horror movie!

Realizing he was about to witness a scene which he probably wouldn't want to explain to his Police Headquarters, Tom Thomas managed to overtake the ambulance and have the driver pull over and stop. It wasn't a moment too soon. Bob's stretcher was teetering on the brink. We had to continue our journey with a medical orderly grimly holding on to Bob's stretcher with one hand and the ambulance doors with the other.

Upon seeing me back in the orthopedic ward at the Andrew Fleming, the nurse in charge suggested I might want to inquire about renting a bed on a permanent basis. She was a young Greek lady by the name of Galanakis.

"Not you again," she said, settling me into the ward. "Will you be asking for another sip of gin? I think we still have some from your last stay."

"Yes, please."

"Don't you have a sip every time you're wounded?"

"Yes, it seems to be turning out that way."

"This must be some kind of record," she said. "Three times wounded and … ."

"Three sips of gin!"

17

Conduct Unbecoming

I have served under many officers during my forty-five years of service. With the exception of a very few, I have done so only out of sheer curiosity for the foolishness they would get up to next.

—Jock Hutton, Squadron Sergeant-Major,
'C' Squadron, Rhodesian, SAS,
speaking with the author, Cape Town: August, 1999

Recuperation from my most recent wounds was cut short a week after I was discharged from hospital. I was sitting at home late one morning sipping a mug of steaming chicken broth liberally laced with Sedgwick's 'Old Brown Sherry' and reading Neville Shute's *Trustee From the Tool Room.* I was imagining myself comfortably ensconced with Mr. Keith Stewart, a character in the book, as he worked on his miniature generators in the warmth of his comfortable basement in England. The phone rang jolting me from my reverie. It was Ron Reid-Daly.

"Can you come to my office right away, Junior? I want to talk with you and Andy Samuels about forming a new group. I'd like to get it going as soon as possible."

When Ron Reid-Daly said "as soon as possible" he meant "now." Andy Samuels was the fellow officer who had seen me off at Mount Darwin the first time I had been wounded. He had recently joined the Selous Scouts from a staff appointment at Brigade Headquarters. Staff work was as alien to Andy as hard work to a unionized stevedore. The war had wrenched him away from a promising farming career, but agriculture's loss had been the

Army's gain. Andy had proven himself to be an extremely capable and courageous officer. Just two years before he had been awarded the Bronze Cross, Rhodesia's third highest award for bravery.

"Can't we discuss it over the phone? The doctor says that I shouldn't be on my feet. Besides, I'm on sick leave for another month."

"Bloody doctors have no sense of urgency and they seldom know what they're talking about. If you can wiggle your fingers, Junior, you can wiggle

323

yourself back to work. I'll see you in my office in an hour."

My fingers still looked like burst frankfurters on a BBQ and I was due to have my dressings changed and the cast on my broken arm replaced within the next two days. I was beginning to wonder whether this might ever happen. I quickly bathed and changed into uniform and was in Ron Reid-Daly's office within the hour.

He and Andy were already poring over an organization chart that had been taped to a side wall. Andy looked up as I walked in, his bald head perspiring in the muggy, midday heat.

"Bax, you skiver. It's about time you got out of your pit and back to work. I'm surprised nobody's charged you with malingering!"

I smiled and let the remark go unanswered. Andy and I had enjoyed a close personal friendship for some years and our two families had become inseparable. Ron Reid-Daly pulled up a chair for me and placed it in front of the chart he had been working on.

"You know that the Rhodesian Government is being pressured by the British and South Africans to engage in settlement talks with the externally-based Nationalist leaders. The South African Government is threatening to cut off economic and military aid unless we agree to start some sort of dialogue with Nkomo and Mugabe."

"What about the peace talks with the internally-based leaders?" I asked, somewhat surprised. I had been led to believe that these talks would put a brake on the insurgency and lead to some sort of political settlement.

"The Americans and British see it as just another ploy to try and get international recognition while Ian Smith remains in power. They say Mugabe and Nkomo are the only two legitimate black leaders that can be engaged in negotiations to end our isolation. Unless we start talking with them soon we're going to start running out of bullets and petrol with which to fight the war. The Americans have put pressure on South Africa to turn off the supply taps if we don't toe the line."

"I'm glad I'm not a politician. Why don't we just take out Mugabe and Nkomo and be done with it? That way nobody will have to talk with them." My fingers were beginning to throb and I was not particularly happy with the idea that the mission Bob Wishart and I had recently undertaken to find a sanctuary for terrorists loyal to the internally-based black leaders might have been in vain.

"Now you're thinking, Junior. Perhaps that pain medication you've been on has stopped clouding your brain. Intelligence reports indicate a surge in terrorist gangs infiltrating Rhodesia from bases in neighboring countries. Mugabe and Nkomo both want to infiltrate as many of their armed supporters into the country as possible before talks begin—and they want them spread over as wide an area as possible. Quite frankly, unless we can do something to counter their plan they'll be talking from a considerable position of strength. We're quickly getting to the stage where we will have neither the manpower nor the resources to cope with the numbers of terrorist gangs operating in the country."

"Well, don't ask me to go looking for gooks on a one-man crusade. I can't even wrap my finger around a trigger and we can't rely on Andy; his bald patch would preclude him from being able to sneak up on anyone undetected." Andy's obscene retort was cut short by Ron Reid-Daly.

"The only way we're going to be able to stop the incursions and stem the tide is to hit the gooks hard in what they think are their safe bases outside the country. We need to find these bases and destroy them. That's where you two come in. I want you to select a small group of specialized individuals to form the nucleus of what is to become the Selous Scouts Reconnaissance Group. Your task will be to coordinate the deployment of reconnaissance teams into neighboring countries to locate terrorist base camps and staging areas. Once you've found them, it will be up to the Air Force, our own Assault Group and the SAS to destroy them."

The deployment of small, specialized reconnaissance teams working deep inside hostile countries to our north was not new to the Selous Scouts. We already had a number of one- and two-man teams who had achieved spectacular successes in the past. Amongst these were Chris Schulenburg, Tim Callow and Dennis Croukamp. They had previously operated free from the encumbrance of any formalized command structure, preferring to work independently through a small mobile headquarters. A need now existed to expand the reconnaissance function under a more formalized structure.

"I was rather hoping for a more mundane duty after my last injury," I replied to the Colonel.

"A more relaxed job is precisely what you're going to have, Junior, but not quite what you had in mind. While Andy works on getting the reconnaissance group operational, you will act as my Intelligence Officer. You'll accompany me to COMOPS HQ each week for the National Security briefings so you can get an overview of what's going on both inside and outside the country.

Once Andy is set up you can then join him armed with the latest available intelligence."

COMOPS, or Combined Operations Headquarters, were situated in Salisbury adjacent to the Prime Minister's office. It was the nerve centre of the war effort and consisted of the heads of the Government agencies directly involved in the war. Lieutenant-General Peter Walls was its Supreme Commander.

I was hoping to get home before Carol arrived back from work.

As I walked through the front door she was sitting in the lounge, furious that I had ignored doctor's orders and gone back to work. Her reaction when I told her about my meeting with the Colonel was similar to that of Golda Meir on being served a pork sausage with her cheese blintzes during her first peace talks in Cairo.

౫౨

A week later I found myself sitting tentatively in the front passenger seat of Ron Reid-Daly's Peugeot staff car headed for what was to be my first visit to the hallowed halls of COMOPS Headquarters. Ron was driving, but his attention was focused on listening to a speaker situated on the front dashboard. It was squawking messages from a high frequency radio installed in the boot

Selous Scouts reconnaissance patrols were seldom compromised. (Dennis Croukamp)

of his car. A forest of aerials extending upwards from the rear bumper gave the vehicle the appearance of a cumbersome sputnik on wheels. One particularly long aerial extending rigidly into the air reminded me of the tail of a rampant warthog. The radio linked Ron to almost every Selous Scout call-sign deployed in the field. One particular message caught Ron's ear and seemed to irk him. A terrorist base-camp in Zambia which was being attacked by the SAS that morning had been found to have been hurriedly vacated. The camp had been located by one of our reconnaissance teams two days before.

"I spoke with COMOPS yesterday and told them the camp was full. They are the only ones outside of the Selous Scouts and Air Force that knew anything about the camp," fumed Ron. "Now, it's empty. I'm beginning to smell a rat, Tim. I've been suspecting for some time there might be a leak coming from somewhere in the halls of COMOPS and the smell seems to be getting stronger by the day."

Combined Operations Headquarters comprised the senior commanders of the Army, Air Force, Police, Special Branch and Central Intelligence Organization. It also included a host of less important, but equally shrill characters, who were seldom shy of having something to say about how to go about winning the war. The problem was that more often than not, everyone seemed to have diverging and sometimes diametrically opposed opinions on how best to go about getting the job done. The result was that trying to form a coherent and winnable national war strategy became as perplexing a task as trying to capture a slippery eel.

The meeting was attended by many officers I didn't recognize. I suspected that most were staff officers who had emerged from their dingy offices like rabbits from their warrens to get an update on the war. Afterwards they would scuttle back to the security of their burrows to write endless staff papers on what frontline soldiers should or shouldn't be doing to win the war. Few if any of the papers would ever be read; fewer still would be implemented.

At the front of the room sitting behind a long mahogany table brooded the 'brains trust' of senior commanders who made up General Walls' management team. Each in turn made his way to a lectern at the front of the room to give his perspective on the security situation and, more important, what needed to be done to improve it. After each presentation a discussion would follow, usually initiated by the General himself. I was struck by the lack of consensus that prevailed amongst the speakers. Collectively they reminded me of an uncoordinated octopus with the General as the head and with each committee member representing a tentacle. Every time the octopus started to move one way, it would be dragged in an opposing direction by one or more of its tentacles. At one stage, debate took place on the advisability of bombing a strategic bridge in Mozambique to disrupt that country's lines of communications. Consensus had just about been reached when the Air Force Commander suddenly got cold feet because, as he put it, this could be construed as an act of war "exceeding the internationally-accepted principle of *hot pursuit*."

"Agreed," chorused Ken Flower, the Director of the Central Intelligence Organization. He was a ruddy-complexioned and sandy-haired Cornishman who had resigned his employment with the British Government to join the British South Africa Police. A few years later he formed the CIO and had become its first Director. "Bomb that bridge and you'll have the South African Prime Minister petulantly banging his shoe on the Parliamentary table threatening to cut off oil supplies." It was like watching a badly-choreographed and disorganized town hall meeting.

The remarks angered Ron Reid-Daly who was sitting next to me. He rose slowly to his feet.

"Gentlemen," he interrupted. His voice was cold, modulated, almost menacing. "What the hell do you, the South Africans or any other gobshites in this room who haven't had a bullet fired at them in anger think we're conducting here, a Boy Scout jamboree?"

The room fell into shocked silence. COMOPS wasn't used to hearing dissenting voices from those outside its sacred walls, even if the voice happened to belong to the Commanding Officer of one its most elite Special Forces units. With the rank of Lieutenant-Colonel, Ron Reid-Daly was one of the lowest-ranking men in the room. As a Captain, I had less status than the tea boy and was beginning to feel less than comfortable.

"Don't get excited, Ron." It was General Peter Walls. He and Ron Reid-Daly shared a close and unique friendship, having fought together in the Malayan jungle while serving with the Rhodesian SAS. "We're fighting a high-density insurgency, not total war. There are other factors we need to consider before destroying the infrastructure of a foreign country, not just military ones."

I admired the General; he spoke with firmness and resolve. It was a pity that the tentacles he relied upon for support seemed unable to act in unison.

Ron Reid-Daly wasn't convinced. "There's a fine distinction between an insurgency and total war when the very survival of your country is at stake. I think we should be more concerned about defeating the enemy than of getting a slap on our wrist from the South Africans or Americans."

I thought this might be the end of the matter. It wasn't. Ron fixed his eyes on Ken Flower and unleashed a final broadside. "If you don't want to do anything about stopping the flood of terrorists coming into the country from across our borders, I will. And I think that the fewer people who know what, when, where and how I intend doing it, the better. I'm becoming increasingly concerned with how many terrorist base camps across our borders have *mysteriously* been vacated just prior to being attacked."

Ken Flower looked miffed, but said nothing. Two months later the telephone in Ron Reid-Daly's office at Andre Rabie Barracks would be tapped. Somebody was determined to find out what the Selous Scouts were up to, one way or another.

I was glad to get out of COMOPS that afternoon. On the way back I suggested to Ron that he allow me back into the field as quickly as possible. It seemed to me that the task of finding and killing terrorists in the bush was infinitely less daunting than having to wrestle with a slippery octopus at Combined Operations Headquarters. It was beginning to appear as though its tentacles might extend into places previously unsuspected, including perhaps a few that were being controlled by Britain's Secret Intelligence Service.

"I think you're right, Tim. Ken Flower knows the location of more externally-based base camps than he's letting us know about. He doesn't want to tell us for fear we'll attack them without letting him know, thereby compromising his efforts at getting Mugabe and Nkomo to the negotiation table. I'm beginning to wonder who's paying his salary, the Rhodesians or the British!"

Ron looked deeply troubled as we headed back to our barracks. "We'll do it ourselves, Tim. Let's get out there and find those bases, and when we do we'll take them out ourselves if we have to. Then we'll see how many are empty just before the troops are choppered in.

Several days later I flew to Kariba to join Andy Samuels who had already established a small base camp at the airport. It was a stone's throw from the Zambian border and an ideal location from which to deploy reconnaissance teams into Zambia. Parked next to our camp was an Air Force fixed-wing turbo prop aircraft piloted by a youngster called Ginger. He had just graduated from the Air Force Academy and this was his first operational deployment. Arriving the following day would be two pseudo-teams and one specialist two-man reconnaissance team under the command of a Rhodesian who knew the African bush as well as the Africans. His name was Ian Waller, better known by his nickname 'Laughing Hyena'.

Andy and I spent the morning after I arrived pondering the best way to find a large terrorist training camp thought to be situated some fifty miles southwest of the Zambian capital, Lusaka. It was reported to be heavily defended by Russian-made anti-aircraft guns. It also happened to be located within a few minutes' flying time of the main Zambian Air Force base at Mumbwa.

Our reconnaissance could be conducted using one of three methods, or a combination of all three … it was just a matter of deciding which method was the most suitable for a particular mission.

One method was to deploy a small pseudo-team. This method was used when the general location of the camp was vague or unclear. Depending on how far inland from the border the camp was thought to be, the team would either walk in or be deployed by helicopter. Once in the general area they would make contact with the locals telling them that they had just returned from Rhodesia and needed to make contact with other terrorists in the area. If there was a camp nearby, the locals would lead our team to it. If not, they would indicate the general direction of the nearest camp. Once the pseudo-team came across a camp they would secretly cache any equipment they were carrying that might compromise their disguise, including the high frequency radio each group carried. Then they would enter the camp and mingle with the real terrorists.

They would remain in the camp for as long as necessary to get the information they needed before slipping away again into the night. It was extremely dangerous work; any slip-up or mistake the team made could blow their cover, resulting in them being captured and then executed. Once they had vacated the camp they would retrieve their cached equipment and contact our headquarters to arrange for a suitable time and place to be picked up by helicopter. The pick-up point would normally be approximately two days' march from the camp to avoid any chance of those inside the camp being alerted by the movement of helicopters. Once back at base, the team would be debriefed and plans made to attack the camp.

Another method was to insert a two-man reconnaissance team at night by parachute using a technique known as HALO, or High Altitude Low Opening. This method was used when conducting a reconnaissance on a camp, the location of which was generally known or suspected. The team would free-fall from an aircraft at high altitude, deploying their parachutes at low altitude to minimize the risk of being seen. Using all the anti-tracking and bushcraft skills they had been taught, they would carefully make their way as close as they could to the camp before setting up a concealed position on some suitable high ground from which to observe it.

Communications between the reconnaissance teams and our headquarters was via the cumbersome and difficult to use high frequency (HF) radios which each team carried, or by the smaller, and more portable very high frequency (VHF) radios which each man carried.

The range of the smaller radios (VHF) was limited to 'line of sight', which meant that either Andy or I would have to get airborne at a prearranged time each day in order to establish a communications link with the team.

High Frequency communication was only used if aircraft were not readily available, or if contact needed to be made with our headquarters outside of a prearranged schedule. These radios required the erecting of long, directional antennas, something that was extremely difficult and dangerous when in close proximity to the enemy. Often the reconnaissance teams would be situated so close to terrorist camps that the only way they could send messages over the radio without compromising their position was by using Morse code. The team would sometimes lie motionless for days making observations on the camp and making detailed notes about its routine. Often they would have to remain there until troops and aircraft could be concentrated for an attack. Their function would then be to pinpoint the location of the camp for the attacking aircraft, using special laser equipment or directional beacons.

The third method of conducting a reconnaissance was simply to jump into an aircraft and look for the camp from the air. The disadvantage of this method was that smaller camps tended to move once the occupants saw an aircraft flying in the vicinity. This wasn't the case with the larger camps which relied on heavy weapons and anti-aircraft guns to defend themselves against attack.

Because our three reconnaissance teams would only be arriving the following day and would need time to set up, it was the third method that Andy and I decided to use to find the Lusaka camp. Once we had identified its location from the air, we could then send Ian Waller in to do a close-in reconnaissance.

The young Air Force pilot wasn't very happy when I told him just before lunch that he and I would be doing an air reconnaissance the following morning to look for the camp.

"What about Zambian MiGs?" he asked, looking extremely concerned.

"They never get airborne when we fly into their airspace. Don't worry about them," I replied.

℘

The following morning Ginger and I gathered our maps and equipment and climbed into the aircraft for an early take-off. We had been in the air for a little over an hour doing grid pattern searches for the camp without finding any trace of it. If the camp was nearby, an hour was too long to loiter without arousing any suspicion and it was time we left the area and headed home. Ginger and I were wearing headphones so we could speak to each other without shouting and at the same time monitor radio traffic both from the Kariba Airport and our own base camp. We were also monitoring the radio frequency used by the Zambian Air Force (ZAF).

We had just flown under a very large bank of cumulus cloud when we heard the first report from the control tower at Kariba Airport that an unidentified aircraft was heading our way on what appeared to be an intercept course. A minute later we heard a radio transmission from the control tower of the ZAF base at Mumbwa urging a MiG that had been scrambled to intercept us to "Hurry up!" The bored response from the Zambian pilot seemed to indicate that he wasn't in much of a hurry to do anything. Ginger and I sat with our backsides crimped to our seats like vice-grips to a hard cushion. We would have been happier if they had been crimped to a parachute. Betting on a lightly-armed turbo-prop plane emerging unscathed from a scrap with a MiG wouldn't excite much interest at many reputable betting institutions. Ginger turned to me and indicated he was going into a steep dive to make a run for it. I looked at him shaking my head and pointed upwards to the huge bank of cloud we were under.

"We have too far to go to the border. The MiG will catch us and have our arses fried before we've gone five miles. Let's go hide in the clouds."

It was then I began to appreciate just how capable young pilots were who had graduated from the Rhodesian Air Force Academy. Ginger climbed effortlessly into the cloud, flipped the plane on to its wing and we circled inside the fluffy cumulus feeling like two tourists on a merry-go-round on a foggy day in London.

The MiG flew aimlessly around with his air-traffic controller excitedly urging the pilot to "Keep looking for the Rhodesian." The pilot didn't seem to share his controller's enthusiasm to keep looking for anything longer than was absolutely necessary. Eventually, on the pretext that he had to "urinate badly," he informed his controller he was returning to base.

We saw the MiG slashing past us like a silver dart as Ginger tipped our plane on to its nose and dived for the treetops to hedge-hop back to Kariba. If the Zambian pilot saw us, his need to urinate must have been greater than his desire to give chase, for he never deviated from his course. We both gave him a middle-fingered salute to hasten him on his way.

We arrived back at Kariba Airport grateful for the MiG pilot's weak bladder. Thirty minutes later we were ensconced in the bar of the Kariba Breezes Hotel feeling considerably more at ease than we had during our carousel ride in the sky.

Two days later we were able to obtain a more precise location of the camp from a terrorist captured by a Selous Scout pseudo-team working to our south. Ian Waller and an African Sergeant, dressed in pseudo-uniforms, were inserted by helicopter into an area eight miles south of the camp and found it the following day. It was called K16, and was occupied by approximately fifty terrorists from Nkomo's ZIPRA movement. The two Rhodesian reconnaissance specialists laid up for three days observing the camp and making detailed notes of its defenses and routine. One night the African member of the team managed to infiltrate right inside the camp and glean valuable information from those inside … such was the incalculable value of our pseudo-operators. The information was eventually relayed back to COMOPS and the camp would later be attacked by a combined air and ground assault resulting in heavy losses for the terrorists.

We remained at Kariba for six weeks during which time we identified the location of two more ZIPRA camps. With the information our reconnaissance teams were gleaning, COMOPS wouldn't run out of targets for a long time to come.

History would show that COMOPS chose to ignore many of them.

Betrayal

"It is not your enemies who will defeat you."
"Then who will it be?"
"The ones with whom you eat."
"With whom I eat?"
"The ones whom you invite to your table." "But they are my friends!"
"It is better to be deceived by your enemies than betrayed by your friends."
—Conversation between the author
and a villager, Makuti, Zambezi Escarpment: 1979

Back in Salisbury for some R&R, Carol and I decided to relocate into town from the Selous Scouts married quarters. We purchased a lovely home called Ladywood Cottage which was located in the northeastern suburb of Marlborough. We had been living there for about a week when I was awakened one night by the sound of somebody trying to break through our bedroom window. Whispering to Carol to remain where she was, I crept silently toward the window and jerked open the curtains. I found myself standing face to face with what I first thought to be an orang-utan that might have escaped from the Salisbury Zoo; the lithe creature appeared to be all arms and legs. Then I realized it was an African who had managed to pry open the window and was in the process of swinging one leg over the sill to get into the bedroom. He got such a fright at my sudden and unexpected appearance that he fell backwards, almost leaving his testicles behind on a brass latch that protruded from the window frame. I secured the window tightly and returned to my bed.

Thirty minutes later I was again awakened, this time by somebody trying to break in through our kitchen window.

Grabbing a Tokarev pistol which I kept under my pillow, I slipped silently out the bedroom window into the chilly night air. It was only then I realized I was stark naked. Keeping in the shadows I crept around to the back of the house to see the same individual now trying to break into the kitchen. Sneaking up behind him I thrust the barrel of my pistol into the back of his neck and asked him what he was doing trying to break into my house again.

"I am unemployed, Baas, and I am thirsty for brandy," came his quick and unsolicited response. This rather impressed me. His tenacity and ability to offer a disarming response to a leading question were important attributes for a Selous Scout pseudo-operator. Grabbing him by his collar I frog-marched him to my front gate and suggested that if he wanted to find gainful employment he should present himself to the Selous Scouts barracks the following morning.

He was still waiting at my front gate when I left for work the next day so I gave him a lift to our training establishment. I hoped he would be more successful doing the selection course than he was at trying to break into my house.

ल०

In January of 1979, I had just returned from another deployment at Kariba when the bug that had been planted in Ron Reid-Daly's office telephone was discovered. He was understandably furious. Directly accusing the Commander of the Army, General Hickman, of complicity in the bugging, Ron was charged with insubordination. He was subsequently required to appear before a court-martial. Before the court proceedings commenced, General Hickman was mysteriously relieved of his command of the Army and placed on the retired officers' list. The court-martial lasted five days at the end of which Ron was sentenced to a mere reprimand. Clearly the court was disgusted by the fact that senior officers of the Army would stoop to such deceitful tactics as bugging the telephone of the Commanding Officer of a specialist unit involved in top secret operations. The Judge Advocate of the Army, Lieutenant Colonel J.P. Reed, was moved to describe the incident as "bizarre, grotesque and outrageous." Shortly after sentencing, Ron Reid-Daly resigned his commission and left the Army, a proud but disgusted soldier.

The fallout from the incident was as quick as it was far-reaching and calamitous. It not only caused the removal from the Army of one of Rhodesia's most outstanding operational officers, but it heralded the beginning of the end of one of its most successful Special Forces units; a unit that had been at the leading edge of the country's counter-insurgency war. The Selous Scouts, suddenly and unceremoniously stripped of its founding Commanding Officer, would never recover. It is said that no man is indispensable but that some are extremely difficult to replace. Unfortunately, no man existed within the Rhodesian Army who could fill the shoes of Lieutenant-Colonel Ronald Francis Reid-Daly, CLM, DMM, MBE. The succession of officers who tried never succeeded. It was not that they weren't fine men in their own right, it was just that the Selous Scouts was simply too unique, too unorthodox and too specialized to have been successfully commanded by anyone else. Both Ron Reid-Daly and the Regiment he founded were finally defeated, not by the enemy, but betrayed by deceitful men within the Army's own corps of officers.

During the weeks and months that followed, the Selous Scouts undertook very few reconnaissance missions. Political considerations and events started taking precedence over sound military judgment. The resolve of the military hierarchy began to falter, squeezed by those in COMOPS who believed that a negotiated political settlement was preferable to a continuation of an aggressive counter-insurgency campaign. To be fair, they had little option. International pressure being exerted by the British and Americans for the Rhodesian Government to engage in peace talks with Nkomo and Mugabe was too persistent, too strong.

COMOPS seemed at sea during this period of 'détente'. They seemed unsure as to how best to deploy the Selous Scouts or even if they should be deployed at all. The result was that we remained in barracks for a considerable period of time doing nothing. I suspected the real reason was simply that Colonel Reid-Daly was no longer around to tell COMOPS *how* we should be deployed. A general feeling of apathy prevailed throughout the Army, but for Andy Samuels and me it became a time of great frolic. After all, if Rome was going to burn, let not the champagne burn with it!

A good friend of mine at the time was a fellow called Andrew Mackay. Andrew was a big, tall, jovial Rhodesian who had an exceptionally sharp wit and an irrepressibly dry sense of humor. He was born and raised in Zambia (Northern Rhodesia) amongst the remote villages and hamlets that dot the wild, sparsely-populated shores of the Zambezi River. It was an upbringing that developed within him a keen sense of freedom, self-reliance and adventure … traits that would remain with him into his adult life. Like many Rhodesians during that period, Andrew found himself having to juggle the demands of a new career with performing compulsory National Service in the Army. During the height of the war he found himself having to spend more time in the bush tracking terrorists than meeting the demands of his civilian employer. He was an adept bushman with a tenacious desire to close with the terrorist gangs he often found himself following; a trait that earned him the call-sign 'Spider Mike'. Later Andrew became a well-known and respected commodity broker and it was in this field that his unorthodox and unconventional upbringing really stood him in good stead. Traveling alone through remote parts of central Africa, Andrew could bamboozle a goods-laden camel from a shady Arab dealer before the unfortunate chandler even realized it was missing. To his friends he became known simply as 'Trader Mackay'.

At the time I first met Andrew he was living in a sumptuous, double-storey white villa called *Broadmead* which he shared with a motley bunch of incorrigible villains he loosely referred to as his "friends." The house had once belonged to Andy Samuel's father, and Andy himself had once lived there with his family before deciding to sell it to his friend Mackay to be used as a praetorian sanctuary for the unaffiliated. A swimming pool in the back garden was so large and ornate that it reminded one of the reflecting pools outside the Taj Mahal. The only difference was that adjacent to Andrew's pool was a large, well-stocked and very rowdy pool bar which was seldom bereft of popping champagne bottles and bikini-clad women eating from trays of sumptuous food being circulated by native servants dressed in white tunics, red fezzes and cummerbunds. If we weren't partying at Broadmead, the three of us would be seen living it up until dawn at one of Salisbury's better-known restaurants and nightclubs.

On one particular occasion a group of us were enjoying a late evening at the El Castilian Restaurant where, some years before, I had asked Carol to marry me. There was a band playing and shortly after midnight when all that remained inside was our small but noisy party of revelers, the band members decided to leave. They left their instruments behind explaining that they would collect them in the morning. With their departure, the owner announced that his restaurant was now closed and would everybody please leave. We declined his polite request but told him we would do our best to keep him entertained by taking over the band's instruments and playing a selection of medleys. He couldn't have been very impressed by our musical talent because he promptly called the police. When two European police officers duly arrived with orders to evict us, Andrew relieved the restaurant owner of his keys, locked the door and suggested that since everybody was now unable to leave, they might as well enjoy themselves. The owner was not amused when the two policemen looked at each other, shrugged their shoulders and decided the suggestion wasn't a bad idea.

There was an American partying with us at the time who had joined the Selous Scouts as a Major, after a proud and distinguished career as an officer with the American Marine Corps. His name was John Murphy and he took it upon himself to become the lead drummer in our ad hoc band doing his best to play a tune which might, if one had a vivid imagination, have sounded a bit like the *Little Drummer Boy*. After listening to his dismal performance for a few minutes, one of the police officers, who by now was on his fourth glass of cognac, politely asked if he could take over the drums to try and do better justice to the tune. The El Castilian was to join a growing list of restaurants to which we were never allowed to return.

ↀ

There followed a continuing period of vacillating instructions and inactivity for the Selous Scouts which had Andy Samuels and me wondering who, if anyone, was in the driver's seat at COMOPS. It was late 1979, and the internationally-brokered peace talks between the Rhodesian Government and the two leading terrorist factions, Nkomo's ZIPRA and Mugabe's ZANLA, were well under way. It was clear that the talks would culminate in a 'one man one vote' election being held, resulting in black majority rule and the birth of a new country, *Zimbabwe,* rising out of the Rhodesian ashes.

Both terrorist leaders had already made known their precondition; any settlement would have to involve the disbandment of the Selous Scouts. Such was their fear and trepidation of the unit that not only did they want it disbanded, but they wanted its members expelled from the country. The writing was on the wall and I began to make plans for Carol and me to leave Rhodesia and move to South Africa.

Another of the provisions of the settlement talks was that both Nkomo and Mugabe would be allowed back into the country to start campaigning for the new elections to be held in mid-1980. Their respective terrorist forces, or guerilla armies as it had become 'vogue' to call them, would be restricted to a number of designated 'assembly areas' located throughout the country. It was against this backdrop that Andy Samuels and I were called one morning into the office of the new Commanding Officer of the Selous Scouts, Lieutenant-Colonel Pat Armstrong.

"Chaps, we've been given the task of killing Mugabe. There's only one proviso—it has to look like an assassination attempt by renegade members of Nkomo's ZIPRA." Andy and I looked at each other in astonishment.

"What are you waiting for, chaps? I have a week in which to get back to COMOPS with your plan. We haven't got much time."

"That's crazy," said Andy. "The gooks in the assembly areas will run riot."

"As soon as Mugabe is dead, the plan is for the Air Force to bomb the assembly areas killing everybody inside." Pat Armstrong spoke with conviction. "Any that survive and who make a run for it will soon be hunted down and killed."

"What then?" I asked. "I suppose Prince Charles will fly in, we'll all doff our hats and sing *God Save the Queen*! Sanctions will be lifted and the rest of the world will shrug their shoulders and say, 'It's the African way'." I was anything but convinced.

At this late stage the plan simply didn't make any sense. However, we accepted that for such a bizarre plan to have been hatched, COMOPS must know something that we didn't.

The plan we developed was simple and carried with it a high probability of success. Best of all it wouldn't leave any trace of having been initiated by the Selous Scouts. Mugabe was due to attend an election rally in the southern city of Bulawayo within two weeks. Thousands were expected to attend. We got one of our black pseudo-operators accredited as one of the few news reporters able to gain entry into the tightly-guarded security area containing the platform and podium from which Mugabe would speak. The operator carried with him a Russian-made tape recorder, the microphone of which would be placed with the other microphones Mugabe would be speaking into. The difference between our microphone and the rest was that ours was filled with a shaped charge full of high explosives. Andy and I would position ourselves on a small hill approximately a mile away from the stadium in which the rally was to be held. We would have with us a portable radio tuned to a station that was to broadcast the rally live. As soon as we heard Mugabe begin his speech, we would simply detonate the explosive charge inside our microphone using a remote detonation device. The result would be like a powerful shotgun shell being discharged into Mugabe's face from a distance of a few inches. At the same time, an explosive charge inside the tape recorder would detonate, completely destroying it. Our operator would then slink away in the ensuing mêlée.

The plan was fine tuned, rehearsed and eventually submitted to COMOPS for approval. Two days later we were given the go-ahead for its implementation. Our pseudo-operator was deployed and had no difficulty getting through security and into the tightly-cordoned area from which Mugabe was to speak. Andy and I, situated on a nearby hill, waited for the rally to begin, nervously chewing on stalks of grass as we counted down the minutes. Thirty minutes before the rally was scheduled to start the high frequency radio which linked us to our Headquarters squawked into life. It was Pat Armstrong.

"It's imperative that you abort the operation. Did you copy?" Pat kept repeating the message over and over with greater urgency.

Andy and I looked at each other, almost unbelieving. "Did you hear that, Andy? They want us to abort."

"I didn't hear a thing," replied Andy, still chewing on his grass. We had gone this far in planning and implementing the operation and Andy was determined it would continue.

"Perhaps the Air Force has just realized they don't have enough bombers to destroy the assembly areas," I suggested, mockingly.

The next message forced even Andy to listen. Pat Armstrong informed us that the operation had been leaked by somebody in COMOPS and that Mugabe's security detail had been made aware of the plan. At that very moment they were removing all microphones from the podium and Mugabe would speak using a bullhorn. Even if we detonated the charge it would explode harmlessly away from its intended target.

It was the ultimate betrayal and I knew at that moment all was lost. Somebody at COMOPS was feeding details of our top secret operations to British Intelligence, who in turn was passing it directly to Nkomo and Mugabe. The finger ultimately pointed firmly in the direction of Ken Flower, the Director of the Rhodesian Central Intelligence Organization, who was privy to the planning of all our external operations. I wondered for how long the deceitful man had been betraying the trust of the Rhodesian people, and jeopardizing the lives of her brave soldiers.

Some weeks later Andy and I were again called into Pat Armstrong's office. The elections had just been held and there was a prevailing concern at COMOPS that, against all expectations, Mugabe had won a landslide victory. Ballot papers from the elections were stored in vaults kept in the basement of Salisbury's Anglican Cathedral until counting could begin. The three of us discussed a COMOPS plan to place explosive charges inside the basement of the Cathedral to blow up the entire building. The ballots would be destroyed and a new election would then have to be held. Before electioneering began, the rampant intimidation which had resulted in Mugabe's sweeping victory would be addressed.

Andy and I looked at each other, then at our new Commanding Officer. All three of us shook our heads in an emphatic *NO!* We would not be party to any more bizarre plots hatched by what appeared to us to be an increasingly irrational command at COMOPS.

‿

Three months later, on 12 July 1980, I resigned my commission from the Rhodesian Army. I had already been asked by the South African Defence Force to assist in forming the nucleus of a copycat regiment of the Selous Scouts in the sparsely-populated northeastern part of South Africa near a town called Phalaborwa. It was a task I accepted with a degree of trepidation, only because I was aware of the vast cultural chasm that existed between the Rhodesian and South African armies. Carol and I agreed to give it a go for an initial period of a year.

A month after I resigned we placed our household furniture into storage in Salisbury with instructions on where we could be reached. Then we loaded our Datsun 120Y with sufficient personal effects to sustain us until we could get settled and headed south into the sunset. The roof rack of the car was so overloaded with suitcases and drooping canvas valises that it looked like a giant bird had just defecated on it.

"It looks rather disgusting and vulgar," remarked Carol, winding up her window. "Do you think they'll let us through the border?"

18
Division of Cultures

"Where are you from?"
"Rhodesia."
"The only thing that separates us is a mere river." "You really think so?"
"Yes. We are like one people." "Are you drunk?"

—Author talking with the Secretary,
Hans Merensky Country Club,
Phalaborwa: September, 1980

O ur arrival in South Africa wasn't heralded by particularly good news. Carol and I stopped in the legislative capital, Pretoria, on the first day and booked into the Culembourg, a rather tired and squalid hotel located in the centre of the city. We were having breakfast the next morning when I was approached by a female employee of the hotel. She was endowed with quite the largest bosoms I had ever seen. Her undersized blouse seemed barely able to contain their voluminousness and I worried they might pop free from their tenuous moorings at any moment. She might have appeared somewhat top-heavy but for an equally large bottom that protruded above her lower extremities like a continental shelf.

"Are you Mr. Bux?" she asked, peering down at me through her ample cleavage.

"No. I'm Mr. Bax," I replied.

"I have a telegram for you, Mr. Bux," she continued, unconcerned with the vagaries of correct pronunciation. She bent her ample frame toward me placing a crumpled piece of paper on the table next to the hard-boiled egg I was trying to eat. It was a telegram from the moving company that had our furniture in storage.

> Dear Mr. Bax. We regret to advise that your furniture and household effects have been totally destroyed by a fire at our storage facility in Salisbury. Best regards and assuring you of our best service at all times, the Management.

I handed the telegram to Carol.

"What on earth are we going to do!" she gasped. Before leaving Rhodesia we had spent a considerable amount of our meager savings buying new oak furniture.

"Order a stiff brandy if they'll give us one," I replied.

I looked around for the busty lady but she had lost interest in us and was busy devouring a large doughnut that somebody had left behind on their breakfast table. It wasn't a terribly auspicious start to the new chapter in our lives.

We arrived in Phalaborwa later that afternoon. The South Africans had constructed a base just outside the town to house their newly-formed 5 Reconnaissance Regiment, or '5 Recce' as it was called. The Regiment was to be formed along similar lines to the Selous Scouts and it was hoped that soldiers leaving that unit would form its nucleus. While the base boasted ultramodern facilities, nobody had thought to incorporate a married quarters, a rather serious oversight given the barrack's location close to a town with its own chronic housing shortage. To overcome the problem, a number of mobile park homes had been hastily created on the outskirts of the town to accommodate the unit's married members. It was to one of these that Carol and I found ourselves directed later that afternoon. It resembled a barren lunar landscape upon which large oblong containers had been scattered. Carol wasn't overly impressed when I informed her that container number two was to be our home for the next year.

For the first four months the only occupants of the base, and of the park homes, were a handful of families whose husbands had served in the Selous Scouts and who, like us, had decided to leave Rhodesia after Independence. After our arrival we heard very little from the South African Special Forces Headquarters under whose command we fell, mainly because no radios or telephones existed at the base with which to communicate. We were simply left to our own devices. When a telephone was eventually installed none of the staff officers at the Headquarters seemed to want to take any responsibility for us. We were like a hot potato that nobody wanted to be left holding.

Eventually, and probably only out of sheer curiosity, the Brigadier in charge of operational planning at the Headquarters decided to pay us a visit. He arrived in a C-130 Hercules with a planeload of curious staff officers anxious to take their first look at the phenomenon of a Rhodesian unit stuck in the middle of the South African lowveldt. They were like zookeepers wanting to

A two-man reconnaissance team, Selous Scouts. (Dennis Croukamp)

get a firsthand glance at a rare species of animal the zoo had recently had the misfortune of acquiring.

The senior Rhodesian officer at our base at the time was a friend of mine called Geoff Atkinson. He and I both held the rank of major and we had got together before the visit to discuss what we should do with the delegation once they arrived.

"The best we can do is to give them a quick tour around the base and then adjourn to the bar," I suggested. "That way they can meet us socially over a drink and convince themselves that we are perfectly normal human beings." Geoff agreed.

On the morning of their arrival we showed them around the base, ending up at midday at the Officers' Mess for a drink. Everything seemed to be going as planned. However, opening the bar at lunch time, a perfectly normal occurrence in any Rhodesian Army Mess, proved to be our first undoing. In the South African Army it was considered a scandalous breach of regulations. What happened next must have had the Brigadier scratching his head about the folly of ever having invited Rhodesians to join the South African Army in the first place.

I was making polite conversation with the Brigadier when we were joined by another Rhodesian, who like me, had previously served in both the Rhodesian Light Infantry and the Selous Scouts. Captain Ian Scott was a lean, scrappy individual who considered social graces a meaningless and unnecessary encumbrance for any soldier involved in a bush war. Few who met him doubted his ability as an exceptional bushman and aggressive frontline soldier, but in a social setting he could be quite uncouth. The three of us had just moved from the bar to an outside courtyard to take advantage of a cool breeze when between us walked a large hunting spider. It was some five inches in diameter with a bulbous yellow backside the size of a squash ball. The Brigadier took a nimble step backwards warning us to be careful.

"You 'Rhodesias' must watch out for those things, they are extremely venomous," he cautioned keeping a wary eye on the hairy creature.

Ian looked down at the spider as if it were nothing more dangerous than a dung beetle. Bending down he scooped it up in his right hand and popped it into his mouth, swallowing it like a hungry hound might swallow a piece of meat. Then pulling a filthy handkerchief from his pocket, he gave his nose a loud honk that sounded like the blast of a ship's horn on a foggy night off the Goodwin Sands.

"They're only dangerous if you let them bite you, Brigadier. Eaten, they are a great delicacy," said Ian nonchalantly, swigging back his beer.

The startled Brigadier looked at Ian with his eyeballs extended out like organ stops. He was quite speechless and continued to stare at Ian as if not quite believing what he had just witnessed. He recoiled backwards in disgust as Ian gave another loud trumpet into his snotty handkerchief.

"Excuse me, Brigadier," he sputtered, a piece of mucus hanging from his nose. "The legs tend to get caught up in one's nostrils. Now, what were we talking about?"

The Brigadier couldn't remember nor did he seem to care. He couldn't wait to board his plane and return to the sanity of his own headquarters.

❧

Our reputation as a bunch of wild, defiant and disorderly bush soldiers was strengthened a month later when we received a surprise visit from yet another delegation of senior officers. They descended upon us like crafty shepherds to an indomitable flock, determined to get us to conform to the rigid protocols and procedures demanded by the South African Defence Force … procedures we had hitherto avoided like the plague.

We had been joined the week before by a former officer of the Rhodesian Light Infantry who had resigned his commission in order to join 5 Recce. His name was Alan Gingles and he was as fiery and outspoken an Irishman as you could ever wish to meet. His short, lean stature belied an exceptionally strong personality that was unafraid of expressing a forthright opinion to anyone who cared to listen, as well as to those who didn't. Not only was he unafraid of speaking his mind, but he did so in a brogue that was as thick as the malt residue inside a barrel of his beloved Bushmills Irish whiskey. It was a tipple he was seldom without in the confines of the Mess.

Unfortunately, it was Alan Gingles whom the South African delegation had the misfortune to run into when they made their unannounced visit to the base late one Friday afternoon. The rest of us had taken the day off to go game viewing in the Kruger National Park, leaving Alan to hold the fort. We had told him we would be back later that afternoon and to meet us in the Mess for a drink.

Unfortunately, it was in the Mess that the South African delegation eventually found Alan, but only after they had been wandering around the base for an hour looking for somebody to speak with.

"It seems that every time we arrive, you 'Rhodesias' are sitting in the bar," announced the leader of the delegation irritably looking at his watch. He was relieved not to have found the base completely deserted but was less than pleased at having found its only occupant sitting in the bar at 4:30 in the afternoon.

"Then you shouldn't have any difficulty finding us in the future," replied Alan, unconcernedly taking a sip from his glass of Bushmills. "And to whom do I have the privilege of speaking?"

"Lieutenant-Colonel Jakkals de Jagger," replied the head of the delegation, running a finger through his stiff moustache. Colonel de Jagger was the head of intelligence at the Special Forces Headquarters. "And where might the rest of the 'Rhodesias' be this afternoon?"

"They're game viewing in the Kruger Park, Jakkals. But they're expected back at any moment to attend our Friday evening prayer meeting."

Jakkals de Jagger bristled at the indignity of being addressed by his first name by the cheeky young Irishman, but talk of a prayer meeting placated him. Perhaps these heathen Rhodesians might be salvageable after all.

"And where do you hold these prayer meetings?" he inquired. "Why, right here in the bar of course. I'm afraid it's one occasion when we do tend to overdo the drinking a bit."

Prayer meetings were a longstanding tradition in the Rhodesian Army where officers within a Regiment would gather in the Officers' Mess bar every Friday evening to socialize over copious amounts of alcohol. It was considered a 'formal parade', and failure by an officer to attend was viewed as seriously as failure to attend any other Regimental duty.

"*Prayer* meetings in the bar?" exclaimed Colonel de Jagger incredulously. "That is precisely what we need to talk to you 'Rhodesias' about. There is talk that you are not even saying your prayers at the morning muster parades." The Colonel lowered his voice to a whisper, as if what he was about to say was so scandalous it couldn't possibly be said out loud. "In fact … there is even a rumor that you are not doing muster parades at all!"

The Colonel drew his shoulders back with hands on his hips, looking gravely down at Alan like a schoolmaster who had just confronted a schoolboy with an accusation he couldn't possibly wriggle out of.

Alan was not to be cowed. "You're quite right about that, Jakkals. Why would anybody want to say prayers on a hot Parade Square when they could just as easily say them in the conviviality of a bar?"

Jakkals was scandalized; so were the rest of his delegation. The Colonel was about to offer a rebuke when Alan continued, "By the way, to change the subject, I've been meaning to ask you chaps about this rugby team you call the Springboks. Do you think it might be a team to give Ireland a warm-up game or two?"

It was probably just as well the South Africans weren't able to pick up on what Alan was intimating. Rugby is the holy grail of South African culture. Making fun of the national team is considered nothing short of treasonous. It was only his brogue, made thicker by his considerable intake of Bushmills that saved the cocky Irishman from being knocked off his barstool that afternoon.

Colonel Jakkals left the following morning, his mission unaccomplished. Soon afterwards the South Africans must have concluded that if they weren't going to get the Rhodesian leopard to change its spots, the best place for the leopard to be was in the bush. We soon found ourselves being deployed to South West Africa to take part in their bush war.

❧

I was thankful to receive a visit from my old friend Ron Reid-Daly during one of my periods of R&R. Ron was now living in Johannesburg where he ran a large security enterprise called Security Services International. The company had just signed a contract to restructure and retrain the fledgling Transkei Defence Force. Transkei was an independent, self-ruled state or homeland, occupying a swathe of South Africa's southeastern coastline.

"I'd like to form a Special Forces Regiment to be based in the coastal town of Port St Johns," said Ron. "There's already a fellow down there running some sort of naval diving academy. You're just the man to go down there and make proper soldiers out of them. I'd like you to use the fellows as a nucleus to form the new Regiment."

I had no idea where Port St Johns was, but it was an offer which I readily accepted. My year's contract with the South African Army was almost over and I had little appetite to renew it.

The failure of the South Africans to successfully incorporate Rhodesians into their 'order of battle' was not theirs alone.

Rhodesians have an indomitable and independent spirit that makes it difficult for them to be assimilated into any foreign culture. South African soldiers are some of the best, most aggressive soldiers in the world, and they have served history proudly in the defence of freedom wherever they have been asked to serve. There is no army in Africa to come close to them, nor a rugby team to subdue the Springboks on their day.

Just before I left Phalaborwa, Carol and I were enjoying evening drinks in our park home with Alan Gingles and his wife, Pauline. She was a strikingly-attractive lady with jet black hair, soft pale skin and green eyes that sparkled like diamonds. Alan was bemoaning the fact that I didn't have any Irish crystal glasses from which to drink the Bushmills we were enjoying.

"I'll send you some when I get home to Ireland," he promised. Shortly after I left the South African Army, Alan was tragically killed on operations. I was devastated. Pauline returned to her family in Ireland and Carol and I heard nothing from her until one day a parcel arrived in the mail. Inside were six Irish Heritage crystal whiskey glasses and a letter from Pauline. In it she wrote … "Alan wanted you to have some decent whiskey glasses, so please accept these as a fulfillment of his promise. It's what he would have wanted."

Wild Coast

"When will the ferry return to this side of the river?" "It will return eventually."
"Do you know when?"
"When the driver awakens."
"The driver is sleeping?"
"He sleeps when he's been drinking."

—Conversation while waiting to
cross the Umzimvubu River,
Port St Johns: September, 1981

My first encounter with divers from the 'naval academy' in Port St Johns occurred on the same day that Carol and I arrived in that picturesque little town. We had driven from our temporary home in Durban the night before and booked into the Cape Hermes Hotel, an elegant, colonial-style lodging situated on the mouth of the Umzimvubu River where it spills into the tumultuous waters of the Indian Ocean. We had just finished a late breakfast at the hotel and were on our way to look at a rambling, bougainvillea-clad villa that had been procured for us to live in. It was situated on a lush hill overgrown with subtropical vegetation and banana trees and enjoyed a panoramic view of the town below and the sweeping expanse of ocean beyond.

As we were driving through the centre of the town, we encountered one of the most bizarre and extraordinary sights I had ever witnessed. A squad of men in full diving gear was flopping its way down the main road. 'Flopping' is all one can reasonably expect to do when walking on a street wearing a wetsuit, flippers, mask and snorkel. At the head of this unlikely-looking group was a well-built man carrying what appeared to be a large cutlass. He might have cut quite an impressive figure were it not for the fact that he kept stumbling over his flippers.

The squad stopped as I pulled up next to them, their masks full of condensation. I wondered at how they could see where they were going. I asked the man with the cutlass what he was doing staggering along a main street in equipment best suited for half a league under the sea.

"These guys are Class A Attack Divers," he replied indignantly. He spoke in a guttural Afrikaans accent. "I'm conducting evaluation training."

"By walking them down a street?"

There is no higher grade of diver in the British Navy than a Class A Attack

Diver and only a few ever qualify. Some showed extraordinary courage during the Second World War by cutting through underwater screens of steel cable protecting the entrance of enemy harbors to blow up the ships beyond with limpet mines. Yet here I was in the presence of twelve of them walking down a street in Port St Johns!

"No, man," he responded, beginning to look uncomfortable in his full-length wet suit. The outside temperature had begun to climb into the high 80s. "I test them in the municipal swimming pool—the deep end, mind you."

"In a swimming pool? If they're class A Attack Divers, shouldn't you be testing them in the ocean?"

"In the ocean—are you crazy, man? That would be far too dangerous, these guys would drown. As it is I have to use this knife to cut them free from their tanks if they panic in the pool."

I soon learned that I had been speaking with Johann Fourie, an Able Seaman who had settled in Port St Johns after being cashiered from the South African Navy. Because of his naval experience, the Transkei Government had asked him to select and train a small group of divers to undertake coastal search and recovery missions. Immediately promoting himself to the rank of 'Naval Captain', he had recruited a motley band of former soldiers and set up offices in some derelict buildings on a hill overlooking the town. After putting

Port St Johns. (Kathryn Costello)

Port St Johns bridge. (Kathryn Costello)

his charges through some rudimentary swimming lessons in the municipal swimming pool and issuing them with some newly-acquired diving equipment, he had pronounced the 'Transkeian Naval Diving Academy' open for business with himself as its self-appointed Commodore. Neither he nor his divers were very happy when shortly after my arrival I incorporated the 'academy' into a newly-formed Special Forces Regiment. They were unhappier still when I insisted on having their diving skills evaluated at sea.

The first diver tested was asked to perform a very basic diving procedure which would take him no further than six feet beneath the surface of some shallow coastal waters. Unfortunately, it was six feet too far. After we had put to sea and jumping reluctantly from the boat, he disappeared below the surface and didn't emerge until hoisted out a few minutes later ... drowned. The rest of the divers who were nervously watching from the shore immediately absconded—as did 'Captain' Johann Fourie.

It was an inglorious end to Transkeian Naval Diving Academy.

&

Port St Johns was a wonderful setting in which to live and work. As a holiday destination, it was unparalleled. It is situated along a stretch of South Africa's southeastern seaboard called the Wild Coast, a rugged almost uninhabited expanse of windswept, rocky cliffs and coral shoals against which the tempestuous, deep blue waters of the Indian Ocean collide, retreat, then collide again in a never-ending rhythm of turbulent confusion. Its jagged shores and coral reefs have become the final resting place of many a proud ship and brave mariner. Below the crashing breakers lie hidden hordes of treasure, their location jealously guarded by an ever-vigilant sea. The picturesque town is as remote as it is undeveloped and nestles in breathtaking beauty between two towering cliffs through which carves the mighty Umzimvubu River. South of the river mouth, protective arms of coral extend out to sea subduing its giant rollers into gentle swells that lap harmlessly on to pristine beaches of white sand.

It wasn't long before our home became a holiday retreat for family and friends—and for others anxious to fade into the obscurity offered by such a remote and inaccessible backwater. Among them was a ragtag group of amateurish and by now, very overweight and unfit former soldiers who had attempted to stage a coup on the resort island of Seychelles.

The group had intended to enter the island on the pretext of belonging to a social rugby club called *Ye Olde and Ancient Order of Froth Blowers*. Flying from the South African port city of Durban, they hoped to bluff their way past the island's customs officials by stuffing their weapons into sports bags. By the time they landed however, the portly fellows had consumed a considerable amount of the plane's ample supply of beer and in the process had divulged their nefarious intentions to some startled fellow passengers. Their disguise wasn't helped going through Customs when one of the officials noticed the barrel of an AK-47 protruding from the bag of one particular bleary-eyed individual. The aspiring 'Soldier of Fortune' had clearly consumed more beer than was good for him during the flight.

Realizing their cover was blown, the 'would be' liberators retreated from the Customs building on to the runway where they hijacked an Air India airliner readying itself for takeoff. An AK-47 pointed at the Indian Captain was all that was needed to convince him to re-route his plane from Bombay to Durban. It also convinced him to comply with the hijackers demand to open a free bar service during the flight.

As ideal a location as my home in Port St Johns was in enabling the gallant, swashbuckling adventurers to retreat into obscurity, they soon became bored and drifted off in search of new and more exciting horizons.

I was rather pleased they decided to leave before Mother and my twin sister Janet arrived on a visit from Canada. Mother would have been quietly disapproving, while Janet would have been more vocal and outspoken in her condemnation. She might well have had them walking the plank from one of the many three-masted barquentines that dotted the coastline.

Thinking that she was coming to a holiday resort of similar sophistication to the Riviera, Janet's holiday attire consisted mainly of cocktail dresses. The most sophisticated nightclub in Port St Johns was an open-sided beach house with a thatch roof that sold bottles of illegally-procured plonk and featured a long-haired creature of doubtful sobriety sitting on a crate of pineapples playing melancholic ballads on an old harmonica. Janet, with her innate ability to have a good time anywhere she traveled, fitted right in—cocktail dresses included!

࿎

There were few medical facilities in Port St Johns and the only doctors available were situated in the capital city, Umtata, which was some 50 miles inland. It was there I took Carol one morning after she announced she might be pregnant. She had already suffered four miscarriages and none of the previous gynecologists she had seen had been able to explain why. The doctor who attended to Carol was a local gynecologist named Brian Hulley. He was a well-known personality in Transkei who liked to spend his free time relaxing at his seaside cottage doing what he loved most—fishing. It was from a weekend of

Port St Johns lighthouse and river-mouth. (Kathryn Costello)

Port St Johns river-mouth. (Kathryn Costello)

Radio 604 Capitol Radio in Port St Johns. (Kathryn Costello)

fishing that he walked into his office that afternoon, smelling like a fishmonger after a busy day at the harbor.

"Are you a fisherman or a doctor?" asked Carol, skeptically taking in Brian's scruffy appearance. His hair was windswept and he had a fishing rapala lure protruding from his shirt pocket.

"I'm both. Do you want to talk fishing or babies?" he replied, striding to a nearby sink to wash his hands.

"Actually, I enjoy fishing but the reason I've come to see you this morning is because I think I'm pregnant. I've already had four miscarriages and no one can tell me why. I would prefer not to have another."

"You've had four miscarriages and nobody can tell you why?" exclaimed Brian, scrubbing vigorously at some stubborn fish scales sticking to his hands.

Carol told him that was correct and explained her history, handing over a large bundle of medical notes she had meticulously kept from visits to previous doctors. It took Brian thirty minutes to sift through them. After reading one he would toss it into a waste bin and go on to the next. Carol was becoming quietly hysterical watching the bundle of notes she had kept for so long being relegated to the rubbish bin. One particular handwritten note caught Brian's interest. He read it again, and giving an exclamation of relief, waved the paper in his hand as if it might be the key to some long unsolved mystery.

"This is just what I was hoping for. It's the *only* note that tells me anything. The rest are all rubbish." He tossed what remained of the bundle into the bin with the rest.

After examining Carol to ascertain that she was indeed pregnant, Brian disappeared into his dispensary and returned a few minutes later with a handful of vials and needles.

"Have one of these injected into your bum each morning before you get out of bed and I'll stake my reputation on the fact that your first child will be born a healthy handful in seven and a half months."

"He doesn't seem very professional," worried Carol on our return to Port St Johns. "Imagine arriving to see a patient looking like you've just stepped off a fishing trawler—and he's thrown all my notes away!"

Seven months later Carol gave birth to a healthy, golden-haired daughter whom we christened Jennifer Sarah Bax. The date was 17 June 1982, and it was the happiest day of my life. Brian had succeeded where all other doctors had failed.

❧

Brian Hulley's Umgazana cottage. (Dr Brian Hulley)

Shortly after Jennifer was born, Brian invited us to join him and his family at their seaside cottage for a weekend of fishing. He had just purchased a powerful, sleek-looking ski boat which seemed as if it should be gracing the dock of a luxury resort on the Mediterranean rather than a scruffy wood jetty on the Wild Coast. We readily accepted his kind invitation and arrived at their cottage late one Friday evening.

The next morning dawned misty and gray, the choppy sea unsettled by a stiff north-easter. Large breakers smashed against the beach in a boiling frenzy of swirling white foam and tumbled angrily over a submerged sandbank that guarded the mouth of the river through which Brian intended launching his new ski boat. After breakfast I was about to echo Carol's sentiments that the sea looked too menacing to send a frigate into let alone a ski boat, when Brian confidently put his arm around my shoulder.

"Come on, it's bad but I've been out in worse. Let's see how she handles a choppy sea."

I knew that Brian was one of Transkei's leading ski boat fishermen and that he had a healthy regard for the sea, so putting my skepticism and fear of seasickness behind me I followed him down to his dock. The relatively calm waters of the river where the boat was moored gave me a false sense of security and I declined to wear the life jacket Brian handed me as I stepped on to the boat.

"Life jackets aren't optional when you launch into a turbulent sea, even in a ski boat this size. Unless you have a divine ability to walk on water, strap it on and strap it tight."

Feeling like a chastised schoolboy I slipped into the jacket making a pretence of clipping the straps around my waist. As we motored slowly toward the river mouth, I marveled at the variety of fishing rods that jutted like saplings from the tubular stainless steel holders attached to each side of the boat. The rods had already been rigged with fishing lures and weights ready for the big catch. It was only when the boat began bucking and plunging its way through the huge offshore breakers that I wished I had taken my companion's advice and securely fastened my life jacket. By then it was too late; I was clinging to the front console of the boat like a frightened child on a violent and extremely uncomfortable roller coaster ride.

We had just plummeted down the back of one particularly mountainous wave and were about to climb another when the propellers of both outboards struck a sandbank, immediately stalling both engines. What happened next seemed to last forever but could only have taken a few seconds. Powerless and rudderless, the boat skewered sideways up the face of the next mountainous wave and just before reaching the crest was unceremoniously flipped upside-down and we found ourselves buried under a huge deluge of furiously churning seawater.

I had been under the upturned boat for what seemed like an eternity before reaching the startling conclusion that before I could swim to the surface, I would first have to dive deeper to clear the sides of the boat. This was no easy feat wearing a life jacket and being hemmed in by a forest of fishing rods with fishing lures snaking everywhere. When I did eventually surface, the life jacket I was wearing had slipped to my lower extremities and was doing a good job of keeping my bottom afloat, but little else. Deciding that my best chances for survival would be to swim for shore I gamely struck out, my arms whirling like propellers. I had been frantically swimming for a while when I realized that I hadn't moved an inch. I was still only a few feet from the upturned boat. Then I realized I was being held fast by a length of fifty-pound fishing line running between my thighs and a rapala fishing lure snagged to the front of my life jacket. My growing sense of unease wasn't helped when I noticed we

Fishing with Brian Hulley. (Dr Brian Hulley)

were rapidly drifting further out to sea. I heard Brian shouting at me through the roar of the surf.

"Stay with the boat. You'll never be able to swim against the outgoing tide and even if you could, the sharks would have your testicles snapped off long before you reached shore."

That didn't sound like a very attractive proposal, and I came as close to walking on water as I had ever come in my haste to scramble aboard the upturned hull. Brian told me not to waste my energy, but to cling to the engines which were leaking huge amounts of fuel into the water.

"The smell should keep the sharks at bay," he gasped, disappearing beneath another huge wave.

I clung to the motor with one hand and kept the other held firmly over my crotch. Fuel or no fuel, I didn't enjoy the prospect of an inquisitive shark poking its nose around my nether regions below the angry surface of the water. Thankfully, it wasn't long before another ski boat was able to rescue us and we were eventually able to make our way back to Brian's cottage. We spent the rest of that weekend firmly anchored to terra firma making a large dent in his ample supply of fine malt whisky.

cx/o

A wide tidal river, the Umzimvubu River separated Port St Johns from a labyrinth of small, quaint and picturesque little cottages that overlooked the beach on the far side of the river. Many of the town's residents lived there as did many of the families whose husbands were involved training the Transkei Defence Force. Amongst them was my good friend, Andy Samuels, who together with his wife, Ellie and their two children had recently arrived from Rhodesia. Also resident at the cottages were a number of disc jockeys working with Capitol Radio, an independent radio station operating out of a grand and elegant-looking double-storey villa on the opposite side of the river.

A large bridge across the river had been opened amidst considerable fanfare and excitement some years before by the country's President. He had even ordered an ox slaughtered in celebration of the great engineering marvel. The bridge was washed away some years later amidst considerably less ceremony. In its place was an old and extremely dilapidated ferry which looked like a World War II landing craft that had been left to rust on Omaha Beach for half a century. The driver, of even older vintage than the ferry, was imbued with a great fondness for liquor. The consequence of his alcoholic intake was that he was prone to taking long and unscheduled siestas when he should have been operating the ferry. Luckily, the craft was attached to a steel cable strung across the river to keep it on course and prevent it floating out to sea during the times when the driver became incapacitated. The ferry was notoriously unreliable and prone to frequent breakdowns, but when it did operate it ferried passengers and cars to and from crumbling concrete ramps on each side of the river where the bridge had once stood.

The unreliability of the ferry service caused havoc with the schedules of the DJ's working with Capital Radio. They would often find themselves stranded on the wrong side of the river and would have to plunge themselves into its shark-infested waters and swim to the other side in order to get to work. The schedules of my co-workers weren't as crucial. There was always another fish to catch as they waited for the ferry, or another cocktail to be sipped.

It wasn't just the ferry driver who was prone to drinking. One evening I was having a party at my house with Andy Samuels and a friend of his called Brian Wyllie who played rugby for the New Zealand All Blacks. Well past midnight Andy and Brian decided it was time to make their way home across the river. Having consumed well over a bottle of J&B whisky, they had considerable difficulty finding their way to Andy's pick-up which was parked directly outside my front door and I wondered how they were going to make it

Andy Samuels. (Debbie Patching)

across the river. I decided I had better travel with them as I was a bit concerned about their ability to negotiate the ferry, if it was still operating at that late hour. Quite why I believed that I might be of assistance I don't know because I had consumed just as much whisky as they had. It just seemed a good idea at the time.

The three of us climbed into the front cab and set off into the night with Andy peering precariously over the steering wheel. He was unable to focus on anything more than a few feet ahead of the vehicle, the result of both his alcoholic intake and the fact that he had neglected to switch on the headlights.

Arriving at the ferry ramp thirty minutes later we were relieved to see it moored on our side of the river. With Brian Wyllie jovially making his best attempt at a rendition of the New Zealand rugby chant, the 'Haka' (no easy feat in the confines of a small pick-up), Andy gunned the vehicle down the ramp towards the ferry. None of us noticed that the ferry wasn't actually moored at the ramp but was drifting some way off. We plunged into the inky, black water in a deluge of spray and steam with Brian Wyllie rapidly switching from the Haka to a rather vulgar version of the Last Rites. In the resulting confusion the ferry driver woke up, and in trying to warn us of the imminent danger we already knew we were in, started operating the only mechanical device that worked on the vessel with any degree of consistency—its foghorn.

Taking this as a signal to abandon ship, Brian Wyllie leaped from the truck and clambered up a nearby tree where he remained for some time looking like a sorrowful chimpanzee.

By a miraculous stroke of good fortune the truck never stalled and Andy was able to reverse it out of the river. With the ferry now firmly against the ramp, and with Wyllie having finally been coaxed from his tree, we were able to resume our journey aboard the ferry. By the time we arrived at Andy's house some hours later, we were feeling decidedly in need of another drink.

🙰

I was sitting in my office one morning planning a training exercise for some of my troops when I received a phone call from the manager of the Umgazi River Bungalows, a well-known tourist resort located a few miles down the coast. The manager's name was Ian Crawford and he told me some rather exciting news.

"Keep this under your belt, but I have the opportunity of getting a few strippers down from Durban in a few days if you guys are interested."

I assured him we would all be interested. An erotic night of burlesque would provide welcome relief from the boredom of sitting at home watching the only television channel available in Port St Johns, the reception of which was so bad that watching it was like peering into an Alaskan winter blizzard.

The show was scheduled for 1 April and that evening, together with five of my colleagues, we arrived at the resort having spun our wives a web of intrigue and deception as to why we would be away for the night. We met Crawford in the bar for a few drinks and he assured us that the strippers were already preparing themselves for the evening's great extravaganza of sleaze.

"How many strippers?" I asked.

"Six, that's one for each of you, the possibilities are endless," replied Crawford with a conspiratorial grin.

After settling our nerves and our excitement with a few more drinks, we followed our host unobtrusively through a side door of the resort's conference hall feeling like truant schoolboys sneaking into an X-rated cinema. The hall was dimly lit and it took us a few minutes to stumble our way to some seats which had been placed in front of a raised platform on which the show was to be staged. On the platform was an unhappy-looking man trying to get a wind-up gramophone to work. The machine looked so old and antiquated I wondered from what museum it might have been borrowed. I was just beginning to wonder whether the malfunctioning gramophone might rob us of our evening's entertainment when it unexpectedly burst into life with a scratchy recording of the theme from the *Pink Panther*. Unfortunately, the machine had been set on the wrong speed making what should have been an enticing musical prelude sound like a slow dirge from a Celtic funeral.

Eventually a red velvet curtain that had been strung across the stage slowly parted and on to the stage strutted a heavily made-up red-headed vixen clad in black fishnet stockings, a white blouse and what looked like a crimson-colored tutu. Behind her were five equally meagerly-clad chorus girls trying to perform something resembling the Can Can, but which looked more like a tired attempt at stretching their aching limbs. The timing and choreography of the dance routine wasn't helped by the fact that, just as the girls arrived on stage, the stylus became stuck on the record and the dirge became an oscillating drone.

I was seated next to a colleague of mine, Chris Robins, with whom I had served in the Selous Scouts. It was just after the redhead had provocatively removed her blouse to reveal a cluster of red freckles that there was a startled exclamation from Chris.

"Hey, that's my wife!"

There was a gasp from the rest of us followed by a stunned silence as we each began recognizing our own wives from amongst the line of aspiring Moulin Rouge chorus girls. Our cover was blown. It had been the ultimate April Fool's joke played by mischievous wives on their unsuspecting husbands. The fact that they had enticed Crawford into joining their prank cost him an evening of drinks, but he was well entertained listening to the wives relating the improbable tales woven by their husbands to explain their absences from home that evening.

❧

I had been living in the remote tranquility of Port St Johns for three years and was becoming quite concerned that the eccentricity of some of its inhabitants might start rubbing off on me. One such character was a local legend named Ben Dekker, an extremely tall individual with long, blond hair who had the build of a Greek God and the reclusive nature of a castaway. His wardrobe consisted of a loin cloth and headband which he sometimes supplemented with a necklace of shells. His home was a cave dug into a cliff-face at the edge of a public beach; the expansive white sands his self-appointed front yard. A tidal rock pool nearby provided a romantic and unique setting for his bathing

Ben Dekker at a party. (Kathryn Costello)

Ben Dekker. (Kathryn Costello)

requirements, which he would occasionally share with some free-spirited female tourist in awe of his renown physical attributes.

My concerns were allayed one afternoon when I received a call from Ron Reid-Daly telling me it was time for me to extract myself from my quiescent environment and join him in Umtata where he had recently been appointed the Commander of the Transkei Defence Force.

"I'd like you to join my Headquarters staff where you can do some work for a change instead of lounging on the beach all day," he said gruffly. "Asking these people to do any work up here is like asking them to run a marathon."

I was quite happy to move. The Special Forces Regiment I had been tasked with forming was now operational, though I doubted it would ever carve its name into the annals of famous fighting regiments. But it was a considerable improvement over its predecessor, the street-walking attack divers of the 'Transkeian Naval Diving Academy.'

Another reason I was happy to move was that it wouldn't be long before my daughter started nursery school. The only school in Port St Johns was a Catholic Convent which had been closed years before when its nuns had absconded after being improperly propositioned by some marauding pirates. The only nun to return was rumored to have become impregnated by one of the cast from the film *Shout at the Devil* which was on location in Port St Johns at the time. The production crew and actors led by the irrepressible Lee Marvin, playing Colonel Patrick O'Flynn, were staying at a seedy hotel in the town called the Needles Hotel, and had introduced the unfortunate nun to the joys of a nip of gin. Thereafter, she had decided to hang up her habit for the less reverent calling of waitressing at the hotel.

After handing over the Regiment to Colin Willis, with who I had been on Cadet Course in Rhodesia, I moved with my family into a newly-built home in Umtata, 50 miles inland from Port St Johns. The date was 2 April 1987.

19

White Mischief

*The Prime Minister has directed that the practice of throwing tea
from the windows of Government buildings must stop. It is inconvenient
for those walking below. Visitors are to adhere to this practice.*

—*Transkei Government Gazette,*
Circular 144: 1988

Prior to the arrival of the Rhodesian training contingent in June of 1981, referring to the Transkei Army as a 'Defence Force' would have been like referring to Durban's Amateur Flying Club as an 'Air Force'. But while members of the latter might well have relished being trained in the art of aerial combat, members of the former positively recoiled at the prospect of any training at all. Their reaction to being retrained and restructured by a team of former Rhodesian soldiers was greeted with nothing short of hysteria. They acted as a troop of monkeys might upon finding a leopard in their midst—with frenzied shock and resentment.

When the training team arrived, of which I was an original member, the so called Defence Force consisted of what might imaginatively have been termed a 'Battalion', and a 'Defence Headquarters' which better resembled the offices of a government welfare agency closed for a long weekend.

The Rhodesians were officially referred to as 'advisors' so as not to create the politically unpalatable impression that whites held command appointments in what was ostensibly a black army. But just as a flying instructor might take over the controls of an aircraft from a trainee pilot during inclement weather, taking over control of the Transkei Army is what we had to do in even the calmest of weather. To them we were simply known as 'white mischief'. We were like a bothersome group of do-gooders who had imposed themselves like unwelcomed guests on a freewheeling fraternity party. It was certainly not without its moments. Sometimes it was like sitting in a ringside seat at Boswell Willkie's Circus.

A week after my arrival at Defence Headquarters, I received a call from my friend, Andy Samuels, whose task it was to advise the Transkei Battalion Commander of his duties. Andy had been working in Umtata for some time and had recently moved his family from Port St Johns into the same neighborhood in Umtata in which I and many other Rhodesian families now resided.

"I think you should get over here and help manage some of the theatrics taking place this morning." Andy sounded is if he was almost at the end of his tether.

I drove out to the Battalion which was situated a few miles

outside the city limits. Andy was sitting in an office he shared with the Battalion Commander and was already halfway through his second packet of cigarettes.

"Where's the Colonel?" I asked.

"Running naked through the Battalion lines," replied Andy, nonchalantly lighting another cigarette.

"At this time of the morning?" I queried. "I could understand it had the bar been open, but it's not even tea time."

"The bar's been open all night. Some Corporal walked into the Officers' Mess early this morning looking for his wife to find her stark naked in the company of the equally naked colonel.

"Goodness me, that's rather unbecoming," I gasped. "What happened next?"

"They ended up chasing each other around the base." "Naked?" I asked, disbelieving.

"Naked. The Corporal chasing his naked wife who was chasing the naked Colonel," replied Andy, exhaling a plume of cigarette smoke through his puckered lips.

"Don't you think you should be doing something about it?" I asked. "We're supposed to be instilling a modicum of decorum into these fellows."

"I've already postponed the parade the Colonel was to have been on this morning," replied Andy. "I also have the Military Police out looking for him. As soon as they've found him I'll send somebody out with his uniform and a note suggesting he might want to consider putting it on before making an appearance on parade."

"Jolly good idea," I replied.

A delegation of reporters from the South African news media was arriving that morning to report on the impact our training team was having on the Transkeians. I hoped that the lusty Colonel would be wearing more than just his beret when they interviewed him.

I soon learned that sex was one of the few activities officers didn't balk at engaging in during working hours, with the officers from Defence Headquarters boldly leading the charge.

∾

In theory, Transkei was an independent, self-governing state within the geographical boundaries of South Africa with complete autonomy over its own affairs. In practice, it was a different story. The frailty of Transkei's ability to manage any Government function, including its affairs of state, was so acute that little could be done without significant assistance from South Africa. To facilitate communication between the two governments, all official communication had to be in English. The problem was that many Transkei civil servants, all of whom were Xhosa-speaking, struggled with the complexities and subtleties of the English language. The result was that much of the correspondence they generated was so perplexing it was often ignored.

In response to a public outcry on the state of the country's crumbling infrastructure, the Prime Minister's Office decided the Government needed to employ more engineers. Instead of recruiting from the private sector, they decided to train engineers from within the ranks of Government departments. A directive was circulated asking for the nominations of civil servants wishing to be trained in the field of 'engine hearing'. Some days later the directive was cancelled to be replaced by another asking for nominations of civil servants wishing to be trained in the field of 'engine earring'. This also was cancelled to be replaced by a final directive stating the Government was reviewing its position on the state of the country's 'crumbling infrastructure', and of the need to train 'engine earrings'. The infrastructure continued to crumble.

On another occasion, an invitation was sent from the Prime Minister's Office to the office of the Minister for Public Works inviting him and his *late wife* to a cocktail function to be hosted by the Prime Minister. The Minister for Public Works responded that he found it objectionable that his "late wife" should be invited anywhere, least of all to a cocktail party because "it is well-known that my wife is deceased."

One day an Afrikaans director of the South African company I was employed by, General Kleinhanse, tried to reach me by telephone from his office in Johannesburg. I was not available, so the call was taken by a Transkei Corporal. He told the General he would have me return his call as soon as possible. When I arrived back in my office later that morning, the Corporal appeared at my door to give me the message.

"Suh, you must phone Jingle Chain House immediately."

"Phone who?"

"Jingle Chain House, Suh," replied the Corporal loudly, as if I might be hard of hearing.

I told the Corporal I didn't know who he was talking about and since he hadn't written down the person's phone number, suggested we should wait to see if the person called back. Unfortunately, when the General did call back I was out to lunch, so the luckless Corporal had to field the call once again.

When I returned to my office, a note had been left on my desk which had me more confused than ever. *"Suh. Jingle Chain House say if you don't phone today you will be fried tomorrow."*

Not having the vaguest idea what the note meant, I made a paper aeroplane out of it and launched it out my twelfth-storey window. It glided lazily downward and crash-landed into the bushy hairdo of an important-looking African lady about to enter the Government building. I hoped she would have better luck understanding the note than me.

❧

Carol and I had become close friends with Andy and Ellie Samuels and hardly a day would go by without our two families getting together for drinks, either at their house or ours. We were at their house one evening when Andy suggested it would be a good idea if he and I joined a group of friends who were planning an inflatable boat trip down the Wild Coast. I knew Andy had recently purchased a Zodiac inflatable but was surprised that he already felt the confidence to take it on a voyage along coastal waters which were as rough as any in the world.

"Oh, charming," said Ellie, draining her gin. "Would you mind getting your insurance policy in order before you go? And while you're at it, would you stock up the bar with more gin, please. Carol and I don't want to run out while we wait for you and Tim to be retrieved from the Falkland Islands."

"Don't be silly. If Thor Heyderal … Heydederdal … " Andy hesitated. He was well on his way through a bottle of J&B and was having difficulty pronouncing the Norwegian explorer's name. "If some Swede or Norwegian, or whoever he was, can sail a balsa raft from South America to the Polynesian Islands without getting lost, I can do the same taking an inflatable dinghy down the Wild Coast."

"Oh, I see, so we're going to have a rubber *Kon-Tiki* impaled on a coral reef somewhere on the Wild Coast with you and Tim wondering where your next bottle of whisky is going to come from."

Ellie didn't share the confidence her husband had in his own seamanship. It was hardly surprising. The extent of Andy's knowledge sailing inflatable boats was taking a sedate ride around a small lake that was located just outside the city limits.

The great voyage was eventually arranged. Nineteen indefatigable seamen were to motor nine inflatable boats down a hundred-mile stretch of the rough coastal waters off the Wild Coast, beginning at Port Shepstone and ending in East London. The trip would last four days. Each boat, comprising two crew members, would carry sufficient provisions to sustain them throughout the voyage; the largest boat would carry three crew members and some spare provisions. The only two who had never put to sea in an inflatable craft before were Andy and me.

The day before the launch, our two families drove down to Port Shepstone in two cars: Carol and Ellie in one and Andy and I in the other towing the rubber dinghy. When we arrived most of the other crew members were already preparing their boats and checking outboard motors. We bade farewell to our wives and joined the rest of the crews, doing some last-minute packing and securing of provisions. We knew the launch the following morning would be bumpy and that everything in the boat would have to be securely tied down. That evening we sat around a fire on the beach enjoying a BBQ and a few drinks while going over our plans for the next day. Then we tucked ourselves into our sleeping bags and tried to get what little sleep we could.

The plan was that the boats would launch as a group early the following morning. Once we were safely through the surf, we could split up and go our separate ways before rendezvousing later that afternoon at a pre-designated point so as to be able to come ashore together. This would ensure that we were never alone during the treacherous times of launching and returning to shore through the surf. Once we were all ashore, we would light a fire on the beach, have a BBQ and a few drinks and then retire for the night. The same routine would be followed each day until we arrived at our destination.

The following morning we awoke to a gusty wind and an unsettled sea. The surf was high and crashed ashore in a jagged, uneven rhythm. Every so often a menacing rogue wave would crash ashore and I began to wish that Andy and I had done some sea trials before deciding to set out on such an ambitious voyage. Andy seemed unconcerned as we heaved our fully-laden rig down the beach and into the shallow surf. The waves looked even bigger now that we were at the water's edge and I was glad Andy was the skipper and not me. I asked him if he was confident about what to do.

"It's easy. We climb the waves before they start to break; it's just a matter of timing. If a big wave breaks in front of us, we turn and run from it then head out again. We'll be through the surf before you know it. I've watched guys do it hundreds of times." Andy seemed a lot more confident than I was.

One by one the boats started up, their outboard motors spewing plumes of blue smoke as the skippers fine-tuned chokes and crew members steadied the bows into the oncoming waves. A shout from the skipper was all it took to have his crew member vaulting over the gunnels and they were off, motors screaming as the heavily-laden crafts ploughed through the broken white water like motorized sledges through swirling snow.

Soon they were powering up the faces of the first incoming waves and hurtling over their crests to be lost from view on the other side. A minute later they would reappear, churning up the face of yet another huge wave, or turning from breaking surf, dodging, weaving and climbing again. They followed each other back and forth through the surf like miniature *frigates of the line* until eventually they were into the calmer, gentler swells of the deep water beyond.

All that is, except for Andy and me! We were still floundering around a few feet from shore nervously waiting for a break in the waves; a break that never seemed to come.

Half an hour later, with the rest of the flotilla impatiently bobbing up and down in the large swells waiting for us, we made our daring move. With a shout from Andy of "Let's go!" we jumped into the boat and shot off through the waves at full throttle like a bat out of hell. I felt as though I was riding a wild stallion which was hellbent on trying to dismount me. Thirty seconds later, it almost succeeded. Andy was propelled off the stern with the elasticity of a gymnast off a trampoline; except Andy was no gymnast. He tumbled through the air in an undignified heap then belly flopped into the sea like an elongated sea lion. Trying to gain his footing, he lost balance and almost managed to amputate his right foot in the whirling propeller. I managed to remain in the boat, but was so entranced by Andy's extraordinary departure I didn't notice the rogue wave bearing down on me with the speed of an express train. The next thing I knew the boat was flipped upside down and swamped beneath a mountain of seawater. I surfaced a minute later minus my trousers to see the upturned craft surfing to shore at precisely the same spot we had launched from moments before. It was an inglorious start to our maritime expedition and put my skipper out of the race for good.

Luckily, one of the three crewmembers from the largest of the rubber dinghies had been watching the pantomime and immediately swam ashore to help me evacuate Andy to a clinic. Then we recovered what we could from our sodden supplies, re-packed the boat and set off through the surf with my new crewmate at the controls. The next four days were relatively uneventful except that we ran out of water on the second day. Our souls and our thirst were saved by an abundant supply of Sedgwick's Old Brown Sherry which Andy had had the foresight to include in our provisions and which sustained us through the remainder of the voyage.

Having adroitly managed to avoid any criticism for his performance as a sea captain, and wishing to re-establish his reputation as a debonair and fearless adventurer, Andy set his sights anew. Our two families were enjoying sundowners one evening on my front lawn in the company of a guest of ours, Molly Currie, who was the sister of Tony Gregg, the former English cricket captain. While we were talking, a large and graceful hot air balloon appeared on the horizon headed in our direction. What I didn't realize at the time was that Molly was an accomplished hot air balloonist and a life member of the Royal Hot Air Balloon Society. Unfortunately, Andy wasn't aware of it either, because he became imbued that afternoon with a considerable amount of hot air of his own.

"I wonder how they steer those things and maintain their correct altitude?" asked Carol, glancing up at the approaching balloon. Before Molly was able to share her expert knowledge, Andy launched into a lengthy monologue on flying hot air balloons which left us all in awe of his expertise.

"I didn't know you were an accomplished balloonist," said Carol, looking surprised.

"Nor did I," echoed Andy's wife.

"They're as easy to fly as a kite," extolled Andy. "What?" gasped Molly.

"I've been in hundreds of the things," continued Andy, relishing his newfound notoriety. "You just hurl a few sandbags over the side when you get too low and fire up the Bunsen burner. To change direction you pull on a guy rope on the opposite side of the rig to the direction you want to turn and that's it. A child could do it."

Molly was speechless.

Ellie was flabbergasted. "I'm very impressed. I never realized I was married to such an intrepid explorer," she stammered. "Perhaps you could take us all on a balloon safari one day."

"It's already planned," replied Andy, with the assurance of a used car salesman. "We'll set off next weekend. I'll just show my credentials to the flying club and we'll be aloft in no time."

Molly suddenly seemed to find her voice. "My dear Andrew, with credentials like yours you'll end up impaled on an electric pylon or lost in the clouds. I've never heard such nonsense about flying balloons in my life!"

With a great flourish, she pulled from her purse her membership card from the Royal Hot Air Balloon Society and presented it to Andy. He stared at it, deflated.

"But Andy, I thought you said you had been in hundreds of balloons before," taunted Carol.

"I have, but I never said I had actually been off the ground in one," conceded Andy, trying to recoup a vestige of honor.

"Thank God for that," sighed Molly.

ೲ

Umtata could by no stretch of the imagination be called an exciting metropolis in which to live, and I jumped at any opportunity of getting away from its drab, filthy streets. One day I had to drive to the South African capital city of Pretoria to collect some medical supplies which the Transkei Army had run desperately short of. One of the medical supplies needed was five thousand vials of penicillin to curb an outbreak of venereal disease amongst Transkei soldiers. The suppurating and debilitating effects of the ailment were beginning to diminish the Army's ability to curb faction-fights. These were a Transkei phenomenon which occurred when one village stole a goat or a cow from another village, resulting in retribution in the form of a mass slaughter. The fighting wasn't only restricted to the two villages concerned. Each would lobby for support from neighboring clans and villages until there would be hundreds of villagers aligning themselves to one side of the dispute or the other. The two warring factions would gather on either side of a nearby valley or field to hurl insults and abuse, then charge towards each other in a frenzied orgy of killing using spears, assegais, machetes and a variety of homemade guns. The area would become a killing field of gigantic proportion. After an hour or so, each side would retreat to its original position leaving hundreds of dead and dying.

The dispute would be considered resolved and everybody would go home and get on with their lives as though nothing had happened.

Travelling with me to Pretoria was a young South African doctor, Pieter Hien, who had been attached to the Transkei Defence Force from the South African Army. We travelled in my newly-acquired Peugeot station wagon and upon our arrival stayed with my friends, Bob and Wendy Wishart. It was Bob I had been with when he lost his leg in the landmine incident in Rhodesia. The following day we drove to the South African Army medical supply depot and loaded my vehicle with vast amounts of supplies before returning to Bob's house later that afternoon. Early the next morning Bob's daughter Mandy rushed into my room asking where my car was.

"In your Dad's driveway," I responded groggily. "Uncle Tim, it's not there, I think somebody's stolen it!"

Sure enough, thieves had broken into my car during the night and driven off with all the medical supplies including the penicillin. The South African Army refused to believe that the supplies had been stolen and declined to give us more. We returned to Umtata two days later minus my newly-purchased station wagon and minus any medical supplies. It wasn't very good news for the Transkei soldiers: the outbreak of venereal disease became an epidemic, so did the faction fighting.

ॐ

One of the most colorful characters in Umtata at the time was a young diamond dealer named Brent Sussens who, together with his Mauritian-born father, ran a lucrative diamond business in the town. Brent had grown up in Mauritius where he quickly displayed amazing entrepreneurial qualities. As a schoolboy he borrowed three rupees from his father one day to watch a soccer match at a stadium close to his home in Port Louis. When he arrived he found a woman at the entrance selling programmes for a rupee each. After ascertaining how many programmes she had left, he ran back to his father and asked if he could borrow a thousand rupees as a short term loan. His flabbergasted father reluctantly agreed. Brent ran back to the stadium, bought what remained of the programmes and started selling them for two rupees each. His ability to make money at anything he put his mind to was a constant source of amazement to me and I resolved to try and learn from his remarkable ability. Brent and his wife Caroline became good friends of ours and would often take me with them on business trips.

Brent would buy old, dilapidated vans for next to nothing and operate them as local taxis, recouping a fortune in fares. Once he bought a huge stockpile of old and unserviceable rifles that were relics from the Second World War. Loading them into a large truck with a few workable ones on top, he sold the entire consignment, including the truck, to a wealthy village chief who was under the impression that he had just purchased a truck full of serviceable rifles.

In Brent's defense, he never alluded to the chief that *all* the rifles were in working order, nor did the chief ask. The savvy businessman merely picked up one of the few serviceable weapons from the top of the pile, gave it to the chief to check out, and asked if he wanted to purchase the entire consignment. The chief, sensing a huge and profitable market for the rifles in the ongoing faction fights, readily agreed. Brent acquired a small fortune from the deal—and the chief a pile of worthless junk.

Making money the entrepreneurial way looked all too easy, even if it did seem slightly lacking in morals. I began to wonder whether accompanying an entrepreneur around for five years might leave one better equipped to earn a vast fortune than attending a university for the same period of time. I was soon to get my answer, getting badly burned in the process.

⁛

I had been working at Defence Headquarters in Umtata for four years when the Transkei soldiers decided that enough was enough; the Rhodesians had been spoiling their party for too long and it was time to do something about it. In the eight years we had been there, we had built and trained their Defence Force into quite a formidable and cohesive organization by African standards. While it was unlikely to distinguish itself with any notable battle honors outside of the arena of quelling chaotic faction fights, it was at least able to operate with a degree of functionality.

One weekend the Army surrounded the small suburb where the dozen or so of us lived and put us all in jail. Luckily our families were spared the ordeal; they were simply given two days to pack up their possessions and leave the country!

I had never been inside a jail before and found it rather intriguing. Not so pleasant was being prodded by the business end of a loaded rifle by a soldier who was shaking so badly from nerves I worried that he might inadvertently discharge his weapon. I was contemplating relieving him of his weapon when an officer appeared and asked Andy Samuels and me to accompany him to the Officers' Mess. There the two of us were escorted into the lounge and asked if we wanted a drink! We were informed that we were not to be kept in jail with the rest because the Transkeians considered the two of us to be "jolly nice fellows." Somewhat embarrassed, he then asked if we would please leave the country immediately as our services were no longer required.

"Would you mind if we finish our drink first?" inquired Andy. "Yes, Sir, of course," responded the Transkei Captain politely. "In that case, could you pour us each another and then we'll be on our way," suggested Andy.

Three hours later we were in my car heading for the South African border town of East London to link up with our families. The rest of the Rhodesian contingent spent an uncomfortable two days in jail before being released and required to leave the country.

They were more than happy to oblige. It was an inglorious end to our Transkei sojourn.

Carol, Jenni and I moved for a short period to the northern suburbs of Johannesburg while we decided what we were going to do. It was decided for us one afternoon by Brent Sussens' father who phoned to ask if we would take care of a vacant farm of his west of the capital city of Pretoria. I had never lived on a farm before, let alone done any farming.

"What's on the farm?" I asked.

"Nothing," he replied. "Just a farmhouse, guesthouse, a large swimming pool and three servants."

"Three servants?" "Three servants." "I'll take it," I replied.

"How will we afford to pay them?" asked Carol, when I had put down the phone.

20

Farming Frolics

There are three ways a man can be sure of losing his money.
Gambling is the quickest, women the most pleasant, and farming
the most certain.

—Jacobus van Tonder, Boer,
De Wildt: November, 1987

There was a knock on the kitchen door. Carol, Jenni and I were enjoying Sunday breakfast in the dining room of the farm we now called home. It was situated in the small rural farming area of De Wildt, an ultraconservative Afrikaans-speaking community near Pretoria. We were the only English-speaking family anyone could ever recall having lived there.

"Who is it?" I shouted between mouthfuls of fried egg and bacon.

It was the herd boy Ellias, one of two farmhands we had inherited. He was standing nervously at the kitchen door dressed in a torn pair of shorts, khaki shirt and homemade sandals made of rubber strips cut from car tyres.

"What is it, Ellias?"

"Boss, one of the cows is sick."

Nobody had told me when we moved on to the farm that we would have to take care of three Brahman cows. I didn't know one end of a cow from the other let alone how to take care of one. I would have felt more qualified offering an opinion about the man on the moon than on what to do with a sick cow.

"I'm sure the cow can stay sick a little longer, Ellias. Come back when I've finished breakfast and I'll see what I can do."

I was playing for time. I didn't have a clue what to do. It wasn't as if I could whisk it off to the vet like a domestic animal. Even if I could, I doubted the old pickup I had recently purchased could get itself to the vet, let alone carrying 1600lbs. of ailing beef. Ten minutes later there was another knock on the door.

"Boss, the cow is *very* sick." Ellias looked worried. I was concerned, too; not for the cow, but for the fact I didn't want to appear the bumbling farmer this early in my farming career.

"I told you to come back after breakfast," I replied in an authoritative voice. I wasn't feeling very authoritative.

After he had left I asked Carol to phone the local vet for some advice. It didn't take us long to find out there were few vets available, especially over a weekend. Farmers tended to take care of their own livestock. We were the only exception. Just then there was yet another knock on the door. This time I became exasperated.

"Ellias, if you knock on that bloody door one more time to tell me the cow is sick, both you and the cow will end up in the hospital."

"But the cow isn't sick anymore," stammered Ellias. I wondered what miraculous turn of events might have occurred that could have resulted in its sudden recovery.

"What do you mean, the cow's not sick anymore?" I demanded.

"The cow is dead, sir."

"Well, that takes care of that then." I was delighted at the ease with which the matter had been resolved and thought that would be the end of it. It wasn't.

"Boss, what must I do with the dead cow?"

It was beginning to sound like Liza in the song *There's a Hole in my Bucket*. I remembered reading somewhere not to allow farm labor to eat dead livestock. It merely induced them to kill more when they felt hungry. One of the easiest ways to kill a cow is simply to feed it a plastic bag. Cows love chewing on plastic and when swallowed, it clogs up their digestive system and they die.

Ellias looked crestfallen when I told him he couldn't eat the animal.

He looked unhappier still when I told him to call the other farmhand to help him dig a hole big enough to bury it. It was late evening before a pit large enough for the dead animal had been dug. I had the cow put inside, poured half a 44-gallon drum of petrol over it, then told Ellias to throw a lighted match into the bottom of the pit.

Africans have a disarming sense of trust and loyalty toward those responsible for their well being. They also have a tendency to take everything you say quite literally. Ellias must have wondered how he was going to get a lighted match into the bottom of a pit stuffed with a dead cow. But that's what he had been told to do, so do it he must. Eagerly watched by the other herd boy and some workers who had gathered from the neighboring farm, he knelt down at the edge of the pit and leaned into it as far as he dared with both arms stretched as far as he could manage. Then he lit the match. The resulting inferno enveloped not only the dead cow but Ellias as well! Another trait deeply-rooted in African culture is a compelling sense of humor and an ability to laugh not only at their own misfortunes, but those of others as well. Ellias was propelled out of the hole like a fiery cannonball and landed at the feet of his colleagues standing nearby. Instead of assisting the poor boy, they rolled on the ground in peels of laughter thinking it was the funniest spectacle they had ever witnessed. Luckily, Ellias only sustained minor injuries, but the laughter that accompanied the group as they made their way back to their living quarters carried on well into the night.

By the following morning the only visible effects on the cow were singed eyelashes, a burnt tail and a body that had become so bloated it had popped completely out of the hole! The herd boys thought this was the result of witchcraft and adamantly refused to go near it again. Carol and I spent the rest of the morning trying to stuff the cow back into the hole so it could be buried. I was told later I should have towed the carcass to a nearby mountain and left it for the vultures—I was learning fast.

The following morning I was visited by a posse of horsemen who trotted down my circular driveway looking like a detachment of soldiers from General De Wet's Boer Army. In the front was a bearded and weathered-looking man wearing a veldt hat, khaki trousers and shirt. He was mounted on a white steed and identified himself as Marnie Maritz, the leader of the local Afrikaner militia. They were armed to the teeth, as if expecting to meet a marauding band of Zulus.

"Are the blacks giving you any problems, Engelsman?" grunted the bearded leader looking down from his mount. 'Engelsman' was the name given by Afrikaners to anyone of English descent.

"Not that I'm aware of," I replied politely.

"If they do, don't bother calling the police, we'll come and take care of them ourselves." He gave me a penetrating look, as if deeply suspicious of an Englishman having taken up residence on his turf. "And don't pay them any more than the minimum wage, Engelsman. They're good for nothing and understand only one thing, the shambok." With that he cantered off with the rest of his posse leaving a calling card of horse manure splattered over my driveway.

I was reminded of a story I had recently read of a BBC reporter conducting an interview with the head of the South African Bureau of State Security (BOSS), General Pieter Van Den Berg. The interview had taken place on the General's farm and when asked about his feelings toward his black farm workers, he gave the reporter a quizzical look.

"Why … they're all stupid, of course."

"But, General," persisted the BBC reporter. "You were almost electrocuted some time ago while welding in your workshop. You must surely acknowledge the role of your black foreman in saving your life by switching off the main electric breaker switch … ."

"No way! No black person would have the good sense to do that," replied the general adamantly. "It was God who instructed him to switch it off."

Such was the disdain shown by many of the rural Afrikaners towards their black workers.

☙

The three-bedroomed farmhouse we lived in was painted yellow and white giving it the appearance of a quaint doll's house. It was nestled under the shade of some huge umbrella trees. Inside was an enormous kitchen and dining room, several lounges and a spacious entertainment area which included a sauna bath overlooking an ornate Olympic-size swimming pool. On the farm were three cows, two farm workers and a house servant. Now that we were comfortably settled, I wondered how we were going to afford to live there. Our cash reserves were insufficient for any prolonged period without income, and I knew nothing about farming. But I was determined to give it a go.

"I think I'll grow mealies," I grandly announced one morning at breakfast. A mealie is the South African vernacular for maize, the country's staple diet.

"That's a great idea seeing that you've never grown a thing in your life," replied Carol. "Where do you propose to find the money to buy tractors and things?"

"I don't need a tractor. All I need do is dig a few furrows, throw some seeds in and keep them well watered. It all sounds very easy. I'm surprised more people haven't tried it."

"And where did you acquire that astonishing bit of expertise?" asked Carol, skeptically.

"I bought a book called *Beginners Guide to Growing Mealies*," I responded smugly. "It was on sale yesterday at CNA. All I have to do is read the directions to Ellias and wait for our first crop to sell."

"I see. And how do you propose we feed ourselves while we wait in breathless anticipation of our first harvest?" Carol seemed less enthusiastic than me.

"I'm going to buy two taxis to operate in the black townships – like Brent use to do." Brent was my entrepreneurial friend from the Transkei who had made a fortune operating African taxis.

The following morning I drove into town and purchased a large sack of mealie seeds together with a beach chair and large colorful umbrella. On my return, Ellias and I carried everything out into a nearby field where I set up my chair and umbrella and sat down to read page one of *Beginners Guide to Growing Mealies*.

"Right, Ellias. Page one tells us to dig a furrow and plant a seed every eight inches."

Ellias dutifully followed my instructions toiling in the heat of the midday sun while I sat under my umbrella directing operations. It was a scheme I hoped would bring untold riches. Before long we had two long rows of mealies planted which, although not very straight, seemed a good enough start. As we were working the neighboring farmer walked over to see what on earth we were doing. His name was Jacobus van Tonder, a huge, weathered Afrikaner who had acres of lush green mealies growing on his farm.

"What the hell are you doing sitting under an umbrella in the middle of the bloody veldt looking like a stranded tourist, Engelsman?" he asked, leaning his leathery frame against the barbed wire fence that separated our two properties.

"I'm growing mealies, Mr. van Tonder," I replied from beneath my umbrella. "What does it look like?" He stared at me in disbelief, as if I might just have told him that the world was oblong. Then he shook his head, obviously lamenting that luck could have dealt him such a cruel blow as to have an Englishman as a neighbor who spent his days sitting beneath a beach umbrella trying to grow mealies. My mealies eventually grew bigger than his, except that he had twenty acres and I only had a few square yards. They tasted good at a Sunday BBQ, but were woefully insufficient to financially sustain us through the year.

Unfortunately, my African taxi enterprise fared considerably worse. A week after spending the last of my dwindling cash reserves purchasing two new Toyota sixteen-seater vans, both were stolen. The two African drivers I hired to drive the taxis into the black townships decided their need was greater than mine and I never saw drivers or taxis again.

Carol, despondent with the limited success of my farming enterprise, had taken up employment in the industrial area of Pretoria managing a rubber factory. The company's name was Precision Rubber Mouldings but traded under the name 'Rubber Tuff'. To one side of her was a company which manufactured scaffolding called 'Laborious Erections', and to the other side was a company manufacturing nuts and bolts called 'Mr. Screwman'.

Anyone seeing the three large signs together could have been forgiven for thinking they had inadvertently wandered into an area of doubtful propriety.

ɛᴐ

We had been on the farm a year when an old friend came to stay with whom I had served in the Rhodesian Army. Bill Duffy was a tall, gaunt Englishman who was the epitome of decorum. Despite having been exposed to the rigors and crudity of Rhodesia's bush war, Bill had never lost his impeccable manners or toffee accent. A few days after his arrival we hosted a dinner party at the farm to which was invited a number of our friends including a business colleague of Carol's. He had an extremely attractive wife who took an instant liking to the polite, swab English gentleman with the pukker accent. She insisted on sitting next to him at the dinner table and seemed to become more enamored with him as the dinner progressed. By the time the main course was served she had succeeded in inserting her calling card up the leg of the poor man's shorts. By the time dessert was served her hand was busy under the table administering more attention to his nether regions than might have been considered decent; especially in the presence of her unsuspecting husband. It was during the serving of Port that Bill, who had been trying to ignore the woman all evening, let out a strangled gasp. With her inhibitions having finally deserted her, the woman's licentious behavior had become too much.

"William, what on earth is wrong? You look as if you're choking, are you alright?" asked Carol, concerned.

"I think the cat just tried to jump on to my lap," he stammered, not knowing what else to say.

"Don't be silly, we don't have any cats," responded Carol.

With that, everybody peered under the table to see what could possibly have caused Bill's distress. By a stroke of good fortune the ends of the overhanging tablecloth spared us from being able to witness the details of Bill's predicament. However, the woman's husband, noticing what he took to be his wife's serviette lying on the floor next to her, reached down to retrieve it.

"I think you dropped your serviette," he said, handing it across the table to her. There was an embarrassed silence in the room as we saw it was not her serviette at all, but an intimate item of her apparel.

ɛᴐ

With the demise of my African taxi service and in need of additional money to supplement Carol's income, I announced one morning that I was getting into the chicken business.

"What do you mean, 'getting into the chicken business'?" queried Carol, suspiciously.

"I'm going to buy and sell chickens."

"That's a great idea … You're highly allergic to chicken feathers and we don't have a place to keep them. You've obviously put a lot of thought into this latest grandiose scheme of yours."

I explained that live chickens were in great demand by residents living in the black townships and the only way they could acquire them was by walking long distances to the nearest poultry farm.

"If I could deliver chickens into the townships, I would be helping the residents while at the same time generating income for our family."

Carol remained unconvinced. "They've been buying chickens from the large poultry growers for years. What makes you think they will suddenly start buying from you?"

"It's very simple psychology, dear. Instead of asking Mohammed to walk to the mountain, we'll be taking the mountain to Mohammed."

Carol remained skeptical, but I pursued the idea and spent the next few days constructing a large chicken trailer capable of carrying five hundred fowl. When it was done I splashed on a lick of bright yellow paint and pronounced the project complete.

"It looks like a reject ostrich enclosure from London Zoo," commented Carol unsympathetically. "Why did you have to draw attention to it by painting it such a gaudy color?"

"Africans like yellow and it will attract attention from a long distance," I replied defensively.

"They won't need to see it," persisted Carol. "Crammed with five hundred chickens they'll be able to smell it for miles. Don't you think you need to give them food and water while they're baking in the sun waiting to be slaughtered?"

She had a point, so later that day I stole as many of her ice cube trays as I could lay my hands on and attached them around the trailer as feeding and watering troughs. Early the following morning I rounded up Ellias, whom I had elevated from 'herd boy' to 'senior chicken sales manager', hitched the yellow trailer to my old Isuzu pickup and drove to the nearest poultry farm to make my first purchase of chickens. With both pickup and trailer crammed with five hundred squawking fowl, we labored our way to a township some six miles away where I had already identified an area to park the trailer. It was a taxi parking area surrounded by hundreds of shanty homes.

It was while travelling down a dirt road close to my intended destination when my first mishap occurred. The trailer got a flat tyre. This posed a serious problem as I had neglected to make provision for a spare wheel. I couldn't remain blocking the road so decided I would keep towing the trailer on its flat tyre. I was making quite good progress and had just about decided that I didn't really need a spare wheel because towing with a flat tyre seemed easy enough, when the second mishap occurred. The trailer caught fire. The flat tyre had become so hot it burst into flames. By the time I managed to stop, the flames were licking up one side of the trailer transforming its bright yellow paint to a sooty black.

Throngs of natives gathered from nowhere to assist and before long we had the fire under control. Luckily only a couple of dozen chickens had succumbed to the flames and smoke, and I used the scorched carcasses to pay the multitudes for their help. I was most distressed that my bright yellow trailer had now been transformed into a blackened, charred mess full of panting chickens on the verge of expiring. Two hours later I managed to purchase a spare wheel and was finally able to get the trailer to its intended destination. By now it was midday and I left the trailer with a reluctant Ellias with instructions to sell as many chickens as he could before they died.

When I returned later that evening I was elated to find the trailer empty and a beaming Ellias gushing at me that all the chickens had been sold. I noticed there was an African taxi parked nearby and as we were busy hitching the trailer to the pickup, the driver walked towards us.

"I see you're selling chickens," he remarked. It is considered rude in African culture to start a conversation with a question. Matters are remarked upon obliquely so as not to offend.

"Yes. I am selling chickens," I acknowledged in confirmation of his astute observation, indicating that I was not offended by what he had said. However, I was extremely wary.

"I am a taxi driver," he offered in a profound expression of the obvious.

"I see you." I replied in polite acknowledgement of his presence and status. He was a slim, wiry man with a mass of shaggy hair which might once have been styled in an Afro.

"This is a taxi rank and I am the taxi marshal."

I knew the conversation was leading up to something and I wasn't sure I liked the direction it was taking. Taxi marshals had complete control over taxi ranks including decision-making over who may and may not operate from them. I chose to let his comment go unanswered, half expecting him to tell me I was not welcome and would not be allowed to return.

"It is rude of you to have parked your trailer here without first discussing it with me and seeking my permission."

I knew he was leading up to telling me that by my actions, I had disrespected the taxi owners and would have to leave. I was about to apologize when he put his hand on my shoulder.

"Don't worry. You are a white man and don't fully understand our culture. The one you left behind with the trailer has told us you are a good employer and I can see in your eyes you have no animosity towards us and that you come in peace."

I could have hugged the man but politely shook his hand instead. "I come in peace," I acknowledged.

He told me I would be allowed to remain selling my chickens as it would be mutually beneficial to both of us; his commuters could buy my chickens on their way home from work and the convenience of their being able to do so would increase his business. But there was a catch.

"You will have to pay us each month for the privilege of using this property." As he spoke, I knew that the price would probably be prohibitive.

"What will I have to pay?"

"A single two-liter bottle of coca-cola and one chicken per month is all we ask of you, white man."

I couldn't believe it. It was a token payment. In return, the taxi marshal undertook to guarantee the safety of my trailer and chickens for as long as it was parked on their taxi rank. It looked like my luck was about to change.

I became good friends with the taxi marshal. His name was Rudi and we ended up becoming firm friends. He was as good as his word and often when I arrived late to collect my trailer there would be a taxi present, the driver patiently guarding it until my return.

❧

One day I was delighted to receive a visit from an old colleague with whom I had served in the Selous Scouts. Pete Donnelly was as hard a specimen of humanity as one could ever expect to meet. His darkly-tanned skin was the texture of tough leather and wearing any form of clothing other than a pair of tattered shorts and slops were anathema to him. His long-suffering wife Sandy, on the other hand, was the epitome of elegant sophistication who had given up a long time ago trying to polish her husband's rough edges. She had even given up trying to refine their two young boys. They had honed the time it took to pluck pigeons shot by their dad and have them roasting over hot coals to thirty seconds. If there were no coals, they were just as happy to eat the pigeons raw.

It turned out that Pete managed a dairy farm midway between my farm and the taxi rank where I sold my chickens. Being able to detour through his farm considerably shortened the distance I had to travel to make my sales. As I was driving past his house one day, I saw him standing on top of a high water tower that had been erected in his garden. He was blowing furiously on an old bugle he had inherited from his dad, and next to him leaning against the water tank was a large hunting rifle. Having huffed and puffed on the bugle, blowing what might have been a vague rendition of *The Ramparts We Watch*, he picked up his rifle and proceeded to fire a volley of bullets in the direction of the African township. I asked him what on earth he was doing.

"Bloody natives are getting restless. Listen to all the bloody noise they're making."

Standing alone on the water tower he looked like he might have been the last remaining member of Watson's patrol defending the approaches to the Khyber Pass during the first Afghan War.

"But they're celebrating a wedding, Pete. They're entitled to make a little bit of noise."

"I don't trust them," said Pete, firing another volley of shot across the valley towards the township. "They'll use the noise of the wedding to sneak up on me and rustle some of my cows. I know the bastards."

With that he picked up his bugle, took another deep breath and gave another long blow. This time I heard only a muffled gargling sound. Luckily none of the native revelers heard it; they might have thought that the lone bastion of civilization standing on the water tower was developing a hernia and have been tempted to come to his assistance. Had they done so, they would have realized the real reason he was having difficulty blowing his bugle was that he was already halfway through a bottle of brandy.

Pete knew a lot about farming and it was through his expertise and coaching that I was able to increase the size of my herd. Eventually, I even became adept at milking my own cows and before long was selling homemade butter and cottage cheese to supplement the income from the chickens. I dismally failed the instructions Peter tried to give on artificial insemination. The first time I tried, I started to retch as I began inserting my hand into the indignant animal. I had more luck castrating young bulls. Pete and I would have their sacks slit open and testicles scooped into a frying pan before the startled beasts even knew they were missing. Then we would light a gas stove that we had brought for the occasion and sit in the field eating a breakfast of fried testicles, eggs and wild mushrooms, while Pete regaled me with even more farming knowledge.

I stopped eating bull testicles the day I found out that I could sell them for extraordinary sums of money to Chinese traders who sent them to their homeland as aphrodisiacs. Ounce for ounce they were worth more than gold, and I could thereafter be seen promenading up and down the streets of Chinatown in Johannesburg with margarine tubs full of bull testicles to sell to the highest bidder.

As well as we were doing, I didn't have the capital to expand the farm to where it would provide the financial returns I thought necessary to secure my family's future. It was during this period that I became close friends with a colleague whom I had worked with in the Transkei. Carel Bosch was a bear of a man who had farmed in Rhodesia before finding himself and his farm

Pete Donelly blowing his bugle. (Pete Donelly)

swept up in the flames of the Rhodesian war. After leaving the Transkei he had been employed by one of South Africa's leading security companies, the COIN Security Group. He had risen rapidly through the ranks to become one of its senior managers. His birthday was on the same day, month and year as mine and consequently we often shared birthday parties. We were enjoying such a celebration on my farm one day when he suggested I apply for a job with COIN.

"The Chairman of the company is a great guy who likes Rhodesians and who is also keen on anyone with a military background. You can continue living on the farm and work for the company at the same time, reaping the financial rewards from both. I could set up an interview for you whenever you want."

"What about tomorrow?" I suggested. I had found myself becoming quite stagnant on the farm and relished the thought of doing something more stimulating than selling chickens and off-loading bull's testicles to horny Chinese businessmen.

"Now Tim, there is one thing I have to make clear," cautioned Carel, not realizing that I would jump at his suggestion with such haste. "COIN Security is a very up-market company. You will probably be working in their posh head office complex in Pretoria, and nobody is going to take too kindly to you arriving in a beaten up Isuzu pickup that belches oily black smoke and drips gallons of oil."

It was true: my gearbox had been leaking oil for some time and would have to be repaired before I could start commuting into Pretoria with any regularity. In fact, the pickup was in such a sorry state of repair that in an effort to avoid being seen travelling in it by her friends, my six-year old daughter refused to be dropped any closer than two blocks from her school. I told Carel I would do my best to get the truck fixed before arriving at the COIN head office for an interview.

The following weekend I invited some friends who were imbued with more mechanical knowledge than me to the farm on the pretext I was having a BBQ. Once they had all eaten and had a few beers I announced the real reason they had been invited over—to help repair the Isuzu's gearbox. They didn't seem to mind, but removing a gearbox while in a doubtful state of sobriety took more time than I had anticipated. By the time it had been removed it was almost dark. Carrying the oily mass of cogs and flywheels into the kitchen, we laid it out on Carol's ornate table whereupon my merry friends gleefully set about refurbishing it. By now they were well on their way through their second bottle of Dimple Haig whisky. Putting the thing back together proved more challenging than taking it apart. By the time the task was pronounced completed, half the gearbox remained lying on the table!

"Don't worry," said the lead mechanic in charge of operations who happened to be a banker from Johannesburg. "It's quite normal when you strip down an Isuzu gearbox to have enough parts left over to build another."

The next morning I arrived at the COIN Security Group head offices for an interview driving an Isuzu pickup that sounded like an Abrams battle tank clanking its way across a metal bridge.

It was November 1988. I was about to take my first tentative steps into the corporate world of scandal, excess and intrigue.

21

Caravan of Camels

"Where will you keep the camels?"
"What camels?"
"The camels for the new contract."
"They can stay in the women's dormitory with the rest." *"You have camels in the women's dormitory?"*
"Yes. They're more reliable than the men."
—*Author talking with branch manager,*
Windhoek, South West Africa: 1988

"Do you have any security experience?"
"No."
"Procurement experience?"
"No."
"Managerial experience?"
"No."

I was being interviewed at the COIN Security Group head offices in Pretoria by Major John Bishop, the company's charismatic and popular Chairman and Chief Executive Officer. He was an impeccably-groomed and well-dressed man with the squat, solid build of an English bulldog. During South Africa's bush war in South West Africa, he had distinguished himself as an aggressive frontline soldier, quickly rising to the rank of major. But first and foremost he was an entrepreneur so he eventually decided to leave the Army to pursue a career in the security industry. It didn't take him long to form his own company, and it quickly grew into one of the largest and most prestigious security enterprises in southern Africa. John's wife Yvonne was the company's no-nonsense Managing Director. Her influence within the company was enormous.

"Did you hire the man?" she asked her husband later that day. They were having lunch with the rest of the Board in the company's stylishly-decorated boardroom.

"Yes. I appointed him our Logistics Manager," replied John, helping himself to another serving of succulent New Zealand lamb from a serving platter being circulated by a steward. The boardroom table had been tastefully set with expensive linens, sterling silver cutlery and exquisite crystal glasses.

"You hired a man with no qualifications?" exclaimed Yvonne. "He was in the Army," replied John, defensively.

"That means he probably drinks too much," chided Yvonne, ordering another bottle of *Muscadet Sèvre et Maine* from the busy steward.

"In that case you should have appointed him to the Board," remarked Monsieur John Beard, the company's suave and debonair French-speaking Director.

❧

There were twenty-seven branches of the COIN Security Group scattered throughout South Africa and South West Africa, and from the morning I arrived I found myself swamped beneath a quagmire of paperwork. Each day a bewildering array of requisitions would arrive on my desk for anything from French kepis to Algerian forage caps, and I began to wonder whether I was working for a security company or an army of legionnaires. I was pondering where to purchase a consignment of ceremonial swords one morning when I received an urgent call from the Chairman's Personal Assistant.

"The Chairman would like to see you in his office immediately." The Chairman's assistant was an extremely attractive and efficient lady who, had it not been for an exaggerated opinion of her own self-importance, might also have been quite personable. She worked in an adjoining office to the Chairman and when I arrived showed me into his office. He was sitting behind an ornate desk peering at a map of South West Africa.

"Tim, I'd like you to purchase twenty camels to be delivered to our branch in Windhoek by early next week." The Chairman spoke casually, as if asking for nothing more complicated than a consignment of boot laces.

"Twenty what?" I asked. "Twenty camels."

I was tempted to inquire whether I should purchase some Arab keffiyea head scarves and cutlasses as well but decided against it in case he said yes. I had no idea where I would acquire them; neither did I have any idea where I would acquire twenty camels.

"Might I ask why you need them, sir?"

The thought of a troop of native guards wearing French kepis precariously swaying atop a caravan of belching camels trying to blend into the South West

John and Yvonne Bishop. (Debbie Patching)

African landscape was more than my imagination could contend with.

"We've just been awarded a contract to guard the railway line running through the Namib Desert," explained the Chairman. "Bandits keep walking off with large segments of track, then selling them back to the Government at inflated prices. Camels will be ideally suited for patrolling the lines. You'll have to purchase them in Windhoek. Your ticket has been booked for tomorrow."

The following day I found myself on an early South African Airways flight to the South West African capital city of Windhoek. We had just reached cruising altitude when an attractive air-hostess walked down the aisle pushing a trolley of beverages.

"Tea or coffee," she asked with a disarming smile.

"No thank you," I replied. "I'll have a gin and tonic please." It wasn't even 7 o'clock and not being an early riser, I was feeling obstreperous at having to catch such an early flight.

"I don't think the bar is open, Sir," she replied, somewhat surprised.

"Well, could you go and check please?"

The air-hostess moved slowly down the aisle pouring delicious-smelling coffee for the rest of the passengers. I immediately regretted having been so cantankerous. Now I would have nothing to sustain me for the remainder of the bumpy, three-hour flight. Five minutes later I noticed somebody peering at me from behind a curtain which separated my seating area from Business Class. The curtain suddenly opened and a smartly-uniformed figure in a peak cap and gold-braided tunic strode purposefully down the aisle towards me. In his hand was a silver tray upon which was set a crystal glass of gin and tonic garnished with lemon. A starched linen serviette draped across his arm completed his rather debonair appearance.

"Are you the gentleman who ordered the gin and tonic?" "Yes," I responded, startled by his unexpected appearance. "I'm the Captain of the aircraft and it's such an unusual request at this time of the morning, I thought I'd bring it to you myself."

"That's very civilized of you, Captain. Thank you very much." I was pleasantly surprised by the service. Perhaps it wouldn't be such a bad flight after all. "Do you think I might have another in half an hour's time, please?"

He wasn't amused. "I opened the bar just for you. I'm closing it again on my way back to the cockpit."

A single gin and tonic didn't go very far but it tasted better than coffee and put me in a better frame of mind for the remainder of my flight.

Three hours later I was met at the Windhoek Airport by the COIN

COIN head office. (Debbie Patching)

Security Branch Manager. He was a short, portly individual who was sweating profusely even in Windhoek's dry, crisp heat. I had heard he was ill-disposed towards anything outside of the regulated routine of his work so wondered what his feelings would be about taking ownership of a caravan of camels. I asked where he thought I might find some.

"Oh, don't worry about that. I have dozens milling around my branch every day looking for work."

"*Camels*? But where would you keep them?" I was surprised by his remarks and even more surprised that camels seemed in such abundant supply. I certainly hadn't seen any since my arrival.

"They can stay in the women's dormitory with the rest, of course." He seemed surprised that I would even have asked.

"You have camels living in the women's dormitory?" The situation seemed to be getting more bizarre by the moment.

"Well, we don't really like to refer to them as 'camels'; it's rather a derogatory term for the women here. But they're hard workers and more trustworthy than the men."

Then I realized there had been a big misunderstanding. "I'm talking about *real* camels … for a contract to guard the railway line in the Namib desert."

"Are you stark raving mad?" he spluttered, breaking into an even greater sweat.

Just then I received a call from the Chairman telling me that the contract for which the camels were required had been canceled. I felt relieved. I didn't feel like I wanted anything further to do with camels. In fact, I felt in need of a drink so suggested we get ourselves out of the heat and into the more accommodating atmosphere of the Windhoek Club.

"I was going to get some *real* camels?" inquired the Branch Manager, reaching for his beer.

"To be quite honest, I don't know anymore," I said, reaching for my own glass. "But if you were, it probably wouldn't have been a very good idea to keep them in the women's dormitory."

We laughed, threw back our beers and ordered another round.

❧

I was barely keeping pace with my work when I was told that a Jubilee was being planned in celebration of the company's tenth anniversary. It was to be held at the company's remote Gijima Training Academy situated some miles outside the city and was to be a spectacle of such grand proportion the Queen's Silver Jubilee would pale by comparison. The more I began to hear about the magnitude of the event the more I began to worry, so it was with some trepidation that I walked into the Chairman's office late one morning to discuss the staggering amount of logistics involved.

"The most important thing we need to be concerned about is the security of the bar stocks," said the Chairman, motioning me to a seat in front of his desk. "It's quite remote out there and we don't want guests arriving at the bar to find that somebody has absconded with the liquor."

I had been expecting to be grilled on my progress in acquiring ceremonial saddles and sabers for the Mounted Cavalry that was to escort the guest of honour—not securing the company's supply of liquor.

"But Chairman, it's by no means assured that the saddles will even be here in time for the parade," I cautioned. "Shouldn't we be more concerned about them than the liquor?"

"Don't worry about the saddles," said the Chairman brushing aside my concerns. "Securing the bar stocks is the immediate concern. If the guests are able get enough to drink after the parade, they won't recall the Cavalry having arrived minus saddles."

I was about to ask why we couldn't use our security guards to protect the bar stocks when the Chairman suddenly seemed to have an idea.

"I know—*Big Bertha*!" he exclaimed, as if in awe of the very name. "We'll lock the bar stocks in *Big Bertha*."

Big Bertha was the pride of the company's fleet of armored vehicles; it was the *Bismarck* of the fleet; indestructible and invincible. The vehicle's thick armor and impenetrable vaults were considered inaccessible by the armed gangs that roamed the highways and byways of Johannesburg looting money and valuables from armored vehicles. It was also the only vehicle considered secure enough by Lloyds of London to transport the millions of dollars-worth of gold bullion the company was responsible for moving each week.

On the day before the big parade, *Big Bertha* was duly taken off its scheduled task of moving gold and dispatched to the company's training academy, its cavernous high-tech vault bulging with liquor. The vehicle was to remain parked at the academy all night and the following morning its precious cargo would be transferred by armed guards to the nearby bar, ready for the party later that day.

The following morning I was on my way to work when I received an urgent call from the academy's manager. He asked if I could get myself out to the academy immediately. The unimaginable had happened: the tenth anniversary parade's entire consignment of liquor had mysteriously disappeared from *Big Bertha's* impenetrable vault!

When I arrived it wasn't too difficult establishing what had happened. The truck's vault lay open with the driver asleep inside. A truck full of liquor proved more of a temptation than millions of dollars-worth of gold had ever been. Opening the vault that night, he had consumed more brandy than he could handle and had passed out leaving the door wide open. The remaining stock had been scooped up in the night by delighted academy staff.

᳄

In March 1991 I was transferred with my family to Cape Town to take over the company's entire operations in the Cape Province. One of the divisions I was responsible for was Armed Banking which was reeling from morale problems due to almost daily attacks on its armored vehicles. A succession of managers had come and gone from the division and I knew that one of the first things I would have to do would be to appoint a new manager.

Shortly after I arrived I became reacquainted with two friends from Rhodesia who would end up having a profound effect on the morale of this division. One was Steven Hatfill, a young American who had left the United States to seek excitement and adventure abroad. He had eventually ended up in Rhodesia where his inquiring mind was soon recognized by the senior Police Special Branch officer attached to the Selous Scouts. It was while he was working on special projects within that unit that his extraordinary medical talents were recognized, and he was talked into getting a medical degree through the University of Rhodesia. After receiving his MD, he left Rhodesia and moved to Cape Town where he was employed by one of the city's leading hospitals conducting scientific and medical research.

The other friend was a dour Scotsman who had been Squadron Sergeant-Major of the SAS before leaving the Rhodesian Army. Jock Hutton had the build and tenacity of a Scottish terrier, and even though he was now in his late sixties, was one of the fittest individuals I had ever known. He had lost none of the grittiness for which he was so well-known as a soldier and it was for this reason I appointed him to manage the ailing Armed Banking Division.

It wasn't long before I started noticing a marked improvement in the Division's morale and I called Jock into my office one day to explain the secret of his success.

"Well, Suhrrr," replied the lean Scotsman leaning over my desk and peering at me from beneath bushy eyebrows—he spoke with a broad Scottish brogue. "I had been noticing that the vehicle crews were looking a wee bit tired on parade each morning. In fact, some of them were looking half asleep. So I went to see Doctor Steve and together we have been up to a wee bit of … skullduggery." Jock leaned further across my desk as if what he was about to reveal might be a major conspiracy. "Every week we give each man a wee injection of a special concoction which the doctor has developed." He straightened himself and looked at me with a sly grin.

"What's in the concoction?"

"That, Suhrr, you will have to find out from the doctor himself. But it works because every morning they are on parade with a big smile." He leaned further over my desk and whispered again. "And an even bigger hard-on!"

That afternoon I made an appointment to see Doctor Steven Hatfill. He worked at a private laboratory in one of the city's leading hospitals. One side of the laboratory was an office and the other side was a restricted area for carrying out research. No one was allowed into the restricted area unless wearing special sterile clothing. When I arrived I didn't see Steve and called out for him.

"I'm in the sterile area, come on in," came the bored response from behind huge racks of test tubes.

"But I'm not wearing proper clothing." "That doesn't matter, come on in anyway."

I walked in to find the doctor standing on a chair having a pee into a sink.

"That can't do the sterilization process much good," I observed.

"Well, the toilets are too far down the corridor … .What can I do for you?"

I asked what it was that he had been injecting into my armed banking crews each week to give them so much energy and vitality.

"Oh, just some vitamin B and other stuff to make them feel good. Do you want me to give you a shot?"

I'd been feeling a bit run down myself lately so readily agreed. Steve prepared a vial of his magic concoction then told me to drop my trousers.

"What effect will it have on me?" I asked, feeling the needle sink into my flesh. I was half expecting to feel like Superman.

"Probably nothing. It's all in the mind," he drawled, spitting a wad of Redman chewing tobacco into a rubbish bin. "But if you think it's going to do you any good, it probably will." It wasn't the first time I had been told about

A COIN formal dinner. (Debbie Patching)

the power of the mind over the body.

Doctor Steven Hatfill was one of the most intelligent and accomplished doctors I ever met. He later returned to the United States and after working for the American Army doing biological research, became Assistant Professor of Medicine at George Washington University in Washington, D.C.

As for Jock Hutton, his exploits in Cape Town became legendary. But he didn't endear himself to the Managing Director, Yvonne Bishop. She arrived at the Branch unannounced one day to do an audit of his division.

"Aren't you a little old to be running a Branch this size?"

Jock sprang up from his chair, bristling. "Too old? *Too old?!* Why don't you bend down and touch your toes, Madame, and I'll show you where the wild goose goes."

A Laborious Union

"Why are you on strike?"
"For our demands." *"What demands?"*
"I don't know!"
—Author talking to striking worker,
Johannesburg: 1997

Two years after my arrival in Cape Town, I was posted back to the company's Head Office in Pretoria. By this time my bona fides within the company had been accepted by Yvonne Bishop, who now seemed less concerned about the drinking habits of her managers than their ability to keep their trousers on in the workplace. Even the slightest rumor of an alleged impropriety would be enough to have her summon a tangled network of informers to her office to inquire into the lurid details. If the rumor couldn't be substantiated, it could always be contrived. Then would come discussion on how to plot the demise of the culprits.

I found myself being recruited by Yvonne into marshalling her 'inner circle' of informers to greater efforts in exposing the identities of the lustful romeos within the company. By some extraordinary quirk of fate, I also found myself being used as a 'confessional' by employees wishing to boast of their workplace infidelities. It didn't take me long to realize that most of the *amours* that came to Yvonne's attention were initiated by those in her inner circle anxious to deflect attention from their own lascivious behavior.

One day Yvonne told me to drop everything I was doing to investigate a report by a Branch Manager that a Supervisor had been caught in a compromising situation with a female employee.

"The Supervisor must be fired immediately," insisted Yvonne. "I can't fire the man until I've completed the investigation," I responded. "The story might not be true."

"Well, hurry up with the investigation, *then* fire him," came her curt response.

It turned out that it was not the Supervisor who had been caught in the act but the Branch Manager. The Supervisor had walked into the Manager's office one afternoon to find him stark naked in a gleeful frolic with his equally naked secretary. I asked Yvonne if she thought the Branch Manager should be fired.

"No. The story can't be true," she responded emphatically. (The Branch

Manager was a long-standing member of her inner circle.)

❦

I had been at the Head Office for some two months when Yvonne called me into her office to tell me she was concerned about the growing militancy of the trade unions to which most of the company's 5,000 employees belonged. There had been rumors of a national strike which, if true, might cripple the company.

"You're the only person in the company who can deal with the trade unions," she told me. "I'd like you to head up the company's Human Resources Division and ensure that none of our guards go on strike."

"That's rather a tall order," I replied. "What do you propose I do, order our guards not to join a national strike if one is called? That would be like ordering a group of squabbling monkeys not to join their friends up a tree."

"I'm sure you can manage. To assist you I'm sending you on a three-day negotiation seminar being presented by Andrew Levi. He's South Africa's best known labour relations expert and he'll explain what to do." Convinced that by sending me on a three-day negotiation seminar she had cunningly torpedoed the union's plans for a strike, Yvonne refused to be drawn into any further discussion on the matter.

As I walked out of the office with my new responsibilities as Human Resources Manager weighing heavily on my shoulders, the Chairman called me into his office. He told me I was to be appointed as his 'Personal Staff Officer'. This was a most prestigious position, akin to being appointed a General's Chief-of-Staff and Aide-de-Camp all in one.

"But Yvonne just put me in charge of Human Resources," I explained.

"Neither job is particularly strenuous," replied the Chairman.

"You can handle both at the same time."

I began to feel rather important. Not only was I Chief Marshal of Yvonne's 'inner circle of informers', but I was now the Human Resources Manager and the Chairman's Personal Staff Officer. It was quite a change from my humble beginning. How could the workers even think of going on strike when confronted with such power?

A short while later, with Andrew Levi's three-day seminar tucked firmly under my belt, I found myself inducted as the newest member into the negotiating team of the powerful South African National Security Employers Association. They didn't think I was very important at all. They were engaged at the time in talks with the trade unions aimed at averting a national strike.

At the negotiation table I found myself seated next to the Association's Chairman and lead negotiator; a portly, bearded gentleman called Don Masterson. It was 10 o'clock in the morning and the heat inside the negotiating room was stifling. Don looked at me and asked if I wanted something to drink. I asked him what he was going to have.

"A cold, dry orange," he growled.

"I'll have one, too, if you don't mind." I didn't know what a cold, dry orange was but it sounded refreshing.

Three minutes later a waiter walked in with two tall glasses of what looked like diluted orange juice. I took a long drink from my glass and almost choked. It consisted entirely of vodka with a splash of orange to give it color. Don looked at me and smiled.

"It's a Russian orange, Junior. If you want to play in the arena of national negotiations with the big boys, you have to learn how to drink with the big boys." Don downed his drink and summoned the waiter for another.

"How on earth are we going to be able to negotiate with the trade unions having consumed half a bottle of vodka?" I stammered.

"It brings us down to their level," replied Don, halfway through his second drink. "They tend to talk absolute gibberish and the only way to understand their demands is to have a substantial amount of liquor under your belt."

As he spoke, a member of the Union negotiating team stood up banging the table. He harangued us for thirty minutes without pause. I was struck by the fact that nobody seemed to be paying him the remotest bit of attention. Then he stopped as abruptly as he had started.

"What did he say?" I whispered to Don, not having understood a word the union official had said.

"He asked if the Union could have a caucus." "A caucus?"

"Yes, a caucus. That's when each side adjourns to separate rooms to formulate their negotiating position."

"I see. Where are we going to go?"

"To the bar, Junior. I see you have a lot to learn."

Two hours later with our capacity to engage in the complex maneuvering of negotiations considerably diminished by vodka, we returned to the negotiating table. The process wasn't particularly successful … three weeks later the trade unions called a general strike.

Even with the considerable wisdom gained from attending Andrew Levi's three-day negotiation seminar I was unable to convince our employees not to join the strike. Not only did they join the rest of the squabbling monkeys up the tree, they occupied the highest branches and became the most vocal.

Yvonne was not amused. I was almost relegated to my old position of Logistics Manager. Life at COIN Security could be quite tenuous.

Some months later my reputation as a skilled negotiator was considerably enhanced. I was representing the company in an important arbitration against the trade union which, had I lost, would have resulted in yet another strike. It was just before lunch on the second day of the arbitration and neither side had made much of an impression on the arbitrator. The case would pivot on the closing arguments to be presented by each side after lunch.

I found myself alone in the arbitration room during the lunch break with everyone else having left to stretch their legs. I noticed a set of car keys on the table which I knew belonged to a new Mercedes Benz recently acquired by the official representing the union … the same man who would be giving the union's closing argument. The arbitration room was situated on the thirteenth floor of a tall building and acting on a whim, I threw the keys out an open window. They landed in a window box four floors below.

After lunch the union representative had just begun his closing argument when he realized his keys were missing. He became so agitated at not being able to find them that he completely lost focus on summarizing his case. This caused the arbitrator to chastise him severely.

The case was awarded in my favor.

My astonishing success gave me a reprieve from being relegated to a lesser position within the company. John and Yvonne indicated their renewed faith in my abilities by telling me the company's Board of Directors would accompany me on my next shop steward's conference. They couldn't have completely trusted me because they invited Andrew Levi to attend as well. The conference took place at a plush facility outside Pretoria. It didn't start off very well. On the first morning the shop stewards were two hours late making their appearance because of having stayed up late the night before making considerable inroads into the resort's bar stocks. Yvonne was furious. I tried explaining that negotiations with the trade union were a tenuous affair requiring infinite patience. No sooner had the shop stewards taken their seats when they requested a caucus.

"What's a caucus?" asked an irritated Yvonne.

"It's where each side adjourns to separate rooms to discuss their negotiating position," explained Andrew Levi.

"No. I won't have it. They were late getting to the meeting and they must stop wasting our time."

Andrew calmly explained that a caucus was a normal negotiation procedure that couldn't easily be denied.

"They're just wasting our time!" fumed Yvonne. "How long will *this* last?"

"Probably all day judging by their hangovers," explained Andrew airily.

Luckily the caucus only lasted a few hours. Yvonne's demeanor was considerably improved when, after returning to the conference room, the senior shop steward stood up and addressed her as "Your Royal Highness." After that, the union could do no wrong. The conference went a long way in buying the company peaceful labour relations, and my own job security for some time to come.

✑

With my reputation as a skilled industrial relations specialist now firmly established, the Chairman asked me travel to Indonesia to run a week's seminar on dealing with trade unions and labour disputes. COIN had by this time considerably expanded its operations and was now operating throughout Africa, the Middle East and Pacific Rim countries. The Chairman had become friendly with a wealthy Indonesian banker whom he had met through an organization to which they both belonged called the 'Young Presidents Organization', or YPO, a global network of young chief executives. The banker owned a number of lucrative businesses in Indonesia, amongst which was a large pulp and paper mill situated deep within the forests of the Riau Province of Sumatra. Our company had recently been awarded the contract to guard the mill and my old friend, Carel Bosch, who had been responsible for me having joined the company in the first place, had been sent to Indonesia to manage the project.

'The workers at the mill have a number of grievances which management doesn't know how to resolve,' explained the Chairman. 'To complicate matters the unions have now become involved and management has no idea how to deal with them.' He went on to tell me there were over a hundred managers at the mill and they would all be attending my seminar.

Two months later I landed in Singapore where I was to spend a night before catching a plane for Indonesia. After booking into some cheap lodgings in the centre of the city, I decided to fulfill an ambition of mine which was to enjoy a Singapore Sling in the elegant opulence of the Raffles Hotel. I was sitting in the hotel's Palm Garden wondering if I could afford a second drink when I was unexpectedly joined by a shady-looking Arab businessman who was in the company of his very attractive daughter. The Arab and I struck up a conversation during which he explained in halting English that he owned a fleet of Arab dhows operating out of Dubai and was now headed for Indonesia looking for cheap lumber with which to build new boats. As our conversation progressed, the Arab began to mistake me for the owner of the pulp and paper mill to which I was headed. I certainly can't recall telling him I was the owner, so it must have been a misunderstanding caused by the language barrier ... fueled by our considerable intake of Singapore Slings. By the time he had bought my fifth drink, I had even managed to convince myself that I *was* the owner of the mill. Sensing an opportunity to lay his hands on some cheap lumber, the Arab invited me to join him and his daughter for dinner at the hotel that evening. Relishing the opportunity of being able to indulge in a quality of fine dining that would ordinarily have been out of my reach, I graciously accepted.

After freshening up at my dingy hotel, I returned to the Raffles Hotel and joined my free-spending host and his daughter in the sumptuous interior of the Tiffin dining room. By my second bottle of *Côtes du Rhône Parallèle 45 Rouge* I was beginning to feel quite impressed with my performance as owner of one of the world's largest lumber mills!

It was only after the Arab suggested I might want to consider spending the night with his lovely daughter in consideration for some favorable terms on lumber prices that I started feeling a little out of my depth. On the pretext of having to go to the toilet, I slipped out of the dining room and hastened through the front foyer of the hotel to the obscurity of my more humble lodgings four blocks away.

The next morning I caught a taxi to the airport for the one-hour flight across the Straits of Sumatra to the Indonesian coastal town of Pekenbaru. There I was met by Carel Bosch whose company I appreciated being in—just in case I happened to bump into my Arab host of the previous evening. I breathed a sigh of relief when, after enjoying a typical Indonesian meal of nasi goreng and fried chicken washed down with glasses of Bir Bintang, we were able to disappear into the relative obscurity of the Sumatra jungle.

The road to the mill was the worst I had ever driven along in my life. Five hours later, after traversing leach-infested swamps and rivers we arrived at the mill. The following day I found myself standing at a lectern presenting an

Industrial Relations course to a room full of Indonesian managers who, with few exceptions, didn't speak a word of English. They would nod their heads wisely at everything I said and would, at the end of each day, stand and politely clap their hands. Then one of them would make a speech in halting English politely thanking me for imparting so much valuable knowledge!

Expertise for running the mill came from a large number of expatriate contractors, mainly from America, Canada, Australia and Finland. They would congregate each evening at a large bar to quaff obscene quantities of Bir Bintang, the local Indonesian beer, while lamenting the inconvenience of earning huge sums of tax-free money in a jungle environment where there was nowhere to spend it. It was while listening to the banter in the bar one evening that I began to realize that it wasn't just the Indonesian workers who had grievances, the expatriate contractors did as well. The most outspoken and vocal of the group were a bunch of Australians who complained bitterly that the only facility at which to spend their money was five miles away.

"What facility is that?" I asked.

"A brothel," replied a leathery Australian who looked like he had spent his entire life in the sun.

"Five miles away," I remarked. "That doesn't seem too far to have to travel if you feel inclined to spend your money on delights of the flesh."

"Yes it is, mate. It's a long way to travel when it's along the worst bloody road imaginable and it takes you five bloody hours to get there!"

In typical Australian fashion they had soon found a solution to their dilemma. The Australians were employed building new concrete silos to expand the mill's capacity. Once they realized they would not be able to convince the brothel's Madame to relocate her establishment closer to her main source of clientele, they simply made it easier for the clientele to get to the brothel.

"How did you do that?"

"Simple, mate," replied the same weathered Aussie. "We just siphoned off the concrete we were supposed to be using for the silos, to build a concrete highway to the brothel. It only takes ten minutes to get there now—want to come along and have a look?"

I declined his kind offer. I was returning home the next day and didn't want to have to explain to Yvonne that my delay was caused by having visited a remote brothel at the end of the only concrete highway in Sumatra. She wouldn't have been very amused.

She would have been even less amused had I told her the highway had been constructed from misappropriated South African concrete for the expansion of the mill.

22

Monkey Business

"Do you see the monkeys?" "Yes. What are they doing?"
"They're playing with some T-shirts."
"T-shirts! In the middle of the African bush?"
"Yes, I think they're our corporate T-shirts."
"What?!"

—*Chairman of COIN Security Group*
talking with his Managing Director,
Near Skukuza Safari Camp: 1998

Shortly after my return from Indonesia I was appointed to the COIN Security Group's Board of Directors. It was like being upgraded from Coach to First Class midway through one's journey. No longer did I have to bring my own thermos of tea to work, nor even yesterday's leftovers for lunch. In the company's luxuriously-appointed top floor suite of offices where directors presided like exalted schoolmasters, the service was five-star. Boardroom stewards circulated all day with silver trays of tea and cucumber sandwiches. Secretaries would flit in and out of offices like eager hummingbirds. The luncheons weren't just meals; they were *grand affairs* of lavish service and excellent cuisine. Seated at the lavishly set boardroom table, directors would be waited on by smartly-dressed stewards serving sumptuous meals from ornate silver platters or pouring delicate wines from bottles wrapped in softly starched linen.

There were always meetings; in fact there seemed to be one for every occasion. There were board meetings, monthly meetings, management meetings, formal meetings, informal meetings and private meetings. However, the most important meetings where *real* decisions were made were the evening meetings. After work each day the bar would open and directors would congregate around it like ducks to a pond to pour their favorite aperitif before taking a seat in the elegantly-furnished rotunda to discuss *les affaires* of the company … and everyone else's affairs. Whether it could be said that directors were fulfilling their fiduciary duties at these meetings was questionable, especially after their second bottle of *Casal de Coelheira* Burgundy. But by the following morning it didn't really matter as most couldn't recall what had been discussed. But there was always the promise of another evening, more drinks and another bottle of wine and another informal gathering to chart the way forward.

Eclipsing even the informal evening meetings in status and importance were the annual conferences. Managers would be summoned from around the globe to be given their sales projections and budgets for the following year and told where their performance might be lacking. The conferences were held at a luxurious tented Safari Camp which had been built on a private game farm owned by the company. Before the construction of the Safari Camp, conferences were held at one of the numerous exclusive private game reserves which bordered the Kruger National Park. It was at one of these conferences that I found myself involved shortly after my appointment to the Board.

The conferences were normally of three or four days' duration and because of the enormous logistics involved in accommodating and feeding so many managers, a small advance party of those attending would drive out the day before to set up camp. A kitchen would have to be set up, sleeping quarters arranged, conference facilities attended to and a host of other housekeeping duties performed. The rest of the conference delegates would fly in the following morning utilizing the company's fleet of executive aircraft. I usually volunteered to lead the advance party and on this occasion was joined by two former Army colleagues of mine, Carel Bosch and Trevor Desfountain. It was Trevor, who as a Captain in the Rhodesian Army, had accompanied me as an instructor during the final forced march of my Officers Selection Course. Also accompanying us was Craig Herwill who had recently been appointed the new Logistics Manager. Craig also happened to be the Pipe Major for the South African Irish Pipe Band.

The morning we were due to leave, Trevor, Carl and I were sitting in Trevor's office drinking cups of strong coffee and feeling hungover from indulging the night before in too much of the vast supply of liquor we invariably took with us to the conferences. The phone rang. Trevor picked it up. It was Ziska, the Chairman's buxom new Personal Assistant.

"The Chairman wants to know why you haven't left yet. You were supposed to have left hours ago."

"We'll be leaving shortly. But before we go, may I come to your office and get an aspirin, please?" Trevor spoke slowly, clutching his sore head.

"An aspirin ... what for?"

John Bishop aghast at seeing monkeys wearing COIN corporate t-shirts! (Debbie Patching)

"Because I have a terrible hangover."

"I don't have any aspirin," said Ziska brusquely. "Besides, you shouldn't be drinking so much before a conference."

"In that case, Ziska, I'm going to have to come to your office and lay my head between your bosoms to get rid of my headache," moaned Trevor.

"You're not hungover, you're still drunk," scolded Ziska. "You'd better leave now or you'll have more than a headache by the time I'm finished with you."

Feeling the worse for wear we piled our stores and equipment into two pickups and set off on the six-hour journey to the game camp at which the conference was being held. It was a luxurious resort south of the Kruger National Park. It consisted of a number of thatched rondavels built around a swimming pool with a panoramic view of a large watering hole teeming with game. We had brought with us a large tent to be used as a conference room and because of its large size and complexity, decided to erect it that afternoon. Unfortunately, Carel Bosch decided it would be a good idea to indulge in some homemade peach mampoer to 'sharpen' our wits before tackling such a herculean task. By the time we had finished the bottle, plus another which he produced from somewhere, we couldn't even focus on the tent, let alone the

Andy Samuels and John Bishop at a COIN conference. (Debbie Patching)

complex instructions that accompanied it. By our third bottle, all thoughts of doing anything that afternoon had vanished and we collapsed instead on some comfortable chairs trying to focus on the animals at the watering hole. They had become skittish because of the appalling noise Craig was making trying to fill his bagpipes with air.

The following morning two events occurred which conspired against getting the conference off to a good start: we were late rising and the remaining delegates arrived early. Instead of seeing the camp fully functional with the conference tent erected so the meeting could begin, the delegates arrived to see Carel, Trevor, Craig and me dressed only in undershorts scratching our heads in bewilderment at the mass of canvas that lay strewn about us. We were unable to figure out how to erect the tent because some mischievous monkeys had run off in the night with the instruction sheet. Worse, the monkeys had raided our stores' vehicle and run off with some cellar casks of wine and a consignment of corporate T-shirts that had been specially made for the conference.

John and Yvonne Bishop were anything but happy with the melée that confronted them and decided to walk to the edge of the camp to view game while the rest lent a hand erecting the tent. Stepping their way gingerly around some empty mampoer bottles, they were aghast to see a troop of monkeys on the camp perimeter staggering around in what appeared to be a state of intoxication. The monkeys were squabbling over a cellar cask of Niederberg chardonnay. Yvonne was not amused when she realized the cask was from COIN Security's own private cellars. Upon seeing some of the monkeys wearing the corporate T-shirts that were to be handed out later that morning, she became quite apoplectic.

The company's Financial Director at the time was an elderly gentleman of comfortable means who treated his job more as an amusing hobby than an important vocation. The first thing he had done when he arrived at COIN was to appoint a Financial Manager to do his work for him; the second was to acquaint himself with the bar where he seemed to spend more time than at his desk. This was his first conference and he seemed quite amused by the chaotic situation that prevailed. In fact, as he explained to me in the bar later that evening, he was secretly hoping the conference might be cancelled.

"Cancelled, but why?" I asked.

"Because, dear chap. I forgot to bring the financial reports needed to present the budget."

"But the budget meeting's tomorrow morning; you haven't got much time to get hold of them." I didn't think I wanted to be sitting next to him when Yvonne Bishop asked for the numbers to be presented.

Returning from a conference in the COIN corporate jet. (Debbie Patching)

Trevor and J.P. Beard. (Debbie Patching)

"Don't worry. I've been around long enough to bluff my way through this sort of thing. I've got my computer with me and will work on a few projections tonight and finish up tomorrow morning before the meeting. Nobody will even realize I left the reports behind."

Unfortunately, the lure of the whisky bottle in the romantic setting of a tranquil sunset in the African bush proved more of a temptation to the Financial Director than preparing himself for the conference. By the time he staggered to bed later that evening, he could barely find his bed let alone his computer. I happened to be sharing a rondavel with him and suggested he might want to take some medication to clear his head and give him a good night's sleep before his presentation the following morning. He readily agreed, but by the time I found the medical box and placed some pain killers and sleeping tablets on his bedside table he was sound asleep. I left the tablets where they were thinking he might need them later in the night. The following morning he woke with his head feeling like it was being compressed in a vice.

"What are these?" he asked, looking groggily at the tablets. "They're the pain killers and sleeping tablets you should have taken last night."

"Well, better late than never," he muttered, tossing down the tablets.

He never made it to the conference tent. Nor did the budget.

Mikhail Kalashnikov

"Dr. Kalashnikov expresses great sorrow for the pain he has caused you."
"Tell him not to worry."
"He would like to offer a token of his sorrow." "He can buy me a vodka."
"It's not enough. He would like to give you his watch."
—The author talking with a Russian Colonel, Johannesburg: 1998

Upon my return from Cape Town, I had moved with Carol and Jennifer into a lovely home in Pretoria's eastern suburbs. Some years later we moved again, this time to a beautiful twenty-five acre plot east of Pretoria called 'Die Wilgers'. It was quite a remote area and the house we lived in was a rambling, single-storey building surrounded by expansive lawns and luscious gardens bordered by thick forests of indigenous trees. Situated a short distance away was a separate guest cottage where friends could stay, coming and going as they pleased. Shortly after we moved on to the plot a colleague of mine from COIN came to stay. He was Alec Shragga, an elderly but fiery gentleman who ran the company's electronics and armed reaction branch in the port city of Durban. Alec's hobby was guns and he was seldom without a pistol strapped to his ankle, a habit which gave rise to his nickname, 'Hotfoot'.

Alec was in Pretoria for a formal dinner which he and I had both been invited to attend. It was being held in honour of a visiting foreign dignitary, the identity of whom had been kept secret. The Greek arms dealer who was hosting the dinner and who had extended the invitation to us told me only that it was somebody he thought I might like to meet. It was only after I had been shown to my seat at the head table that I realized it was Dr. Mikhail Kalashnikov, the Russian inventor of the AK-47. Not only was I seated at his table, I happened to be seated directly opposite him. He was flanked on either side by two dour-looking Russian colonels who acted both as Kalashnikov's personal bodyguards and his interpreters.

Conversation at the dinner table centered mainly on the success of the AK-47 and the fact that "it was still being used by many armies in the world as their primary assault weapon of choice." And … "for those armies that weren't using the weapon, most had copied its unbeatable design to manufacture equivalent rifles of their own." Midway through the second course I was getting tired of listening to the accolades given to the weapon and decided to voice a few opinions of my own. I had already armed myself with a few glasses of Russian vodka and in a voice louder than I had intended, told one of the Russian colonels that "I" thought the AK-47 was one of the most *inferior* weapons in the world. A startled hush enveloped the room.

The Colonel recoiled at my remark as though it might have been the most insulting thing he had ever heard. Glowering at me menacingly from across the table, he asked in his thick Russian accent what could possibly have led me to conclude that the world's top-selling military weapon was 'inferior'.

"Because, my dear Colonel," I said, taking another sip of vodka. "I have been shot nine times by an AK-47 and am still alive to be talking to its inventor today. You must surely agree, Colonel, that such a weapon would have to be considered inferior."

"Nine times, that is impossible," growled the Colonel looking at me with grave suspicion.

"Nine times, old chap. I have the scars to prove it. Would you like to have a look?" Not wishing to cause even more of a spectacle, the Colonel declined.

Wondering what all the fuss was about, Dr. Kalashnikov leaned over to the Colonel and asked what I had said. The Colonel spoke for a few minutes with Kalashnikov listening intently. After the two exchanged a few words the Colonel leaned across the table toward me, his voice softer … almost apologetic.

"Dr. Kalashnikov expresses great sorrow for the pain he has caused you."

"Tell him not to worry. My body is stronger than his bullets." "He would like to offer you a token of his sorrow," exclaimed the

Colonel.

"He can buy me a vodka," I suggested.

"It's not enough. He would like to give you his watch."

I watched in astonishment as Dr. Kalashnikov solemnly removed his wristwatch and handed it to me across the table. It was a large, heavy timepiece with the insignia of the Russian Armed Services embossed on its face. I handed Kalashnikov my own watch in exchange, and we both shook hands across the table. After dinner, Kalashnikov insisted on having a photograph taken of us standing together shaking hands. It was a token gesture from a proud and distinguished engineer for a debt of remorse honorably settled.

Later that night, Alec and I were invited to the hotel at which the Russian delegation was staying. It wasn't long before I had them singing the revolutionary songs that our Selous Scouts' pseudo-gangs had sung deep in the Rhodesian bush to lure communist guerillas to their position to be killed or captured.

Finally, long past midnight it was time to bid our Russian hosts farewell. I poured Alec into the front seat of my car and we set off down the highway toward home. Halfway home I needed to relieve myself so pulled over to the side of the highway and stopped the car. Leaving Alec sleeping peacefully in his seat, I got out of the car and was busy peeing into a drainage ditch on the side of the road when I heard a sudden commotion behind me. Alec started shouting and the next thing I knew shots were being fired in my direction. I dived for cover into the drainage ditch, wondering what was happening. Looking up, I saw Alec swaying unsteadily above me waving his pistol in the air. He was shouting at the top of his voice.

"Tim, where have they taken you, the bastards? I'll shoot the whole damn lot of them." With that he fired more rounds that went whistling above my head.

"Alec, what the hell are you shooting at!" I yelled from the bottom of my ditch.

"There you are," said Alec, peering down at me through the darkness. "What the hell are you doing lying down *there?*"

"I was busy having a pee, you idiot. Now if you would just put that gun away I can finish what I was doing and we can both go home."

"You're lucky I didn't shoot you," said Alec, extending a hand to help me out of the ditch. "When I woke up to find the car stopped and you missing I thought the bastards had hijacked you."

"It's lucky your aim is so shaky after having had so much to drink, you bloody fool." I had successfully survived being shot nine times by an AK-47. I didn't fancy my chances of survival after being shot at close range by a hollow nose .45 colt.

It was an unexpected ending to an unexpected evening.

Where Danger Lurks

"It's not where the dogs bark, that danger lurks.
It's from the silence of the shadows, where you hear no bark."

—Matabele Wisdom

As tranquil as it was living in the quiet seclusion of our home it was not without its problems. Violent crime in South Africa had reached endemic proportions and my family was not immune. Our property was surrounded by a ten-foot diamond mesh fence and seldom would a week go by that we didn't have armed intruders cutting through the fence at night trying to break into our house. Invariably we would be awakened by our two Ridgebacks barking, and I would quickly reach for my shotgun and slip through the bedroom window into the shadows of the night to investigate. Carol would reach for a pistol she always kept under her pillow, collect Jennifer from her bedroom, and together they would huddle in our bedroom waiting for me to return. Then would start a deadly game of cat and mouse with me searching the thickly-wooded property to intercept the intruders before they managed to get into the house.

I knew never to concern myself with areas in which the dogs were barking; feeding them only mornings, at night hungry Ridgebacks can be relied upon to keep anyone at bay. The intruders would taunt the dogs to keep them occupied at one end of the property, while others would sneak through the fence at the opposite end unhindered by the distracted dogs. Usually a couple of rounds discharged from my shotgun would be enough to dissuade the intruders from pursuing with their intentions and they would sneak off into the darkness in search of easier pickings. The dogs would stop barking, the owls would resume their hooting, Jennifer would be returned to her bedroom and the family would sleep fitfully through the rest of the night.

The intruders seemed to become more brazen with each passing week. One night we had three attempted break-ins, so the next day I had a motion detector alarm system installed around the perimeter fence. This made things much easier for me. A soft buzzer next to my bed would alert me that my fence had been breached and a control panel nearby would indicate precisely where. The motion detector was rigged to the exterior lights on my property, but unlike a conventional system where security lights were activated when the alarm was triggered, my lights were rigged to switch off, plunging the property into total darkness. Now, not only did I know where the intruders had cut through the fence but I was able to get there quickly and undetected.

Locating the cut in the fence was easy. The intruders would tie a white plastic bag on the fence where they had cut it so they could easily find the opening when making their escape. My *modus operandi* was simple. As soon as my alarm was triggered I would immediately make my way to where I knew the breach to be. I knew the property like the back of my hand and didn't need a light to know were I was going. Once I had found the breach I would move the plastic bag some ten yards further along the fence, and then find a suitable ambush position nearby. I would then fire two shots into the still night and wait. This would cause the intruders to stop dead in their tracks, turn and run back to the fence. They would find the plastic bag and try to crawl through the breach—but there would be no breach. As they fumbled around in the dark they would suddenly find themselves illuminated by a million-candle halogen flashlight taped to the barrel of my eight-gauge semi-automatic Remington 1100 shotgun pointed directly at them. Staring down the one-inch barrel of my shotgun as they stood hemmed and illuminated against the fence, they didn't stand a chance. Flinch and they would be dead.

One area of my property was thickly-wooded and it became a favored infiltration route for the intruders wishing to pit their skills against a wily old soldier like me. It didn't remain a favored infiltration for long. I hung triple-barbed fishing hooks from the tree branches so the hooks dangled five feet off the ground. I attached the hooks to the branches using thin steel fishing line difficult to see at night. Two nights after my traps had been set, the intruders struck again. Having been alerted to a breach in the fence, I was about to enter the forest when I heard somebody screaming in the woods. Quickly making my way to where the sound was coming from I switched on my flashlight to see a scruffy, reptilian-looking individual attached to a stout black wattle tree by a one-inch fishing hook caught in his cheek. His brave comrades hadn't stuck around to help, nor had they bothered to retrieve his weapon which still lay on the ground next to him.

Although the intrusions into my property began to diminish, the constant threat of armed intruders breaking into neighboring houses began to affect my family, so we left the solitude of our remote lot for the relative safety of a gated community in Johannesburg.

❧

In 2001 the company for which I had worked for twelve years changed. It had grown into one of the most successful security enterprises in the southern hemisphere with tentacles reaching across the globe. But it was still a private company financed solely out of the back pockets of its two co-founders, John and Yvonne Bishop. Unfortunately, it grew too big too quickly and the day inevitably came when it was forced to sell out to a large publicly-funded conglomerate based in Johannesburg. The new management wasted little time in making their intentions known to change the company's traditions and culture. John and Yvonne adamantly opposed the changes and it soon became clear that in order for the changes to take place the two of them would have to be removed.

Loyalty is a tenuous commodity which can be as fleeting as the mist. Management within the company suddenly found itself in the unenviable position of having to decide whether to remain loyal to the new masters or to the old warriors. Loyalty to one would mean betrayal to the other and it wasn't long before the corridors of the company became awash with deceit, intrigue and deception.

Managers started treating each other with the same degree of mistrust and suspicion that Parisians must have shown during the inglorious days of the Vichy Regime. For the Parisians the consequence of misplaced loyalty was death, while for the COIN managers it was only dismissal. But the ramifications were still far-reaching.

Most chose to close ranks with the new masters and to be fair, that was probably the right thing to do. But for an old soldier like me, deserting John and Yvonne would have been like leaving a wounded comrade to die on the battlefield, and I had been wounded too many times in the past for that to happen.

I was sitting with John and Yvonne in the quiet solitude of their beautiful thatched home in Pretoria the day they were both removed from the company; a company they had given so many years of their life building into a global enterprise.

I knew I would be next in the firing line.

"Would you mind if I poured myself a gin?" I asked. "I should think you two would probably like one as well."

John nodded his head and motioned me towards his well-stocked bar.

I poured the drinks and carried them to where we were sitting overlooking Pretoria's western suburbs and the rolling hills beyond. The sun had begun to set and darkness was beginning to cast its shadowy veil across an uneasy African landscape.

"Cheers!" I said.

The three of us raised our glasses in a toast to an uncertain future. "How odd that we should be doing this," I remarked.

"Doing what?" asked John. "Having three sips of gin … ."

Post Scripta

A

Armstrong, Pat   Living in South Africa.

B

Bax, Carol   Living in the United Kingdom.
Bax, Jennifer   Living in the United Kingdom.
Bishop, John   Living in South Africa.
Bishop, Yvonne   Deceased. Laid to rest in South Africa.

C

Chait, Sergeant Andy   Killed in Action with 'C' Squadron, Rhodesian SAS.

F

Fitzsimmons, Bruce   Killed in a motor vehicle accident, South Africa.
Flower, Ken   Deceased.
Fortier, Mark   Living in Lake Placid, Florida.
Fortier, Todd   Killed in a motor vehicle accident, United States.

G

Gillespie, Athol   Killed in a motor vehicle accident, South Africa.
Griffin, Terry   Living in South Africa.
Griffiths, Dr. Charlee   Practising medicine in Australia.

H

Hart, Winston   Living in New Zealand.
Hatfill, Dr. Steve   Assistant Professor of Emergency Medicine
                                       George Washington University, USA
Herwill, Craig   Living in South Africa.
Hulley, Dr. Brian   Living in South Africa.
Hutton, Jock   Living in the United Kingdom.

K

Kriel, Neil — Living in South Africa.

L

Laframboise, M'sieur Pierre — Killed in a lumber accident, Chapleau, Canada.

Lambert, Doug — Living in the Middle East.

Lockley, Dick — Retired and living in South Africa.

M

Mackay, Andrew — Living in Australia.

Masterson, Don — Succumbed after a brave fight with illness, South Africa.

McNeilage, Pete — Retired in United Kingdom.

Myers, Rev. Elizabeth — Living in the United States.

N

Nell, Jannie — Killed in Action with the Selous Scouts.

P

Pearce, Capt. Martin — Killed in Action with 'C' Squadron, Rhodesian SAS.

R

Rawlins, David — Living in Zimbabwe.

Reid-Daly, Lt. Col. Ron — Succumbed after a brave fight with illness, 2010.

S

Samuels, Andrew — Succumbed to illness. Laid to rest in South Africa.

Samuels, Ellie — Living in South Africa.

Samler, Keith — Living in South Africa.

Scott, Ian — Living in South Africa.

Schulenburg, Chris — Living in South Africa.

Shragga, Alec — Deceased. Laid to rest in South Africa.

Snelgar, Bruce — Killed on Operations, Rhodesia.

Strong, Jeremy — Retired and living in the United Kingdom.

T

Thomas, Tom	Living in South Africa.
Tourle, Sergeant-Major Al	Killed by a lion, Zambezi Valley, Rhodesia.

W

Walker, Vic	Living in the United Kingdom.
Walls, General Peter	Deceased. Laid to rest in South Africa.
Walsh, George	Deceased. Laid to rest in United Kingdom.
Williams, Theo	Living in Angola.
Willis, Colin	Living in Botswana.
Wishart, Bob and Wendy	Living in South Africa.

Index

Antonowitz, Sergeant-Major Bruce, 249, 251, 309
Armstrong, Lieutenant-Colonel Pat, 338-340, 418
Atkinson, Geoff, 344
Aust, Lieutenant-Colonel Charlie, 144, 146, 193

Baginski, Mr, 79
Baldwin, Flight Lieutenant 'Baldy', 210
Baldwin, Ginger, 329, 332-333
Barrett-Hamilton, Major, 136, 139-140
Bax, Carol, 22, 212-213, 215-216, 223, 271, 274-275, 285-290, 297, 299,301, 320-321, 326, 334, 337-338, 341-343, 348-349, 353, 355, 368-369, 371-372, 375-382, 412, 415, 418
Bax, Janet, 21, 26-28, 33-34, 36-38, 40-44, 46-48,56, 59, 61-62, 67-68, 70-71, 73, 75, 79-80, 83-85, 172, 175, 299-301, 353
Bax, Jennifer Sarah, 22, 355-356, 412, 415, 418
Bax, Shelagh, 26-27, 31-32, 34, 39, 43, 46-48, 56, 59, 62, 66-68, 70-71, 73, 276
Beard, John, 390, 411
Bellingham, Major, 303, 306
Bishop, Major John, 389, 408-409, 418
Bishop, Yvonne, 391, 397-397, 409-410, 418
Bosch, Carel, 386, 402-403, 407-408
Boyd-Sutherland, Major, 111-112
Burundu, Corporal, 270

Callow, Tim, 262-263, 325
Cary, Steve, 191, 198
Chait, Sergeant Andy, 161, 167, 169, 418
Chidomo, Corporal, 310-311
Coetzer, Sergeant-Major Paul, 114
Collett, Dale, 266, 269, 284
Coster, General Keith, 175, 193, 259
Croukamp, Dennis, 173, 190, 194, 209, 214, 219-221, 233, 239, 243, 250, 254-256, 266, 268, 293, 325-326, 344
Currie, Molly, 371

Dace, Colin, 196-197
De Jagger, Lieutenant-Colonel Jakkals, 346-347
Dekker, Ben, 362-363
De Rosie, Monsieur Jean Bateese, 88, 90-91, 93
Desfountain, Captain Trevor, 148, 150, 407

De Wet, General, 378
Dick, Superintendent 'Major' Ron, 128, 278-281, 283, 299
Donnelly, Pete, 384
Donnelly, Sandy, 385
Dos Santos, Captain José, 178, 180-182
Duffy, Bill, 381
Duma, Corporal, 112, 298
Duncan, Major 'Butch', 253, 261, 263, 278
DuPloy, Lieutenant Johan, 216

Eberhardt, Richard, 105-108
Ellias (herd boy), 376-380, 382-383

Father, 24-31, 33-36, 38-40, 43, 56, 60-66, 68, 71, 72, 74, 79, 80, 83-85, 156
Field, Major Reg, 69
Fitzsimmons, Sergeant Bruce, 243, 265, 269, 273-274, 418
Flower, Ken, 328-329, 340, 418
Fortier, Mark, 276, 418
Fortier, Todd, 276, 418
Fourie, Johann, 350, 351

Galanakis, Nurse, 321
Geoffrey, Corporal, 315-316, 318-319
Gillespie, Captain Athol, 160-161, 292, 418
Gingles, Alan, 346, 348
Gingles, Pauline, 348
Goodwin, Zoë, 49, 52, 54, 76
Grant, Reverend Peter, 299
Gregg, Tony, 371
Griffin, Terry, 126, 135, 146, 148, 159, 161, 165, 171, 174, 201, 206, 418
Griffiths, Anne, 286, 288-290
Griffiths, Dr. Charlee, 221, 224-225, 228-231, 286-290, 418

Harrison, Air Vice-Marshal, 41
Hart, Winston, 177, 179, 185, 418
Hatfill, Dr. Steve, 395-397, 418
Herwill, Craig, 407, 418
Hickman, General, 335
Hien, Dr. Pieter, 373

Hopwood, Dave, 200, 202
Hulley, Dr. Brian, 353, 356, 358, 418
Hutton, Sergeant-Major Jock, 323, 395, 397, 418

Kamathi, Dedan, 310
Kirrane, Sergeant-Major Trevor 'Rockjaw', 131, 140
Kleinhanse, General, 367
Krause, Charlie, 236
Kriel, Major Neil, 279, 281, 419

Laframboise, Monsieur Pierre, 88, 90-91, 93, 419
Laing, Bruce, 272-273
Lambert, Major Doug, 196, 203, 205-207, 218, 220, 233, 419
Lamprecht, Major, 112
Lead, Lady Mary, 42
Levi, Andrew, 399, 401
Lockley, Major, Dick, 151-154, 158, 160-161, 164, 172, 419

MacIntyre, Lieutenant-Colonel Derry, 193, 201, 215, 277
Mackay, Andrew 'Trader', 336-337, 419
Maclean, Lieutenant-Colonel Sandy, 142-143, 149
Marais, Marius, 207-208, 218
Maritz, Manie, 378
Masterson, Don, 400, 419
May, Jimmy, 139
McNeilage, Sergeant-Major Pete, 255, 257, 419
Moore, Rod, 108
Moses, 239-240, 243, 245-248, 252
Mother, 21-22, 24-27, 31, 33-34, 36, 38-41, 43-48, 50, 56, 59, 61-62, 66-71, 73-77, 79-80, 86, 89, 94, 98, 114, 122, 124, 149-150, 172-173, 175, 212, 243, 247, 276, 285, 299, 301, 353
Mugabe, Robert, 307, 324-325, 329, 336, 338-340
Myers, Reverend Elizabeth, 277, 419

Nangle, Mr., 274-276, 278
Nel, Jannie, 263-265, 269-270, 419
Nkomo, Joshua, 307, 324-325, 329, 333, 336, 338, 340
Noble, Keith 'Fingers', 200, 202

O'Connor, Sean Connor, 88-90, 93

Pearse, Martin, 143, 145, 161, 173, 177, 183, 186, 193, 212, 214
Percy, 200, 202, 234

Rabie, Sergeant Andre, 278, 292, 297, 304, 307, 329
Rawlins, David, 156, 161, 419
Reed, Lieutenant-Colonel J.P., 335
Reid-Daly, Lieutenant-Colonel Ron, 122, 139, 187, 200-201, 230-232, 249, 251, 259-260, 279-280, 282, 297, 302, 304-308, 314, 323-325, 328, 335-336, 347, 364, 419
Robins, Chris, 362
Rothschild, Dr. Alexander, 295
Rudi, 384

Sachse, Bert, 292
Samler, Detective Inspector Keith, 302, 304, 419
Samuels, Captain Andrew, 222-223, 323, 329, 336, 338, 359-360, 366, 368, 375, 409, 419
Samuels, Ellie, 368, 419
Schulenburg, Chris, 241, 243, 325, 419
Scott, Captain Ian, 345, 419
Shragga, Alec, 412, 419
Skeepers, C.J., 131, 133
Smith, Ian, 204, 277, 313, 324
Smith, Sergeant, 133-134, 136-138
Snelgar, Bruce, 186, 419
Stanley, Earnest, 104-105, 107, 109, 112
Stokes, Colonel, 275
Strong, Captain Jeremy 'Jerry' Treadwell, 152, 155, 162-163, 281, 419
Sussens, Brent, 373, 375
Sussens, Caroline, 373

Tarr, Sergeant-Major Robin, 120, 122
Tarr, Major Rod, 191-193, 203
Thomas, Tom, 257, 315, 321, 420
Thorley, George, 124, 126, 130, 278
Tourle, Sergeant-Major Al, 131, 420
Tucker, Matron Shirley, 274-275

Van den Berg, General Pieter, 378
Van den Berg, Ziska, 407-408
Van der Riet, Sergeant-Major Piet, 260, 264, 272
Van Rooyen, Johan, 315, 319
Van Schalkwyk, Trooper, 186-187
Van Tonder, Jacobus, 376, 380
Von Kauffman, Miss, 49-50

Walker, Colonel Vic, 305, 420
Walker, Sergeant, 140
Waller, Sergeant Ian 'Laughing Hyena', 329, 331, 333
Walls, General Peter, 326-328, 420

Walsh, Major George, 215, 420

Watson, Brenda, 104

Williams, Theo, 161-163, 420

Willis, Colin, 147, 161, 165, 170, 177, 191, 199, 203, 210, 364, 420

Wishart, Detective Chief Inspector Bob, 309-310, 314, 324, 420

Wishart, Mandy, 373

Wishart, Wendy, 373, 420

Worthington-Thomas, Lieutenant Roger, 99-100, 102

Wrottesley, Honorable Mark, 144-147, 149

Wyllie, Brian, 359-361

Related titles published by Helion & Company and GG Books

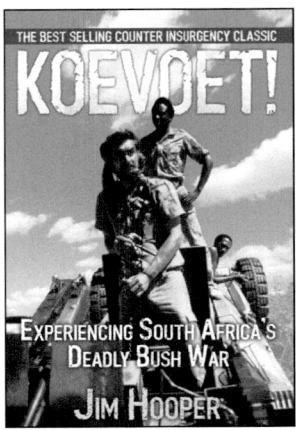

Koevoet! Experiencing South Africa's Deadly Bush War
Jim Hooper
312pp Paperback
ISBN 978-0-957058-70-6

LZ Hot! Flying South Africa's Border War
Nick Lithgow
174pp Paperback
ISBN 978-1-908916-59-4

A Whisper in the Reeds. 'The Terrible Ones': South Africa's 32 Battalion at War
Justin Taylor
224pp Paperback
ISBN 978-1-908916-58-7

HELION & COMPANY
26 Willow Road, Solihull, West Midlands B91 1UE, England
Telephone 0121 705 3393   Fax 0121 711 4075
Website: http://www.helion.co.uk